# Dave Brubeck and the Performance of Whiteness

# Dave Brubeck and the Performance of Whiteness

Kelsey Klotz

# OXFORD
UNIVERSITY PRESS

Oxford University Press is a department of the University of Oxford. It furthers
the University's objective of excellence in research, scholarship, and education
by publishing worldwide. Oxford is a registered trade mark of Oxford University
Press in the UK and certain other countries.

Published in the United States of America by Oxford University Press
198 Madison Avenue, New York, NY 10016, United States of America.

© Oxford University Press 2023

The publisher gratefully acknowledges support from the AMS 75 Publication
Awards for Younger Scholars Fund of the American Musicological Society,
supported in part by the National Endowment for the Humanities and
the Andrew W. Mellon Foundation.

All rights reserved. No part of this publication may be reproduced, stored in
a retrieval system, or transmitted, in any form or by any means, without the
prior permission in writing of Oxford University Press, or as expressly permitted
by law, by license, or under terms agreed with the appropriate reproduction
rights organization. Inquiries concerning reproduction outside the scope of the
above should be sent to the Rights Department, Oxford University Press, at the
address above.

You must not circulate this work in any other form
and you must impose this same condition on any acquirer.

Library of Congress Cataloging-in-Publication Data
Names: Klotz, Kelsey A. K. author.
Title: Dave Brubeck and the performance of whiteness / Kelsey Klotz.
Description: New York : Oxford University Press, 2023. |
Includes bibliographical references and index.
Identifiers: LCCN 2022027319 (print) | LCCN 2022027320 (ebook) |
ISBN 9780197525074 (hardback) | ISBN 9780197525104 (epub)
Subjects: LCSH: Brubeck, Dave—Criticism and interpretation. |
Jazz—History and criticism. | Music and race—United States—History—20th century.
Classification: LCC ML410.B868 K56 2022 (print) |
LCC ML410.B868 (ebook) | DDC 781.65092—dc23/eng/20220613
LC record available at https://lccn.loc.gov/2022027319
LC ebook record available at https://lccn.loc.gov/2022027320

DOI: 10.1093/oso/9780197525074.001.0001

1 3 5 7 9 8 6 4 2

Printed by Sheridan Books, Inc., United States of America

*To Zachary*

# Contents

| | |
|---|---|
| Acknowledgments | ix |
| Introduction: Buying the Myth | 1 |
| 1. "Any Jackass Can Swing": Sounds in Black and White | 31 |
| 2. Professors, Housewives, and Playboys: The Jazz Converts | 73 |
| 3. (In)Visible Men: White Recognition and Trust | 119 |
| 4. "We Want to Play in the South": Brubeck's Southern Strategy | 157 |
| 5. Negotiating Jewish Identity in *The Gates of Justice* | 199 |
| Conclusion: Evading Whiteness | 259 |
| *Selected Bibliography* | *281* |
| *Index* | *291* |

# Acknowledgments

From the beginning of this project, I have benefited from the encouragement and support of family, friends, and a variety of academic colleagues, communities, and institutions. I am thrilled to be able to recognize and share my appreciation for many of them here.

First, I am indebted to the faculty and staff at the University of the Pacific Library in Stockton, California, and especially at the Holt-Atherton Special Collections, where the Brubeck Collection was held while I conducted the archival research for this book, and under whose auspices I was awarded travel grants to complete my work. I particularly thank Mike Wurtz, Nicole Grady, and Trish Richards, each of whom welcomed me, and who have created an incredibly supportive archival environment. Thanks also to Keith Hatschek at UoP for his continued kindness.

Parts of this book stem from my dissertation, completed at Washington University in St. Louis. Since graduating, I have enjoyed the continued community of past and current graduate students—Liza Dister, Darren LaCour, Kathryn Nunnally, Ashley Pribyl, and Felipe Tinoco, have especially continued to offer encouragement and advice. Additionally, Daniel Fister's keen editing eye and knowledge of critical race theory provided critical feedback on several parts of this book. Many thanks are due also to Patrick Burke, my advisor, who was continually available for thoughtful advice and feedback on my work, and to Gerald Early, whose thoughtful questions during my time writing for the publication *The Common Reader* helped to shape and focus both my writing voice and my approach to this work.

The year I spent as a postdoctoral fellow at the Fox Center for Humanistic Inquiry at Emory University (2017–2018) was incredibly intellectually stimulating, and this book has been immeasurably enriched by both the time I was able to dedicate to it in cozy offices surrounded by an interdisciplinary gathering of fellows, and the conversations and debates we had when brought together. In particular, I thank Walter Melion, Keith Anthony, Colette Barlow, and Amy Erbil, as well as Kiera Allison and Christopher Willoughby, whose doors were always open for long and intense discussions about our work, lives, and teaching. Members of the Emory University Department of Music were also inviting, especially Stephen Crist, whose generosity and humility, together with his depth and breadth of knowledge about Brubeck and his archive, offered support and mentorship well beyond the fellowship. Thank you, Stephen.

Since coming to the University of North Carolina at Charlotte in 2018, I have benefited from the kindness and support of colleagues in the Department of Music and the College of Arts + Architecture, especially Aly Amidei, Nadia Anderson, Will Campbell, Carlos Alexis Cruz, Jason Dungee, Mira Frisch, David Gall, Lee Gray, Jay Grymes, Hannah Harrell, Hali Hutchison, Kim Jones, Jessica Lindsey, Brook Muller, Lisa Newman, Elena Payne-Wiens, Joe Skillen, Sheena Smallwood, and Fred Spano.

I have benefited from the generosity, wisdom, critical feedback, advice, suggestions, and support of many, without whom this project would not be the same. I would like to thank Suzanne Ryan, who initially shepherded the proposal for this book into a contract and offered mentorship afterward, and Lauralee Yeary, whose patient guidance got the manuscript to press. I also thank Ingrid Monson and anonymous reviewers who provided crucial feedback on the proposal and finished manuscript. I am grateful to Rebecca Furgerson Sloan, who was generous with her knowledge of her family's history of hosting jazz musicians and other prominent Black activists and entertainers as they traveled across Iowa in the 1950s, and who allowed her sister's meaningful words to Brubeck to be quoted in chapter 4. Likewise, I thank Katherine Cruse, who provided permission for photographs by Lonnie Wilson to be featured in chapter 2.

I am lucky to have found supportive intellectual homes in jazz studies, musicology, and ethnomusicology. Within these academic communities, I am grateful to Christopher Coady, Judah Cohen, Eugenia Conte, Jillian Fischer, Ken Ge, John Gennari, Denise Gill, Sunaina Kale, Tammy Kernodle, Mark Lomanno, Mark McCorkle, Daniel Melamed, Ingrid Monson, Darren Mueller, Ruth Mueller, Lewis Porter, Ken Prouty, Fritz Schenker, Gabriel Solis, Rami Stucky, Kimberly Hannon Teal, Sherrie Tucker, Sarah Town, Mikkel Vad, Christi Jay Wells, and Dave Wilson for their feedback, emotional and professional support, and intellectual stimulation at various points in this project. Without David and Shirley McKamie's early mentorship at Truman State University, I would never have considered musicology as a potential path; I am grateful for their lasting support. I also thank Mark Kligman, Danielle Stein, Samantha Madison, Alexander Hallenbeck, and the UCLA Jewish Music Studies working group for their insights that helped to shape chapter 5, and for inviting me to discuss my work on *The Gates of Justice* (1969). I am especially appreciative of Jeff Janeczko, curator for the Milken Archive of Jewish Music, for his thoughtful comments and assistance on the essay version of chapter 5. I am also humbled to have received an AMS 75 PAYS Subvention to support the publication.

Within the intellectual communities listed above, I have been especially grateful for the following women who have each had an indelible impact on me as a person, teacher, and scholar: Eugenia Conte, my rad SEM mainstay, who is (the best kind of) delightful, and who gracefully manages the delicate balances between accountability and assurance; Liza Dister, whose insights never cease to influence the way I approach my work, and whose ability to combine boundless compassion with a keen critical eye offers a crucial model in social justice work; Denise Gill, whose attentive mentorship combined empathy with academic rigor, and who is a dedicated advocate; and Sherrie Tucker, in whose intuitive mentorship I found a generous and kind champion, and who seemed to know exactly what I needed to hear at precisely the moments I needed to hear it most.

I am grateful also to my family, including Dan and Martine Kline, Jared and Leslie Kline, Arlene Kockler, and Gregory, Deanna, and Rachel Klotz. Much love and a lifetime of gratitude also go to Rich and Tammy Kline, who have supported and encouraged me whole-heartedly from the very beginning (and who continue to post positive reviews on their refrigerator).

But most of all, and with all of my heart, I thank my partner, Zachary, who has been on this path with me from the beginning, who has been the project's best champion (and who designed its cover), who has brainstormed with me, been a constant sounding board, and never seemed to mind being used as a human thesaurus, and whose love sustained the work. With you, I am the luckiest.

# Introduction

## Buying the Myth

Dave Brubeck was a jazz musician and composer who engaged directly in the massive social and historical moments in which he lived. He formed an integrated army band during World War II (the Wolf Pack), engaged in cultural diplomacy for the US State Department during the Cold War (and subsequently wrote *The Real Ambassadors*, a musical featuring Louis Armstrong that boldly made plain the racial hypocrisy involved in such cultural diplomacy), became involved in the civil rights movement by insisting that audiences accept his interracial quartet, and composed musical works that (implicitly and explicitly) protested the Vietnam War, treatment of Native Americans, and Christian hypocrisy and indifference to racial justice. Upon his death, many of Brubeck's obituaries highlighted his unusual and at times innovative musical approaches, including his heavy-handed touch at the piano, the complex rhythms and meters featured on the album *Time Out* (1959), his penchant for polytonality, and the inclusion of musical influences from around the world.[1] Many also positioned him as a white ally by emphasizing his 1960s civil rights advocacy, which notably resulted in his canceling a twenty-five-date tour of the South when twenty-two colleges and universities refused to let Eugene Wright, the Quartet's bass player, who was Black, perform with the otherwise all-white group.[2]

---

[1] See, for example, John Blake, "What the Tributes to Dave Brubeck Missed," CNN, December 22, 2012, https://www.cnn.com/2012/12/21/us/dave-brubeck-appreciation/index.html; Taylor Ho Bynum, "The Brilliance of Dave Brubeck," *New Yorker*, December 6, 2012, https://www.newyorker.com/culture/culture-desk/the-brilliance-of-dave-brubeck; John Fordham, "Dave Brubeck Obituary," *The Guardian*, December 5, 2012, https://www.theguardian.com/music/2012/dec/05/dave-brubeck; Don Heckman, "Dave Brubeck Dies at 91; Jazz Legend," *Los Angeles Times*, December 5, 2012, https://www.latimes.com/local/obituaries/la-me-dave-brubeck-20121206-story.html; Eyder Peralta, "Legendary Jazz Musician Dave Brubeck Dies," NPR, December 5, 2012, https://www.npr.org/sections/thetwo-way/2012/12/05/166570705/dave-brubeck-legendary-jazz-musician-dead-at-age-91; Ben Ratliff, "Dave Brubeck, Whose Distinctive Sound Gave Jazz New Pop, Dies at 91," *New York Times*, December 5, 2012, https://www.nytimes.com/2012/12/06/arts/music/dave-brubeck-jazz-musician-dies-at-91.html; Matt Schudel, "Dave Brubeck, Worldwide Ambassador of Jazz, Dies at 91," *Washington Post*, December 5, 2012, https://www.washingtonpost.com/local/obituaries/dave-brubeck-worldwide-ambassador-of-jazz-dies-at-91/2012/12/05/a9fa70e4-3959-11e0-bb8c-90acdd319fdd_story.html.

[2] This book was completed in summer 2021, one year following the death of George Floyd, and when many news sources began to change their approach to the capitalization of Black/black and White/white. In this book, I capitalize Black, as the term Black in a racial or cultural meaning conveys "an essential and

Despite his well-documented civil rights work, and despite the fact that he was a white musician working within a predominantly Black field, Brubeck often struggled to position his career in racial terms. In a 2001 interview, journalist Hedrick Smith asked him to do just that—to consider the role Brubeck's race might have played in how critics and audiences heard and understood his music. Smith asked, "Have you ever felt that jazz was seen as an African American music, and therefore, African Americans should go first?"[3] Brubeck first situates his answer broadly, considering the changes and shifts jazz historiography itself might play in the coming decades, while also leaving room for his own skepticism of framing the question around race:

> You know, that's a strange thing, because that question is going to be asked forever. And the answers are going to change, as historians know more, or know less, or buy the whole myth.

Brubeck quickly shifts away from this meta-approach to jazz history. He continues on with arguments he has often recycled across his career: he cites his heroes, who were mostly Black and included Duke Ellington, Art Tatum, Teddy Wilson, Billy Kyle, and Fats Waller. He reminisces on Black musicians who highly valued the music of white musicians, reflecting, "And then I think of all the wonderful things that Black musicians admired about white musicians"; and concludes with an all too familiar call for colorblindness, repeated across the century by both Black and white musicians:

> Like George Shearing said, "I can't tell the difference," you know, because he's blind. And he said one time, "I don't care if somebody is purple, as long as they can play."

---

shared sense of history, identity and community among people who identify as Black." Others, such as the National Association of Black Journalists, capitalize Black and White both for symmetry and to call attention to White as a similarly raced group identity that has otherwise gone unrecognized by many white people. I do not capitalize white, in part because it risks an association with or affirmation of white supremacists and white nationalists. While I expect and respect that my readers can differentiate between white supremacist ideologies and the performances of whiteness described in this book, I also appreciate that capitalization can both confer and reflect power and visibility. There is power in recognizing "White" as a visible racial identity; however, there is also power in amplifying the statements and contributions of Black musicians and writers who have been historically oppressed. "Explaining AP Style on Black and white," *AP News* July 20, 2020, https://apnews.com/afs:Content:9105661462; Mike Laws, "Why We Capitalize 'Black' (and not 'white')," *Columbia Journalism Review*, June 16, 2020, https://www.cjr.org/analysis/capital-b-black-styleguide.php; Nell Irvin Painter, "Why 'White, Should Be Capitalized, Too," *Washington Post*, July 22, 2020, https://www.washingtonpost.com/opinions/2020/07/22/why-white-should-be-capitalized/?utm_campaign=wp_week_in_ideas&utm_medium=email&utm_source=newsletter&wpisrc=nl_ideas.

[3] Dave Brubeck and Hedrick Smith, "Talking with Dave Brubeck: Dave on the Racial Barrier," *Rediscovering Dave Brubeck*, Public Broadcasting Service, December 16, 2001, http://www.pbs.org/brubeck/documentary/facts.htm, accessed June 1, 2020.

While Brubeck's answer began as a meditation on jazz historiography and historians' shifting approaches to race, he concluded by emphasizing that there was, in fact, one right answer to Smith's question—a colorblind approach—further asserting, "And that's the answer."

Now, more than one hundred years since Brubeck's birth, twenty years since that PBS interview, and a decade since his passing, the question remains: How can we—historians, writers, musicians, audiences—understand the legacy and impact of a musician like Dave Brubeck? It is undeniable that Brubeck leveraged his fame as a jazz musician and status as a composer for social justice causes, and in doing so, held to a belief system that, during the civil rights movement, modeled a progressive approach to race and race relations. It is also true, however, that it took Brubeck, like others, some time to understand the full spectrum of racial power dynamics at play in post–World War II, the early Cold War, and civil rights America. His position as a highly visible white man in the predominantly Black jazz field, particularly in the 1950s, both helped and hindered his progress in this regard. As ethnomusicologist Ingrid Monson contends, "The 'advanced consciousness' of the racially progressive white person did not alter the fact that public accommodation laws in the South and segregated practices in the North conferred certain benefits upon white musicians, whether they actively desired them or not."[4] Brubeck harnessed what historian David Roediger would refer to as his "wages of whiteness" to become an active anti-racism advocate—even while he maintained what historian George Lipsitz calls a "possessive investment in whiteness."[5]

This book approaches Brubeck as a lens through which to understand the broader American culture at mid-century; as such, though it details much of the music and events in his life in the 1950s and 1960s, it is not only biographical. Through interviews with Brubeck and work in his archive, other scholars and writers have created detailed accounts following various areas of his life.[6]

---

[4] Ingrid Monson, *Freedom Sounds: Civil Rights Call Out to Jazz and Africa* (Oxford: Oxford University Press, 2007), 73.

[5] David R. Roediger, *The Wages of Whiteness: Race and the Making of the American Working Class* (London: Verso, 1991); George Lipsitz, *The Possessive Investment in Whiteness: How White People Profit from Identity Politics* (Philadelphia, PA: Temple University Press, 1998).

[6] Andy Birtwistle, "Marking Time and Sounding Difference: Brubeck, Temporality and Modernity," *Popular Music* 29 (2010): 351–371; Darius Brubeck, "1959: The Beginning of Beyond," in *The Cambridge Companion to Jazz*, ed. Mervyn Cooke and David Horn (Cambridge: Cambridge University Press, 2002), 177–201; Philip Clark, *Dave Brubeck: A Life in Time* (New York: Da Capo Press, 2020); Stephen Crist, *Dave Brubeck's Time Out* (Oxford: Oxford University Press, 2019); Stephen Crist, "Jazz as Democracy? Dave Brubeck and Cold War Politics," *Journal of Musicology* 26 (2009): 133–174; Stephen Crist, "The Role and Meaning of the Bach Chorale in the Music of Dave Brubeck," in *Bach Perspectives: Bach in America*, ed. Stephen Crist (Urbana: University of Illinois Press, 2003), 179–216; Ted Gioia, "Dave Brubeck and Modern Jazz in San Francisco," *West Coast Jazz: Modern Jazz in California, 1945–1960* (Berkeley: University of California Press, 1992), 60–85; Fred M. Hall, *It's About Time: The Dave Brubeck Story* (Fayetteville: University of Arkansas Press, 1996); Keith Hatschek, "The Impact of American Jazz

These accounts have done critical work documenting the life and music of an influential and much-beloved musician, and since his passing, they have remembered him well.

This book explores yet another of the myriad ways such musicians can be remembered within the broader cultural contexts in which they were active.[7] I focus on Brubeck's intersectional identity to understand the ways in which his identity, and particularly his racial identity, shaped not only his experience within jazz but also the experiences of his critics and audiences at mid-century.[8] As Matthew Frye Jacobson argues, 1930s immigration politics marked the beginning of a view of "monolithic whiteness"; that is, an American whiteness that tended not to distinguish between European countries of origin.[9] As the civil rights movement began to take form, Jacobson writes, "both the progressive and the regressive coalitions that formed around questions of segregation and desegregation solidified whiteness as a monolith of privilege."[10] In other words, between the 1930s and the 1960s, white Americans across the political spectrum participated in the consolidation of language, culture, and privilege around an increasingly singular notion of whiteness.

This project uses Brubeck's performance of whiteness across his professional, private, and political lives as a starting point to understand mid-century whiteness and white supremacy more fully. In doing so, I ask,

---

Diplomacy in Poland During the Cold War," *Jazz Perspectives* 4, no. 3 (Fall 2010); Keith Hatschek, *The Real Ambassadors: Dave and Iola Brubeck and Louis Armstrong Challenge Segregation* (Jackson: University Press of Mississippi, 2022); Mark McFarland, "Dave Brubeck and Polytonal Jazz," *Jazz Perspectives* 3 (2009): 153–176; Michael Spencer, "'Jazz-mad Collegiennes': Dave Brubeck, Cultural Convergence, and the College Jazz Renaissance in California," *Jazz Perspectives* 6 (2012): 337–353; Kevin Starr, "Brubeck! Jazz Goes to College," *Golden Dreams: California in an Age of Abundance, 1950–1963* (Oxford: Oxford University Press, 2009), 381–410; Ilse Storb, *Dave Brubeck: Improvisations and Compositions—The Idea of Cultural Exchange* (New York: Peter Lang, 1994).

[7] As Krin Gabbard writes of 1920s white jazz musicians Bix Beiderbecke, Frankie Trumbauer, Joe Venuti, and Red Nichols, there are white jazz musicians whose musical styles "ought to be understood as something other than white theft of black capital." But while musical styles may not be reducible to white theft of Black capital, white capital was too often valued more highly, regardless of where the musical style originated. Krin Gabbard, *Jammin' at the Margins: Jazz and the American Cinema* (Chicago: University of Chicago Press, 1996), 15.

[8] Intersectionality, as theorized by legal scholar Kimberlé Crenshaw, focuses on how aspects of one's identity create overlapping modes of discrimination, and how those modes of discrimination are linked. Thinking intersectionally encourages scholars to understand how different aspects of one's identity may combine and overlap, resulting in both discriminations and privileges. Kimberlé Crenshaw, "Mapping the Margins: Intersectionality, Identity Politics, and Violence Against Women of Color," *Stanford Law Review* 43 (1990–1991): 1241; Patricia Hill Collins, *Intersectionality as Critical Social Theory* (Durham, NC: Duke University Press, 2019).

[9] Matthew Frye Jacobson, *Whiteness of a Different Color: European Immigrants and the Alchemy of Race* (Cambridge, MA: Harvard University Press, 1998), 93.

[10] Ibid., 95.

- What does "sounding white" mean in jazz, and (how) did Brubeck "sound white"?
- What made critics and audiences understand Brubeck as respectable, and why was he considered unique in this regard?
- What do attempts at anti-racism look like within white supremacist structures in the 1950s and 1960s?

But while the title of my book indicates that Brubeck is a primary subject, this book concerns itself equally with whiteness as performed by his fans, critics, and other jazz musicians, and how these various stakeholders in Brubeck's life used him in their own identity formation within systems that placed a higher value on whiteness. Therefore, the questions asked in this book not only revolve around Brubeck but also around his audiences and critics, and include:

- To what extent was Brubeck's whiteness made by others, and to what extent did he and they both seek and receive benefits that stemmed from their own white privilege?
- How did audiences and critics use Brubeck to craft their own identities centered in whiteness?
- How did he reflect whiteness in various mid-century American communities, and what did that reflection do for those communities?

By focusing on Brubeck, the project also makes a second key contribution to a turn in critical whiteness studies similar to that of historian and anti-racist scholar Ibram X. Kendi, critical whiteness studies scholar Robin DiAngelo, and philosopher Shannon Sullivan: namely, that racism is perpetuated daily by white folks who also attempt anti-racist actions and support anti-racist policies. Though his legacy is tightly bound to his civil rights efforts, neither Brubeck nor those who critiqued and loved him are perfect vessels for anti-racism—no one is. His story reveals how whiteness retains its hold on its beneficiaries, even when they intend to reject it.

## "Revealing" Whiteness

This project navigates a number of challenges, including one that any work in critical whiteness studies bears: how to discuss and critique whiteness without centering whiteness in unhealthy and unhelpful ways. However, as Sullivan argues, "While we might think that white people have spent too much time focused on themselves . . . the opposite is the case. White people have barely begun to constitute themselves with white affects and other habits that are worthy of admiration."[11] In other words, many white people have not had to consider themselves as white—as being racialized subjects whose lives and livelihood have been shaped to some extent by whiteness. As James Baldwin wrote about white people decades ago, "They are in effect still trapped in a history which they do not understand and until they understand it, they cannot be released from it."[12]

Because white people have largely not understood their own "white racial frames," the field of critical whiteness studies has often focused on the "invisibility" of whiteness, or on "revealing" the sights and sounds of whiteness.[13] As Lipsitz articulates, "As the unmarked category against which difference is constructed, whiteness never has to speak its name, never has to acknowledge its role as an organizing principle in social and cultural relations."[14] Richard Dyer and Ruth Frankenburg, two early scholars in the academic field of whiteness studies, noted the ways in which race has often been assigned to people of color—as something "they" have, as an issue pertaining only to racial "Others."[15] Insisting that whiteness be made visible, Dyer explains that "as long as race is something only applied to non-white peoples, as long as white people are not racially seen and named, they/we function as a human norm. Other people are raced, we are just people."[16] The problem with white people's insistence on seeing themselves/ourselves as "just human" is that such color-blind approaches deny the lived realities of race for people of color. The visibility of race, and therefore of whiteness, is essential to breaking down legacies of racist structures, as journalist Reni Eddo-Lodge argues in her book, *Why I'm No Longer Talking to White People About Race*.[17]

If whiteness is by and large invisible to many white people, then the privileges that stem from whiteness likewise remain unseen. At its simplest, white privilege describes the everyday, unearned benefits of being white; it does not deny any hardships white people may have faced or currently face in their lives but rather recognizes that skin tone typically does not contribute to those hardships. However, many critical whiteness studies question the notion that whiteness is simply invisible. For example, feminist scholar Peggy

---

[11] Shannon Sullivan, *Good White People: The Problem with Middle-Class White Anti-Racism* (Albany: State University of New York Press, 2014), 122.
[12] James Baldwin, "A Letter to My Nephew," *The Fire Next Time* (1962; New York: Vintage, 1992), 8.
[13] Joe R. Feagin, *The White Racial Frame: Centuries of Racial Framing and Counter-Framing* (New York: Routledge Press, 2009).
[14] Lipsitz, *Possessive Investment*, 1.
[15] Richard Dyer, *White: Essays on Race and Culture* (New York: Routledge Press, 1997); Ruth Frankenburg, *White Women, Race Matters* (Minneapolis: University of Minnesota Press, 1993).
[16] Dyer, *White*, 1.
[17] Reni Eddo-Lodge, *Why I'm No Longer Talking to White People About Race* (London: Bloomsbury, 2017).

McIntosh explains that "whites are carefully taught not to recognize white privilege," but rather, "whites are taught to think of their lives as morally neutral, normative, and average, and also ideal, so that when we work to benefit others, this is seen as work which will allow 'them' to be more like 'us.'"[18] Philosopher Charles W. Mills calls such lack of racial knowledge on the part of whites (as well as some people of color) white ignorance.[19] White ignorance is a non-knowing that includes both false belief and the absence of true belief; it can stem from "straightforward racist motivation," but it does not have to. Indeed, as Mills writes, colorblindness is a form of white ignorance often not based in bad faith but which nevertheless refuses to recognize the "long history of structural discrimination that has left whites with the differential resources they have today."[20] Media scholar John Fiske describes one method of white ignorance and maintenance of power as exnomination, or "the means by which whiteness avoids being named and thus keeps itself out of the field of interrogation and therefore off the agenda for change."[21] Through exnomination, Fiske explains, "whiteness cannot be part of the problem, or part of the solution, because it is not even 'there.'"[22] Philosopher Linda Martín Alcoff argues that "whiteness went unnamed because white presence required no explanation or justification, not because it was invisible."[23] She describes the "facticity of whiteness," as a lived experience and way of navigating the world (and of being navigated around) that exists beyond self-ascription; it is this "facticity of whiteness" that belies any notion of the invisibility of whiteness, whether or not whiteness is recognized.[24]

Of course, neither the invisibility of whiteness nor the ignorance of whiteness negates its rewards; as American studies scholar Sherrie Tucker notes, white people do not "have to choose or know about [their] privilege to benefit from it."[25] Importantly, Fiske asserts that whiteness is "not an essence but a power whose techniques differ according to the conditions of its application. The most common can be cataloged, though not exhaustively, for new techniques will always be developed to meet new conditions."[26] In recent years, white privilege has become a banner under which many particular

---

[18] Peggy McIntosh, "White Privilege: Unpacking the Invisible Knapsack," *Peace and Freedom*, July/August 1989.
[19] Charles W. Mills, "White Ignorance," in *Race and Epistemologies of Ignorance*, ed. Shannon Sullivan and Nancy Tuana (Albany: State University of New York Press, 2007), 11–38.
[20] Ibid., 21, 28.
[21] John Fiske, *Media Matters: Race and Gender in U.S. Politics*, 2nd ed. (Minneapolis: University of Minnesota Press, 1996), 42.
[22] Ibid., 44.
[23] Linda Martín Alcoff, *The Future of Whiteness* (Cambridge: Polity Press, 2015), 71.
[24] Ibid., 9.
[25] Sherrie Tucker, *Dance Floor Democracy* (Durham, NC: Duke University Press, 2014), 314.
[26] Fiske, *Media Matters*, 42.

benefits have gone unnamed. This book details some of these privileges for mid-century white Americans, focusing particularly on intellect, respectability, recognition, and heroism. Naming these privileges specifically and tracing their appearance in mid-century jazz and popular culture offers a method of making whiteness visible, and of breaking down an otherwise monolithic term. As Alcoff explains, whiteness is not a monolith; whiteness is not simply one, unchanging form or entity across history, but rather is "a historically evolving identity-formation that is produced in diverse locations, while constantly undergoing reinterpretation and contestation."[27]

Like much of the work of critical whiteness studies, then, this project reveals elements of whiteness that many white audiences, critics, and musicians found to be invisible at mid-century—privileges and benefits that for some whites remain hidden even today, couched in rhetoric around "mainstream" culture. However, some critiques of whiteness studies writ large have focused on the field's framing around invisibility and revelation. These studies ask for whom whiteness is invisible, drawing attention to the well-documented experiences of people of color for whom whiteness is necessarily visible and always has been. As feminist scholar Sara Ahmed, scholar and activist bell hooks, author Toni Morrison, philosopher George Yancy, and others argue, though whiteness remains invisible to many white people, people of color see whiteness and experience the negative manifestations of white privilege daily, whether through overt acts of racism, legacies of racist policies, or microaggressions.[28] Writing in the early 2000s, Ahmed explains that "the power of whiteness is maintained *by being seen*; we see it everywhere, in the casualness of white bodies in spaces, crowded in parks, meetings, in white bodies that are displayed in films and advertisements, in white laws that talk about white experiences, in ideas of the family made up of clean white bodies."[29] Though there existed only limited language to distinguish "white culture" and "whiteness" in the 1950s, Black writers across the twentieth century (and indeed, in the nineteenth century) created ways of describing the hegemonic whiteness that categorized Black lives as Other, different, or outside the mainstream.[30] Even as this book

---

[27] Alcoff, *The Future of Whiteness*, 22.

[28] Sara Ahmed, "Declarations of Whiteness: The Non-Performativity of Anti-Racism," *Borderlands E-Journal* 3, no. 2 (2004); bell hooks, "Representing Whiteness in the Black Imagination," in *Displacing Whiteness: Essays in Social and Cultural Criticism*, ed. Ruth Frankenberg (Durham, NC: Duke University Press, 1997); Toni Morrison, *Playing in the Dark: Whiteness and the Literary Imagination* (Cambridge, MA: Harvard University Press, 1992); George Yancy, *Look, A White! Philosophical Essays on Whiteness* (Philadelphia, PA: Temple University Press, 2012).

[29] Ahmed, "Declarations of Whiteness," para. 14.

[30] A very small sampling includes Amiri Baraka [LeRoi Jones], "Jazz and the White Critic," *Black Music* (New York: Murrow, 1960); Combahee River Collective. "The Combahee River Collective Statement," in *Home Girls: A Black Feminist Anthology*, ed. Barbara Smith (New York: Kitchen Table Women of Color Press, 1983); Kimberlé Crenshaw, "Mapping the Margins: Intersectionality, Identity Politics, and Violence

focuses on whiteness, it attempts to do so with an ear toward Black experiences and voices.[31] As Toni Morrison writes in defense of her book, *Playing in the Dark: Whiteness and the Literary Imagination*, against those concerned with centering whiteness in literature, "My project is an effort to avert the critical gaze from the racial object to the racial subject; from the described and imagined to the describers and imaginers; from the serving to the served."[32]

## Sounding White

Given the invisibility of whiteness to many white people, it follows that whiteness is also largely inaudible (again, for many white people). Sound studies scholar Jennifer Lynn Stoever theorizes the audible racial distinction constructed by white ears and made visible by white discourse as the "sonic color line," which "produces, codes, and polices racial difference through the ear, enabling us to hear race as well as see it."[33] Just as race is a social reality (that spent much time masquerading in the lie of a biological reality), the sonic color line is also a "socially constructed boundary that racially codes sonic phenomena such as vocal timbre, accents, and musical tones." Within musicology, ethnomusicology, and jazz studies, the academic fields that shape this project, and subsequently, the fields with which this book primarily engages, much work has been done to deconstruct essentialist notions of race and music. The field of New Jazz Studies in particular hosts many examples of scholars deconstructing jazz historical narratives based on damaging stereotypes of Black people and essentialist notions of how Black music "should" sound.[34] As jazz studies scholar Scott DeVeaux argued in his pivotal 1991 article, "Constructing the Jazz Tradition: Jazz Historiography," "The narratives we have inherited to describe

Against Women of Color," in *Critical Race Theory: The Key Writings That Formed the Movement*, ed. Kimberlé Crenshaw, Neil Gotanda, Gary Peller, and Kendall Thomas (New York: New Press, 1995), 357–383; W. E. B. Du Bois, *The Souls of Black Folk* (Chicago: A. C. McClurg, 1903); W. E. B. Du Bois, "The Souls of White Folk," *Darkwater: Voices from Within the Veil* (New York: Harcourt, Brace, 1920); Ralph Ellison, *Invisible Man* (1952; repr., New York: Vintage International, 1995); bell hooks, *Ain't I a Woman?* (Boston, MA: South End Press, 1981); bell hooks, "Representations of Whiteness in the Black Imagination," in *Killing Rage: Ending Racism* (New York: Holt, 1995), 31–50; Audre Lorde, *Sister Outsider* (Trumansburg, NY: Crossing Press, 1984); Sojourner Truth, "Ain't I A Woman?" Women's Rights Convention, Old Stone Church, Akron, OH, 1951, https://www.nps.gov/articles/sojourner-truth.htm

[31] See *Black on White: Black Writers on What It Means to Be White*, ed. David R. Roediger (New York: Schocken Books, 1998).
[32] Morrison, *Playing in the Dark*, 90.
[33] Jennifer Lynn Stoever, *The Sonic Color Line: Race and the Cultural Politics of Listening* (New York: New York University Press, 2016), 11.
[34] Any listing of these numerous texts on jazz and race would ultimately be incomplete. Some that inform this work include Patrick Burke, *Come In and Hear the Truth: Jazz and Race on 52nd Street* (Chicago: University of Chicago Press, 2008); Christopher Coady, *John Lewis and the Challenge of*

the history of jazz retains the patterns of outmoded forms of thought.... If we, as historians, critics, and educators, are to adapt to these new realities, we must be willing to construct new narratives to explain them."[35]

Many scholars have contributed crucial theories at the juncture of critical race studies and music, including music theorist Philip Ewell's "Music Theory and the White Racial Frame," musicologist Matthew D. Morrison's hermeneutic tool "Blacksound," sound studies scholar Jennifer Lynn Stoever's "sonic color line," sound studies scholar Nina Eidsheim's "sonic blackness," historian Barbara Savage's "aural blackface," African American studies scholar Daphne A. Brooks's "sonic blue(s)face," and literary theorist Eric Lott's "love and theft."[36] This project contributes a vital deconstruction of the performance of whiteness—its images, its sounds, and its power—in a genre that appeared to promote Black men, even as it was structured by a white-dominated music industry. For example, the first chapter analyzes white-coded musical narratives by mid-century white jazz critics such as Leonard Feather, Ralph Gleason, Barry Ulanov, Jack Maher, Martin Williams, and Arnold Shaw. Descriptions of jazz by these and other writers filtered the musical sounds audiences heard, leading them to understand Brubeck's aesthetic choices within a European classical musical frame; such decisions conferred assumptions of intelligence

---

"Real" Black Music (Ann Arbor: University of Michigan Press, 2016); Scott DeVeaux, The Birth of Bebop: A Social and Musical History (Berkeley: University of California Press, 1997); John Gennari, Blowin' Hot and Cool: Jazz and Its Critics (Chicago: University of Chicago Press, 2006); Robin D. G. Kelley, Africa Speaks, America Answers: Modern Jazz in Revolutionary Times (Cambridge, MA: Harvard University Press, 2012); Tammy Kernodle, "Black Women Working Together: Jazz, Gender, and the Politics of Validation," Black Music Research Journal 34, no. 1 (Spring 2014): 27–55; George Lewis, "Improvised Music After 1950: Afrological and Eurological Perspectives," Black Music Research Journal 16, no. 1 (Spring 1996): 91–122; Ingrid Monson, Freedom Sounds: Civil Rights Call Out to Jazz and Africa (Oxford: Oxford University Press, 2007); Ingrid Monson, "Fitting the Part," in Big Ears: Listening for Gender in Jazz Studies, ed. Nichole T. Rustin and Sherrie Tucker (Durham, NC: Duke University Press, 2008), 267–287; Guthrie Ramsey, The Amazing Bud Powell: Black Genius, Jazz History, and the Challenge of Bebop (Berkeley: University of California Press, 2003); Guthrie Ramsey, Race Music: Black Cultures from Bebop to Hip-Hop (Berkeley: University of California Press, 2003); Nichole Rustin-Paschal, The Kind of Man I Am: Jazzmasculinity and the World of Charles Mingus Jr. (Middletown, CT: Wesleyan University Press, 2017); Sherrie Tucker, Swing Shift: "All-Girl" Bands of the 1940s (Durham, NC: Duke University Press, 2000). Others can be found in Patrick Burke's broad review: Patrick Burke, "Race in the New Jazz Studies," The Routledge Companion to Jazz Studies, ed. Nicholas Gebhardt, Nichole Rustin-Paschal, and Tony Whyton (New York: Routledge Press, 2019), 185–196.

[35] Scott DeVeaux, "Constructing the Jazz Tradition: Jazz Historiography," Black American Literature Forum, 25, no. 3 (Autumn 1991): 553.

[36] Daphne Brooks, "'This Voice Which Is Not One': Amy Winehouse Sings the Ballad of Sonic Blue(s)face Culture," Women and Performance: A Journal of Feminist Theory 20, no. 1 (March 2010): 37–60; Nina Sun Eidsheim, "Marian Anderson and 'Sonic Blackness' in American Opera," American Quarterly 63, no. 3 (September 2011): 641–671; Philip Ewell, "Music Theory and the White Racial Frame," Music Theory Online 26, no. 2 (September 2020), https://mtosmt.org/issues/mto.20.26.2/mto.20.26.2.ewell.html; Eric Lott, Love and Theft: Blackface Minstrelsy and the American Working Class (New York: Oxford University Press, 1993); Matthew D. Morrison, "Race, Blacksound, and the (Re)Making of Musicological Discourse," Journal of the American Musicological Society, 72, no. 3 (Fall 2019): 781–824; Barbara Dianne Savage, Broadcasting Freedom: Radio, War, and the Politics of Race, 1938–1948 (Chapel Hill: University of North Carolina Press, 1999); Stoever, The Sonic Color Line.

and respectability on him over Black jazz musicians making similar aesthetic choices, like the Modern Jazz Quartet. American studies scholar John Gennari explains these critics' importance to future understandings of jazz: "The meanings we attach to the music and the musicians—how we make sense out of what we hear and see and feel—are very deeply influenced by the filters that stand between us and the sound that comes out of the musicians' bodies and instruments."[37] Narratives that coded particular sounds as "white" then impacted the way audiences, both within and outside the active jazz community, understood jazz musicians and their music.

Part of the invisibility/inaudibility of whiteness stems from its ability to appear as a universal norm or a dominant discourse.[38] This invisible universality extends to the field of sound. As an example, Stoever contrasts the successful careers of Freeman Fisher Gosden and Charles Correl, who played the overwhelmingly popular blackface minstrel characters Amos and Andy, with Black actor Frank Wilson's struggles to receive employment because he sounded "too much like a white man"; as Stoever argues, "The inaudibility of whiteness does not mean it has no sonic markers, but rather that Americans are socialized to perceive them as the keynote of American identity"—a keynote only available to certain racialized bodies.[39] Monson similarly refers to the inaudibility of whiteness not as a lack of sounds perceived as white but rather as "a stubborn unwillingness of many non-African Americans to recognize that their social vantage point is not universal."[40]

This universal tendency is, of course, not a new phenomenon, nor is it wholly unique to the United States, the central focus of this book. In her study of eighteenth-century German dramas, German historian Wendy Sutherland argues that particular concepts "emerge[d] as standard universal terms framing the Enlightenment and the universally enlightened individual"; such concepts included "*Vernunft* (reason), *Verstand* (intellect), *Kultur* (culture), *Geschmack* (taste), *Geist* (mind), *das Schöne* (the beautiful), and *das Erhabene* (the sublime)."[41] As Sutherland explains further:

> This dream of white perfection, which must be reinforced through black imperfection, appears to have gained a solid footing during the Enlightenment, which

---

[37] John Gennari, *Blowin' Hot and Cool: Jazz and Its Critics* (Chicago: University of Chicago Press, 2006), 4.
[38] As Dyer argues, "Most of the time white people speak about nothing but white people, it's just that we couch it in terms of 'people' in general." Dyer, *White*, 3.
[39] Stoever, *The Sonic Color Line*, 12.
[40] Ingrid Monson, "On Ownership and Value: Response," *Black Music Research Journal* 30, no. 2 (Fall 2010): 377.
[41] Wendy Sutherland, *Staging Blackness and Performing Whiteness in Eighteenth-Century German Drama* (New York: Routledge, 2016), 10.

contributed significantly to this construct of imagined perfection. How the Enlightenment presents itself and its terms as universal and normative is in fact a reflection of a construction of whiteness, which by nature is universal, normative, and therefore invisible.[42]

Like Sutherland, I argue that white people exercised the discursive privilege to define themselves around particular traits of whiteness, and that they used racist stereotypes of racial Others to confirm a pre-existing ideal self-definition. In other words, the construction of whiteness was deployed not only as a response to blackness but as a way of confirming and affirming the moral value of traits white people (who alone had the discursive power to define both whiteness and blackness) already recognized in themselves. By linking these traits to race through Enlightenment thinkers, lawmakers, various branches of Christianity, and pseudo race science, whites assumed a moral supremacy—a white *moral* supremacy that was used to justify oppression and exploitation of Black bodies and labor. Black and other non-white bodies served to confirm that although the specific traits of whiteness may change from generation to generation, the ostensibly normative moral supremacy of whiteness could remain unchanged. Uncovering these norms, naming the ways in which they are raced, and tracing how they subtly shift across time, Ahmed explains, contests their dominance.[43]

By this point, it is already likely clear that much of the work of this book focuses on the Black/white racial binary within the United States. This risks silencing the experiences of other people of color and oversimplifies the complexity of race and power dynamics. Furthermore, as Indigenous studies scholar Aileen Moreton-Robinson (Quandamooka) argues, the prevalence of the Black/white racial binary demonstrates an "unequivocal acceptance that the United States is a white possession," and "eras[es] the continuing history of colonization and the Native American sovereign presence."[44] At the same time, the Black/white racial binary reflects much of the focus on American "race relations" in the book's period of study. However, as Stoever explains, "The black/white binary has never been about descriptive accuracy, but rather it is a deliberately reductionist racial project constructing white power and privilege against the alterity and abjection of the imagined polarity

---

[42] Ibid., 12.
[43] Ahmed, "Declarations of Whiteness," 2004.
[44] Aileen Moreton-Robinson, *The White Possessive: Property, Power, and Indigenous Sovereignty* (Minneapolis: University of Minnesota Press, 2015), 60, 51.

of 'blackness' and the transfer of this power across generations and (white) ethnicities."[45]

Another caveat along similar lines: whiteness itself is also not a monolith; as Lipsitz suggests, "All whites do not benefit from the possessive investment in whiteness in precisely the same ways."[46] Whiteness is performed differently by white people in unique circumstances, based on their intersecting identities and particular locations. Performances of whiteness necessarily include, intersect with, and incorporate other performances of identity, including gender, sexuality, class, religion, and able-ness, to name a few. Brubeck's performance of whiteness is inseparable from his performances of masculinity, heterosexuality, Christianity, middle-class belonging, and other factors; each makes up a part of his experience and informs his performance of whiteness, and none can be extracted from the other. However, as with many performances, certain habits, actions, and phrases become so familiar as to fade into the background to be repeated in later generations. It is those familiar performances surrounding Dave Brubeck and his music with which this book concerns itself.

## The Performance of Whiteness

Throughout the book, I understand whiteness to be a performance—but what does it mean to perform race? Race exists as a lived reality that has been used to justify the dehumanization of racial Others through slavery, acts of violence and terror, legal discriminations, and daily microaggressions; however, it is also a construct, with spoken and unspoken rules, behaviors, and speech acts defined and re-defined over the course of centuries—what Ahmed and Sullivan call habits, after philosopher Pierre Bourdieu's *habitus*, or what we do and say without thinking.[47] To understand whiteness as a habit is to understand it as fundamental to white bodies being in and interacting with the world. For that reason, as Sullivan writes, "Habits of white privilege are both capable of transformation and incredibly difficult to change because they are dynamic, temporal compositions of the self."[48]

---

[45] Stoever, *The Sonic Color Line*, 21.
[46] Lipsitz, *Possessive Investment*, 22.
   See also Nancy Isenberg, *White Trash: The 400-Year Untold History of Class in America* (New York: Penguin Random House, 2016).
[47] Pierre Bourdieu, *Outline of a Theory of Practice* (Cambridge: Cambridge University Press, 1977). Sullivan further notes that "racial categories are historically, socially, economically, and psychologically constructed—and are nonetheless real for being so." Sullivan, *Revealing Whiteness: The Unconscious Habits of Racial Privilege* (Bloomington: Indiana University Press, 2006), 128.
[48] Sullivan, *Revealing Whiteness*, 4.

These habits were and are built in the interactions between the self, identities deemed to be like the self, and Others; in other words, such habits were built through collective performances, beginning with the performances of dominance exerted by empires of white supremacy. Following philosophers Maurice Merleau-Ponty and Simone de Beauvoir, who understood the body as "an active process of embodying certain cultural and historical possibilities," gender theorist Judith Butler argues that acts that define one's identity demonstrate similarities to theatrical performances.[49] Theorizing performance in relationship to gender, Butler continues: "The act that one does, the act that one performs, is, in a sense, an act that has been going on before one arrived on the scene."[50] In other words, a performance of race understands the racialized body as the site of a "legacy of sedimented acts rather than a predetermined or foreclosed structure, essence, or fact."[51] Similarly, sociologist Joe R. Feagin describes the "white racial frame" as a "dominant racial frame that has long legitimated, rationalized, and shaped racial oppression and inequality in this country."[52] Like other strongly held views one might possess, Feagin explains that "the dominant [white] racial frame becomes implanted in the neural linkages of a typical brain by the process of constant repetition of its elements—which are heard, observed, or acted upon repeatedly by individuals over years and decades."[53] Put another way, the white racial frame consists of shared experiences, socialization, and language—performances—that continually privilege a white social frame.

Such performances are not singular acts, nor are they intended to refer only to work on the musical stage; rather, they are repeated norms that guide everyday life for many individuals within a particular culture. As such, as philosopher Jacques Derrida underscores, performativity is not about individual agency, but rather performativity highlights broad social conventions and structures.[54] Capturing the temporal spectrum of past, present, and future

---

[49] Judith Butler, "Performative Acts and Gender Constitution: An Essay in Phenomenology and Feminist Theory," *Theatre Journal* 40, no. 4 (December 1988): 521. See also Simone de Beauvoir, *The Second Sex*, trans. H. M. Parshley (New York: Vintage, 1974); Maurice Merleau-Ponty, "The Body in Its Sexual Being," in *The Phenomenology of Perception*, trans. Colin Smith (Boston: Routledge and Kegan Paul, 1962).

[50] Ibid., 526.

[51] Ibid., 523.

[52] Joe R. Feagin, *The White Racial Frame: Centuries of Racial Framing and Counter-Framing*, 3rd ed. (New York: Routledge, 2020), x. Music theorist Philip Ewell has analyzed European classical music as possessing a white racial frame, in terms of what composers and theorists are routinely uplifted as representing the best framework, what time period and national origin the most celebrated classical music stems from (eighteenth-, nineteenth-, and early twentieth-century German music), what racial theories are acceptable, the prevalence of a belief in meritocracy, and the use of "diversity" language over anti-racism. Philip Ewell, "Music Theory and the White Racial Frame," *Music Theory Online* 26, no. 2 (September 2020), https://mtosmt.org/issues/mto.20.26.2/mto.20.26.2.ewell.html

[53] Feagin, 15.

[54] Jacques Derrida, "Signature, Event, Context," in *Margins of Philosophy*, trans. Alan Bass (Chicago: University of Chicago Press, 1984).

inherent in everyday performances, performance studies scholar Diana Taylor explains performance as simultaneously a doing ("the *now* of performance"), a done (a product that "might be experienced or evaluated at some different time"), and a re-doing (the repetition of past performances through both present actions and future experience).[55] As a "doing," performance encapsulates the ways in which we learn particular societal norms through imitation, repetition, and internalizing; for Taylor, performances "operate as vital acts of transfer, transmitting social knowledge, memory, and a sense of identity through reiterated actions."[56] As a "done," performance simultaneously takes on particular meanings and shapes meaning-making, considering how the meanings of performances "change depending on the time and context and framing of their realization."[57] As a re-doing, performances are continually re-performed and in this way normalize particular behaviors across time.

In *Dave Brubeck and the Performance of Whiteness*, I use performance as a theoretical tool with which to analyze the norms and repeated habits of whiteness at mid-century.[58] As James Baldwin emphasizes, "The great force of history comes from the fact that we carry it within us, are unconsciously controlled by it in many ways, and history is literally present in all that we do."[59] So, too, is the performance of whiteness a historical performance that is embodied and replayed in the present. The sites of these performances are as wide-ranging and as varied as the actors involved. In other words, performance here means not only what Brubeck and his bandmates did on stage but their actions, statements, and music off-stage. Performance includes what critics (both jazz and mainstream) wrote about which musicians and where; it includes the audiences who went to the club, college auditorium, or festival to hear them; it encompasses the magazines they read and the advertising campaigns of which they became part; it includes the managers, booking agents, record producers, and other members of the broader music industry and the musicians they programmed to perform what songs in what spots; it

---

[55] Diana Taylor, *Performance*, trans. from Spanish by Abigail Levine, adapted into English by Diana Taylor (Durham, NC: Duke University Press, 2016), 7, 9. Taylor follows Merleau-Ponty, who also claimed that the body was both a "historical idea" and "a set of possibilities to be continually realized." Butler, "Performative Acts and Gender Constitution," 521.

[56] Ibid., 25.

[57] Ibid., 40.

[58] Similarly, Reva Marin investigates various presentations of white identity (including Jewishness) among white jazz autobiographers in *Outside and Inside: Race and Identity in White Jazz Autobiography*. Marin describes these autobiographers as searching for a jazz identity in the midst of political and social upheavals in the United States, writing, "The effort of white jazz musicians to become insiders, or conversely to justify their outsider status, assumes great significance within their narratives." Reva Marin, *Outside and Inside: Race and Identity in White Jazz Autobiography* (Jackson: University of Mississippi Press, 2020), xxii.

[59] James Baldwin, "White Man's Guilt," *Ebony* 1965; qtd. in *Black on White: Black Writers on What It Means to Be White*, ed. David R. Roediger (New York: Schocken Books, 1998), 3250–3325.

includes the Brubeck Collection (initially held at the University of the Pacific and now at Wilton Library), the saving, preserving, and cataloguing (and decisions around each of these) of vast quantities of artifacts of the Brubecks' lives, and decisions regarding Brubeck's legacy (including permissions, re-releases, and concert celebrations)—in short, the performance of race with which this book concerns itself is simultaneously one centuries-old performance of whiteness, *and* many performances delivered in particular, individual settings at various points in time.

Understanding whiteness as a performance in which all white people are engaged offers methods to reflect on and critique the habits that buttress the performance of whiteness, and to identify and dismantle the modes of performance that support white supremacy. As cultural anthropologist Victor Turner explains, "We will know one another better by entering one another's performances and learning their grammars and vocabularies."[60] The performance of whiteness in the United States at mid-twentieth century was a cumulative effort: even if the parties involved (Brubeck, his promoters, critics, and audiences) had vastly different motivations, the result was an image that overwhelmingly corresponded with the unspoken narratives and traits of whiteness.

## White Supremacy

Because performances are simultaneously located in the present and across history, they include (and implicate) more than a single individual. As Sullivan writes,

> A person's relationship to her race is not merely a matter of how she projects herself into the world, and merely having good intentions in terms of attempting to disidentify as white does not erase her whiteness. A person's race is the product of transaction with her world due to her social "location" in it, which means that other people help constitute the racialization of her experience through their perceptions of and reactions toward her.[61]

In thinking about whiteness as a racial category, and especially as something beyond individuals, it is important to understand that intent plays very little

---

[60] Victor Turner, "From a Planning Meeting for the World Conference on Ritual and Performance," qtd. in Taylor, *The Archive and the Repertoire* (Durham, NC: Duke University Press, 2003), 280.
[61] Sullivan, *Revealing Whiteness*, 159.

role in the performance of whiteness. In other words, even when someone holds positive intentions, even actively seeks to perform anti-racist actions, they are still participants in a broader white performance that is and has always been about more than that individual. Monson makes this clear in *Freedom Sounds: Civil Rights Call Out to Jazz and Africa*, writing,

> Perhaps the greatest difference between black and white musicians in the 1950s ultimately lies in the fact that the latter had access to structural white privilege, no matter what their individual relationship to the blues and African American aesthetics more broadly, while black musicians experienced structural racial discrimination, no matter what their individual relationship to Western modernism and mainstream culture.[62]

Importantly, Monson highlights the "disjunction between an individual's self-conscious identity (whether ethnic or political) and that person's treatment as a citizen within the larger sociology of race relations in the United States." It was not an individual citizen's choice to be part of their performance of race, nor does that individual have power or control over the habits of that performance. Monson further underscores that "American social structure and the economic structure of the music industry with its de jure and de facto segregation of black and white ensured this."

This book thus understands white supremacy as a structure that supports, protects, and values white people and whiteness as it simultaneously dominates, silences, and de-values non-whites. White supremacy is *not only* the Ku Klux Klan or neo-Nazis, though both organizations are explicitly white supremacist; white supremacy is not simply the use of Confederate flags, Hitler salutes, hoods, or burning crosses, though these are often signs of white supremacy. All of these examples foreground individuals involved in overtly racist activities; while they may act as signifiers of white supremacy, white supremacy itself is much broader, encompassing a full range of performances of race and racism embedded in what sociologist Evelyn Nakano Glenn describes as the "rules and social practices that are widely shared within the local community or region" that inform individual actors.[63] As Eddo-Lodge contends,

---

[62] Monson, *Freedom Sounds*, 73. George Lipsitz explains that focusing on individual intent narrows focus to a small part of racism and racist acts: "As long as we define social life as the sum total of conscious and deliberative individual activities, we will be able to discern as racist only *individual* manifestations of personal prejudice and hostility. Systemic, collective, and coordinated group behavior consequently drops out of sight." (*Possessive Investment*, 20).

[63] Evelyn Nakano Glenn, *Unequal Freedom: How Race and Gender Shaped American Citizenship and Labor* (Cambridge, MA: Harvard University Press, 2002), 2. Musicologist Loren Kajikawa likewise analyzed the ways in which American schools and departments of music maintain legacies of white supremacy by fetishizing European classical performance standards and reproduction of past works, restricting access through auditions, and maintaining "universal" musical standards of aesthetic quality that are based

"*Structural* is often the only way to capture what goes unnoticed—the silently raised eyebrows, the implicit biases, snap judgements made on perceptions of competency."[64] DiAngelo explains further, "White supremacy in this context does not refer to individual white people and their individual intentions or actions but to an overarching political, economic, and social system of domination.... [R]acism is a structure, not an event."[65] Understanding race as performance exposes the connections and disconnections between an individual and the political, social, and economic contracts and structures of which that individual is part. The performance of whiteness at once reveals an individual performance as well as its function within broader performances of whiteness.

## Feeling White

White Americans have been implicitly and explicitly taught to "not see" race, as McIntosh argues. This means that race and race talk can challenge white readers, producing a host of emotional responses that overwhelmingly attempt to maintain control—control over one's self and livelihood, over the terms by which race is discussed and the vocabulary used, and over people of color (including their reactions and language). As critical race studies scholar Paula Ioanide demonstrates in *The Emotional Politics of Racism: How Feelings Trump Facts in an Era of Colorblindness*, "The presumption that we can combat systemic gendered racism, nativism, and imperialism by generating more empirical facts and more reasonable arguments is severely challenged by the reality that people's emotions often prevent and inhibit genuine engagements with knowledge."[66] DiAngelo calls the heightened emotional reaction on the part of whites to charges of racism (or even discussions about racism) white fragility.[67] Brubeck also felt his whiteness deeply, even while

---

in European classical music values (such as prioritizing melody and harmony over rhythm or timbre). Loren Kajikawa, "The Possessive Investment in Classical Music: Confronting Legacies of White Supremacy in U.S. Schools and Departments of Music," in *Seeing Race Again: Countering Colorblindness Across the Disciplines*, ed. Kimberlé Crenshaw, Luke Charles Harris, Daniel Martinez HoSang, and George Lipsitz (Berkeley: University of California Press, 2019), 155–174.

[64] Eddo-Lodge, *Why I'm No Longer Talking*, 64.
[65] Robin DiAngelo, *White Fragility: Why It's So Hard for White People to Talk About Racism* (Boston, MA: Beacon Press, 2018), 28.
[66] Paula Ioanide, *The Emotional Politics of Racism: How Feelings Trump Facts in an Era of Colorblindness* (Stanford, CA: Stanford University Press, 2015), 2.
[67] DiAngelo, *White* Fragility, 28. While white fragility has been critiqued as an ineffective method of implicit bias training, and though DiAngelo herself is a complicated white figure within the field of critical whiteness studies, white fragility remains an important lens through which to view Brubeck, his critics, and his audiences. For criticism of DiAngelo, see Daniel Bergner, "'White Fragility' Is Everywhere. But Does Antiracism Training Work?" *New York Times*, July 15, 2020, https://www.nytimes.com/2020/07/15/magazine/white-fragility-robin-diangelo.html; Jonathan Chait, "Is the Anti-Racism Training Industry

maintaining colorblind ideologies, and when challenged, his responses varied between surprise, anger, fragility, confidence, and a desire to work harder on social justice causes.

Part of the emotional challenge for Brubeck, along with other white people, comes from the way we have been enculturated to conceive of ourselves as individual moral actors operating outside of a racial group. As Dyer writes,

> A white person is taught to believe that all that she or he does, good and ill, all that we achieve, is to be accounted for in terms of our individuality. It is intolerable to realize that we may get a job or a nice house, or a helpful response at school or in hospitals, because of our skin colour, not because of the unique, achieving individual we must believe ourselves to be.[68]

Understanding racism as simply a result of bad moral values (as opposed to "good" moral values) reinforces the notion that racism is about individuals rather than structures of white supremacy. It might be tempting to call Brubeck a "good" or "nice" white person; however, whether or not Brubeck is a "good person" is beside the point. Indeed, as Sullivan contends, even the question of whether or not Brubeck is a "good white person" "contains a psychological privilege . . . of always feeling that they ["good" white people] are in the right."[69] The iconography of mid-century anti-Black racism tends to focus on images of the KKK, or southern white sheriffs and police officers with batons and vicious dogs.[70] Brubeck's story challenges contemporary stark conceptions of mid-century white supremacy, which, with the passage of time, have become painted in black and white rather than shades of gray. In other words, the way many white people frame racism is on one particular extreme end of a spectrum of racism—a spectrum that is far broader than colorblind ideologies allow.

---

Just Peddling White Supremacy?" *New York Magazine*, July 16, 2020, https://nymag.com/intelligencer/2020/07/antiracism-training-white-fragility-robin-diangelo-ibram-kendi.html; Carlos Lozada, "White Fragility Is Real. But 'White Fragility' Is Flawed," *Washington Post*, June 18, 2020, https://www.washingtonpost.com/outlook/2020/06/18/white-fragility-is-real-white-fragility-is-flawed/; John McWhorter, "The Dehumanizing Condescension of *White Fragility*," *The Atlantic*, July 15, 2020, https://www.theatlantic.com/ideas/archive/2020/07/dehumanizing-condescension-white-fragility/614146/; Kelefa Sanneh, "The Fight to Redefine Racism," *New Yorker*, August 12, 2019, https://www.newyorker.com/magazine/2019/08/19/the-fight-to-redefine-racism; George Yancy, interviewed by Woojin Lim, "To Be Black in the US Is to Have a Knee Against Your Neck Each Day," *Truthout*, July 18, 2020, https://truthout.org/articles/george-yancy-to-be-black-in-the-us-is-to-have-a-knee-against-your-neck-each-day/.

[68] Dyer, *White*, 9.
[69] Sullivan, *Revealing Whiteness*, 184.
[70] As Eddo-Lodge argues, "People feel that if a racist attack has not occurred, or the word 'nigger' has not been uttered, an action can't be racist." Eddo-Lodge, *Why I'm No Longer Talking*, 63.

The maxim "seeing is believing" holds true for many white folks in discussions about racism; that is, racism does not seem to exist for some white people until and unless they are able to witness it. History bears this out: violent images of Emmett Till; the 16th Street Baptist Church in Birmingham, Alabama; Selma, Alabama's "Bloody Sunday"; and the assassination of Martin Luther King Jr. each galvanized white support for key policy changes during the civil rights movement. While the more recent videos and stories representing the deaths and inhumane treatment of Michael Brown, Michelle Cusseaux, Tamir Rice, Eric Garner, Natasha McKenna, Breonna Taylor, George Floyd, and so many other Black women and men at the hands of police have resulted in fewer large-scale policy changes, they have nevertheless resulted in greater support for movements like #BlackLivesMatter. Despite these moments, some white Americans claim that they are not racist, in large part because they can see neither the pain inflicted by racist microaggressions with which they have been enculturated for generations, nor the racism that persists at structural levels—the racism that affords many whites more generational wealth, better schooling, greater social mobility, better healthcare, and so on. White possessive investment in moral rectitude obscures many of these forms of racism; as DiAngelo writes of "nice" white progressives, "Niceness requires that racism only be acknowledged in acts that intentionally hurt or discriminate, which means that racism can rarely be acknowledged."[71] In other words, many white Americans have been able to see racism only in a particular way—one that too often results in lethal violence and Black trauma. As jazz scholar Dale Chapman summarizes, "What has in fact occurred, in this era of 'racism without racists,' is that the application of racist discrimination has simply shifted to other, less visible registers of social interaction."[72]

Like many other white Americans, Brubeck also was able to see particularly violent forms of racism clearly. This is evident in a scene from the Ken Burns *Jazz* documentary in which Brubeck emotionally recalled an extremely impactful interaction from his young childhood with the first Black man he ever saw when he was growing up in rural Ione, California.[73] During most of

---

[71] Robin DiAngelo, *Nice Racism: How Progressive White People Perpetuate Racial Harm* (Boston: Beacon Press, 2021), 49.

[72] Dale Chapman, *The Jazz Bubble: Neoclassical Jazz in Neoliberal Culture* (Berkeley: University of California Press, 2018), 17.

[73] Ken Burns's *Jazz* has been critiqued for the ways in which it presents a master narrative of jazz that omits much in the name of preserving bebop as a type of jazz ur-text. See further George Lipsitz, "Jazz: The Hidden History of Nationalist Multiculturalism," *Footsteps in the Dark: Hidden Histories of Popular Music* (Minneapolis: Minneapolis University, 2007), 79–106; Catherine Gunther Kodat, "Conversing with Ourselves: Canon, Freedom, Jazz," *American Quarterly*, 55 no. 1 (March 2003): 1–28; Tracy McMullen, *Haunthenticity: Musical Replay and the Fear of the Real* (Middletown, CT: Wesleyan University Press, 2019), 108–109.

his interviews throughout the documentary, Brubeck is steady—he looks into the camera, smiles often, and speaks with a strong voice. But in this scene, Brubeck becomes emotional, tears springing to his eyes as he explains the moment when his father asked the Black man (Brubeck identifies the man as his father's friend) to open his shirt for Brubeck. Brubeck pauses, and looks up, above the camera as the memory comes to him. He starts, "There--" and abruptly stops, leans over, head down. When he lifts his head again, tears are in his eyes. "There was a *brand*. On his chest." He pauses again, this time for a long time, turning his head to the side, very clearly fighting back tears. As he raises his head to camera level, he starts, "My dad," his voice breaking at the mention of his father, "said 'These things can't happen.'" As his eyes return to the camera, he shakes his head slightly, before looking away again. And then, with great passion, he returns to the camera, nodding his head affirmatively: "*That's* why I fought for what I fought for." His strength and determination remain clear, even as (or perhaps because) his voice wavers, and becomes thinner and higher pitched.

It is an emotionally affective moment—one that for some viewers demonstrated that Brubeck understood deeply that the racial violence, evidenced by the scar on the man's body, was wrong, and a moment that Brubeck's son, Chris Brubeck, would credit with changing the narrative surrounding Brubeck from being a "square" to having an important impact on jazz history.[74] But the story Brubeck shares also demonstrates a familiar episode in which white viewers can see particular acts as racist while in other spaces maintaining colorblind ideologies that deny racist treatment in systemic ways. Indeed, one fundamental paradox of colorblind ideologies is that white innocence exists simultaneously with anti-Black racial violence. As philosopher George Yancy contends, other less physically violent forms of racism threaten white innocence because those forms of racism implicate the systems in which we live:

> White people must be prepared to accept the lie that is their whiteness. It's not about fragility. It's about white people's desire to maintain their white power,

---

[74] As Brubeck's son, Chris Brubeck, would later explain, "Anyone that was in the jazz press took the time to watch the entire Ken Burns *Jazz* series, and it started generating this new assessment of Dave.... [Instead of saying] 'He's too straight; he's boring; he's corny,' they started thinking, 'He's a real human being that has a big heart and cares about people. There's a hell of a good man who plays music originally and well, and let's appreciate him.' It's part of what made the last quadrant, or fifth, of his life so beautiful. All the axes that were being ground suddenly were laid to rest." Morgan Enos, "What Do We Overlook About Dave Brubeck on His 100th Birthday? Authors, Musicians, and Family Members Reflect," *Discogs Blog*, December 4, 2020, https://blog.discogs.com/en/dave-brubeck-birthday-overlooked-moments/.

white privilege and white innocence. History has given them the blinkers, the shelters to use to protect them from facing the lie and violence of whiteness, their whiteness.[75]

White racial innocence is far more easily maintained if racism must be seen to be believed. In the Ken Burns scene, the audience sees an impactful performance of white innocence. This does not mean that this moment is not a true representation of Brubeck's feelings about the memory, nor that the moment at the river was not incredibly important to him; indeed, litigating the sincerity of this moment is entirely beside the point. As Taylor writes, these performances are *not* necessarily "theatrical, put-on, 'pretend,' or conscious acts."[76] Rather, understanding this moment as a performance allows it to be contextualized alongside other performances and re-performances of whiteness across time. It is a performance of white innocence that ostensibly provides evidence of "sincerity" and of "goodness," and whose end result separates one "innocent" white person (and those who share in that performance) from white racist, violently anti-Black individuals. But in their focus on individual acts of physically violent racism, performances of white innocence ultimately leave broader structures of white supremacy safely in place.

For white scholars, disrupting white racial innocence will almost certainly result in feelings of white fragility, but as Yancy explains, "Undoing whiteness will certainly *not* happen by simply understanding that whiteness is a site of fragility."[77] One of my own moments of such disruption occurred as a graduate student fellow at Washington University in St. Louis's Center for the Humanities in Fall 2015, one year after the killing of Michael Brown. While the protests throughout Ferguson and St. Louis in 2014 had largely passed by Washington University in St. Louis (WashU), the academic year that followed featured several academic dialogues aimed at engaging with St. Louis's historical and contemporary experiences with racial discrimination. In early October, the Center hosted an event called "Arts in Struggle: An Afternoon of Creativity, Community and Dialogue on the Struggle for Racial Justice," as part of the Greater St. Louis Humanities Festival. Held in a local art gallery, it featured visual art by Damon Davis and De Andrea Nichols, a spoken word performance by Cheeraz Gormon, and a screening of Katina Parker's documentary, *Ferguson: A Report from Occupied Territory*. The event culminated

---

[75] George Yancy, interview with Woojin Lim, "To Be Black in the US Is to Have a Knee Against Your Neck Each Day," *Truthout*, July 18, 2020, https://truthout.org/articles/george-yancy-to-be-black-in-the-us-is-to-have-a-knee-against-your-neck-each-day/

[76] Taylor, *Performance*, 31.

[77] Yancy, *Truthout*.

in a panel moderated by WashU assistant professor of African and African-American Studies, Jonathan Fenderson.[78]

During the panel I was sitting with others from the Center for Humanities—a row of white academics (and a couple of friends). There were also a handful of Black community members in attendance. In the question-and-answer section, it became clear that what I and others from the Center had considered to be thought-provoking and important was traumatizing for two Black women in attendance in particular—an entire afternoon focused on Black death, pain, and trauma, seemingly for the edification of the predominantly white scholars in the room. One woman's response remains fresh in my memory: "You are killing our babies," she told us.

I recoiled at what I perceived to be a horrendous accusation—after all, I had very clearly not killed anyone. For days afterward, my internal responses vacillated between shame, disappointment, anger, and confusion: Why would this woman want to alienate the "good" white people trying to make a difference, trying with the best intentions to learn and do better? How could she think that of us, of me? Put simply, my response focused on the disruption of my white racial innocence, which ultimately centered me and my hurt; it individualized her comment, reacting against the notion that I should be considered responsible for the actions of other white people, or that I was part of a broader system of white supremacy. My response thus unfairly equated my pain with hers, and it centered my individuality, intentions, and innocence (hallmarks of white privilege) over hers.

Whiteness studies has an uncomfortable obsession with "goodness" that is impossible to miss; the construct of goodness is unavoidably scattered throughout this chapter in quotes by Sullivan, Dyer, and DiAngelo, just as it fills remembrances of Brubeck's life. Even attempts to unpack the term reek of a cloying desire to, if not absolve oneself or one's allies, then to align oneself and one's allies with "not racists." "Goodness" seems to confer innocence on the "right" white folk, but it is also a shield that deflects attacks against that same white innocence. As Yancy suggests, being "good" "does not exempt you from the relational dimensions of white privilege and power."[79] The good/bad racist binary further obscures systemic racism by focusing on one racist individual; according to Eddo-Lodge, "We tell ourselves that good people can't be

---

[78] Tila Neguse, "'Art and Activism Are Inseparable': Artists Share Their Social Justice Work and Ideas," *Center for the Humanities*, September 29, 2015, https://humanities.wustl.edu/features/Arts-in-Struggle-St-Louis-Humanities-Festival?_ga=2.184067494.1421195242.1592402051-1258598002.1489291557.

[79] George Yancy, "Guidelines for Whites Teaching About Whiteness," *Teaching Race: How to Help Students Unmask and Challenge Racism* (Hoboken, NJ: John Wiley, 2019), 31.

racist.... We tell ourselves that racism is about moral values, when instead it is about the survival strategy of systemic power."[80]

## Anti-Racism

The power, privilege, and effects of whiteness must first be known to be disavowed and dismantled. It is useful to think about some of the aspects of whiteness performed by Brubeck during his career through a frame of anti-racism as Kendi defines it: "a powerful collection of antiracist policies that lead to racial equity and are substantiated by antiracist ideas."[81] Anti-racist people, therefore, support anti-racist ideas (that racial groups are equals) and anti-racist policies (that "written and unwritten laws, rules, procedures, processes, regulations, and guidelines that govern people" should sustain racial equity between racial groups). Brubeck refused to perform in the South without Eugene Wright, his Black bassist, and he refused to stay in segregated hotels while on tour; in these actions, he supported anti-racist ideas (that Wright was his equal) and anti-racist policies, by rewarding integrated hotels and colleges with his business. His longer-form compositions in the 1960s often included frank social justice messages: *The Real Ambassadors* (1962) addressed the hypocrisy inherent in the State Department's use of Black jazz musicians to support the United States' diplomatic agenda abroad while racism continued unchecked at home; *Gates of Justice* (1969) used texts from the Jewish sage Hillel, Martin Luther King Jr., and the Bible to inspire continued civil rights activism among Jewish audiences and to re-kindle Black-Jewish relations. In writing these compositions, Brubeck publicly championed anti-racist ideas, and *The Real Ambassadors* explicitly critiqued racist policies.

However, anti-racism is not a permanent state of being; rather, it is a process of constant striving to commit anti-racist acts, and to make anti-racist statements. In distinguishing between being "not a racist" and being anti-racist, Kendi asserts that the former is essentially neutral, and basically says, "I am not a racist, but neither am I aggressively against racism."[82] But as Kendi explains, "There is no neutrality in the racism struggle." One cannot simply *be* "not a racist," nor can they always be anti-racist. Brubeck is not automatically and permanently an anti-racist simply by taking anti-racist measures in his musical actions, no matter how important. Brubeck also remained

---

[80] Eddo-Lodge, *Why I'm No Longer Talking*, 63–64.
[81] Ibram X. Kendi, *How to Be an Anti-racist* (New York: One World, 2019), 1.
[82] Ibid., 9.

simultaneously committed to an unrealistic notion of colorblindness that frequently denied the experiences of people of color, particularly within the music industry, and race politics of Brubeck's era ultimately benefited him in both material and symbolic ways.

Some white folks will have a problem with that last sentence—that Brubeck benefited in material and symbolic ways because he was white. I know this because I have spoken with them in classrooms during lectures, academic conference rooms in presentations of my research, and by telephone as I worked with various stakeholders throughout this project. Before this book was published, reactions spanned the gamut and included both support of what some referred to as "activist musicology" and questions rooted in white fragility seeking to preserve Brubeck's (and the questioner's own) white innocence. Even as I was completing the book, I felt pulled to the white anxiety I both heard and imagined, as I recognized familiar performances of whiteness in others, performances that I have put on before. In one conversation, I was repeatedly questioned on how various future audiences might perceive Brubeck after reading various portions of the book. It took an entire month and the advice of a close mentor to realize how such encounters had already begun to threaten the arguments in my nearly fully drafted project. White tears and fears combined in anxiety over Brubeck's "goodness," and I had begun to write and edit within those all too familiar performances of whiteness. But fear of what? A fear of the rupture of white innocence, of what comes with the loss of solidarity in the performance of whiteness, of a new kind of unenculturated performance? I had unintentionally provided the answer to Ahmed's question: "Is a whiteness that is anxious about itself—its narcissism, its egoism, its privilege, its self-centeredness—better?"[83] It was all too easy to slip back to familiar, even if emotional, performances of white anxiety and innocence, and to unfairly equate my intellectual fears with the very real fears of racial violence that were literally happening all around me in the wake of George Floyd's death.

Put simply, I have had to constantly critique and re-critique not only my work but my approach to the work. Kendi's focus on anti-racism demands that attention be given to anti-racists and their methods in a constant striving toward justice rather than simply focusing on racists:

> What if antiracists constantly self-critiqued our own ideas? What if we blamed our ideologies and methods, studied our ideologies and methods, refined our ideologies and methods again and again until they worked? . . . Self-critique allows

---

[83] Ahmed, "Declarations of Whiteness," 2004.

change. Changing shows flexibility. Antiracist power must be flexible to match the flexibility of racist power, propelled only by the craving for power to shape policy and their inequitable interests.[84]

Kendi's focus on self-critique moves beyond the tendency to focus on "bad" feelings like shame or guilt when reflecting on whiteness, but it does not become what Ahmed describes as a discourse of love or narcissism when she writes of fears that "whiteness studies could even become a spectacle of pure self-reflection, augmented by an insistence that whiteness 'is an identity too.'"[85] The goal is not to categorize Brubeck as either anti-racist or not anti-racist (or racist, for that matter), but to interrogate Brubeck's image, reception, and sound within broader systems of whiteness, white privilege, and white supremacy to create a fuller picture of the performance of whiteness in mid-century America.

Therefore, this book should not be considered a form of anti-racism. Arguing against the performativity of anti-racism, Ahmed offers further warnings for projects in critical whiteness studies that warrant re-stating in full here:

> I am arguing that whiteness studies, even in its critical form, should not be about re-describing the white subject as anti-racist, or constitute itself as a form of anti-racism, or even as providing the conditions for anti-racism. Whiteness studies should instead be about attending to forms of white racism and white privilege that are not undone, and may even be repeated and intensified, through declarations of whiteness, or through the recognition of privilege as privilege.[86]

In other words, simply undoing white racism or white privilege, though a crucial task, is not anti-racist; recognizing whiteness or declaring white privilege, as most critical whiteness studies attend to, does not do anything to support equality among racial groups. Neither recognition nor analysis of modes of white privilege as performed in this book ensures anti-racist policies, actions, or behaviors. I point to performances of whiteness and white privilege replayed over time and particularly prominent in the United States at mid-century, but the work itself focuses on, as Ahmed writes above, "attending to forms of white racism and white privilege that are not undone, and may even be repeated and intensified."[87]

---

[84] Kendi, *How to Be an Anti-racist*, 214.
[85] Ahmed, "Declarations of Whiteness," para. 5.
[86] Ibid., para. 58.
[87] For example, musicologist Carol Oja details some of the materials found in Sarah Corbin Robert's archive. Robert served as president general of the Daughters of the American Revolution (DAR) when they

## Chapter Outline

How is whiteness performed and re-performed? How do particular traits become inscribed with whiteness, and further, how do those traits, now racialized in a listener's mind, filter the sounds a listener hears? By pairing visual cues with musical codes of whiteness, I argue that we can hear the multiple layers upon which whiteness operated at mid-century for musicians, critics, and audiences more fully through a detailed examination of the specific privileges granted to Brubeck, his critics, and his audiences at mid-century.

Chapter 1 focuses on how jazz critics performed race in their musical discussions of Brubeck's music. In a series of debates appearing in *Down Beat* magazine in 1955, critics assessed the merits of the Dave Brubeck Quartet in direct comparison with the Modern Jazz Quartet, an all-Black group, in terms of counterpoint, spontaneity, swing, and commercial success. While many studies in jazz focus on the relationship between blackness, rhythm, and authenticity, I introduce the concept of white intellectual privilege to examine a specific privilege granted to white cool jazz musicians like Brubeck—that is, critics' assumptions that his music was uniquely intellectual by virtue of its connections to European classical music, particularly through counterpoint. By comparing the music of each quartet through critics' descriptions, I demonstrate how critics inscribed Brubeck's sound within a rhetoric of white intellectual privilege while denying the same association to the Modern Jazz Quartet, who also included extensive counterpoint in their music. The chapter also examines Brubeck's own colorblind approach to jazz and race.

Chapter 2 focuses on Brubeck's conversion of new audiences to jazz in the 1950s. His method was to promote an image of respectability, which he deployed in mainstream publications, advertisements, and personal appearances in which he performed the role of jazz authority figure. With this image, he found entrance to the predominantly white spaces of suburban homes, college campuses, and mainstream magazines. In their overwhelming support of Brubeck and his music, white, middle-class, and

---

refused to allow famed singer Marian Anderson to perform a concert in Constitution Hall because she was Black. Robert's archive contains new details into this pivotal historical moment—details that further implicate the DAR in the racist decision not to allow Anderson to perform and which reveal the insidious and covert ways in which white supremacy was wielded by this group of white women. Nevertheless, the DAR decided to open the archive, even allowing more offensive documents to be viewed on their public website. As Oja suggests, DAR's decision marks a move toward anti-racism, in that it could support the work of dismantling past racist ideas and policies. However, it is not itself an anti-racist action as opening the archive presents no policy supporting equality among racial groups, and indeed, potential viewers are not obliged to enact anti-racist ideas or policies upon encountering the documents. Carol J. Oja, "Segregating a Great Singer: Marian Anderson and the Daughters of the American Revolution," *Times Literary Supplement*, July 17, 2020, 10–11.

upper-middle-class mainstream audiences quite literally bought into the notion that their thoughtful appreciation of his music could link themselves to his sonic and visual images of intellect and respectability. This chapter offers three case studies focusing on spaces and audiences that had the most to gain from Brubeck's respectability: Boston's Storyville club, fans who described themselves as housewives, and *Playboy* audiences.

Brubeck's 1954 appearance on the cover of *Time* magazine introduced him to a large, predominantly white readership and contributed significantly to the rapid growth of his career. He was the second of four jazz musicians to appear on *Time*'s cover at mid-century. The others featured were all Black: Louis Armstrong (1949), Duke Ellington (1956), and Thelonious Monk (1964). In chapter 3, I analyze these stories using theories of recognition by Ralph Ellison, who writes that recognition means achieving a form of psychic agreement, and Judith Butler, who emphasizes mutual active engagement. I interrogate the shifting levels of power, invisibility, visibility, and recognition between Brubeck, Armstrong, Ellington, Monk, and *Time*'s mainstream audience.[88] In addition, by focusing on "mainstream" or non-jazz audiences in chapters 2 and 3, I demonstrate the important roles these audiences (who are often portrayed as outsiders to jazz) played in defining jazz within the broader commercial music industry.

While the first three chapters analyze Brubeck's pre-1960 career, sound, and image, the fourth and fifth chapters consider the relationships between Brubeck, his audiences, and whiteness within the context of the civil rights movement. Chapter 4 focuses on the activities surrounding his 1960 tour of the South. In January 1960, Brubeck made headlines after twenty-two segregated colleges and universities across the American South refused to allow his interracial quartet to perform. Brubeck had been quietly rehearsing his activism leading up to the scheduled southern tour: he had previously canceled concerts in Dallas (1957), South Africa (1958), and at the University of Georgia (1959), and had a near miss at East Carolina College (1958). New details in his steps toward race activism highlight the ways in which he leveraged his whiteness to support integration efforts, even as he continued to benefit from a system of racial capitalism that privileged his voice over those for whom he advocated. Ultimately, Brubeck adopted a new musical and promotional strategy aimed directly at southern audiences, a strategy that married commercial interests with political ideology by banking on his ability to draw "new" audiences to jazz.

---

[88] Ralph Ellison, *Invisible Man* (1952; repr., New York: Vintage International, 1995), 14; Judith Butler, *Undoing Gender* (New York: Routledge, 2004), 131.

Chapter 5 examines the musical culture surrounding Brubeck in the late 1960s, as the civil rights movement appeared to some to be splintering. When the Brubeck Quartet officially disbanded at the end of 1967, Brubeck made the shift to classical composition. Among his first commissions was the cantata *The Gates of Justice* (1969), which premiered at Rockdale Temple in Cincinnati, Ohio. Commissioned by the Union of American Hebrew Congregations (UAHC) with the College Conservatory of Music at the University of Cincinnati, Brubeck was tasked with composing a cantata that would address what many Jewish leaders perceived as the rapidly deteriorating relationship between Black and Jewish communities. I position the work within its original context, presenting musical analysis alongside conversations among Black and Jewish leaders across the 1960s. I reveal the ways in which the cantata, though explicitly intended to speak to Black-Jewish relations, also re-solidified a particularly Jewish identity in an era of increasing discomfort with white assimilation among Jewish communities. In selecting Brubeck for the commission and by framing the cantata as a work with specific resonance among Jewish audiences, I argue that Rockdale Temple and the UAHC's leaders ultimately attempted to draw a greater contrast between Jewishness and mid-century American whiteness.

To conclude, I consider Brubeck's relationship to his alleged Native American ancestry within the context of the fraught arguments over race, ownership, belonging, and jazz in the 1990s. Rather than attempt to seek the "truth" of Brubeck's ancestry, revealed in detail in jazz critic Gene Lees's *Cats of Any Color: Jazz, Black and White* (1994), the conclusion is a critique of white possessive investment in a settler understanding of Indigeneity and multiculturalism. In grappling with Brubeck's relationship with Native American sounds in his choral composition *Earth Is Our Mother* (1992) and claims of ancestry amid a white backlash against Black musicians and writers like Wynton Marsalis, Stanley Crouch, and Albert Murray who asserted a new focus on Black musicians in jazz, I examine a final performance of whiteness: a performance of white evasion that maintains white dominance, even as it asserts its racial justice credentials.

## Loving Brubeck

As an author, I am mindful of the negative reactions possible in a project that scrutinizes Brubeck's race, particularly for his family and friends, and the musical communities who loved and knew him. Though Brubeck passed away in the early stages of the dissertation research that would ultimately become part of this book, the hours spanning the 2010s and early 2020s I spent researching in his archive, watching him, listening to his voice and his music, reading his words, charting his movements across the country, and playing transcriptions of his music at the piano gave me some sense of knowing him. As musicologist Ashley Pribyl suggests of similar archival research, "As I read through someone's papers, I get to know them as a person. I learn to recognize their handwriting, their pet-names for their friends and family, sometimes even their inside jokes.... They become a friend to me, even though I am a stranger to them."[89]

In the name of loving and of knowing, I focus on Brubeck's whiteness, and that of his audiences and critics, not to critique him unfairly for not always being who I wanted him to be in the twenty-first century. Indeed, as Lipsitz asserts, "There has always been racism in the United States, but it has not always been the same racism."[90] Instead, I focus on performances of whiteness by and surrounding a musician who attempted to dedicate himself to civil rights work to show how deep the perpetual performance of whiteness runs—how invisible it is to the social justice-minded. I do so as a reminder that many white people are still unable to fully name the harm that performance does. I focus on Brubeck, in short, because I believe he still has lessons left to teach us about the crucial questions of race in America, if we are willing to listen to his performance.

---

[89] Ashley Pribyl, "Mourning Harold Prince: A Scholar's Perspective," *New York Public Library*, June 10, 2020, https://www.nypl.org/blog/2020/06/10/mourning-harold-prince-scholars-perspective.

[90] Lipsitz, *Possessive Investment*, 4. Similarly, Alcoff writes that the solution to whiteness and its relationship to racism "will not be found in a flaccid universal humanism, nor in a pursuit of white redemption, nor in a call to a race-transcendent vision of class struggle. Rather, the solution will be found in facing the truths about who we are, how we got here, and then developing an offensive strategy for achieving a future in which we can all find a place" (204).

# 1
## "Any Jackass Can Swing"
### Sounds in Black and White

For much of his career, Dave Brubeck was considered by many to be something of an outsider to jazz. According to jazz critics, Brubeck did not swing and was too far outside jazz's legacy, while for mainstream music critics, Brubeck seemed "respectable," his music "intellectual"—contrasts that implicitly drew attention to Brubeck's whiteness in different ways. Some of Brubeck's perceived outsiderness likely stemmed, at least in part, from his entry into jazz, which seems to have come from the combination of a highly developed ear (possibly the result of dyslexia, which made it difficult for him to read music); hearing Duke Ellington, Art Tatum, and Stan Kenton on the radio; a classical background that included lessons from his mother, a classically trained pianist; and later, study with French modernist composer Darius Milhaud. In a time when other jazz musicians might have been working their way up through big bands, in small gigs in big cities, cutting contests, or by hearing and studying the "greats" in performance, Brubeck's relative isolation growing up in Ione, California, and attending college in Stockton, California, before his deployment in World War II, ensured a different path. Indeed, in his early career, Brubeck seemed to be using jazz to attain a career in composition—an approach supported by Milhaud, who encouraged his students to take full advantage of jazz in their compositions as their American birthright. In articles in *Down Beat* magazine published in 1952 and 1954, during Brubeck's rise to fame, Brubeck suggested that his life as a jazz musician might only be temporary and that eventually he planned to settle down and compose "serious" music.[1] More than fifteen years after those articles, Brubeck did eventually focus on classical composition. Still, Brubeck remains in the memories of many today as a jazz musician, to one degree or another.

The details of how the Brubeck quartet formed have been explained elsewhere, but a brief recounting here sets the stage for the musical debates

---

[1] Nat Hentoff, "Brubeck Has Double Life as Jazzman, Classic Composer," *Down Beat*, December 3, 1952, 6; Nat Hentoff, "Jazz Fills Role of Classical Composition, Brubeck Learns," *Down Beat*, June 2, 1954, 2.

*Dave Brubeck and the Performance of Whiteness*. Kelsey Klotz, Oxford University Press. © Oxford University Press 2023.
DOI: 10.1093/oso/9780197525074.003.0002

ahead.² Following service in World War II (where he narrowly escaped the Battle of the Bulge by creating an interracial army band, and where he also first met alto saxophonist Paul Desmond), Brubeck attended Mills College on the GI Bill in pursuit of a master's degree in music, which he never completed. At Mills College, he studied with Darius Milhaud, who became a monumental figure in Brubeck's life (he and Iola Brubeck named their first child Darius). With Milhaud's students, as well as Desmond and vibraphonist and percussionist Cal Tjader, Brubeck formed an octet, a group that performed original compositions and arrangements. Brubeck later claimed that the octet should have rivaled the *Birth of the Cool* nonet in terms of innovations to small ensemble jazz composition. In the late 1940s, as he tried to get the octet off the ground, Brubeck gigged around the Bay Area in trios and quartets, and was by his accounts incredibly financially insecure. At one point, as Ted Gioia documents, Desmond stole a regular gig from Brubeck.³ Brubeck refused to speak to or play with Desmond, though by 1950 Desmond had essentially launched a crusade to re-join Brubeck's group (he studied recordings, memorized their book, and offered to babysit). Brubeck's wife, Iola, intervened in the relationship, allowing Desmond in the house when Brubeck had forbidden it, and a thaw began. Brubeck officially extended an offer to Desmond after Brubeck nearly broke his neck in a diving accident in Hawaii. Brubeck was still in traction and had only recently learned he would be able to play the piano again; Iola Brubeck wrote the letter to Desmond on Dave Brubeck's behalf. Around 1949, just before the original quartet formed, Iola Brubeck began a letter-writing campaign, offering the trio to various local colleges for student body assemblies or dances, and the octet for more formal concerts. As the quartet became more of a focus, Iola Brubeck gradually began to write to colleges farther afield, until the Brubeck Quartet became a known entity on college campuses.

The original quartet, which officially formed in 1951, included Brubeck and Desmond as regular members. The bass and drum seats rotated fairly often: drummers included Herb Barman (1951), Lloyd Davis (1952–1953), and Joe Dodge (1953–1956); bassists included Roger Nichols (July–August 1951), Freddie Dutton (September 1951), Gene England (October 1951), Wyatt Ruther (November 1951–December 1952), Ron Crotty (December 1952–1954), Bob Bates (1954–1955), Norman Bates (1955–1957), and Joe

---

[2] Philip Clark, *Dave Brubeck: A Life in Time* (Cambridge, MA: Da Capo Press, 2020); Stephen A. Crist, *Dave Brubeck's* Time Out (Oxford: Oxford University Press, 2019); Fred M. Hall, *It's About Time: The Dave Brubeck Story* (Fayetteville: University of Arkansas Press, 1996).

[3] Ted Gioia, *West Coast Jazz: Modern Jazz in California, 1945–1960* (Berkeley: University of California Press, 1992).

Benjamin (1958). The quartet shifted between all-white and integrated formations in its early years: while all of the quartet's drummers were white, bassists Freddie Dutton, Wyatt Ruther, and Joe Benjamin were Black. In the mid-fifties, during Brubeck's steep ascent to fame, the quartet was often all-white. In 1956, Joe Morello joined on drums, and in 1958, Eugene Wright joined on bass; together with Brubeck and Desmond, these four comprised the classic quartet, which played together until the quartet disbanded in 1967. The classic quartet was integrated, featuring Brubeck, Desmond, and Morello, who were white, and Wright, who was Black.

Brubeck's popularity truly manifested in 1954. The group had begun to place highly in critics' polls by the music magazine *Metronome* in 1952 and 1953, and then in 1954, Brubeck signed a record deal with Columbia Records. In November 1954, he became only the second jazz musician to be featured on the cover of *Time* magazine (following Louis Armstrong in 1949). *Time*'s coverage (detailed in chapter 3) was laudatory and presented him as a serious jazz musician, unlike most others in jazz. Following the *Time* cover, the jazz press reacted en masse. As jazz historian Grover Sales explained,

> Brubeck's *Time* cover fanned the long-smoldering resentment within the black jazz community against the commercial dominance of white "cool" and its genteel restraint.... Feeling *Time* should have honored Ellington, among others, black musicians were put out because they held Brubeck to be peripheral to important developments, outside the mainstream of modern jazz, a founder of no schools, and an inspirer of few disciples.[4]

*Down Beat* critics who had previously offered positive or at least lukewarm criticism of Brubeck became part of a months-long conversation about the legitimacy of his music within the world of jazz. Such conversations continued throughout his career, leading Gioia to conclude, "Brubeck's music is loved or hated, and rarely viewed with indifference.... About Dave Brubeck there is no consensus."[5]

But in 1955, some vocal *Down Beat* jazz critics did find a consensus: whether or not they liked Brubeck's music, they overwhelmingly believed that he remained an outsider to the history of jazz, detached from its legacy, and with little potential contribution to its future. As their pens flew and typewriters clacked in defense of jazz tradition, jazz critics Leonard Feather, Nat Hentoff, and Ralph Gleason added to the growing discourse of whiteness surrounding

---

[4] Grover Sales, *Jazz: America's Classical Music* (1984; repr., New York: Da Capo Press, 1992), 168–169.
[5] Gioia, *West Coast Jazz*, 66.

descriptions of Brubeck's music around the key themes of improvisation, counterpoint, and swing. In their use of these terms, critics implicitly defined jazz along racial lines, in part constructing and building on what Ingrid Monson refers to as "one of the worst discursive legacies of the 1950s and 1960s"—the racial coding of "intellectual and unemotional" as distinctly white.[6] This chapter identifies part of what defined jazz's 1950s "sonic color line," a phrase by sound studies scholar Jennifer Lynn Stoever that explains how music and sound are affixed to "essential notions of racial identity, constructing the grammar of the sonic color line and casting it far beyond any immediately visible onstage presence."[7]

## Critics' Debate

The critics' debate began with Leonard Feather's February 1955 "Blindfold Test," which was a popular feature in *Down Beat*, a leading jazz magazine read by jazz audiences and musicians alike. Its premise was simple: Feather played ten recordings for top jazz musicians, who then guessed the performer. The appeal of each feature was the promise of hearing what a well-known musician supposedly really thought about their fellow musicians, but as historian Eric Porter notes, the tests often also supported Feather's own "colorblind" theory of jazz.[8] Most of these columns appeared without much remark from other critics and readers.[9] However, this was not the case for one seemingly unexceptional test given in 1955 to Shorty Rogers, a white Los Angeles-based trumpeter usually associated with West Coast jazz.[10]

Two of the recordings Feather played featured the Dave Brubeck Quartet (DBQ) and the Modern Jazz Quartet (MJQ), an all-Black group that had formed out of the rhythm section of the Dizzy Gillespie big band in 1951, around the same time as the Brubeck Quartet. The MJQ's members included John Lewis (artistic director and pianist), Milt Jackson (vibraphone), Percy

---

[6] Ingrid Monson, *Freedom Sounds: Civil Rights Call Out to Jazz and Africa* (Oxford: Oxford University Press, 2007), 295.
[7] Jennifer Lynn Stoever, *The Sonic Color Line: Race and The Cultural Politics of Listening* (New York: New York University Press, 2016), 82.
[8] Eric Porter, *What Is This Thing Called Jazz? African American Musicians as Artists, Critics, and Activists* (Berkeley: University of California Press, 2002), 118.
[9] A notable exception is Roy Eldridge's 1951 "Blindfold Test," in which Feather attempted to prove that Eldridge could not, as Eldridge had claimed, tell a white player from a Black player. Leonard Feather, "The Blindfold Test: Little Jazz Goes Color Blind," *Down Beat*, July 13, 1951, 12. Detailed in Monson, *Freedom Sounds*, 80.
[10] Leonard Feather, "The Blindfold Test: Shorty Shows Catholic Taste, Picks MJQ, Ory," *Down Beat*, February 9, 1955, 13.

Heath (bass), and Kenny Clarke (drums), who was replaced by Connie Kay in 1955. The MJQ remained an active performing ensemble until 1974.

After correctly identifying the MJQ's recording of "Vendôme," Rogers responded, "This record, to my way of thinking, has just about everything. The spontaneous and the preconceived construction work, the very wonderful contrapuntal writing, canonic imitation, without being pretentious about the whole thing." After he correctly identified a DBQ recording of "Here Lies Love," Rogers directly compared the MJQ and DBQ: "I enjoy more of a balance of preconceived composition work combined with the spontaneous, such as you find with the Modern Jazz Quartet." For Rogers, the main difference between the MJQ and the DBQ was a perceived distinction between "preconceived composition" and spontaneity, in which the MJQ balanced both and the DBQ focused on spontaneity. This reversed the standard script written by critics for Black and white musicians, which normally held that white musicians relied on pre-composition while Black musicians were "naturally" gifted improvisers.

Rogers's comparison between the MJQ and the DBQ exacerbated the growing feeling among many critics that the DBQ had gained more popularity than its musical ability warranted, and spurred a debate among *Down Beat*'s columnists about both quartets that played out across the magazine's pages for months to come. In the following issue, Leonard Feather focused on the disparities in recognition and financial well-being between the MJQ and DBQ.[11] Brubeck, Feather wrote, had received much more media and commercial attention than the MJQ had; by February 1955, Brubeck had been featured on the cover of *Time* magazine and had signed to the Columbia record label. Feather argued that, in contrast, the MJQ had "paid their dues in jazz for longer, wearier, more disheartening years than Brubeck and his sidemen have ever known."[12] Further, despite the MJQ's financial lack, Feather insisted that they had offered more to jazz through their experiments in form and "the jazz language." Whereas Rogers's comparison had implicitly asked how the quartets' musical approaches differed, Feather asked how two quartets with such *similar* musical approaches could have such differing levels of recognition. For Feather, the only answer lay in the difference in the racial makeup of the quartets.

In subsequent issues, critics Nat Hentoff and Ralph Gleason escalated the fever pitch largely against Brubeck, again invoking the MJQ as a better

---

[11] Leonard Feather, "Feather's Nest," *Down Beat*, February 23, 1955, 7.
[12] Ibid.

example of similar musical approaches.[13] But while Feather directly tied the difference in recognition between the groups to racial disparities, both Hentoff and Gleason's comments implicitly embedded race into a conversation about music. In doing so, they each relied on stereotypical relationships between Black jazz musicians and swing, while also contributing to an invisible discourse about the sound of whiteness.

Down Beat offered two conclusions to this debate. The first came in June 1955 from Feather, whose own columns four months earlier had initiated the conversations.[14] This time, Feather made it even more clear that race was the only meaningful distinction between the two quartets in terms of their recognition by mainstream media and subsequent financial well-being. Then, in August, Down Beat featured an interview with Brubeck that offered him a chance to rebut all that had been said against him.[15] Brubeck took on many of the criticisms from Feather, Hentoff, and Gleason, including his purported lack of swing, and cited his commercial success, culminating in his Time magazine cover, as the real reason critics attacked him. Like Feather, he directly addressed the issue of race that had implicitly and explicitly formed the center of this debate.

The rest of this chapter is organized around the themes that emerged from these debates: economic opportunities, spontaneity versus composition (primarily borne out through each quartet's use of counterpoint), swing, and colorblindness. These discussions reveal in myriad ways the extent to which critics understood Brubeck's whiteness to be an indelible and defining feature of his sound. Ultimately, the racial distinction between the quartets served as the linchpin for critics' challenges to Brubeck's authenticity within the jazz genre.

## Race and Economic Opportunities in the Music Industry

Recognizing a larger conversation about recognition, visibility, and race in the quartets' respective record labels, positions in polls, and performance locations, Feather focused on the economic and marketing disparities between the MJQ and DBQ:

---

[13] Nat Hentoff, "Counterpoint," *Down Beat*, March 9, 1955, 6; Ralph Gleason, "Perspectives," *Down Beat*, April 6, 1955, 18.
[14] Leonard Feather, "Feather's Nest," *Down Beat*, June 15, 1955, 24.
[15] Don Freeman, "Dave Brubeck Answers His Critics: A Lot of Them Are Being Unfair, Insists Jazz' Controversial Pianist," *Down Beat*, August 10, 1955, 7.

> On the one hand, you are delighted that an intelligent, ambitious, clean-living, and talented fellow like Brubeck can win so many fans and, in effect, do so much for jazz; on the other hand, you are distressed that an intelligent, ambitious, clean-living, and talented fellow like John Lewis, mentor of the MJQ, can have accomplished so much more, musically, while gaining so much less ground, economically.[16]

Feather's phrasing suggested that the only distinction between the two "intelligent, ambitious, clean-living, and talented" fellows was their race. Initially relying on his readers to infer the racial distinction between Brubeck and Lewis, Feather implicitly critiqued race-based narratives that assumed that traits such as intelligence, ambitiousness, clean-living, and talent were inherent to Brubeck as a white man but which assumed that these traits were unique to Lewis as a Black man by using them to describe both men. Put simply, Feather argued that Brubeck's privileged status as a white man gave him more financial, institutional, and media opportunities for recognition and economic gains.

The MJQ and DBQ's access to various economic opportunities, including the labels each group recorded on, their placement in polls, and where and to whom they performed, differed greatly. In 1955 the MJQ was still recording on Prestige, an independent jazz label owned by Bob Weinstock that featured primarily Black jazz musicians such as Miles Davis, John Coltrane, Sonny Rollins, and Thelonious Monk. The label also featured white "cool" musicians such as Lennie Tristano, Lee Konitz, and Stan Getz. In the year following the *Down Beat* debate, 1956, the MJQ would sign to Atlantic Records, which by 1958 was the second largest independent jazz label in the United States.[17] Though Brubeck started on an even smaller regional label in 1951— the San Francisco-based Fantasy Records, he signed to the major record label Columbia within just three years. On Columbia, Brubeck had access to wider distribution and promotion and a broader audience than he had on Fantasy, or than the MJQ had on either Prestige or Atlantic. Jazz musicians recorded by Columbia were typically among the most commercially popular jazz musicians and in the 1950s included Louis Armstrong, Duke Ellington, and Miles Davis.

In the early to mid-1950s, the DBQ frequently made both *Billboard* popular album charts and jazz charts. The week following Brubeck's November *Time* magazine cover, the DBQ's *Jazz Goes to College* (released June 7, 1954) landed a number 13 spot on the "Best Selling Popular Albums" chart for LPs.[18] *Jazz*

---

[16] Feather, "The Blindfold Test," 7.
[17] Gary Kramer, "Atlantic and R&B Trend Developed Side by Side," *Billboard*, January 13, 1958, 39.
[18] "Best Selling Popular Albums," *Billboard*, November 13, 1854, 56.

*Goes to College* remained on the "Best Selling Popular Albums" chart through March 19, 1955. On March 19, 1955, *Brubeck Time* (1955) entered the pop chart at number 15 before peaking at number 5 in the April 30, 1955 issue of *Billboard*.[19] The DBQ's next album, *Jazz: Red, Hot and Cool* (1955), followed suit, reaching number 8 on the November 12, 1955 list, almost exactly one year after Brubeck's *Time* cover was published.[20] These charts were for popular music and were not jazz specific. The first list featuring the DBQ also included Hollywood actors and singers Mario Lanza and Judy Garland as well as popular bandleader Glenn Miller and jazz singer June Christy.

A look at the *Billboard* jazz charts, which were based on album sales, reveals that Brubeck was also a more popular choice for these jazz audiences than the MJQ. The MJQ's first appearance on *Billboard*'s jazz lists in October 1955 put them at number 10 for their eponymous album, *Modern Jazz Quartet* (1953).[21] The DBQ appeared twice on the same list, with *Brubeck Time* at number 2, and *Jazz Goes to College* at number 3. Likewise, in January 1956 the MJQ's *Concorde* (1955) reached number 6 on the jazz charts, with the DBQ at numbers 1 and 3 for *Jazz: Red, Hot and Cool* and *Jazz Goes to College* on the same charts. During the jazz critics' debates in 1955 over the DBQ and MJQ featured in *Down Beat*, the MJQ did not appear on *Billboard*'s best-selling lists for jazz, while the DBQ continued to make consistent appearances.

The DBQ seemed to have greater appeal to *Down Beat*'s jazz audiences during this period as well. In *Down Beat*'s readers' polls for 1953–1955, the DBQ was named the number 1 combo each year.[22] In 1953, readers ranked the MJQ at number 18 with a mere thirty votes, compared to the DBQ's 973. In 1954, the MJQ zoomed to the number 2 spot, garnering 564 votes to the DBQ's 925. The ranking stayed the same in 1955, with the DBQ rising to 1,050 votes, and the MJQ also rising to 880 votes. While the MJQ gained significant traction in the readers' polls, they remained second place to the DBQ during the period of this study.

An easy guess as to why the DBQ and MJQ's positions in the polls differed so greatly is the distinction in each quartet's visibility in mainstream and jazz media. In addition to the difference in capital (especially regarding studio time, advertisement, and media placement) between each quartet's label, each quartet had distinctly different touring and performance schedules. The DBQ quickly became known for their college tours. College tours, to which the

---

[19] "Best Selling Popular Albums," *Billboard*, March 19, 1955, 24; "Best Selling Popular Albums," *Billboard*, April 30, 1955, 26.
[20] "Best Selling Popular Albums," *Billboard*, November 1955, 94.
[21] "Billboard Buying and Programming Guide-Best Selling Packaged Records: Jazz," October 1, 1955, 34.
[22] "Readers' Poll," *Down Beat*, December 30, 1953; December 29, 1954; December 28, 1955.

DBQ had earlier (and as a predominantly white group, likely easier) access than the MJQ, had the added benefit of young, excited audiences who were new to jazz and had the potential to grow into long-term financial supporters.

The MJQ performed primarily in nightclubs on the east coast in their early years, before branching out to college tours and concert hall dates (Brubeck claimed responsibility for paving the way for the MJQ in colleges).[23] Ralph Gleason, one of *Down Beat*'s West Coast representatives, suggested that the MJQ had a narrow sphere of influence when he explained in 1954, "The only reason I can think of why I didn't vote for the Modern Jazz Quartet in the recent *Down Beat* critics' poll is the simple fact that up to then I had not heard them."[24] Just one month before Gleason's comments, Nat Hentoff wrote, "If enough club owners around the country will now take an initial venture on the [Modern Jazz] Quartet, the MJQ could become as big as Brubeck," suggesting that at issue was club owners' reticence to feature a new, ostensibly untested group.[25]

The difference in economic opportunity remained Feather's primary focus. In June, toward the end of the *Down Beat* debate, Feather reminisced on a conversation he had recently had with Brubeck, drawing the issue of race more explicitly into the debate. Brubeck, Feather reported, felt the critics had been unfair in saying the DBQ had never struggled or had "lean" times. Feather wrote in response to Brubeck's charge,

> [Brubeck] concedes, though, that he never has had to face the psychological, economic, and other barriers that the MJQ members met from the day they were born.
>
> When Dave's name is submitted for a television show, his agent is never told, 'Sorry, but we already have one white act booked for that week.' When he's offered to a smart night club, the rejoinder is never, 'We'd rather not encourage white trade by booking a white act.'[26]

Feather doubled down, explaining to *Down Beat*'s primarily white audience, "Foolish though those statements sound, they are simply a reversal of what happens every day of the week to many of the finest combos and bands in America." By reversing the usual journalistic practice of only identifying people of color, Feather upended the normative assumptions of white universality and invisibility by labeling Brubeck white, highlighting the material advantages granted to Brubeck by television executives and nightclub

---

[23] Ralph J. Gleason, "Brubeck: 'I Did Do Some Things First,'" *Down Beat*, September 5, 1957, 14.
[24] Ralph J. Gleason, "Perspectives," *Down Beat*, November 17, 1954, 15.
[25] Nat Hentoff, "Caught in the Act: Modern Jazz Quartet: Birdland, New York," *Down Beat*, October 6, 1954, 32.
[26] Feather, *Down Beat*, June 15, 1955.

managers throughout his career—a privilege that for Feather, had unfairly magnified the Brubeck quartet in the public eye.

## Spontaneity versus Composition: Approaches to Counterpoint

While the economic differences between the MJQ and the DBQ were never far from critics' pens, Gleason and Hentoff, among other writers, sought to more directly debate the musical merits of each quartet. In doing so, they deployed musical descriptions to establish a racially coded language of jazz authenticity. In his blindfold test, Rogers praised the MJQ for its incorporation of counterpoint; however, counterpoint was more often a mainstay in critics' descriptions of the DBQ's music. Counterpoint and canons also brought easy comparisons to European classical music—the music of Johann Sebastian Bach in particular; however, I argue that critics based such comparisons more often on their racialized expectations of each quartet than on musical sounds.[27]

### The DBQ's Approach to Counterpoint

Though the DBQ's later repertoire included original compositions by Brubeck, some of which, like "The Duke" and "In Your Own Sweet Way," were covered by other jazz musicians, the DBQ's early repertoire was filled mostly with arrangements of standards.[28] In his arrangements, Brubeck often included both pre-planned counterpoint and space for improvised counterpoint. Pre-planned contrapuntal sections were typically found as arrangements of the head melody while improvised counterpoint featured a follow-the-leader style of simultaneous improvisation between Brubeck and Desmond.

Jazz critics frequently commented on Brubeck's ability to perform counterpoint, whether improvised or composed. In his review of the *Jazz at Oberlin* album (1953), critic Red Nordell of the *Christian Science Monitor* wrote, "The Brubeck-Desmond teamwork appears to advantage in the contrapuntal opening and closing of 'The Way You Look Tonight.' "[29] Likewise,

---

[27] For his part, Shorty Rogers did not adhere to racial binaries in his descriptions, complaining of Brubeck in the *Blindfold Test*, "I would have liked to hear more composition work, although I know Dave prefers to limit his composition work more to his piano solos."

[28] I detail the performance history of "In Your Own Sweet Way" here: Kelsey A. K. Klotz, "Performing Authenticity 'In Your Own Sweet Way,'" *Journal of Jazz Studies* 12, no. 1 (2019): 72–91.

[29] Red Nordell, Review of *Jazz at Oberlin College* by Dave Brubeck, *Christian Science Monitor*, January 19, 1954, 15.

Dick Carter, a fan of Brubeck's, wrote to Brubeck in 1956 explaining that his favorite recording of Brubeck's was "The Way You Look Tonight": "The contrapuntal interplay between you and Paul assumes a delicate, flowing gracefulness which I think, excels some of your other fugal exchanges."[30] "The Way You Look Tonight" from the DBQ's *Jazz at Oberlin* album (1953) features both pre-composed and improvised counterpoint as typically performed by the DBQ. Example 1.1 is a transcription of the head melody,

**Ex. 1.1.** "The Way You Look Tonight," Counterpoint between Brubeck and Desmond in head melody. Author's Transcription. Melody by Jerome Kern, © 1936. Used by permission.

[30] Personal Letter, Dick Carter to Dave Brubeck, June 14, 1956, Brubeck Collection, Wilton Library, Wilton, CT.

in which Brubeck begins with the melody, accompanied by Paul Desmond's alto saxophone obbligato in running eighths. The pair switches roles in measure 7, at which point Desmond performs the melodic line while Brubeck plays something akin to a bass line. The melody ends in measure 10 of the example.

This pattern, in which one musician follows the other with a switch in the middle, is similar to Brubeck and Desmond's approach to improvised counterpoint. Example 1.2 is a transcription of the AAB sections of the AABA chorus featuring improvised counterpoint. In the first A section, Brubeck provides space for Desmond's improvisation by playing quarter notes and half

**Ex. 1.2.** "The Way You Look Tonight," Improvised counterpoint. Author's Transcription.

**Ex. 1.2.** Continued

notes, while Desmond plays scalar eighth note passages. The second A section begins with Brubeck harmonizing Desmond's sequential melody for the first six measures. In essence, though Desmond and Brubeck are improvising, Brubeck follows Desmond's ideas, further evidenced by a triplet ornament, performed first by Desmond in m. 25 and then by Brubeck in m. 26. In m. 27, however, Brubeck is the first to introduce an eighth-note passage, and Desmond quickly begins to fill his line with eighth notes. By the beginning of the B section, it is clear that Desmond is now following Brubeck's improvisation, as Brubeck plays an idea in m. 33 that Desmond returns in m. 34. In m. 34, Brubeck begins a descending scalar passage, to which Desmond again responds in m. 36, this time elongating the passage. In m. 39, the two begin playing the lick on the same pitch at the same time. Brubeck immediately stops playing the idea, letting Desmond take over. Perhaps it is Brubeck's insertion of rests or perhaps both Brubeck and Desmond understand that they need to transition to the melody in the final A section, but each begins playing in longer note values in m. 41, thus calming the rhythmic activity. Brubeck and Desmond's counterpoint ultimately is a balance of leading and following between the two musicians; whereas Brubeck follows Desmond by providing him the space to improvise and by supporting him more harmonically, Desmond follows Brubeck by playing Brubeck's musical phrases back to him.

For many audiences and critics, the DBQ's improvised counterpoint was a highly impressive display of skill between Brubeck and Desmond and suggested a magical, unspoken language between the two. In T. George Harris's *Time* feature of Brubeck (1954), Harris included a conversation between Desmond and Brubeck working out the musical details of their counterpoint (Harris did not specify which musician said what):

> "What are we going to do?"
> "Well, I'm going to take an eight-bar intro..."
> "Then I play counterpoint to you and you take the rest, but the rest of what?"
> "Why don't we do like we always do, keep things going and kick it around and see if something happens?"
> "If we goof the counterpoint, which we certainly will, playing it for the first time, keep going."
> From then on, nothing further was said—they communicated through what Brubeck regards as a kind of mental telepathy.[31]

Though Harris included this account to gesture toward an ostensibly magical and unspoken language between Brubeck and Desmond, it actually highlights the importance of pre-planning, even when improvising. Brubeck or Desmond suggests that they will likely "goof the counterpoint" because they will be "playing it for the first time," implying that it usually took several takes for them to get the counterpoint right.

While the musical content of the pair's improvised counterpoint was rarely planned extensively, it was governed by practical constraints, as evidenced

---

[31] T. George Harris, "Man on Cloud No. 9," *Time*, November 8, 1954, 75–76.

in a conversation between Desmond and Brubeck as they recorded "When the Saints Go Marching In" in the mid-1950s.[32] Desmond does the math for the song, calculating that they could play eight choruses in two minutes and suggesting they do some counterpoint: "You can't hardly goof." Brubeck responds affirmatively, and tells Desmond to do five choruses, leaving three for Brubeck. Desmond re-calculates, suggesting two choruses of counterpoint and one for the melody to end the song. Furthermore, a memo written by Desmond in the 1950s analyzing the quartet's commercial viability suggests that the men recognized counterpoint as an effective marketing strategy: Desmond observed that the quartet should continue to work on improvising in fugues, as it was both commercially successful and rarely done by other groups.[33]

## The MJQ's Approach to Counterpoint

The comparison between the DBQ's music and the MJQ's music initially drawn by Shorty Rogers reveals the stark distinctions in the terms critics used to describe the two quartets. While the DBQ's counterpoint was loosely defined, the MJQ's was typically quite strict, adhering more closely to European classical rules of counterpoint. For example, Lewis's composition "Vendôme" follows fugue form and features improvisation in the episodes (Fig. 1.1). Further, the exposition loosely adheres to the rules for a fugue: Jackson begins by playing the three-measure long subject, and Lewis plays the answer on the dominant three measures later. Jackson enters with a slightly altered version of the subject three measures after that, which Lewis

| Form | Exposition | | | | Episode 1 | Entry | Episode 2 | Entry | Episode 3 | Entry | Episode 4 | Final Entry | | |
|---|---|---|---|---|---|---|---|---|---|---|---|---|---|---|
| Vibraphone | $S_1$ | | $S_2$ | | Improvised solo | S | | S | Free counterpoint | S | Improvised solo | S | S | Coda |
| Piano | | $A_1$ | | $A_2$ | | A | FC | Improvised solo | | | | A | A | Coda |
| Length in Measures | 3 | 3 | 3 | 3 | 16 | 3 | 4 | 11 | 3 | 14 | 4 | 37 | 4 | 4 | 4 |

Figure 1.1. "Vendôme," form chart. Transcription by Author. "S" indicates subject. "A" indicates Answer. "FC" indicates free counterpoint.

[32] "When the Saints Go Marching In," Dave Brubeck Quartet [likely recording *Jazz Impressions of the USA* (1956)], Brubeck Collection. "When the Saints Go Marching In" never made it onto the album.
[33] Paul Desmond, "Quick Memo to Myself," ca. 1950s, Paul Desmond Papers, Holt-Atherton Special Collections, University of the Pacific, Stockton, CA.

also answers in his left hand three measures later. "Vendôme" does not have a countersubject in the exposition (a traditional fugue would layer the countersubject and answer). While the DBQ's improvised counterpoint typically occupied another "solo" chorus, Lewis usually created compositions and arrangements for the MJQ that integrated counterpoint within the form of the piece. Nevertheless, even when critics noted Lewis's attention to form, they did not refer to "Vendôme" as a fugue, nor did they discuss Lewis's ability to compose fugues.

Critics were, however, quick to ascribe Brubeck's music to his background in European classical music, specifically calling out excerpts for sounding like fugues and counterpoint. For instance, one reviewer described the DBQ's recording of "Look for the Silver Lining" as "fugish."[34] "Look for the Silver Lining" has the head-solo-head form typical of many jazz performances.[35] Brubeck and Desmond insert improvised counterpoint in the final solo chorus, which is no doubt what the reviewer had in mind when describing the piece as "fugish." The counterpoint is imitative, but is decidedly different from an actual fugue form; when compared to "Vendôme," "Look for the Silver Lining" bears none of the structural elements of a fugue, such as an exposition, entries, or episodes.

Despite the fact that Brubeck's repertoire included no strict counterpoint, fugues, or canons, critics also repeatedly pointed to Brubeck's counterpoint as evidence of his connection to the great master of contrapuntal music: Johann Sebastian Bach. As early as 1952, a reviewer called Brubeck's counterpoint "Bachian," even though none of the pieces reviewed contained either improvised counterpoint or arranged counterpoint moving in anything other than homophony.[36] Direct comparisons between Brubeck and Bach continued into the mid-1950s, such as when *Metronome* critic Al Zeiger again called Brubeck's music "Bachian" in 1955, or when, in 1958, Hugh Thomson of the *Toronto Daily Star* described the Brubeck Quartet's music as "Bach jazzed up."[37] It is possible that Brubeck encouraged such comparisons; as Stephen Crist notes, Brubeck consistently referred to Bach as an important musical influence throughout his career.[38] However, even when writers acknowledged

---

[34] Review of "Look for the Silver Lining," by the Dave Brubeck Quartet, *Down Beat*, December 3, 1952, 15.

[35] Dave Brubeck Quartet, "Look for the Silver Lining," *Stardust*, with Paul Desmond, Wyatt Ruther, and Lloyd Davis. © 1952 by Fantasy Records.

[36] Review of "A Foggy Day" and "Lyons Day," by Dave Brubeck, *Down Beat*, March 21, 1952, 14.

[37] Al Zeiger, "Dave Brubeck: A Musical Analysis," *Metronome*, August 1955, 19, 38; Hugh Thomson, "Music Review: Massey Hall Shook Up by Jazz Cool, Sizzling," *Toronto Daily Star*, November 7, 1958.

[38] Stephen Crist, "The Role and Meaning of the Bach Chorale in the Music of Dave Brubeck," in *Bach Perspectives: Bach in America*, vol. 5 (Champaign: University of Illinois Press, 2002).

distinctions between Brubeck and Bach, they often did so from the perspective of fitting Brubeck (and the jazz he played) within a European tradition. As composer and French horn player Gunther Schuller expounded at a 1955 Music Inn Roundtable,

> There again, it may seem like very little counterpoint, compared to the contrapuntal masterpieces of Bach or of Brahms, or whoever. And yet, if you consider that this is being composed on the spot, and that one man is trying to compose, via a direct inspiration, two or three lines running simultaneously—again, I as a classical composer, I sit down and I work these things out and sometimes it takes me a very long time. And it took Beethoven sometimes years to work out some of these things. And here's a man who sits down and sometimes just plays it right off. Now, I don't say it's always as great as Beethoven, and maybe, I don't know, if you want to be fair, maybe it never is. But the attempt, the will, the vision to do something of that kind on the spot, is to me, again, one of the great steps forward in jazz.[39]

Although Lewis's counterpoint was more strictly composed than Brubeck's, critics did not compare Lewis to the eighteenth-century contrapuntal master—even when Lewis directly quoted pieces by Bach. The MJQ's arrangement of "Softly, as in a Morning Sunrise" features a canon taken directly from Bach's *Musical Offering* as an introduction to the head melody (Ex. 1.3). Lewis's transcription mirrors Bach's nearly exactly, with the theme appearing in the bass line with Lewis and Jackson in canon above. The canon is not strict, as Jackson's melodic line in m. 4 differs from Lewis's line in m. 5, but the second imitation in mm. 5 and 6 re-asserts the measure-long imitation point. Even still, *High Fidelity* critic John Wilson was struck instead by what he heard as the group's jazz roots, writing of "Softly, as in a Morning Sunrise,"

> For all the monkish solemnity with which they sometimes approach their work, the Quartet is essentially a direct and swinging group as almost every selection on this disk demonstrates. . . . [John Lewis's] playing is utterly jazz even while part of his thinking is firmly rooted in the classics (there is a fine sample of his surprisingly low down piano behind Jackson's solo on "Softly, As In a Morning Sunrise").[40]

---

[39] "Jazz Today," Music Inn Roundtable #4, August 26, 1955, Audio recording, Marshall Winslow Stearns Collection, Institute of Jazz Studies, Rutgers University-Newark, Newark, NJ. Author's transcription.
[40] John S. Wilson, Review of *Concorde*, by the Modern Jazz Quartet, *High Fidelity*, February 1956, 109.

**Ex. 1.3.** "Softly, as in a Morning Sunrise," Introduction performed by the Modern Jazz Quartet. Author's transcription.

## White Intellectual Privilege

Despite both quartets' frequent use of counterpoint, critics were far more likely to discuss the DBQ's counterpoint or relationship to Bach than that of the MJQ.[41] Moreover, nearly every article that connected the MJQ to fugues

---

[41] Articles linking the DBQ to counterpoint, canons, fugues, or "Bachian" sounds between 1952 and 1955 include Review of "A Foggy Day" and "Lyons Day," by Dave Brubeck. *Down Beat*, March 21, 1952, 14; Barry Ulanov, "Dave Brubeck," *Metronome*, March 1952, 17; Review of "Look for the Silver Lining," by Dave Brubeck, *Down Beat* December 3, 1952, 15; Barry Ulanov, Review of "My Romance," etc., by Dave Brubeck. *Metronome*, April 1953, 24; Barry Ulanov, "A Talk with Dave Brubeck," *Metronome*, April 13, 1953, 29–30;

or counterpoint prior to and throughout the *Down Beat* debate was written by Nat Hentoff.[42] This can in part be explained by the DBQ's higher level of popularity and recognition between 1952 and 1955. Still, it is evident that critics were less likely to discuss specific European classical musical traits when performed by an all-Black ensemble such as the MJQ, whom critics implicitly understood as holding a stronger tie to jazz.[43] Similarly, critics took for granted that the DBQ, a usually all-white quartet at that time, would perform music with sonic similarities to European classical music.[44]

That white critics would consider Black musicians' primary musical contributions to be jazz rather than classical music stems from a legacy of European and American reliance on Cartesian dualisms. Simon Frith argues that Western epistemological distinctions based on problematic Cartesian dualisms—disembodiment versus embodiment, seriousness versus fun, mind

---

Review of "Give a Little Whistle," etc., by Dave Brubeck, *Down Beat*, July 15, 1953, 19; Nat Hentoff, "Caught in the Act: Dave Brubeck Quartet, Birdland, NYC," *Down Beat*, April 21, 1954, 7; Review of "Balcony Rock," etc., by Dave Brubeck, *Down Beat*, August 11, 1954, 12; Barry Ulanov, Review of "Balcony Rock," etc., by Dave Brubeck Quartet, *Metronome*, September 1954, 22; Al Zeiger, "Neo-classicism: Jazz and Classical," *Metronome*, November 1954, 60–61; T. George Harris, "Man on Cloud No. 7," *Time*, November 8, 1954; John S. Wilson, Review of *Dave Brubeck at Storyville 1954*, by Dave Brubeck Quartet, *High Fidelity*, January 1955, 74; Barry Ulanov, Review of "On the Alamo," etc., by Dave Brubeck Quartet, *Metronome*, January 1955, 22; John S. Wilson, Review of *Brubeck Time*, by Dave Brubeck Quartet, *High Fidelity*, April 1955, 69; Al Zeiger, "Dave Brubeck: A Musical Analysis," *Metronome*, August 1955, 19, 38; H. S. Rummell, "Bach to Brubeck and Back," *High Fidelity*, November 1955, 42–44, 120, 122; John S. Wilson, Review of *Jazz: Red Hot and Cool*, by Dave Brubeck Quartet, *High Fidelity*, November 1955, 73.

Articles linking the MJQ to counterpoint, canons, fugues, or "Bachian" sounds between 1952 and 1955 include Nat Hentoff, "Counterpoint," *Down Beat*, January 12, 1954, 6; *Metronome Yearbook*, 1954; Nat Hentoff, "Caught in the Act: Modern Jazz Quartet: Birdland, New York," *Down Beat*, October 6, 1954, 32; Nat Hentoff, "Counterpoint," *Down Beat*, January 13, 1955, 6; Nat Hentoff, "The Modern Jazz Quartet," *High Fidelity Magazine*, March 1955, 36+.

[42] By 1958, more critics, including Max Harrison, Martin Williams, John S. Wilson, Whitney Balliett, and Joe Goldberg, began to discuss the MJQ's counterpoint, fugues, and canons. This is likely due to Lewis's relationship with Gunther Schuller and the Third Stream movement, which combined jazz and European classical elements into a new genre. Schuller coined the term "Third Stream" in 1957. While Brubeck would periodically insist that he had been doing Third Stream all along, and indeed, in the late 1950s he embarked on some more overtly classical-jazz fusion projects with the quartet, he was never explicitly tied to the movement.

[43] While most Black newspapers did not cite specific musical techniques employed by either the DBQ or the MJQ, the more detailed articles on the MJQ describe their music as "well planned, arranged," or "serious." However, these articles often came a few years after the *Down Beat* debate. "New Chicago Jazz Group Triumphs in Loop Debut," *Chicago Defender*, September 14, 1957, 18; "Critic Calls Modern Jazz Quartet Hit," *Chicago Defender*, June 28, 1958, 19.

[44] Contemporary critics have started to find the flaws in mid-century critics' focus on Brubeck's "fugish" or seemingly classically influenced playing. For example, as critic Philip Clark insists, "When people talk about Dave, there's all this stuff about how he was into fugues, polytonality, and polyrhythms, but there's another side of him. . . . I saw him play a lot, and occasionally, in the middle of a solo, he'd just slam a chord down to see what would happen." Jazz historian Ted Gioia highlighted the disconnect between what critics wrote about Brubeck's music and musical background and how Brubeck tended to approach his music, explaining, "The funny thing is that the stereotypes about Dave tell you how well-schooled and formally trained he was, but he had a looser and less academic approach to the creative process than almost any jazz musician I've met." Morgan Enos, "What Do We Overlook About Dave Brubeck on His 100th Birthday? Authors, Musicians, and Family Members Reflect," *Discogs Blog*, December 4, 2020, https://blog.discogs.com/en/dave-brubeck-birthday-overlooked-moments/.

versus body, and intellect versus physicality—were a primary way white critics and audiences understood the difference between white and Black musicians and their music throughout the nineteenth and twentieth centuries.[45] While other scholars have focused on deconstructing the link between blackness and primitivism and rhythm (including swing) in jazz, focusing on Brubeck reveals the tacit understanding of some critics that white musicians had unique access to European classical musical techniques.[46] Examining white intellectual privilege, I argue, allows scholars a way to discuss the seemingly normative narratives written for white musicians. My phrase "white intellectual privilege" reflects what feminist scholar Peggy McIntosh calls "white privilege," but also makes clear the mode of privilege to which I am referring: the assumption that white people are uniquely intellectual.[47] Further, "white intellectual privilege" also makes clear one particular aspect of what Joe R. Feagin refers to as the "white racial frame," a viewpoint often unexamined by white people that holds standards or norms of whiteness as an "ideal type."[48]

The relationship critics highlighted between Brubeck and Bach, counterpoint, fugues, or the numerous other references to European classical music and composers not documented here, is based on an implicit assumption that white musicians like Brubeck were uniquely capable of performing and composing challenging works of "high" art. For many white critics—and some Black critics—musical intellect was demonstrated through deployment of European classical techniques, references to European classical works and composers, and education in European classical methods.[49] Essentially, musical intellect, as defined by the European tradition, implied whiteness. David Ake describes a similar association critics made between Bill Evans and

---

[45] Simon Frith, "Rhythm: Race, Sex, and the Body," in *Performing Rites: On the Value of Popular Music* (Cambridge, MA: Harvard University Press, 1996): 123–144.

[46] Kofi Agawu, "The Invention of 'African Rhythm,'" *Representing African Music* (New York: Routledge Press, 2003), 55–70; Simon Frith, "Rhythm: Race, Sex, and the Body," in *Performing Rites: On the Value of Popular Music* (Cambridge, MA: Harvard University Press, 1996), 123–144; Ted Gioia, "Jazz and the Primitivist Myth," in *The Imperfect Art* (New York: Oxford University Press, 1988); Ingrid Monson, "The Problem with White Hipness: Race, Gender, and Culture Conceptions in Jazz Historical Discourse," *Journal of the American Musicological Society* 48, no. 3 (Autumn 1995): 396–422.

[47] Peggy McIntosh, "White Privilege: Unpacking the Invisible Knapsack," *White Privilege and Male Privilege*, ed. Michael Kimmel and Abby Ferber (Boulder, CO: Westview Press, 1988), 13–26.

[48] Joe R. Feagin, *The White Racial Frame: Centuries of Racial Framing and Counter-Framing*, 3rd ed. (New York: Routledge, 2020), 14.
In his crucial article, "Music Theory and the White Racial Frame," music theorist Philip A. Ewell deconstructs some of the ways the field of music theory perpetuates a white racial frame. Much of what he describes applies to how critics often implicitly granted greater value (intellectual and artistic) to jazz musicians they perceived as sounding "classical." Philip A. Ewell, "Music Theory and the White Racial Frame," *Music Theory Online* 26, no. 2 (September 2020), https://mtosmt.org/issues/mto.20.26.2/mto.20.26.2.ewell.html.

[49] Burton Peretti, *The Creation of Jazz: Music, Race, and Culture in Urban America* (Urbana: University of Illinois Press, 1992), 61. Peretti writes, "Black ministers, lawyers, doctors, and educators—what W.E.B. Du Bois called the 'talented tenth'—strove to exercise civic leadership for all blacks in the realms of culture, morals, religion, and politics. Their values and culture were often close to those of genteel, Victorian whites, which called

intellect, which was particularly apparent when they noted Evans's interest in philosophy and European literature, but left out similar descriptions of other "book-smart" jazz musicians like Charlie Parker, Charles Mingus, and Max Roach. Ake explains that the discourse surrounding these musicians "ignores their 'literary' side, replaced by lurid tales of drug-induced excesses and bizarre behavior."[50] On the other hand, Evans's own entrenchment in drug abuse was "passed over or dismissed as 'personal problems.'"

Whether they liked his music or not, critics overwhelmingly described Brubeck in terms of his intellect, either directly (by calling him or his sound intellectual), or indirectly (by mentioning his impending master's degree, noting his studies with Milhaud, or linking his music to the sounds of either Bach or European classical modernists). Further, the language used by critics in jazz publications like *Down Beat* and *Metronome* and in mainstream magazines with national reach, including *Time*, *Vogue*, and *Life*, trickled down to regional coverage of these musicians. In other words, language linking Brubeck to intellect through European classical composers and techniques appeared as often in *Time* as it did in student publications like *The Davidsonian*, the newspaper of Davidson College in Davidson, North Carolina; students Bill Cunningham and Bob Talbert re-performed the white intellectual privilege seen in national newspapers, writing that Brubeck was a "well-versed and scholarly musician" whose "touch at the piano is that of a concert pianist who can evoke the feelings of Bach, Beethoven, Chopin, and Scarlatti with the harmonic and rhythmic expressions of jazz."[51]

## Creating a White Jazz Lineage Through Cool Jazz

Brubeck was one part of a broader white racialization of cool jazz in the 1950s, which was achieved primarily through descriptions of intellectual engagement.[52] According to critics, cool jazz represented restrained emotion or the complete absence of emotion, and cool musicians' incorporation of

for a strict code of education, self-control, male authority, female domesticity, and industriousness." Though Peretti's focus is on the 1920s, the same tension existed throughout the mid-twentieth century between largely middle-class African Americans who downplayed the importance of jazz as an African American art form and African Americans who celebrated jazz as the result of a uniquely Black experience.

[50] David Ake, "Body and Soul: Performing Deep Jazz," *Jazz Cultures* (Berkeley: University of California Press, 2002), 98.
[51] Bill Cunningham and Bob Talbert, "Progressive Music with Brubeck Here March 10," *The Davidsonian*, March. 4, 1955, 1.
[52] Though many now trace the beginnings of cool jazz to the interracial *Birth of the Cool* nonet, fronted by Miles Davis, cool is nevertheless now widely associated with whiteness. Kelsey A. K. Klotz, "Racial Ideologies in 1950s Cool Jazz," PhD diss., Washington University in St. Louis, 2016.

European classical musical techniques in particular achieved this definition. Arnold Shaw elaborated the point in a 1954 article for *Esquire*, describing white musicians such as Dave Brubeck, Gerry Mulligan, Lennie Tristano, Cal Tjader, and Stan Getz.[53] Shaw emphasized cool jazz's aspirations to the status of European music through emphasis on the "musical mind," writing that cool jazz privileged the same musical elements as European classical music: "Chords and counterpoint have become basic, instead of rhythm." He highlighted cool as a tool to protect the integrity of the mind from emotional distractions, writing, "Reason and knowledge count, not feeling. And the elaboration of a musical idea to its logical conclusion is considered the highest achievement." Shaw and other white jazz critics placed emotion and intellect, or the body and the mind, on opposite ends of a spectrum, where intellect, demonstrated by the "cerebral" techniques of European classical music, was cool and emotion was the natural response of a hot body. By relying on Cartesian dualisms and naming mostly white musicians as the most skilled exponents of cool, these critics made plain the racial ideologies that informed their writing.

A 1952 article by Barry Ulanov written for *Vogue* magazine highlights specific musical techniques that, for Ulanov, made cool the ideal form of jazz. Like Shaw, he explained, "The new music called 'cool' is more restrained than the jazz of the past, more ordered, more controlled, more subtle," but he also emphasized its relationship to "authentic" jazz, adding that "it is still an improvised music."[54] For Ulanov, cool jazz's seeming inclusion of European classical musical techniques made it the ideal jazz genre—one that had "evolved" from "obstreperous, imaginative but untutored childhood into maturity." Calling it a parallel movement to twelve-tone modernist classical music, Ulanov firmly placed cool jazz within a lineage of European classical music, writing, "It rests upon the pillars of all music, the great supports that buoyed the polyphony of Bach and gave depth to the elegance of Mozart. The performances of these men represent at least a partial unfolding of the resources latent in jazz." In his descriptions, Ulanov created a language of ownership white male musicians and audiences could use to claim jazz as their own. Nearly all of the men Ulanov detailed in his article were white (tenor saxophonist Lester Young and alto saxophonist Charlie Parker were named as the first steps of cool jazz's development), and all but tenor saxophonist Stan Getz revealed their indebtedness to European classical musical techniques,

---

[53] Arnold Shaw, "The Cool Generation," *Esquire*, May 1954, 42.
[54] Barry Ulanov, "Cool Jazz," *Vogue*, March 15, 1952, 79.

according to Ulanov. (Ulanov found other ways to ensure Getz's whiteness, describing his tone as the "soft, clean, clear air of the new sound" and his image as a "scrubbed schoolboy look and bright blue eyes.") Ulanov noted that alto saxophonist Lee Konitz represented cool jazz's new trend toward "thinking" musicians, in that his music was "carefully planned and executed" and he demonstrated much "consciousness" in his musical decision-making. Of clarinetist John Laporta, Ulanov explained, "If one probes enough, one may also stimulate words, and then one of the most alert musical minds in jazz may begin the constructive but relentless analysis of his own music and anybody and everybody else's—from Bach . . . through Mozart to Schoenberg, Berg, and Bartók." After summarizing Brubeck's achievements in polytonality and jazz chamber ensemble writing through his octet, Ulanov finished his article with a description of pianist Lennie Tristano's musical "experiments," which through "technical skill and intuitive resources" created jazz that was "atonal, contrapuntal, and improvised."

While Ulanov interpreted cool musicians' use of European classical techniques as proof of the genre's merit over jazz genres that came before, other critics and musicians heard the same techniques as proof of the genre's inauthenticity within the field of jazz.[55] Regardless the motive, both critics who valued and those who did not value cool jazz normalized a discourse of cool jazz as "intellectual" through references to European techniques, and the label "cool jazz," to which Brubeck was tied, reinforced the notion that white jazz musicians were emotionally distanced and intellectual performers, leaving the implicit assumption that Black jazz musicians were naturally emotional players.

Mainstream critics' descriptions of the similarities between cool jazz and European classical music served two primary purposes: (1) in claiming that cool jazz was intimately intertwined with European art music, critics could argue that jazz *was* an art music, thus providing an uplift for the genre that was happening around the country in the 1950s as jazz made its way onto college campuses, was used for cultural diplomacy by the US State Department, and was celebrated at places like Newport and Lenox; and (2) critics could minimize or erase entirely the role of Black music and musicians in jazz. Composer and musicologist George Lewis documents similar efforts in histories of experimental music that position "spontaneous" music as the result of European and European-American heritage. According to Lewis, these texts

[55] See, for example, Marshall Stearns, *The Story of Jazz* (London: Oxford University Press, 1970), 236–237.

whitewash improvisers like Charlie Parker in favor of aleatoric or "spontaneous" composers like John Cage. As Lewis writes, "coded qualifiers to the word 'music'—such as 'experimental,' 'new,' 'art,' 'concert,' 'serious,' 'avant-garde,' and 'contemporary'—are used in these texts to delineate a racialized location of this tradition within the space of whiteness; either erasure or (brief) inclusion of Afrological music can then be framed as responsible chronicling and 'objective' taxonomy."[56]

This is not to suggest that Black musicians did not also perform techniques associated with European classical music.[57] However, even if Black musicians used these musical tools to associate themselves with intellect, sophistication, and refinement, as John Lewis seemed to, critics by and large considered these musicians to be unique as compared to other Black jazz musicians—and certainly not the foundation of a new, "fully evolved" musical style.[58] As historian Burton Peretti writes regarding Black musicians of the 1920s, "Whatever attitudes they held or steps they took to associate their work with dominant traditions, however, musicians always ran up against white America's refusal to acknowledge their achievement."[59] Monson advances this argument into the 1950s, writing, "In the binary logic that characterized racial thinking in the United States, if hard bop was black, then the cool sound was white, regardless of the number of influential African American musicians who also played in a cool manner."[60]

Trumpeter Miles Davis acknowledged similar limitations in the musical genres he could access within mid-century societal constraints. In his autobiography, Davis recalled his dissatisfaction with the Juilliard symphony orchestra: "I knew that no white symphony orchestra was going to hire a little black motherfucker like me, no matter how good I was or how much music I knew."[61] Contrast these experiences with those of a musician such as Dave Brubeck, who was assumed by the United States State Department in 1958

---

[56] George Lewis, "Improvised Music After 1950: Afrological and Eurological Perspectives," *Black Music Research Journal* 16, no. 1 (Spring 1996): 102.

[57] See also Christopher Coady, *John Lewis and the Challenge of 'Real' Black Music* (Ann Arbor: University of Michigan Press, 2016). Coady argues that Lewis's compositional approach fit squarely within African American middle-class musical traditions, writing, "We might also think of Lewis's use of western art music conventions as emerging from the experience of being part of the African American middle class" (111). In other words, European classical music was not, at mid-century, solely a white phenomenon, nor was Lewis's deployment of classical music particularly subversive for either him or Black middle-class audiences.

[58] I have written elsewhere about Lewis's relationship to the politics of respectability: Kelsey A. K. Klotz, "On Musical Value: John Lewis, Structural Listening, and the Politics of Respectability," *Jazz Perspectives* 11, no. 1 (Fall 2018): 25–51.

[59] Peretti, *The Creation of Jazz*, 73.

[60] Monson, *Freedom Sounds*, 81.

[61] Miles Davis, *Miles: The Autobiography*, with Quincy Troupe (New York: Simon and Schuster, 1990), 59.

to possess equal skills in performing both classical music and jazz (which he did not), and the intellectual privilege associated with being white is made all too clear.[62]

## Swinging Within and Outside Jazz

While counterpoint and descriptions of Brubeck's musical intellect coded the DBQ's music as "white," critics also used a primary jazz criterion, swing, to code the DBQ, and Brubeck in particular, as "not Black." In his article, Feather argued that Brubeck was "not primarily a swinging pianist," explaining, "It even has been implied that you will find less jazz piano in eight minutes of Brubeck than in eight bars of John Lewis. Or 10 seconds of Bud Powell. Or one finger of Count Basie."[63] Pitting Brubeck against Black pianists, Feather's comment potentially implies that as a white pianist, Brubeck could not be presumed to swing as well. No doubt motivated by Feather's critique, Hentoff argued that while the MJQ was "easily and consistently superior to Brubeck's quartet," Brubeck could, in fact, swing. Gleason, writing one month after Hentoff, sided with Feather—Brubeck could not swing.

Critics often used swing as a litmus test that defined whether or not a musician was an "authentic" jazz musician—and that test often rested implicitly or explicitly on racial authenticity. As Monson argues, part of sounding "white" in the 1950s was based on critical judgments that determined whether or not white musicians "failed to live up to aspects of African American aesthetics, usually swing or emotional presence."[64] Music theorist Matthew Butterfield's survey of critical attempts to define swing demonstrate that even when critics attempted to defined swing as "music itself," distinct from any social context, race became an implicit part of the conversation: "Used casually, swing operates today (as it always has) as a term of praise referencing an African American rhythmic impulse or quality, a racially specific rhythmic sensibility that is attractive, engaging, and hip. By contrast, when we describe music as 'not swinging,' we mean that it is rhythmically bland, square, and decidedly unhip—in a word, we mean it is 'white.'"[65] In other words, authenticity and blackness were unspoken parts of a definition of swing that critics and

---

[62] Brubeck quickly telegrammed the US State Department, instructing them to stop promoting him as a dual jazz and classical pianist prior to his 1958 tour of the Iron Curtain.
[63] Feather, "Feather's Nest," *Down Beat*, February 23, 1955.
[64] Monson, *Freedom Sounds*, 76.
[65] Matthew Butterfield, "Race and Rhythm: The Social Component of the Swing Groove," *Jazz Perspectives* 4, no. 3 (2010), 306.

musicians could use to threaten white musicians' place in a commercial industry from which they otherwise benefited greatly.

## Does Dave Brubeck Swing?

The question of whether or not the DBQ was a "swinging" group frequently plagued the quartet. For instance, Jack Maher wrote in a 1956 review of *Jazz at the College of the Pacific*, "I won't go so far as to say that the Quartet doesn't swing, but I do think that it does somewhat lack that humanly funky feeling that makes jazz a distinctly personal experience."[66] Rather than state directly that Brubeck or the DBQ did not swing, Maher used adjectives like "funky," "human," or "personal," which imply the necessary and interrelated relationships between the body, intuition, blackness and swing. Other critics were more direct: John Mehegan wrote in 1957 that Brubeck did not swing, and Martin Williams complained in a review that Brubeck frequently started to swing, but would inevitably abandon it.[67]

These critics rarely defined swing, instead relying on an implicit understanding that swing had a universal definition (even if they could not agree on whether Brubeck could swing). The fact that there was no universal definition of what it meant to swing became a crucial part of critics' debates surrounding Brubeck's ability to swing. Unable to rely on stereotypically racialized notions of swing to account for Brubeck's music, critics who believed in Brubeck's ability to swing usually made their case by offering a swing spectrum. For them, Brubeck may not have swung like Count Basie, but that did not mean he did not swing at all. In 1953, two years before the critics' debates over the DBQ and MJQ, Hentoff first defended Brubeck's ability to swing, writing "that each man swings his own way, if he swings at all, and that his way of swinging is as individual as his phrasing, his ideas, his tone. That ways of swinging have to do with ways of looking at life, and with all kinds of personal background factors."[68] Hentoff was not alone. *Metronome* critic Al Zeiger, writing against critics who thought the DBQ did not swing, argued that swing contained a variety of potential meanings, both for the performing musicians and for the listener: "It [Swing] is a subjective evaluation of one's own musical understanding. Something may not swing for you, but it may swing for someone

---

[66] Jack Maher, Review of *Jazz at the College of the Pacific*, by Dave Brubeck. *Metronome*, August 1956, 24.
[67] John Mehegan, "Jazz Pianists: 2," *Down Beat*, June 27, 1957, 17; Martin Williams, Review of *Jazz Impressions of Eurasia*, by Dave Brubeck. *Down Beat*, February 5, 1959, 23. *Jazz Impressions of Eurasia* featured white drummer Joe Morello and African American bassist Joe Benjamin.
[68] Nat Hentoff, "Counterpoint," *Down Beat*, April 8, 1953, 6.

else."⁶⁹ *Down Beat* critic Don DeMichael agreed, writing, "The big question in many persons' minds is: Does Brubeck swing or doesn't he? It depends on how you define 'swinging'—there's more than one way, you know. I feel that he can swing but often doesn't."⁷⁰ That these critics felt the need to create a new, broader definition of swing to accommodate Brubeck suggests that the issue was crucial to appreciating Brubeck as a jazz musician. As with critics who invoked counterpoint and Bach to claim a white jazz lineage, critics who claimed a swing spectrum likewise seemed intent on reshaping narratives surrounding jazz authenticity that did not rely on blackness.

Likewise, Gene Lees explained in detail the effect of listeners' subjectivity on the perception of swing. Regarding *Gone With the Wind* (1959), Lees wrote, "'But *that* doesn't swing!' some dissident voice may cry. What he means is that it doesn't swing *him*."⁷¹ Lees explained his understanding of swing by providing an example of two friends who are tapping their feet to music:

> Now if the group plays closer to the way you feel time than to the way your friend feels it, then you are going to be swung harder than he is. And you may conceivably get into a dispute over whether the group swung or not, failing to recognize that you are discussing a subjective reaction in yourselves, not an objective reality.⁷²

Even though Lees argued for the subjectivity of swing, thus defending Brubeck against those who would claim he does not swing, Lees was one of the only critics who asserted that swinging was not a "jazz absolute," suggesting that Lees was interested not only in decoupling blackness from swing, but in decoupling notions of jazz authenticity from swing, as well. For most critics and fans, swing was an objective property of jazz music, and it continued to have the juridical power to cast some musicians into the darkness of "not jazz."

Musicians also debated Brubeck's relationship to swing. In addition to critiquing Brubeck's chord-heavy approach to the piano, Miles Davis told *Down Beat* in 1955 shortly after a revelatory "come back" performance at the Newport Jazz Festival, "Do I think [Brubeck] swings? He doesn't know how."⁷³ Davis's interview irritated more than Brubeck, however; Charles Mingus wrote an open letter in response, in which he dedicated a significant amount

---

⁶⁹ Al Zeiger, "Dave Brubeck: A Musical Analysis," *Metronome*, August 1955, 19, 38.
⁷⁰ Don DeMicheal, Review of *Southern Scene*, by Dave Brubeck. *Down Beat*, June 23, 1960, 30.
⁷¹ Gene Lees, "About This Man Brubeck... Part 1," *Down Beat*, June 22, 1961, 23.
⁷² This description mirrors Brubeck's own later description of swing as a fluid construct in Les Tomkins, "Jazz? It's as Much European as African, Claims Dave Brubeck," *Crescendo*, June 1964, 18–19.
⁷³ Nat Hentoff, "Miles: A Trumpeter in the Midst of a Big Comeback Makes a Very Frank Appraisal of Today's Jazz Scene," *Down Beat*, November 2, 1955, in *The Miles Davis Reader*, ed. Frank Alkyer (New York: Hal Leonard, 2007), 36.

of space defending Brubeck's ability to swing, writing that it was unimportant to consider, "not because Dave made *Time* magazine—and a dollar—but mainly because Dave honestly thinks he's swinging. He feels a certain pulse and plays a certain pulse which gives him pleasure and a sense of exaltation because he's sincerely doing something the way he, Dave Brubeck, feels like doing it."[74] Mingus continued, suggesting that even by Davis's swinging standards, Brubeck should be considered a swinging musician: "As you said in your story, Miles, 'if a guy makes you pat your foot, and if you feel it down your back, etc.,' then Dave is the swingingest by your definition, Miles, because at Newport and elsewhere Dave had the whole house patting its feet and even clapping its hands." In his defense of Brubeck, Mingus suggests that Davis's issue is not with Brubeck's music but more with the recognition and financial gains Brubeck experienced after the *Time* article (published one year earlier), and re-focuses the conversation about swing to center on personal expression and emotional connection—two of jazz's other markers of authenticity.[75]

Of course, not all musicians shared in Mingus's defense—and even Mingus didn't always defend Brubeck's ability to swing. In a Blindfold test published just six months before he would excoriate Miles Davis for criticizing Brubeck (June 1955), Mingus offered commentary on "Bop Goes the Leesel," performed by Lee Konitz (who Mingus correctly identified). Mingus focused most of his ire on Brubeck and Desmond, who were not on the record: "This makes me mad, because it's not jazz, and people are calling this kind of beat jazz. Dave Brubeck gets the same beat. And it's leading Lee [Konitz] to think this swings, because Desmond has made it like that, and they call it swing. . . . It's like five dead men, this record. No stars, man."[76] Given that this Blindfold Test was published in the same issue as Feather's last entry into the Brubeck debate, Mingus could have been responding to the months-long conversation surrounding Brubeck's validity. As Eric Porter explains, Mingus recognized that Brubeck had by that point become a leading definer of jazz and swing, over and above Black musicians like himself struggling to gain similar recognition.[77] Likewise, as one unidentified Black jazz musician explained to Nat Hentoff, the assumption that Black musicians could swing and white

---

[74] Charles Mingus, "An Open Letter to Miles Davis," *Down Beat*, November 30, 1955.

[75] For more on Mingus's emphasis on and expression of emotion, see Nichole Rustin-Paschal, *The Kind of Man I Am: Jazzmasculinity and the World of Charles Mingus Jr.* (Middletown, CT: Wesleyan University Press, 2017).

[76] Leonard Feather, "50 Stars for Bird! Mingus Exclaims," *Down Beat*, June 15, 1955, 25, 33. Mingus also criticized Brubeck when commenting on "Margo" by Teddy Charles: "The composition is the kind of thing people should be listening to. . . . Dave Brubeck can never do that, man. He could play the notes—but it wouldn't sound like that. But he wouldn't want to play like that anyway."

[77] Porter, *What Is This Thing Called Jazz?*, 119–120.

musicians could not often benefited white musicians who were perceived to swing, while at the same time denying Black musicians recognition of the skill it took to swing: "I was on the same bill with Brubeck, and his combo got nearly all the attention even though they were playing nothing. It's like people took it for granted that we could swing because we were Negroes, but thought it was something to make a fuss about when whites do it."[78] Put simply, through Brubeck, critics and musicians engaged in fraught negotiations surrounding swing, and especially its relationship to blackness and its role as a key defining feature of "authentic" jazz. Such negotiations threatened to reframe swing in colorblind terms—a move some Black jazz musicians understood as an act of erasure.

## Brubeck's Swing Spectrum

For his part, Brubeck unsurprisingly preferred to be considered through a wide swing spectrum; as he told critic Don Freeman: "The critics say I don't swing. I say we always swing—sometimes we don't swing very much, but it's always enough to be considered jazz."[79] Brubeck was more direct in a personal letter to British critic Steve Race, explaining that while he is "constantly" told he does not swing, "I assume that any jackass with the normal feeling for jazz can swing."[80] But while Brubeck asserted his ability to swing, he maintained his authority to choose an amount of swing. If, as seems likely, critics deemed swing to be primarily the unequal relationship of pairs of eighth notes, a spectral understanding makes sense in listening to Brubeck's music. For instance, in "The Way You Look Tonight," Brubeck and Desmond play straight eighths throughout the introduction and melody, while Desmond's solo and the improvised counterpoint features swung eighth notes. Brubeck plays his solo with straight eighth notes. Likewise, "Brother, Can You Spare a Dime?" features a swung melody and Desmond's solo is swung, but Brubeck incorporates passages with both swung and straight eighth notes in his solo, and Desmond and Brubeck perform the improvised counterpoint with straight eighth notes. Brubeck's typical improvisatory style likewise supports his flexible approach toward swing. Often, Brubeck's solos feature chord-heavy half and quarter

---

[78] Qtd. in George E. Pitts, "Race Prejudice Runs Throughout World of Jazz," *Pittsburgh Courier*, June 6, 1959, 22.
[79] Don Freeman, "Dave Brubeck Answers His Critics: A Lot of Them Are Being Unfair, Insists Jazz's Controversial Pianist," *Down Beat*, August 10, 1955, 7.
[80] Personal letter, Dave Brubeck to Steve Race, June 17, 1955, Brubeck Collection, Wilton Library, Wilton, CT.

note passages, and he rarely relies on the standard bebop piano convention of a running melodic line in the right hand supported by chords in the left hand. Additionally, Brubeck often accents beats 1 and 3 in these passages, rather than 2 and 4, which most jazz musicians stress. This accentuation, combined with Brubeck's emphasis on half and quarter note passages, often belies a swing feel, which is likely at least part of what caused such consternation among critics regarding Brubeck's ability to swing.[81]

Brubeck at times seemed to revel in demonstrating his versatility in different styles, and this extended to swing. Of Brubeck's compositions, "Two Part Contention" is most indebted to counterpoint, both through the title's clear reference to J. S. Bach's Two-Part Inventions and in both solo and quartet performances.[82] But in introducing the tune during his 1956 Newport performance, Brubeck draws attention to the quartet's approach to swing, rather than its counterpoint:

> It's in three sections, and these sections are marked by tempo changes by Joe Dodge on drums. The first part that you will hear will be the two lines, one played by Paul Desmond on alto saxophone, the other by the bass player Norman Bates, and we'll develop the whole three sections from this original thematic material. [counts the tune off][83]

Brubeck begins his description of the piece not by describing the counterpoint but by highlighting the larger structure—a three-part form designed around tempo changes. Each of the tempo changes allowed the DBQ to show off a different approach to swing. The first section, which features the contrapuntal head melodies, improvised counterpoint, and a solo by Desmond, has a typical Brubeck feel, mixing straight eighth notes with light swing throughout Desmond's solo. In the Newport recording, the quartet performed this section at about 180 bpm. The second section primarily features Brubeck's solo. Brubeck leads the quartet through the transition into a new tempo area. At

---

[81] Paul Desmond was rarely accused of not swinging. However, there are two signal differences between Desmond and Brubeck that might account for this: (1) Desmond's solos frequently featured lots of swinging eighth notes, and (2) critics frequently understood Desmond to be constrained by the DBQ configuration, and thus, many critics seem to have been sympathetic to Desmond's plight. Critics' primary objection lay with Brubeck.

[82] The form of each chorus is a fairly typical 32-bar AABA structure: in the Newport recording, the A sections feature Desmond and Bates (bass) in counterpoint, while Brubeck joins the group on piano in the B section, taking over the second counterpoint for the bass, which shifts to a simplistic line featuring one bass note per measure. Brubeck drops out for the final A. In the Newport recording, Brubeck and Desmond begin the solo section with two choruses of improvised counterpoint, characteristically trading lines and space and responding to one another, until Desmond begins his solo.

[83] Dave Brubeck Quartet, *Dave Brubeck and Jay & Kai at Newport*, Columbia CL 932, 1956. Author's transcription.

132 bpm, this section has a heavy, old-fashioned swing feel—the kind of showy feel and tempo shift that often inspires audience applause and propels an ensemble through a finale-style coda. The strong bass back beat and heavy cymbals accompanying Brubeck's solo highlight the old-school swing feel of this section. The third section features solos by both Desmond and Brubeck before ending with a short version of the head melodies. This final section is the fastest, clocking in at 240 bpm at Newport. Here, the DBQ swings in a more modern cool style, with the faster tempo necessitating more agility from the bass and drums, evening out the accents of the previous tempo. Like the first tempo, this is a characteristic example of the DBQ at fast tempo, with both Desmond and Brubeck eschewing fast, running lines for longer note lengths and (in Brubeck's case) an emphasis on thick chords. Throughout "Two Part Contention," the quartet clearly performs the counterpoint critics loved to highlight, but a closer listen to both the tune and to Brubeck's explanation not only reveals his implicit argument that he could swing (and swing in a variety of ways), but it also re-asserts his right, as a jazz musician, to possess a personal interpretation of swing.

## Does the MJQ Swing?

To be clear, the MJQ did incorporate more swing passages in their music than the DBQ, or at least more than Brubeck did as a soloist. However, the MJQ, like the DBQ, did not always include swung eighth notes throughout their pieces. For instance, "Vendôme" features straight eighth notes in its episodes, and while Jackson's solo is swung, Lewis's solo is not. In "Softly, as in a Morning Sunrise," the MJQ plays a straight eighth-note introduction before the swung melody and solos, and also ends the piece with a straight eighth-note conclusion. In fact, much of the MJQ's written counterpoint features straight eighth notes, or at the very least either confusion between whether or not to swing between Lewis and Jackson or an agreement for each musician to take differing approaches.[84] However, the MJQ's early to mid-1950s repertoire also featured a number of pieces in which all the musicians swung eighth notes throughout, and most of the time, improvised solos were clearly swung.

Despite the MJQ's somewhat similar use of a swing spectrum, critics consistently praised the MJQ for their ability to swing. Hentoff offered qualifiers

---

[84] In the case of "Django" and "Milano," Lewis does not swing the melody and Jackson does. Modern Jazz Quartet, "Django" and "Milano," *Django*, with Milt Jackson, John Lewis, Percy Heath, and Kenny Clarke. © 1956 by Prestige.

to Brubeck's ability to swing, writing of the "ingredients" that defined the MJQ's importance: "Undeniable skill of each of its members and the remarkable command of dynamics and shading of the unit as a whole. Those ingredients also include the group's taste, its relaxed, subtly swinging beat, and the warmth of feeling it generates."[85] *High Fidelity*'s John S. Wilson described the MJQ's typically "strong, gutty, swing," while Don DeMichael dismissed critiques of the MJQ's experiments with Third Stream by asserting the group's "intense swinging."[86] In a 1965 article evaluating the MJQ's career, DeMichael again asserted the primacy of swing to the quartet's music, thereby claiming it as authentic jazz: "Though the quartet's music has become increasingly intricate, the four men have never lost sight of the jazz essential—swing."[87]

Even Lewis himself initially focused criticism of the quartet around rhythm. As musicologist Christopher Coady documents, in a 1953 column by Hentoff, John Lewis framed the quartet's sound in terms of rhythmic authenticity, even as Hentoff initially centered musical questions around compositional form; Lewis explained, "In jazz, except for the best Dixieland people and a few others, there's often been a rhythmic dullness. The bass, drums, and piano should do more than simply supply chords and a basic pulsation. . . . In our work we also stimulate counterpoint rhythmically this way: when someone is playing a solo, the other instruments will play ideas in the background, ideas subordinate to those of the soloist. They don't slip back and just keep time."[88] As Coady explains, "Such comments can be seen to temper Hentoff's questioning around form, framing Lewis's work for the *Down Beat* audience as authentic jazz in the established language of authenticity"—that is, around rhythm and swing, even as Lewis simultaneously highlights the MJQ's contrapuntal approach to swing.[89]

## Jazz Legacy

Ultimately, for Hentoff and Gleason, the difference in swing between the MJQ and the DBQ reflected a difference in musical intent, and therefore contribution to a broader jazz legacy, which became another method of measuring

---

[85] Nat Hentoff, "Caught in the Act: Modern Jazz Quartet: Birdland, New York," *Down Beat*, October 6, 1954, 32.
[86] John S. Wilson, Review of *Pyramid*, by the Modern Jazz Quartet. *High Fidelity*, June 1960, 88; Don DeMichael, Review of *Odds Against Tomorrow*, by the Modern Jazz Quartet, *Down Beat*, January 18, 1960, 34.
[87] Don DeMicheal, "John Lewis: Structure and Freedom: A Reappraisal of the Modern Jazz Quartet," *Down Beat*, June 17, 1965, 24.
[88] Nat Hentoff, "Counterpoint," *Down Beat*, December 30, 1953, 8.
[89] Coady, *John Lewis*, 71.

each group's authenticity to jazz. Hentoff explained that "Brubeck in his playing goes in for himself. He's not contributing directly to the over-all jazz tradition." Likewise, Gleason respected that Brubeck "played his own music the way he wanted to," but believed that the MJQ would make a "lasting contribution" to jazz, implying that their legacy would live longer than Brubeck's would.[90] Hentoff's main argument was that because Brubeck fulfilled his own musical goals, Brubeck was a worthy jazz musician. He couched this somewhat forgiving analysis of Brubeck's playing by writing that Brubeck had little influence on the field of jazz and that most musicians had little desire to express the emotions Brubeck wanted to express. However, Hentoff carefully distinguished Brubeck from the MJQ, writing that what made Brubeck a "vital jazzman" was that he broke away from the tradition.[91] Hentoff thus placed Brubeck in a liminal position, in which the very thing that made him a true jazz musician was his willingness to operate outside of jazz. In other words, Brubeck gained an outsider status based on his relationship with the sounds of whiteness (counterpoint, Bach, etc.)—a relationship that, ironically, the very same critics helped to develop.

## Cats of Any Color: Colorblind Jazz

The racial distinctions made in critics' discussions of the two quartets' music were not lost on Brubeck, who answered his critics in an article by Don Freeman in August 1955 (five months after Shorty Rodgers's *Blindfold Test*).[92] In his response, Brubeck directly addressed his understanding of the racial critiques he had received: "Dave said they're criticizing him for all kinds of things now—'for not, of all things, being a Negro!' 'Tell me,' he declared, "what does that have to do with the music we play?'"[93] Brubeck seemed dumbfounded by claims that his group would not be authentically linked to jazz because they were white. Despite the regularity with which Brubeck cited Black musicians who had a significant impact on him (including Duke Ellington, Art Tatum, Teddy Wilson, and Fats Waller, among others), Brubeck's statement seems to question the link between authentic jazz and blackness more broadly, and was therefore part of a larger emerging critical discourse of colorblindness in jazz. This discourse, as Monson writes, argued

[90] Gleason, "Perspectives."
[91] Hentoff, "Counterpoint."
[92] Don Freeman, "Dave Brubeck Answers His Critics: A Lot of Them Are Being Unfair, Insists Jazz' Controversial Pianist," *Down Beat*, August 10, 1955, 7.
[93] Ibid.

that "musical traits were shared across the color line," even if the benefits reaped were not equally shared.[94] As cultural historian Jon Panish explains, colorblindness at once accepted racial differences in situation as a product of sociology rather than biology, but nevertheless, implicitly upheld whiteness as the "*invisible* norm and standard of success."[95] According to Panish, such a move toward what whiteness studies scholar Ruth Frankenberg describes as "color-evasiveness" and "power-evasiveness" "encourages us to ignore race and its effects on the distribution of wealth, power, status, and opportunity in society."[96] Historian and critical race theorist Ibram X. Kendi equates colorblindness with the notion of being "not racist," explaining the failure of colorblind neutrality: "As with the 'not racist,' the colorblind individual, by ostensibly failing to see race, fails to see racism and falls into racist passivity."[97]

Within jazz, colorblind discourses allowed Black jazz musicians to claim genius and talent within a society that typically assumed neither of them; however, as Monson explains, the same colorblind discourse also allowed white musicians to dismiss any seemingly unequal priority given to jazz's Black heritage. Colorblindness could not recognize systemic inequities within the music industry and thus retained legacies of racial essentialist language used by critics, musicians, and audiences to understand the jazz genre. As Stoever writes, "From its earliest manifestations, color blindness never seriously threatened the link between 'whiteness' and 'Americanness,' because it did not challenge—or even acknowledge—the sonic color line disciplining American listening . . . to 'match' certain sounds, voices, and environments to visual markers of race."[98]

Beginning very early in his career, Brubeck frequently explained that jazz was an equal meeting of European and African musical aesthetics that could only have taken place in America—a description that prioritized a colorblind approach to jazz history by glossing over any power differentials in that meeting. In a 1950 article Brubeck wrote for *Down Beat* based on lectures for a class he and Iola Brubeck co-taught at the University of California extension, Brubeck summarized how he thought jazz developed. He wrote, "Jazz is

---

[94] Monson, *Freedom Sounds*, 78. As Monson writes, Black musicians also deployed colorblind discourse; doing so underscored the importance of the music as a universal experience (and also promoted meritocratic hiring practices). For example, Miles Davis famously explained his hiring Lee Konitz on alto saxophone for what would come to be known as the *Birth of the Cool* nonet, "I wouldn't give a damn if he was green with red breath. I'm hiring a motherfucker to play, not for what color he is" (qtd. p. 82).

[95] Jon Panish, *The Color of Jazz: Race and Representation in Postwar American Culture* (Jackson: University Press of Mississippi, 1997), 7.

[96] Ruth Frankenberg, *White Women, Race Matters: The Social Construction of Whiteness* (Minneapolis: University of Minnesota Press, 1993), 14.

[97] Ibram X. Kendi, *How to Be an Antiracist* (New York: One World, 2019), 10.

[98] Stoever, *The Sonic Color Line*, 231.

an improvised musical expression based on European harmony and African rhythms," explaining that these two cultures "face[d] a similar problem in the United States" in that they had both been "uproot[ed] from their native soil" and "transplanted to a new continent" with a different "spiritual climate":

> Jazz was born from spiritual necessity. The Negro, who had suffered most from his uprooted life, was the first to find the expression (in the early spirituals, work songs, and blues). But there were enough white men who suffered from the same spiritual impoverishment in this traditionless age, and who were motivated by the same longing for emancipation and a new life in the Promised Land—to bring forth a jazz that was neither black nor white—but American.[99]

In retrospect, Brubeck's belief in European immigrants' and enslaved Africans' common oppression shockingly misunderstands the very real distinctions in agency, freedom of choice, and the power of racial status between these groups in roughly 350 years of transatlantic crossings. Further, such beliefs claimed ownership over Black musical production and aesthetics that, when packaged and sold to audiences expecting an "authentic" performance, then overwhelmingly resulted in greater economic capital for white musicians than for their Black counterparts. However, within the context of the 1950s, Brubeck's views were far from unique, and indeed demonstrated a strain of progressivism in that he clearly valued the contributions of Black musicians, equally with the contributions he heard from Euro-American musicians.[100]

In the civil rights movement, Brubeck's actions against segregation would demonstrate a strongly held ideological belief that all people were created equal. However, his colorblind approach to race in 1955 was born out of his own lived experiences, which often did not require or inspire any acknowledgment of structural racial issues. Brubeck's colorblind response to criticisms aimed at his authenticity seems to reflect a defensiveness regarding his position as a white jazz musician. As jazz historian Reva Marin explains, "Central to this colorblind perspective is its insistence that the history of jazz has been unfairly represented as the exclusive or primary domain of black music and culture, and that, as a result, the contributions of white

---

[99] David Brubeck, "Jazz' Evolvement as Art Form," *Down Beat*, January 27, 1950, 12.
[100] Brubeck kept this belief in an equally biracial jazz history, doubling down on his insistence that white musicians also played an important role in jazz's formation; see Les Tomkins, "Jazz? It's as Much European as African, Claims Dave Brubeck," *Crescendo*, June 1964, 18–19; Martin A. Totusek, "Dave Brubeck Interview," *Cadence*, December 1994, 5–17; Dave Brubeck, "A Long Partnership in Life and Myth," an oral history conducted in 1999 and 2001 by Caroline C. Crawford, Regional Oral History Office, Bancroft Library, University of California, Berkeley, 2006.

jazz musicians as creators, innovators, and stylists have been obscured or deliberately misrepresented."[101] Brubeck's experiences were shaped by what sociologist Eduardo Bonilla-Silva refers to as a white habitus—"a racialized, uninterrupted socialization process that *conditions* and *creates* whites' racial taste, perceptions, feelings, and emotions and their views on racial matters."[102] Whether or not he recognized it, Brubeck's decisions about what and how to play took place within a racially stratified and segregated society. For example, while Brubeck contemplated pursuing classical music after World War II, his teacher, Darius Milhaud, insisted that his students take advantage of their American heritage and pursue jazz.[103] In other words, Brubeck was convinced by a white European classical master that he could, and should, reap the benefits of being an American by claiming the country's ostensibly only truly original musical style—a style that by the time of Brubeck's studies with Milhaud after World War II, had already seen white musicians like Benny Goodman, Tommy Dorsey, Glenn Miller, and Artie Shaw gain a level of fame unheard of by most Black musicians. For Brubeck to decide to pursue jazz, particularly in contrast with John Lewis's experiences, reflects the privilege Brubeck had in making such a choice; further, he was able to successfully leave a door open to return to classical musical composition.[104] As composer and trumpeter Bill Dixon argued decades later, "It must be remembered that white men *elect* to play jazz; their musical horizons are not bound by an enforced social tradition that relegates them to one area of musical expression."[105]

Brubeck's colorblindness was not a static ideology or discourse. As jazz writers critiqued his music, Brubeck tended to retreat to a defensive performance of colorblindness; however, he simultaneously recognized the importance of being aligned with Black musical aesthetics. When his music gained praise for what would stereotypically be considered Black musical aesthetics

---

[101] Reva Marin, *Outside and Inside: Race and Identity in White Jazz Autobiography* (Jackson: University of Mississippi Press, 2020), xxi.

[102] Eduardo Bonilla-Silva, *Racism Without Racists: Color-Blind Racism and the Persistence of Racial Inequality in the United States*, 3rd ed. (New York: Rowman and Littlefield, 2010), 104. Emphasis original.

[103] Dave Brubeck, "'Jazz' Evolvement as Art Form," *Down Beat*, January 27, 1950, 12; "Time Takes a Look at Dave Brubeck," *Blue Note News*, January 2, 1953 [repr. *Time*, November 10, 1952]; Ralph J. Gleason, "Dave Brubeck Remembers 'They Said I was Too Far Out,'" *Down Beat*, August 8, 1957, 17–19, 39; John S. Wilson, "Loyal Fans of Dave Brubeck Flock to Carnegie Hall Concert," *New York Times*, April 7, 1966.

[104] Nat Hentoff, "Brubeck Has Double Life as Jazzman, Classic Composer," *Down Beat*, December 3, 1952, 6; Nat Hentoff, "Jazz Fills Role of Classical Composition, Brubeck Learns," *Down Beat*, June 2, 1954, 2.

[105] Qtd. in Monson, *Freedom Sounds*, 272. Even aside from his musical career, Brubeck had other means to support his family. As he told Gene Lees, Brubeck's father, Pete Brubeck, had given Dave four Holstein cows when he graduated from grammar school. He explained, "He kept those separate in his herds. I could always come back to the ranch." Gene Lees, *Cats of Any Color: Jazz, Black and White* (Cambridge, MA: Da Capo Press, 2001), 47; for more information on the relationship between race and inherited wealth in the United States, see Thomas M. Shapiro, *The Hidden Cost of Being African American: How Wealth Perpetuates Inequality* (Oxford: Oxford University Press, 2005).

(swing, the blues, and spontaneity), he seemed more apt to emphasize the importance of African and African American musical aesthetics to jazz. Many Black musicians defended him at various points in his career (including Charlie Parker, Mary Lou Williams, Billy Taylor, and Charles Mingus), and he would re-tell memorable stories of their support throughout his career, enacting a form of "credentialing."[106]

Perhaps the story he told most was that of pianist Willie "The Lion" Smith. Smith praised Brubeck's playing in one of Feather's blindfold tests, reflecting on Brubeck's performance on "St. Louis Blues": "I like the piano because he plays like the guys I told you about at the brickyards in Haverstraw, New York, where the blues was BORN."[107] The Brubecks celebrated Smith's assessment; Iola Brubeck wrote to Smith to thank him for the appraisal, telling him, "It did my heart good to hear a veteran speak out in favor of the spirit of the Blues, as played by my husband's Quartet," and explaining that she was going to send the article to Dave Brubeck, who was touring India with the US State Department, and that it would make him happy.[108] Indeed, it did make Dave Brubeck happy, and throughout his career, he pointed to this moment, as well as another in which Smith referred to Brubeck as his son, as evidence of his ability to swing.[109] Brubeck's frequent recounting of Smith's approval of his blues playing makes clear the authority Brubeck understood Smith to have—an authority based in performance as well as racial authenticity.

Similarly, Stephen Crist recounts a roundtable given at the Music Inn after the release of *Time Out* (1959), in which Willis James, chair of the music department and director of the Glee Club at Spelman College, went to the podium and sang. According to Brubeck's recollections, shared in a 2001 interview with his son, Darius Brubeck, James asked the crowd, "Can any of you tell me what time signature that was in?" Brubeck explained that despite the many musicians in the audience, no one responded. James continued, "That was an African work song; it was in five-four time, and the Dave Brubeck Quartet is on the right track." Brubeck reminisced, "That was such an important statement in my life to have somebody with his background telling these musicians that what I was doing was on the right track. . . . To be vindicated

---

[106] According to Robin DiAngelo, credentialing "describe[s] the ways in which white progressives attempt to prove that they are not racist." Robin DiAngelo, *Nice Racism: How Progressive White People Perpetuate Racial Harm* (Boston: Beach Press, 2021), 58.

[107] Willie "The Lion" Smith, with Leonard Feather, "The Blindfold Test: The Lion Roars," *Down Beat*, April 17, 1958, 39.

[108] Iola Brubeck to Willie "The Lion" Smith, April 15, 1958, Brubeck Collection, Wilton Library, Wilton, CT.

[109] Dave Brubeck, interview with Carey Frampkin, October 17, 1981, Chicago, Brubeck Collection, Wilton Library, Wilton, CT.

in what I was trying to do was wonderful."[110] As with Brubeck's accounting of Smith's approval, James's approval was particularly meaningful for Brubeck because it (1) linked the Brubeck Quartet and Brubeck specifically not only to an African American musical heritage but also to an African musical heritage; (2) came from a Black scholar and performer of Black musics; and (3) was performed in front of a group of mostly jazz musicians.[111] In other words, Brubeck believed he could access narratives of jazz authenticity by buttressing his claims of authenticity with support from Black musicians, while simultaneously denying that Black-coded musical elements were part of the music he created, a perspective that positioned his success in jazz as evidence of the genre's meritocracy.

Of course, white jazz musicians often attempted to defend themselves against claims that their music was racially inauthentic. However, Brubeck differs from some other white musicians like trombonist Jack Teagarden, pianist Russ Freeman, baritone saxophonist Pepper Adams, and alto saxophonist Art Pepper in that he not only argued that he, as a white man, could swing, too, but also that he did not have to swing all of the time to be considered "authentic." While, as Monson writes, such a defensive posture by white musicians and their advocates "simply confirms the centrality of the African American legacy in shaping the musical aesthetics of the mainstream jazz tradition," Brubeck both took pride in having the support of Black musicians, thus anchoring him more securely to jazz's Black aesthetics, *and* questioned the racial binary defining jazz.

Indeed, the whole 1955 *Down Beat* debacle surrounding Brubeck and the MJQ can be read as an assertion of Brubeck's aesthetic agency in relation to an emerging jazz discourse tying jazz authenticity to blackness and reflects a reckoning, on Brubeck's part, that jazz might not reflect the colorblind existence he experienced as a white man outside of jazz.[112] He seemed surprised that well-meaning critics like Feather, Hentoff, and Gleason could use his race to write him out of jazz, a genre to which Brubeck felt he had already contributed significantly.[113] Though Brubeck may have been the center of this particular debate, Monson explains that Brubeck was simply one part of a larger picture of race relations within jazz at mid-century:

---

[110] Darius Brubeck, "Jazz 1959: The Beginning of Beyond" (MA thesis, University of Nottingham, 2002), 143–144. Interview from July 25, 2001, qtd. in Crist, 46.
[111] Of course, that James was speaking about Paul Desmond's composition, "Take Five," and not one of Brubeck's did not stop Brubeck from seeing this as a statement of support for Brubeck himself.
[112] Monson, *Freedom Sounds*, 73–74.
[113] For more critical approaches to jazz colorblindness, see John Gennari, *Blowin' Hot and Cool: Jazz and Its Critics* (Chicago: University of Chicago Press, 2006); Nichole Rustin [Paschal], "*Cante Hondo*: Charles Mingus, Nat Hentoff, and Jazz Racism," *Critical Sociology* 32, no. 2–3 (2006): 317.

In response to the commercial and popular success of white jazz musicians, which was viewed by many as depriving African American musicians of a fair economic return on their creativity, many African American jazz musicians of the 1950s and 1960s seemed determined to emphasize and develop black difference rather than witness a repeat of the 1930s, when Benny Goodman was crowned the King of Swing. The racialized power differentials in the music industry, in other words, led to a dynamic that offered African American musicians a choice between emphasizing difference and earning recognition as black artists or emphasizing sameness and having the history of African American leadership in the music erased in a sea of colorblindness.[114]

The connection between Goodman and Brubeck had already been suggested in a 1953 *Down Beat* article titled "Coronation Ceremonies Nearing for Brubeck," which outlined Brubeck's accomplishments as a "modern" jazzman whose music might "make the road ahead one whit easier, for similarly splendid combos— the Gerry Mulligans, the Lennie Tristanos, the Buddy DeFrancos, et al."[115] The fact that each of those combos was white, combined with the impending victory critic Jack Tracy envisioned ("In the meanwhile, begin preparations to hail the new king. He'll be crowned any time now") set up the coming storm surrounding Brubeck's music and his recognition, authenticity, and aesthetic agency. Though some critics would continue to promote varying degrees of colorblindness throughout the 1950s and 1960s, the Brubeck debacle that occurred over a span of months in 1955 made clear jazz's emerging racial principle—that colorblindness may be ideal, but it denied the social reality of race that had already overwhelmingly benefited white musicians in jazz's short history.

## Conclusion

The long-lasting impact of this debate extended well beyond the 1960s and is particularly evident in a 2007 oral history interview, in which Brubeck debated whether or not he belonged in the "cool" school:[116]

> When people talk about cool, I recommend that they listen to an NBC broadcast from a club, live, in Los Angeles. "This Can't Be Love" and "Look for the Silver

---

[114] Monson, *Freedom Sounds*, 106.
[115] Jack Tracy, "Coronation Ceremonies Nearing for Brubeck," *Down Beat* February 11, 1953, 3.
[116] Joe Goldberg, *Jazz Masters of the Fifties* ([1965]; New York: Da Capo Press, 1983), 131.

Lining." And to this day, I think that's some of the most spontaneous, hard swinging, far from West Coast 'cool' so to speak.[117]

Brubeck then exclaims, "How can they call us cool? I mean, that is *wild*." Although Brubeck did not elaborate further on what made these recordings more "spontaneous" and "hard swinging" than others in the Brubeck Quartet discography, each includes the tell-tale sign of an energetic Brubeck performance: large, block chords played in repeated rhythmic motives.[118] "Look for the Silver Lining" also features Brubeck shouting "Play!" to Desmond just one measure before the two engage in a particularly spirited bout of improvised counterpoint.

In his 1953 review of the sides, Barry Ulanov, one of the first jazz critics to describe Brubeck as a cool musician, wrote that "this is the Brubeck Quartet at its best, swinging, putting down fresh lines . . . discovering the capacities of their instruments anew," suggesting that Brubeck was not alone in considering this performance as challenging the boundaries of cool.[119] However, as the *Down Beat* review of the same recording indicates, some reviewers still focused more on the triplet ornaments, sequenced motives, and counterpoint that marked the record as belonging to cool jazz; regarding "Look for the Silver Lining," the reviewer wrote, "There are fuguish moments in the last chorus," while the summary of "This Can't Be Love" noted that it had "some of Desmond's coolest, smoothest work." However, the reviewer also described Brubeck in terms generally considered to be outside cool, explaining that "This Can't Be Love" contained "some intense, jumpy Brubeck."[120]

Throughout his interview with Gioia, Brubeck is occasionally fuzzy about the details of his early career; his wife, Iola Brubeck, and his manager, Russell Gloyd, work to fill in any gaps. But in this moment, Brubeck quickly recalls two recordings from a single LP dating from 1952 that he believed proved that he was *not* a "cool" musician, suggesting that this was a battle Brubeck had fought before, and one which he was always prepared to fight. Importantly, Gioia did not ask Brubeck whether or not he thought his quartet was cool—the word "cool" was not part of the question.[121] Instead, Brubeck's detailed

---

[117] Dave Brubeck, August 6–7, 2007, interviewed by Ted Gioia, Jazz Oral History Program Collection, Archives Center, National Museum of American History, Smithsonian Institution.

[118] Dave Brubeck Quartet, "Look for the Silver Lining" and "This Can't Be Love," © 1952 Fantasy 521.

[119] Barry Ulanov, Review of "At a Perfume Counter," "Frenesi," "This Can't Be Love," and "Look for the Silver Lining," *Metronome*, January 1953, 25.

[120] Review of "Look for the Silver Lining," "This Can't Be Love," "At a Perfume Counter," and "Frenesi," *Down Beat*, December 3, 1952, 15.

[121] Brubeck, interview with Ted Gioia (2007), 51–52. Gioia asked, "Let me ask you about the early quartet recordings. Those are quite extraordinary recordings, because they sound very spontaneous, but they are

and fervent response was the result of Gioia asking how much of the quartet's music was planned and how much was spontaneous—a question that had been implicitly linked to 1950s debates over the racial authenticity of cool, including Shorty Rogers's comments. For Brubeck, to be called cool—even to hint at it—was an accusation that he did not swing, did not improvise, and had no emotion in his music—elements that were associated with blackness, and that therefore would remove (and for some in the jazz community, *had* removed) his quartet from narratives of authentic jazz. Brubeck may have understood jazz to be colorblind, but he also understood that jazz's racial connotations, held by many critics and audiences, had the power to cast his music as inauthentic.

Perhaps Brubeck's seeming racial inauthenticity is, at least in part, why so few present-day jazz musicians cite Brubeck as a major influence. In a 2020 reflection on Brubeck's career and music, jazz scholar Lewis Porter notes, "Among jazz musicians, jazz critics, and 'hardcore' jazz fans, Brubeck's piano playing has largely been either vilified or ignored. If a pianist says his or her main influence is Brubeck, that will almost guarantee a negative reaction in those circles."[122] After recounting major collections and textbooks in which records by and information about Brubeck is either nonexistent or scarce, Porter notes how well known Brubeck was and is, and asks, "If Dave was as famous as Louis, Duke and Miles Davis, why do they each get a full chapter in every jazz history text, while he gets no more than a page?" The reason, Porter explains, is that many in jazz believe that Brubeck "is an excellent composer, but his piano playing is heavy-handed and doesn't swing"—a charge levied at Brubeck beginning with the debates outlined in this chapter but which carried through the rest of his career.

Brubeck's own response to such accusations, that "any jackass can swing," was an uncharacteristic moment of near crudeness that shows the level of frustration he had at such charges.[123] For Porter, this moment expresses Brubeck's approach to swing, outlined above: "He followed this [comment] by

also very well planned and conceived. I'm trying to understand, what kind of preparation or rehearsal? How planned were they? How did you get that kind of combination between the planned and the spontaneous?"

[122] Lewis Porter, "Reconsidering the Piano Legacy of Dave Brubeck, in a Deep Dive Centennial Special," *WBGO*, February 20, 2020, https://www.wbgo.org/post/reconsidering-piano-legacy-dave-brubeck-deep-dive-centennial-special.
[123] Later, even Brubeck was surprised by his statement. In a different interview, Hedrick Smith asked Brubeck, "You once said to a critic, 'Anybody can swing.' What did you mean?" Brubeck begins his response saying, "It was even worse than that. I said, 'Any jackass can swing,'" suggesting that this was something of an uncharacteristic response (at least publicly) for him.
Dave Brubeck and Hedrick Smith, "Talking with Dave Brubeck: Dave on the Racial Barrier," *Rediscovering Dave Brubeck*, Public Broadcasting Service, December 16, 2001, http://www.pbs.org/brubeck/documentary/facts.htm, accessed July 15, 2021.

trying to explain that swing is not everything; it's more important to try and innovate. What I think he was trying to say is: *What would swing have to do with the solo you just heard?* [emphasis original]" In other words, Brubeck understood jazz to highlight individual expression—and he believed that swing, a defining feature of jazz for many, could be a matter of individual expression, too. But perhaps what Brubeck did not consider—what his colorblindness may have prevented him from considering—was that the very privilege that allowed him to pick and choose when to swing, that assumed swing to simply be a musical device equal to any other, and that granted him wide recognition and the status of "intellectual," was part of what his critics objected to all along.

# 2
# Professors, Housewives, and Playboys
## The Jazz Converts

"He's [a] Jazz Evangelist" read the headline of a 1958 interview with Dave Brubeck in the *Detroit Times*. Writer Arnold Hirsch explained, "Dave Brubeck, firmly established as one of the high priests of modern jazz, last night revealed he's also a musical evangelist."[1] As Brubeck began to reveal to Hirsch how he "spread the word of jazz," Detroit-based jazz impresario Ed Sarkesian interrupted the pair, explaining, "It was 1953 that jazz took hold and got out of the cellars. And it was Dave who started it." Though presented by Hirsch as unimpeachable evidence of Brubeck's privileged position in jazz, Sarkesian's comments inspire a number of questions about the place of jazz in the early 1950s. What does he mean by "jazz took hold," and for whom did it take hold? When jazz came up from the cellars, where did it go? And what was Brubeck's role?

As early as the 1940s jazz critics and audiences worried over jazz's apparently imminent demise; with the increasingly sober economic realities of the postwar popular music industry, many big band leaders found it harder to support an ensemble of twelve, fifteen, or eighteen musicians, and their decline worried jazz fans across the United States in the late 1940s and early 1950s. By that point, it seemed clear that jazz had lost its position as "America's Popular Music." While jazz combos maintained popularity among jazz audiences, mainstream audiences simply seemed to have lost interest.

That is, according to Sarkesian, until Dave Brubeck entered the scene and completely changed the jazz market; Brubeck's college tours, which he began even before the quartet was formed, targeted a younger, whiter audience than was assumed to typically listen to jazz, and introduced a future "mainstream" consumer audience to jazz as performed by Brubeck, who Hirsch writes, "brought classical harmony and style to the jazz field." Hirsch further explains that Brubeck "had the feeling the college kids were ripe for the intelligent jazz sounds of Brubeck & Co."[2] For Sarkesian and Hirsch, Brubeck's "intelligent"

---

[1] Arnold Hirsch, "He's Jazz Evangelist," *Detroit Times*, August 19, 1958.
[2] Decades later, Iola Brubeck explained in a Library of Congress interview that she and Dave Brubeck wanted to perform at colleges because young people did not expect jazz to be primarily entertaining, and

and "classical" sounds—terms often used to describe the music of white cool jazz musicians (see chapter 1)—ultimately had an uplifting effect on jazz. Using his music, Brubeck managed to elevate jazz from cellars to "respectable" gymnasiums and auditoriums on college campuses across the United States, and "jazz took hold" in mainstream markets that had not listened to it since the Swing era. As jazz and film scholar Steven Elworth observed decades later, "Brubeck was extremely popular on the white college circuit, where his image was seen as that of an exemplary white jazz musician who was also an artist and intellectual."[3]

Brubeck's success touring colleges helped to catapult him to fame largely through his ability to present a credibly aspirational image to mainstream audiences. Even from the beginning of his career, mainstream press coverage (i.e., *Time, Life, Good Housekeeping*, and other non-jazz-oriented publications) explicitly assumed Brubeck's respectability to be unique among others in the field of jazz—a fact that did not escape him. On a 1954 television broadcast with Dave Garroway, Garroway asked Brubeck if his picture on the cover of *Time* magazine, which had appeared just one week earlier, lent "a certain amount of respectability to the jazz business," asking whether or not that respectability was good for jazz.[4] Brubeck answered, "Well, I think it's good, because the thing that's held jazz back has been the environment. And every time a club is run decently, there's an audience, a wonderful audience, that usually won't go into a nightclub."

According to Brubeck, groups and musicians like the Brubeck Quartet, Gerry Mulligan Quartet, and Stan Getz, all white, were helping to "make converts" of non-jazz audiences—a statement that pre-dated Hirsch's similar assertion by four years. The way such musicians were able to "make converts" was by placing jazz in white-coded spaces. Simply put, if a club was "respectable" or "decent," and if it avoided a stereotypical "environment," "new" audiences would go.[5] As musicologist Guthrie Ramsey explains, "As musicians push against a listening community's acceptable codes of musical

---

they believed that music students understood that Brubeck was performing "a new vocabulary and a new language," and music students "could sort of grasp what was going on." Iola Brubeck with Denise Gallo, "Jazz Conversation: Lyricist Iola Brubeck," Library of Congress, April 10, 2008, https://www.loc.gov/item/webcast-4797/.

[3] Steven B. Elworth, "Jazz in Crisis, 1948–1958: Ideology and Representation," in *Jazz Among the Discourses*, ed. Krin Gabbard (Durham, NC: Duke University Press, 1995), 65

[4] Dave Garroway, *Friday with Garroway*, NBC Radio Collection, November 12, 1954, Motion Picture, Broadcasting & Recorded Sound Division, Library of Congress, Washington, DC.

[5] Importantly, Brubeck speaks of respectability within the space of a jazz club, not a concert hall. As Scott DeVeaux writes, jazz ensembles had already been finding ways of benefiting from the respectability inherent to a concert hall setting. Scott DeVeaux, "The Emergence of the Jazz Concert, 1935–1945," *American Music* 7, no. 1 (Spring 1989): 6–29.

behavior, they are usually articulating who they believe they are in the world through displays of musical prowess, stylistic challenge, and experimentation."[6] Speaking in the racially coded language of critics who defined the sounds of cool jazz around white intellectual privilege, Brubeck's statement highlights the position of new jazz audiences previously scared away by racist stereotypes that linked jazz, blackness, and primitivism. Further, he and other white cool musicians could serve as gatekeepers to "new" jazz audiences; these audiences, as Amiri Baraka explained, "liked a little culture with their popular music," and ostensibly had greater buying power—facts that were exploited by white musicians, their promoters, and advertisers.[7] While other white jazz musicians (namely, Benny Goodman and Paul Whiteman) have likewise been credited with or have taken credit for introducing respectability to jazz, the ongoing conversations surrounding Brubeck's respectability in the early 1950s, paired with the rise in postwar capitalism and jazz's increasing presence on college campuses and in concert halls, demonstrates the extent to which the Brubeck phenomenon was experienced by white mainstream audiences as something new.

Brubeck converted new audiences to jazz early in his career. His method was to promote an image of respectability that was automatically coded as white—an image of which "respectable" audiences (or audiences who considered themselves to be respectable) would approve and to which they could relate. Brubeck, his wife Iola, and record producers deployed this image in mainstream publications, advertisements, and personal appearances in which he performed the role of jazz authority figure. With this image, he contributed to pre-existing mainstream assumptions regarding respectability and race in jazz nightclubs, and he found entrance to the predominantly white spaces of suburban homes, college campuses, and mainstream magazines. Thanks to the Brubeck quartet's college tours, and albums such as *Jazz at Oberlin* (1953), *Dave Brubeck & Paul Desmond at Wilshire-Ebell* (1953), *Jazz at the College of the Pacific* (1953), *Jazz Goes to College* (1954), and *Jazz Goes to Junior College* (1957) that capitalized on those tours, Brubeck was and remains strongly associated with college jazz; as Paul Lopes writes, "The Dave Brubeck Quartet came to personify a new legitimacy for jazz music as the jazz art world successfully pursued the college market as a new source of income and prestige."[8]

But colleges were not the only spaces to which Brubeck's legitimacy—his whiteness—granted his quartet special access. His moves within

---

[6] Guthrie Ramsey, *The Amazing Bud Powell: Black Genius, Jazz History, and the Challenge of Bebop* (Berkeley: University of California Press, 2013), 141.
[7] Amiri Baraka, *Blues People: Negro Music in White America* (New York: HarperCollins, 1963), 214.
[8] Paul Lopes, *The Rise of a Jazz Art World* (Cambridge: Cambridge University Press, 2002), 235.

predominantly white spaces, from college auditoriums to Boston's Storyville night club to living rooms to penthouses, further reveal the extent to which whiteness granted respectability to not only Brubeck but also to his mainstream audiences and their engagement with his music as well. Brubeck's more mainstream jazz communities in Boston's Storyville, living rooms, and penthouses occupy a liminal space in jazz historiography, despite their typically higher degrees of privilege outside of jazz. As musicologist Kimberly Hannon Teal demonstrates, "Jazz places show contested ideas about and varying experiences with what might be considered a large-scale, shared jazz community; individually, each venue holds different benefits, challenges, pathways, and barriers for every performer and listener who accesses music there—and those who can't or don't."[9] Likewise, jazz places created, maintained, and occupied by mainstream audiences offer a host of different benefits, challenges, pathways, and barriers, and they also inspire new questions surrounding accessibility.

In focusing predominantly on white mainstream audiences, this chapter is not meant to suggest that Brubeck was not also popular among many Black audiences (both Amiri Baraka as a young college student and Barack Obama were fans). In a 2001 interview with Hedrick Smith and aired on PBS, Smith noted the common set of assumptions among jazz musicians that West Coast jazz was cool jazz, that cool jazz was white jazz, and that this was a way to de-authenticate or "put down" white musicians. Smith asked Brubeck, "Did you feel that you were handicapped because you were West Coast and white?" Brubeck's response was no, and he cited the Quartet's popularity among Black audiences in both colleges and nightclubs, including the Apollo in Harlem and all around the South. Brubeck seemed frustrated that "the critics don't like to remember that we were doing both. They like to pigeonhole us into intellectual college, university concert halls. It's not true at all."[10] Brubeck is correct on every account here: that his itinerary included dates in Black colleges, universities, and nightclubs, and that critics often overlooked those dates. This chapter focuses on what Brubeck calls the "pigeonhole" critics created to describe his music. By focusing on Brubeck's white audiences—in particular, the "mainstream" audience on whom much of the marketing around Brubeck focused—this chapter confronts the assumptions inherent in "respectability" at midcentury—namely, that respectability was a privilege automatically granted to white tastemakers, power brokers, and audiences based

---

[9] Kimberly Hannon Teal, *Jazz Places: How Performance Spaces Shape Jazz History* (Berkeley: University of California Press, 2021), 8.
[10] Dave Brubeck, "Talking with Dave Brubeck," interview with Hedrick Smith, *Rediscovering Dave Brubeck*, PBS, December 16, 2001, https://www.pbs.org/brubeck/talking/daveOnRacial.htm.

on their intersecting race, class, gender, and sexual identities. With Brubeck in the marketplace, white, middle- and upper-middle-class audiences could quite literally buy into the notion that through their thoughtful appreciation of Brubeck's music, they could further bind themselves to his image of intellect and respectability.

## A Respectable Image

From the beginning of his career, mainstream publications welcomed Brubeck in features and interviews, and they frequently mentioned him in passing to assert jazz's newfound respectability and intellect. That *Vogue, Esquire, Good Housekeeping, Playboy,* and *Time,* magazines targeting white, middle- to upper-middle-class audiences, would feature lengthy articles with color pictures praising jazz marks a shift in the jazz audience at mid-century. These magazines featured predominantly white models (*Playboy* did not feature a Black model in its pages until 1965 with Jennifer Jackson, and its first Black cover model was Darine Stern in 1971; *Vogue*'s first Black cover model, Beverly Johnson, appeared in 1974). The publications were marketed to consumers with enough income to purchase magazines whose prices were between 35 cents ($3.16 today) (*Good Housekeeping*) and 50 cents ($4.42 today) (*Vogue, Esquire,* and *Playboy*). Readership included an audience who saw some value in certain kinds of music beyond entertainment and who could conceivably bring that mindset and listening attention to "serious" modern jazz musicians such as the Dave Brubeck Quartet. Brubeck's success in these magazines also demonstrates that, to some extent, his popularity among white audiences had also transcended gender.

While jazz critics were often suspicious of jazz musicians who were too popular with mainstream audiences, Brubeck did not share such feelings, and he and his promoters specifically targeted them as a yet untapped market. In fact, he frequently boasted of his ability to bring a "wider" jazz audience, and his appearances in 1950s advertisements promoted an "alternative" (i.e., respectable) jazz image. Brubeck's whiteness intersected with his self-positioning as a heteronormative, middle-class family man with a classical pedigree that reinforced the system of white privilege from which he benefited.[11] Put simply,

---

[11] Though Brubeck's earnings placed him in the upper middle class or upper class for much of the 1950s, I refer to his middle-class status in this chapter as an important part of his self-presentation. As Shannon Sullivan writes, the "rhetoric of the middle class holds sway" and is "inseparable from the American Dream and the Protestant work ethic." In other words, the middle class here operates as more than an economic category—as a social, cultural, and educational category as well. Shannon Sullivan, *Good White People: The Problem with Middle-Class White Anti-Racism* (Albany: State University of New York Press, 2014), 7.

the fact that Brubeck was featured on mainstream advertisements was not only because he wanted a "wider" audience; advertisers also used him as part of their marketing strategy because he appealed to audiences with purchasing power. Brubeck's privilege as a white, heterosexual, middle-class man granted him visibility and access to mainstream media that many other jazz musicians—particularly Black jazz musicians—did not have.[12] In this way, the system of commercial white privilege acted as a loop: white consumers' interest in products advertised by white celebrities spurred further marketing decisions to feature white celebrities. As Timothy Taylor explains, "Cultivating one's personality was a way to stand out from the crowd, the mass, and this could be accomplished through consumption, purchasing goods that could be used to define oneself."[13] Not only could Brubeck's audience define themselves by purchasing a Brubeck record, but Brubeck could cultivate his own public personality through the marketplace.

With endorsements, Brubeck explicitly selected products that would bring a new audience to jazz—an audience that after hearing him, would presumably become interested in similar jazz musicians. Essentially, he viewed himself as a kind of brand ambassador for jazz. In defending his decision to be part of an advertising campaign for a lipstick company, Brubeck told *Down Beat* reporter Don Freeman in 1956, "The only reason I went for the lipstick deal was that it might promote the good of jazz among people who might be strangers to it—the *Vogue* readers, for example."[14] In the lipstick advertisement, Brubeck is featured playing the piano in profile, with model Suzy Parker draped over the piano in a bright red dress with matching lipstick, cigarette in hand. The same photo was used on Brubeck's album, *Jazz: Red Hot and Cool* (1955) (Fig. 2.1). In the mid- to late 1950s, Columbia and other record companies released several albums featuring beautiful white women (or parts of beautiful white women); indeed, this seemed to be an important part of their advertising and marketing strategy.[15] But this Brubeck cover is different from many of these because of the

---

[12] Reva Marin notes Benny Goodman's similar "respectable" image construction throughout his career, writing, "Beginning in the early 1940s, the public image that Goodman had cultivated from the beginning of his career—mild-mannered and fatherly, industrious and grateful for the opportunities he had received in his own country—had seemingly begun to bear fruit, as Goodman was appointed to positions befitting his reputation as the leading statesman of jazz, the representative of American democracy through popular music." Brubeck's role as a cultural ambassador for the US State Department in 1958 further cements this particular similarity. Reva Marin, *Outside and Inside: Race and Identity in White Jazz Autobiography* (Jackson: University of Mississippi, 2020), 112.

[13] Timothy Taylor, "Music and Advertising in Early Radio," *Echo* 5, no. 2, http://www.echo.ucla.edu/volume5-issue2/taylor/taylor-3.html, accessed April 2, 2020.

[14] Don Freeman, "Dave Brubeck Not Pink over Red, Hot, and Cool," *Down Beat*, January 25, 1956, 9.

[15] See, for example, the Pat Moran Trio's *This Is Pat Moran* (1958), the Art Van Damme Quintet's *Manhattan Time* (1956), Erroll Garner's *Penthouse Serenade* (1955), and the George Shearing Quintet's *Velvet Carpet* (1956). The original cover of Miles Davis's *Miles Ahead* (1958) featured a white woman on a

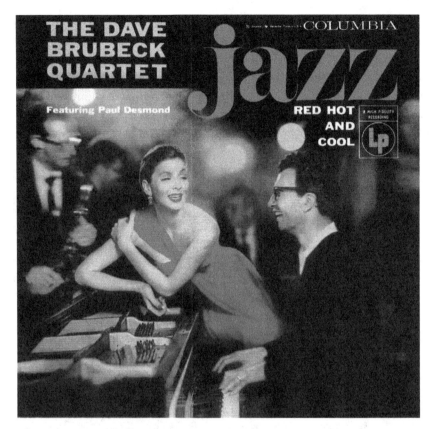

**Figure 2.1.** Album cover, *Jazz: Red Hot and Cool*. © 1955 Sony Music Entertainment. Courtesy of Sony Music Entertainment.

clear product placement (that this was both an advertisement and an album cover), and because Brubeck is foregrounded fairly equally with Parker. The other figures in the image are blurred in a haze of smoke and stage lights, but the air around Parker and Brubeck is clear, and while her pose may seem suggestive, his visible wedding ring ensured viewers that nothing untoward was happening in this otherwise private scene. In other words, the advertisement promoted Brubeck's image as a respectable man—a man who could be welcomed into a white suburban living room—who happened to play jazz music. The women viewing the advertisement in the pages of *Vogue* could be assured that they, too,

---

sailboat, to which Davis strenuously objected (in his autobiography, he says he asked Columbia producer George Avakian, "Why'd you put that white bitch on there?"). Future pressings were sold with an album cover featuring a photo of Davis performing. Davis's later album, *Someday My Prince Will Come* (1961) featured Davis's wife, Frances Davis, in a strapless outfit gazing directly into the camera, upsetting the tradition of featuring only white women on jazz albums.

could effortlessly entertain a "respectable" musician like him, if only they would buy Helena Rubinstein lipstick.

Likewise, a 1958 Bethlehem Steel advertisement, published in *Business Week*, presented Brubeck to the public as a man capable of providing for his family through an in-depth look at his thoroughly modern home in Oakland, California, high on a hill across the bay from San Francisco (Fig. 2.2). The ad's placement in *Business Week*, a publication meant for company managers who

**Figure 2.2.** Pages 1 and 2 of Bethlehem Steel Advertisement, 1958. Brubeck Collection, Holt-Atherton Special Collections, University of the Pacific Library. © Dave Brubeck.

### Dave Brubeck and his "tree house"

If the highest attribute of a home is to express the personality of its owners, the home of Dave Brubeck, jazz pianist extraordinary, is an architectural triumph. Like his music, Brubeck's home is imaginative, bold in concept. Moreover, it answers the functional requirements of the owners, and the problems of a perplexing site.

The lot itself is beautiful, with tall trees and a magnificent view of the Bay. But it's also narrow (50 x 100), steeply sloped, and virtually all rock. Here Brubeck wanted to build a home for a large family without marring the site's natural beauty.

Architect David Thorne had the answer. He formed a sort of "hand" by anchoring five steel "fingers" to a mass of rock. These beams cantilever in two directions, *creating* a 3000-sq-ft level floor for the entire living area. How this was done is explained on the next page.

Thus Thorne preserved the site, leaving trees and boulders intact. The structure appears to spring from solid rock, yet its spectacular cantilever seems to soar, giving a "tree-house" effect.

**Brubeck at Home**

"The way I look at it, this house expresses much of my wife's personality and my own. To us it's a house that is full of common sense. It's completely open and honest. We have nature all around us. I feel that if inspiration can come from good surroundings, I'll find it here."

**Figure 2.2.** Continued

subscribed by submitting their title and employer, targeted predominantly white and white-collar businessmen—men who, like Brubeck and unlike many other jazz musicians, could build new homes. The pamphlet included floor plans and pictures of the Brubeck home, including one featuring him, his wife, Iola, and four children. The home had a modern design and seemingly defied rules of gravity through the use of Bethlehem steel beams, but more important for Brubeck, it served as an introduction to his family and their home. As he explained in the pamphlet, their home was an expression of both his and his wife's personalities; nevertheless, his description also claims the design as more practical (masculine) than decorative (feminine): "To us it's a house that is full of common sense. It's completely open and honest."[16] In these ads, Brubeck and his public relations team promoted him as a respectable public figure fulfilling traditional heteronormative roles of masculinity and positioning himself within a modern, non-decorative design space.

Brubeck made it clear that his appearance in such advertisements was meant to bring a *new*, middle-class, white *Vogue*-reading audience to jazz. Brubeck understood himself to be a gateway to jazz for his audience, and his own "respectable" image as an honest family man was an important element in attracting this "new" audience. As he explained in a 1957 *Down Beat* interview, his "fan mail frequently mentions how they have become interested in jazz through us, even though they never liked it before. And that, by playing our records, they've become interested in most of the other jazz records of serious jazz artists."[17] He was also uniquely recognized as a potential jazz educator, having taught a jazz history course at the University of California Berkeley extension as early as 1950, and having spoken at the 1955 Music Educators' National Convention (MENC). But Brubeck did more than educate his audience: in serving as an entry point to jazz, he could subsequently claim a corner of the jazz market.

Brubeck's fan mail also linked his respectability to his Christianity well before Brubeck explicitly turned to religious compositions.[18] For example, Dave Holland, a sophomore at St. Olaf College in Northfield, Minnesota, wrote to Brubeck in 1958, asking if Brubeck felt jazz and Christianity could be understood together.[19] He explained Brubeck's importance as a jazz evangelist, expressing his hope that Brubeck might bring a sea change of support for modern music at a Christian college like St. Olaf. The perception of Brubeck as a "respectable" jazz musician was paramount for Holland: he notes that jazz was not thought of highly on the rural, Lutheran campus, but that Brubeck nevertheless had had a stunning effect on the classical music–oriented students, writing that though "music men on campus" had little respect for jazz, they could still respect Brubeck. Importantly, Holland directly connects

---

[16] Bethlehem Steel advertisement, ca. 1950s. Promotional Materials, Brubeck Collection, Wilton Library, Wilton, CT.

[17] Ralph Gleason, "Brubeck: 'I Did Do Some Things First,'" *Down Beat*, September 5, 1957, 14.

[18] Brubeck at times encouraged this connection, such as when he contributed three short essays on his faith to *Guideposts*, a nonsectarian spiritual magazine: "Fragile Moments . . . When God Speaks in Whispers" (January 1958), "Words That Changed My Life" (April 1958), and "Short Cut to Freedom" (July 1965).

[19] Dave Holland to Dave Brubeck, personal letter, February 18, 1958, Brubeck Collection, Wilton Library, Wilton, CT.

Brubeck's seemingly unique ability to provide moral guidance and convince religious people of jazz's moral potential with his respectability.

While Brubeck's "respectability" was well established by the time he signed with Columbia Records in 1954, there is no doubt that Columbia's investment in jazz's potential as a "respectable" music aided Brubeck's swift rise in popularity, particularly among mainstream audiences. Part of this no doubt stems from Columbia record producer George Avakian's own experience as a jazz enthusiast at Yale University and his friendship there with Marshall Stearns, who would later found the Institute of Jazz Studies, and whose 1956 *The Story of Jazz* was among the first book-length studies of jazz published. Avakian also taught one of the first university courses about jazz in 1948, at New York University, and as musicologist Darren Mueller explains, was one of the first industry professionals to approach the production of jazz albums similarly to those of classical albums.[20] As Mueller writes, there is a notion of respectability that undergirds Avakian-produced jazz albums; that notion can be felt particularly in the venues featured on live LPs produced by Avakian: college campuses, Carnegie Hall and other concert halls, a military base, and Newport, Rhode Island. As jazz scholar John Gennari explains, jazz at the Newport Jazz Festival, which began in 1954, and the Lenox School of Jazz in Lenox, Massachusetts, "symbolized the refining impulses of an educated, curious, urbane, and diverse audience. Jazz's cultural capital accrued by virtue of its association with northeastern social elites, its propaganda value as a form of interracial 'democratic' public culture, and its symbolic status as a serious American 'art' legitimated by intellectuals and jazz critics."[21] It seems no surprise, then, that Brubeck, one of Columbia's highest-selling jazz musician and a frequent performer and guest at the Newport Jazz Festival and Lenox School of Jazz, would also be touted as one of its most "respectable," in advertising, marketing, reviews, and recording decisions. Brubeck was a key figure in jazz's increasing drive toward white respectability: As a 1958 headline for the *New York National Enquirer* put it, "Jazz Climbs Up the Social Ladder—with a Mighty Shove from Dave Brubeck."[22] Put simply, Brubeck's desire for respectability was well matched at Columbia, which also offered greater access to the "new" jazz audiences Brubeck targeted.

---

[20] Darren Mueller, *At the Vanguard of Vinyl: A Cultural History of the Long-Playing Record* (Durham, NC: Duke University Press, Forthcoming).

[21] John Gennari, *Blowin' Hot and Cool: Jazz and Its Critics* (Chicago: University of Chicago Press, 2006), 210.

[22] "Jazz Climbs Up the Social Ladder—With a Mighty Shove from Dave Brubeck," *New York National Enquirer*, March 16, 1958.

It was not just that these audiences were new, but that these audiences, who read *Time, Vogue,* and *Playboy*, and who were often college educated and predominantly white, ostensibly engaged with jazz differently than past jazz audiences—at least according to mainstream audiences and writers who were unfamiliar with the numerous jazz critics, club owners, and musicians who were also college educated. According to critics, these audiences were capable of comprehending the Brubeck Quartet's complicated musical lines; because of this, they were an intelligent audience and could grant Brubeck's new musical lines the respect and attentive listening he and other cool musicians apparently deserved over other jazz musicians. This chapter focuses on three spaces outside of college tours in which Brubeck converted his audiences: Boston's Storyville night club, living rooms across the country, and *Playboy's* penthouse. In each space, his respectability and "serious" music played an important role in his new audiences' conception of themselves as jazz listeners.

## Brubeck in the Jazz Club: Storyville

When Brubeck described a "decently" run club that attracted a "respectable" audience to Garroway in 1955, what sort of listeners might he have had in mind? What does respectability look and sound like? And what happens when a "respectable" audience does not listen "seriously"? Popular music scholar Simon Frith argues that critics determined audiences' modes of listening through their physical engagement with music—what musicologist Christi Jay Wells calls "choreographies of listening"—and mapped such distinctions onto binary understandings of racial difference.[23] According to Wells, "choreographies of listening" not only describe audience members as listeners with bodies but also as active agents in the performative practice of listening.[24] Wells explains,

> When applied to jazz listening spaces, choreography indexes the implicit and explicit assumptions people make about their role in the event (dancer, musician, concertgoer, etc.), how they should thus orient their body in space to communicate what it means for them to listen to the music being played (or that they are

---

[23] Simon Frith, "Rhythm: Race, Sex, and the Body," in *Performing Rites: On the Value of Popular Music* (Cambridge, MA: Harvard University Press, 1996), 123–144.
[24] Christi Jay Wells, *Between Beats: The Jazz Tradition and Black Vernacular Dance* (Oxford: Oxford University Press, 2021).

playing), and what their listening body communicates about the soundscapes and attendant values present in the space.[25]

Frith writes that in critical discourses, white audiences demonstrated passive postures and were often quietly seated to allow for deep thought, whereas critics described Black audiences' bodies as actively engaged, often in dance, and were therefore also assumed to be non-thinking. It bears repeating that Frith's analysis is of the critical discourse—not how Black and white audiences actually engaged with the music. He explains that such acts of listening are place-based: "When rock (or jazz) acts move into seated concert halls, for example, it is often to register that the music is now 'serious,' should now be appreciated quietly."[26] The assumption in each choreography of listening is that "serious" music demands "respectful" attention, whereas "fun" music does not, and further, that racialized musical spaces likewise grant privileged access to choreographies of listening assumed to be respectable. As George Lipsitz writes, "White identity in the United States is place bound.... [B]ecause of practices that racialize space and spatialize race, whiteness is learned and legitimated, perceived as natural, necessary, and inevitable. Racialized space gives whites privileged access to opportunities for social inclusion and upward mobility."[27]

In 1953, Brubeck named Boston's Storyville jazz club as his favorite performance venue on the East Coast.[28] The club was instituted by Boston native and Boston University graduate George Wein. In 1950, Wein, the son of a physician, shocked his family members by opening a jazz club in the Copley Square Hotel. Unashamed of what he described in his autobiography as "jazz's seamy origins," he took the name of his club, "George Wein's Storyville: The Birthplace of Jazz," from New Orleans's former legal red-light district, linking his club to historical narratives of authentic jazz.[29] Wein's desire to associate his club with "jazz's seamy origins" simultaneously clashed with his goal, shared with Brubeck, to make jazz "respectable," and he made sure to distance his own Storyville from the reputation of its predecessor; he called his Storyville a "respectable place," and in describing what "respectability" meant

---

[25] Wells, *Between Beats*, 12.
[26] Frith, "Rhythm," 125.
[27] George Lipsitz, *How Racism Takes Place* (Philadelphia, PA: Temple University Press, 2011), 6.
[28] Nat Hentoff, "Counterpoint," *Down Beat*, July 1, 1953, 8.
[29] George Wein, *Myself Among Others*, with Nate Chinen (Cambridge, MA: Da Capo Press, 2003), 76. Storyville, in New Orleans, had long been associated with the beginnings of jazz history, as was evident in Wein's subtitle, "The Birthplace of Jazz." Cornetist Buddy Bolden, trumpeter Joe "King" Oliver, trumpeter Louis Armstrong, and pianist Jelly Roll Morton, all known as innovators in early jazz, grew up and played in and around Storyville.

for his club, he drew upon implicitly racist distinctions by emphasizing that Storyville was a "true music room. Storyville was never a joint. We had no floor show, no drug dealers or resident hookers. We kept things clean."[30] Though Storyville, New Orleans, had long held a reputation as "the wickedest city in America . . . [and] was notorious for promiscuous race mixing," the reality was that Storyville, New Orleans, was much more about the intersections of white supremacy and patriarchal masculinity.[31] Wein's distinction between his Storyville and a "joint" perhaps reflects his assumption, as a white, mid-century northern Jew, that Storyville, New Orleans, was implicitly associated with blackness; as historian Emily Epstein Landau writes, "Storyville is remembered to add an element of danger, the *frisson* of transgression, to jazz music—to make it sexy."[32] For his part, Wein underscored his understanding of jazz's racy beginnings by insisting that *his* Storyville was "clean."[33]

In their descriptions of the Storyville audience, critics frequently focused on the audience's seemingly careful and attentive listening, connecting the club's quiet atmosphere to the narratives of respectability described by Wein. Cyrus Durgin, a music reporter for the *Daily Boston Globe* and self-described "longhair," wrote about the "attentive" listening that happened at the club.[34] For Durgin, Storyville was an example of how jazz had become a "serious" music, calling it Boston's "best temple of jazz."[35] He offered the Gerry Mulligan and Dave Brubeck Quartets, both white groups, as proof of jazz's shift toward "attentive listening performances":

> Some people do talk, but not many, and conversation is frowned upon. Most of the customers are there to listen, to Mulligan's closely-woven musical strands that sound not unlike syncopated Bach, or to Brubeck's resourceful piano style, with its moving voices of counterpoint and its fascinating shades of harmonic and instrumental color.

---

[30] Wein, *Myself Among Others*, 127, 85. By the end of 1950, Storyville closed, due to a miscommunication with the management of the Copley Square Hotel. Wein re-opened the club in the Hotel Buckminster, closer to both Boston University and Fenway Park, in 1951. Like the Copley Square Hotel, the Hotel Buckminster was located in a racially segregated neighborhood. The Buckminster Storyville was not as successful as the Copley Storyville until Wein booked white British jazz pianist George Shearing in September 1951. In 1953, Wein moved Storyville back to the Copley Square Hotel. In his recollections of Storyville, Wein does not specify which location he means (Hotel Buckminster or the Copley Square Hotel), suggesting that his concept of Storyville as a space remained largely unchanged, regardless of the actual place it occupied.

[31] Emily Epstein Landau, *Spectacular Wickedness: Sex, Race, and Memory in Storyville, New Orleans* (Baton Rouge: Louisiana State Press, 2013), 2; Alecia P. Long, *The Great Southern Babylon: Sex, Race, and Respectability in New Orleans, 1865–1920* (Baton Rouge: Louisiana State Press, 2004).

[32] Landau, *Spectacular Wickedness*, 205.

[33] Wein, *Myself Among Others*, 85.

[34] Cyrus Durgin, "Jazz Moves to Newport as Serious Music Form," *Daily Boston Globe*, June 20, 1954, C79.

[35] Durgin likely took this phrase from *Daily Boston Globe* writer John William Riley's 1951 article covering the new opening of Storyville; Riley also referred to the club as "Boston's new temple of jazz." John Wm. Riley, "Theatre Talk: New Night Club Enters, Another Gets a Face-Lift," *Daily Boston Globe*, October 19, 1951, 20.

Durgin argued that Mulligan and Brubeck deserved attentive listening because their music, tied as it was to European classical music, was "serious," a term associated with privileged art discourse. In his use of terms laden with import from high art discourse and the European classical musical tradition, Durgin's account bears witness to the pervasive whiteness embedded in the sounds of white musicians in spaces like Storyville. That Storyville audiences focused on listening to "serious" music suggests that they, apparently unlike other jazz audiences, were likewise serious, and further, contributed to the respectability Wein desired of his nightclub.

Of course, many jazz musicians had considered jazz "serious" and worthy of modern art status since bebop (and earlier, for that matter). As jazz scholar Scott DeVeaux writes, the narrative surrounding bebop was one that eschewed the commercial trappings of the Swing era. Within jazz discourse, the narrative surrounding bebop highlighted artists who "force[d] radical and disorienting innovations upon a reluctant and bewildered audience, in this way guaranteeing a minority role in American culture for jazz as 'avant-garde' art."[36] However, though this narrative connecting bebop with modern art music was fairly standard for jazz audiences, or for some of the readers of *Down Beat*, it remained primarily an "insider" story. For mainstream audiences, including many of Durgin's readers of the *Daily Boston Globe*, the idea that jazz could be "serious" or "thoughtful" seemed novel, or "hip." Dizzy Gillespie highlighted this distinction in his autobiography, writing, "Around 1946, jive-ass stories about 'beboppers' circulated and began popping up in the news. Generally, I felt happy for the publicity, but I found it disturbing to have modern jazz musicians and their followers characterized in a way that was sinister and downright vicious."[37] Though Gillespie places some blame on the behaviors of some bebop followers, he clearly implicates the non-jazz, mainstream press by citing *Time* magazine coverage of bebop that defined the music and its culture as "hot jazz overheated, with overdone lyrics full of bawdiness, references to narcotics and doubletalk."[38] Put simply, there was a broad gulf between jazz followers' understandings of jazz as an art music and mainstream or new jazz fans' failure to recognize that jazz already had an art discourse.

---

[36] Scott DeVeaux, *The Birth of Bebop: A Social and Musical History* (Berkeley: University of California Press, 1997), 8.
[37] Dizzy Gillespie, *To Be Or Not . . . to Bop* (1979; Minneapolis: University of Minnesota Press, 2009), 278.
[38] "Be-bop Bebopped," *Time*, March 25, 1946.
   Of course, jazz magazines like *Down Beat* often perpetuated the same stereotypes. An article written just one month earlier than the *Time* article mourned the "loss" of the 52nd Street jazz scene to beboppers, bemoaning, "They come with their zoot suits, long haircuts, reefers and 'zombie' jive to night spots that feature top jazz talent. Soon they become the 'atmosphere' that pervades the spots. . . . Keep the zombies away . . . they are lousing up jazz." "Zombies Put Kiss of Death on 52nd St. Jazz," *Down Beat*, February 25, 1946, 3.

In marking spaces like Storyville as "listening spaces," mainstream audiences like Durgin confronted their own assumptions that jazz was not an art music and would not require "serious" listening. Brubeck and Mulligan's jazz were portrayed as exceptions—jazz that needed quiet spaces, presumably like Storyville. But for all of Cyrus Durgin's and George Wein's insistence that Storyville was a "quiet" place for listening to jazz, albums and radio broadcasts recorded live at Storyville suggest otherwise.[39] Many of these recordings contain audience noise and conversation, though most seem to balance the recording toward the music and away from audience noise.[40] However, Gerry Mulligan and Dave Brubeck's live recordings feature audience noise particularly prominently.

Mulligan's December 1956 recording at Storyville offers a glimpse of the typical audience noise jazz musicians had to contend with—even in this apparently "quiet," "respectable" space. Audience chatter is prevalent throughout the tracks, but perhaps the most striking moment is found on "Limelight."[41] At the onset of the song, an audience member's high-pitched, shrill whistling is heard above both Mulligan and valve trombonist Bob Brookmeyer's melody and the usual din of the audience. The whistling is heard several times, but, as jazz musicians typically do, Mulligan and Brookmeyer continue on. Mulligan begins the first solo after the melody, and in the third measure of his second AABA chorus, the whistling patron interrupts Mulligan. Within this chorus, the whistler interrupts Mulligan a total of three times, and each time, Mulligan stops playing until the whistler stops. The final time, Mulligan verbally reprimands the whistling patron, telling him,

> Ok, wise guy. You care to step outside, *whistler*? You and me have got a few words to say. I mean I've been putting up with some noisy audiences but that's the most in*sult*ing thing that *any*body *ev*er did.

This encounter—Mulligan's speech and his silence afterward—lasts the rest of the chorus, and the rhythm section adds an extra A section, allowing him to enter again on the downbeat of his third chorus, for a total of 18 bars of interrupted performance. Mulligan and his quartet continue on as if nothing had happened, and are thanked by the audience with hearty applause at the end of the piece.

---

[39] Hentoff, "Counterpoint," July 1953. Hentoff also referred to Storyville's "relative silence."
[40] For instance, the audience can be heard softly in the background on live Storyville recordings by Billie Holiday, Charlie Parker, Lee Konitz, and Stan Getz. In general, the audience is best heard in piano, bass, and drum solos, but the constancy suggests that the conversations are consistent throughout the performance.
[41] Gerry Mulligan Quartet, "Limelight," *Gerry Mulligan Quartet at Storyville*, by Gerry Mulligan, ©1956 by Pacific Jazz. Author's transcription.

While Mulligan's outburst may have been unique, it nevertheless indicates that the Storyville audience was far noisier than Durgin or Wein described. Brubeck shares a similar Storyville experience. On a Brubeck recording from October 22, 1952, at Storyville, a patron whistles along with Desmond on the melody of "You Go to My Head."[42] Rather than accost the patron as Mulligan did, the characteristically non-confrontational Desmond simply deviates enough from the melody to throw off the whistler, who eventually stopped. The audience also plays a prominent role throughout the Brubeck Quartet's 1954 recorded performances at Storyville; their conversations, laughter, and tinkling glasses are never far from the record listener's ears, suggesting that what Durgin and Wein referred to as "respectable" had little to do with careful or quiet listening.

Unlike other popular Boston nightclubs such as the Savoy and the Hi Hat, Storyville was located in a primarily white neighborhood. Wein later explained in his autobiography that the club's Copley Square location was ideal for the affluent neighborhood surrounding it: "In terms of location, clientele, and the quality of the music, Storyville could be the first club poised to compete with the Savoy and the Hi Hat, both in an African American neighborhood." According to Boston's 1950 census results, the Copley Storyville was neatly tucked into an almost entirely white neighborhood (Copley Square was on the border of a distinctly white and a distinctly Black neighborhood).[43] According to Wein, Storyville's audience was primarily white and college educated but did not draw audiences under the drinking age of twenty-one: "Once we caught on, our audience was mostly made up of professors from the different local colleges. . . . The club attracted blacks when I had certain artists booked, but for the most part the audience was white and middle class."[44]

Despite recorded evidence of Storyville's more casual sonic atmosphere, Durgin and Wein insisted that Storyville was a place for "serious" listening; for both, "serious" listening seemed to sound white. Indeed, the images of the Brubeck Quartet at Storyville seems to suggest the kind of focused listening

---

[42] Dave Brubeck Quartet, "You Go to My Head," *Dave Brubeck & Paul Desmond*, with Paul Desmond, Ron Crotty, and Lloyd Davis, ©1952 by Fantasy Records.

[43] Frank L. Sweetser, "Ethnicity Non-White, City of Boston, 1950," *The Social Ecology of Metropolitan Boston: 1950*, Boston University (Division of Mental Hygiene, Massachusetts Department of Mental Health, 1961), 45–46. Sweetser makes an exception to tracts G-3 and G-4, which contained most of Boston's Chinese population.

[44] George Wein with Marc Meyers, "Interview: George Wein (Part 1)," *Jazz Wax*, July 23, 2008, http://www.jazzwax.com/2008/07/interview-georg.html; George Wein drew a wide variety of musicians to the club; however, his main staples included Dixieland Revival musicians such as the Bob Wilber sextet and Jimmy McPartland, "modern" jazz artists like Charlie Parker, Mulligan, Brubeck, the Modern Jazz Quartet, Lee Konitz, George Shearing, and Stan Getz, and popular jazz singers such as Billie Holiday, Anita O'Day, and Sarah Vaughan.

described by Durgin and Wein—all visible bodies are focused on the stage and the Brubeck Quartet, all bodies seem still. But the tables and the items left casually on them remind us that Storyville was a social place—a nightclub—in which it was not only acceptable to drink and smoke, talk and laugh, but in which such behaviors were expected alongside live musical performance. In other words, their interest was not necessarily "serious," in a pure definition of the word, unburdened by cultural connotations. Even if Brubeck's music was more "complex," more "intellectual" for its references to European classical music, as critics often claimed, Storyville's ostensibly "respectable" audiences could choose to focus their listening entirely on the Brubeck Quartet—or not. In fact, in the 1950s, Brubeck preferred differentiated engagement from his audience; as he explained to the *Boston Globe*, "That's why I like playing at Storyville, where half the audience can dance, while the other listens."[45] But regardless of the form of engagement that took place when Storyville's audiences listened to Brubeck, critics and commentators granted those audiences the privilege of respectability not accessible to previous jazz audiences—even some white jazz audiences like the 1930s jitterbugs, whose interest in jazz was derided as silly or thoughtless, and whose engagement in jazz fan culture seemed distinct from Brubeck's more "selective" audience.

Nor was respectability assumed of many Black artists—even those whose actions and modes of self-presentation were aligned with what Evelyn Brooks Higginbotham refers to as the "politics of respectability."[46] Though critics like Amiri Baraka blamed Black middle-class churches for "always pushing for the complete assimilation of the Negro into white America," Higginbotham argues that the "politics of respectability" promoted by those churches included both conservative and radical impulses.[47] In her discussion of the turn of the twentieth century women's movement in the Black Baptist Church, Higginbotham writes that "although the black church offered women an oppositional space in which to protest vigorously social injustice, this space remained, nonetheless, situated within the larger structural framework of America and its attendant social norms."[48] In other words, the politics of respectability *did*, to some extent, reinforce white, upper- and middle-class Protestant values, and it was, like W. E. B. Du Bois's concept of double consciousness, highly attuned to the critical and racist "gaze of white America."

---

[45] John Wm. Riley, "Brubeck's Key to Jazz: Improvise, Let Audience In," *Boston Globe*, January 21, 1954.
[46] Evelyn Brooks Higginbotham, "The Politics of Respectability," in *Righteous Discontent: The Women's Movement in the Black Baptist Church, 1880-1920* (Cambridge, MA: Harvard University Press, 1993), 185–229.
[47] Baraka, *Blues People*, 125.
[48] Higginbotham, "The Politics of Respectability," 187.

However, the politics of respectability also included an element of subversion through its adherents' insistence that Black bodies could not only operate within white spaces, but that Black Americans could perform better than their white counterparts, and thus, as Higginbotham writes, could yield a "sense of moral superiority over whites." Importantly, respectability is only considered political when it is not inherently granted, as it was with Boston's predominantly white Storyville audience.

A prominent example of jazz respectability cited by historians and critics alike was the Modern Jazz Quartet (MJQ).[49] The MJQ's presentation as serious, tuxedo-attired Black men playing "chamber style," "learned" jazz fulfilled many of the tenets of mid-twentieth century Black respectability politics. As Ingrid Monson writes, "In a social climate that associated jazz musicians with heroin addiction and dissoluteness, the MJQ confronted white audiences in the United States and Europe with a conservative black masculinity that they seldom realized existed."[50] Musicologist Christopher Coady further notes that while white mainstream publications and jazz publications alike tended to frame the "respectable" elements of the MJQ's style (the visual style, on-stage presentation, and classical musical elements) as a movement away from African American culture, critics in the black press tended to understand the MJQ as the "realization of a long-awaited style of jazz that could effectively showcase folk elements while simultaneously rejecting liberal values of 'rebelliousness' and 'emotional abandonment.'"[51] Therefore, the key distinction between the respectability of the Brubeck Quartet and the respectability politics of the MJQ, from the perspective of both the mainstream and jazz presses, is the degree to which white audiences assumed respectability of the former and were confronted with unexpected respectability by the latter.

White cool jazz musicians like Brubeck did not have as far to go to meet commercial audiences as did Black jazz musicians, either figuratively or literally. In tracing bebop's move from "Harlem jook spaces to the wider commercial world of 52nd Street," Guthrie Ramsey argues that "bebop's geographical journey, such as it was, altered the social processes of marginalization, concealment, and boundary making by revealing them as hegemonic strategies

---

[49] Lewis was not the only musician for whom the politics of respectability works as an interpretive frame; from the Fisk Jubilee Singers to Duke Ellington to the album *Charlie Parker with Strings* to gospel singers like Mahalia Jackson to Motown to Wynton Marsalis and his neotraditional approach to jazz, respectability politics has been both an effective and controversial marketing and social justice strategy by which Black musicians have presented themselves to or have been received by their audiences.
[50] Ingrid Monson, *Freedom Sounds* (Oxford: Oxford University Press, 2007), 96.
[51] Christopher Coady, *John Lewis and the Challenge of 'Real' Black Music* (Ann Arbor: University of Michigan Press, 2016), 13. Coady quotes the following article in this excerpt: "Modern Jazz Quartet Top Unit to Emerge from 1940 'Bop' Era," *Chicago Defender*, April 25, 1963, 29.

that organized race, gender, and class differentiation."[52] However, the moves made by cool jazz musicians among white-dominant spaces (white jazz clubs, college campuses, suburban living rooms, etc.) did not alter social processes of marginalization, concealment, and boundary making. Indeed, the acceptance of predominantly white cool jazz musicians into these typically white spaces (as portrayed by the mainstream press) further marginalized Black jazz musicians in these spaces, concealed the extent to which white musicians often received higher paying gigs and better marketing placements, and reinforced already segregated boundaries between white and Black listening spaces—all under the guise of "respectability." Within the white racialized space of Storyville, white audiences could partake in jazz while maintaining their respectability—no matter how attentively they listened.

Brubeck's music also occupied and transformed particularly gendered spaces—from the living room to the penthouse—as men and women alike found themselves able to claim Brubeck's music as part of their own identities. Indeed, part of what defined the seeming "newness" of Brubeck's "respectable" audience was its gender—and more specifically, that he could draw both women *and* men to jazz.

## Performing Respectability Across Gender: Cool's "New" Audience

Brubeck's apparent respectability hinged on his masculinity and heteronormativity as much as it did his whiteness. In mainstream advertisements, performances, speaking engagements, and television/radio appearances, Brubeck demonstrated a strong adherence to social norms that inscribed white masculinity for white audiences in the 1950s. He was educated, showed near constant devotion to his wife, was a breadwinner and nondenominational Christian, and provided for his wife and children (most obviously in the construction of their modernist home in the hills of Oakland). Though women had listened to and participated in jazz from its beginning, Brubeck's appeals to respectability ensured that white, middle- and upper-middle-class housewives could profess their enjoyment of his music without risking association with the stereotypes that had previously been tied to female jazz fans (whether that was the frantic jitterbug, the woman of loose sexual morals, or the macho lesbian). In other words, they, too, could enjoy the privileges of respectability. On the other hand, Brubeck's white, middle-, and upper-class

---

[52] Ramsey, *The Amazing Bud Powell*, 25–26.

male audiences could appreciate his music for its intellectual content and further, could access discourses of masculinity through his association with jazz.

As has often been discussed in jazz scholarship, jazz was one of few realms where Black men could assert their masculinity without fear of reprisals from white audiences. In fact, in order to maintain their authenticity as jazz musicians, audiences and critics expected Black jazz musicians in particular to participate in overt displays of masculinity—even if musicians like the members of the Modern Jazz Quartet or, later, Ornette Coleman, offer clear examples of the diversity of Black masculinities operating in the 1950s.[53] Indeed, as jazz studies scholar Nichole Rustin-Paschal argues, such expectations became a defining part of the jazz genre, and jazz musicians themselves began to expect the same of their fellow musicians.[54] However, the relationship between Black male jazz musicians and masculinity threatened to further perpetuate racist stereotypes with their roots in blackface minstrelsy. For example, the fact that jazz historian Ted Gioia describes the Primitivist Myth (that a jazz musician was considered to be "the inarticulate and unsophisticated practitioner of an art which he himself scarcely understands") using only male musicians demonstrates the extent to which race and gender were both implicated in this stereotype.[55] As Ingrid Monson explains,

> The unfortunate implication is that the "real" African American is someone who comes very close to embodying the most persistent stereotypes of African American men that recur throughout American history: the Zip Coon image of the urban, black dandy transmitted through the minstrel show; and the Buck image of black men as physically and sexually aggressive, perhaps most obviously employed in D. W. Griffith's *Birth of a Nation*.[56]

Racist stereotypes of the "oversexed primitive" (whether male or female) pervaded white representations of African Americans inside and outside the jazz field (of which Norman Mailer's 1957 "The White Negro: Superficial Reflections on the Hipster" is only the most infamously and bombastically primitivist example).[57] According to Monson, "The 'subcultural' image of

---

[53] David Ake, "Regendering Jazz: Ornette Coleman and the New York Scene in the Late 1950s," in *Jazz Cultures* (Berkeley: University of California Press, 2002), 62–82.
[54] Nichole Rustin-Paschal, *The Kind of Man I Am: Jazzmasculinity and the World of Charles Mingus, Jr.* (Middletown, CT: Wesleyan University Press, 2017).
[55] Ted Gioia, "Jazz and the Primitivist Myth," in *The Imperfect Art* (New York: Oxford University Press, 1988), 36.
[56] Ingrid Monson, "The Problem with White Hipness: Race, Gender, and Cultural Conceptions in Jazz Historical Discourse," *Journal of the American Musicological Society*, 48, no. 3 (Autumn 1995): 419.
[57] Norman Mailer, "The White Negro: Superficial Reflections on the Hipster," *Dissent*, 4 (1957): 279.

bebop was nourished by a conflation of the music with a style of Black masculinity that held, and continues to hold, great appeal for white audiences and musicians."[58] By engaging with such representations of primitivized and sexualized Black men, white men—whom Eric Lott identifies as bohemians and Mailer refers to as hipsters—ostensibly achieved access to a particularly racialized mode of masculinity.[59] James Baldwin would come to describe such experiences like this: "It is still true, alas, that to be an American Negro male is also to be a kind of walking phallic symbol."[60]

In his discussion of Black free jazz saxophonist Ornette Coleman's aversion to the overt sexuality of jazz culture in the late 1950s and early 1960s, musicologist David Ake explains that the relationship between jazz and sex has "long been central to the jazz community's understanding of itself."[61] But as Monson demonstrates, the relationship between jazz and sex has long been central to mainstream culture's understanding of the jazz community as well, which makes women's engagement with jazz, whether as performers or listeners, a delicate dance. As Sherrie Tucker explains in her work on "all-girl" bands during World War II, "white women playing swing edged ever so near to one of the most inflammatory social taboos of the white U.S. imagination: racial mixing involving white women."[62] At mid-century, a flurry of Supreme Court decisions challenged the legality of segregation, from *Shelley v. Kraemer* (1948), which found that racially restrictive property covenants violated the Fourteenth Amendment, to *Brown v. Board of Education* (1954), which ordered the integration of schools, to *Bailey v. Patterson* (1962), which ordered the integration of inter- and intrastate transportation facilities. Such decisions resulted in a frenzy of official policies that covertly reinforced Jim Crow–era laws enforcing segregation and often hinged on the protection of white women from the myth of the Black male rapist, the threat of racial mixture, and the depurification of the white race. Ultimately, many cultural gatekeepers continued to prioritize segregation in cultural spheres during this time as well; many venues, particularly but not only in the South, required segregated audiences and forbade integrated musical groups from performing.

[58] Monson, "The Problem with White Hipness," 402.
[59] Eric Lott, *Love and Theft: Blackface Minstrelsy and the American Working Class* (New York: Oxford University Press, 1993), 50.
[60] James Baldwin, "The Black Boy Looks at the White Boy," in *The Price of the Ticket: Collected Nonfiction, 1948–1985* (New York: St. Martin's/Marek, 1985), 290.
[61] David Ake, "Re-Masculating Jazz: Ornette Coleman, "Lonely Woman," and the New York Jazz Scene in the Late 1950s," *American Music* 16, no. 1 (Spring 1998): 38.
[62] Sherrie Tucker, *Swing Shift: "All-Girl" Bands of the 1940s* (Durham, NC: Duke University Press, 2000), 245.

However, even in the early 1950s, mainstream publications were already beginning to define cool jazz primarily through its relationship to whiteness, meaning that Brubeck's "new" white, female audience no longer risked racial mixture when listening to jazz; the sounds that entered their ears emanated from almost entirely white musicians and were heard as white. Removed from the threat of racial mixing, white female listeners could participate in the particular jazz subculture that was "cool," even if critics and musicians from within jazz created a discourse of femininity around cool jazz and other predominantly white styles to distinguish it from "authentic" jazz. For example, jazz critic Ralph Gleason's critique of Brubeck made a direct connection between the "authentic" musical elements of jazz and Brubeck's masculinity when he wrote that the Brubeck Quartet "didn't swing for me and was lacking a certain, shall we say, masculinity."[63] Even if Brubeck was demonstrably straight, his masculinity remained unconvincing to some jazz critics and musicians used to jazz's typical discourses of masculinity.

Often, jazz musicians and critics evoked stereotypes regarding sexuality in order to question cool musicians' masculinity. This was the case when hard bop pianist Horace Silver described cool jazz as "faggot-type jazz," further equating it with "jazz with no guts," a comment that recalls trumpeter Dizzy Gillespie's similar belief that white cool musicians like Konitz and Tristano lacked guts and sweat, arguing, "You're supposed to sweat in your balls in this music."[64] In an era in which white cool jazz musicians generally received much more commercial attention than most Black musicians, whatever their genre, Black musicians often promoted definitions of authenticity through intersecting discourses of race, gender, and sexuality. In doing so, Ramsey suggests, bebop musicians seeking status as performers of complex music were able to assert their own musical ability by relying on legacies of western classical narratives that assigned genius to men.[65] As Ake writes, "Given the extreme marginalization of the African-American male during the 1950s, it should come as no surprise that some musicians would be reluctant to let go of one of their few domains of perceived power."[66]

However, many mainstream audiences would have had little knowledge of language used by jazz critics, musicians, and audiences to code white

---

[63] Ralph Gleason, "Perspectives," *Down Beat*, April 6, 1955, 18.

[64] Gillespie, *To Be or Not*, 360. I have written elsewhere on the relationship between sweat and critical discourses surrounding Black masculinity: Kelsey A. K. Klotz, "'Your Sound Is Like Your Sweat': Miles Davis's Disembodied Sound Discourse," *American Studies* 58, no. 4 (2019): 5–23.

[65] Guthrie Ramsey, "Making the Changes: Jazz Manhood, Bebop Virtuosity, and a New Social Contract," in *The Amazing Bud Powell: Black Genius, Jazz History, and the Challenge of Bebop* (Berkeley: University of California Press, 2013), 121–144.

[66] David Ake, *Jazz Cultures* (Berkeley: University of California Press, 2002), 82.

jazz musicians as "feminine" or "feminized," and therefore inauthentic. For these audiences, Brubeck did not lack masculinity, and neither did many of his fellow cool jazz musicians; jazz's relationship with blackness and masculinity seemed enough to transfer that masculinity to white jazz musicians. *Time* magazine's coverage of Brubeck, for example, highlighted his physical prowess and dominating personality in the following description of his on-stage demeanor: "Normally as peaceable as a lullaby, Brubeck has been known to come off the bandstand in the middle of a number and threaten to silence a noisy customer with his muscular hands, which, until a few years ago, were expert at roping cattle."[67] Such descriptions of Brubeck's "manliness" highlights the importance of Brubeck's masculinity to the critics framing him but also suggests his ability to be read as stereotypically masculine, at least by mainstream audiences. Given the intersection of jazz, popular, and European classical music discourses in which he was written, gendered dynamics could have been tricky for Brubeck. Instead, the audiences targeted by *Vogue* and *Good Housekeeping* took to him easily and were able to engage with his music in a variety of ways, from academic study to entering performance spaces they earlier might not have (such as Storyville) to playing jazz records and performing his music on their own pianos.

## Brubeck in the Living Room

In 1956, music editor George Marek declared to the readership of *Good Housekeeping* magazine that jazz had become respectable (two years before Arnold Hirsch proclaimed it in the *Detroit Times*). Citing college courses, concerts in Carnegie Hall, "good" radio stations dedicating time to jazz, and the "careful" production of LPs, he outlined evidence of a shift coming from within the genre, drawing stark distinctions between old and new jazz performers:

> Jazz used to be the boy with dirty hands whom you wouldn't let come into your house. Jazz was born in the gin mills; the dubious night spots; the after-hour clubs of New Orleans, Chicago, and Kansas City.... And now, with clean hands, it is to be found in the concert halls, the music conservatories, and by way of respectable and carefully produced LP records, in the nicest living rooms.[68]

---

[67] T. George Harris, "The Man on Cloud No. 7," *Time* Magazine, November, 8, 1954, 67.
[68] George Marek, "From the Dive to the Dean: Jazz Becomes Respectable," *Good Housekeeping*, June 1956, 120.

Using fairly explicit racial stereotypes, Marek associates jazz's past with places that were, in the 1950s, considered places of blackness, and further, contrasts jazz's past with its present location in places of overwhelming whiteness: concert halls, colleges, and even, as he describes later in the article, "the most conservative element, the suburban community."[69] In doing so, he made clear whose dirty hands were not allowed in the houses of *Good Housekeeping*'s predominantly female readers. In a 2008 interview, Iola Brubeck reflected on Dave Brubeck's mother's conception of jazz musicians, which matched Marek's "boy with dirty hands." She explained that Elizabeth Brubeck had once told her about a piano student who had wanted to learn a piece of music by a popular bandleader. According to Iola Brubeck, her mother-in-law admitted that her response to the student had been, "You don't want to learn the music of someone you would not invite into your own home, would you?"[70] Marek's article, along with Brubeck's respectability, set a new standard for white middle-class women: that it was newly acceptable to invite jazz (or at least some kinds of jazz) into the living room.

Brubeck was a key figure in Marek's identification of a new trend in jazz performance. Linking Brubeck to polarizing European classical modernists like Igor Stravinsky and Alban Berg, Marek's argument suggested that if the audience liked Brubeck, they were part of a forward-thinking branch of jazz modernists, soon to be accepted into the realm of high art. But though Marek may have thought that he was identifying a new trend in jazz performance, what he actually described was a change in jazz's reception, and further, a change in the genre's audience, whom he, like Brubeck, referred to as "converts." This audience not only listened to jazz but listened and "behave[d] normally," and even studied it. According to Marek, this mid-century audience was welcomed at Boston University, New York University, Juilliard, Princeton, and Yale; they were found at Newport, "the old stronghold of high society"; and this audience was at home in concert halls. This audience listened carefully to European classical music, even complicated modernist compositions. Put simply, this

---

[69] Of course, both Black and white musicians sought access to concert halls, in part for the respectability conferred by the space (often raced white), and also for the financial benefit—as DeVeaux explains, "A single performance in a concert hall could generate as much income as a full four- or five-show day in a theater" (17). Scott DeVeaux, "The Emergence of the Jazz Concert, 1935–1945," *American Music* 7, no. 1 (Spring 1989): 6–29; Kelsey Klotz, "On Musical Value: John Lewis, Structural Listening and the Politics of Respectability," *Jazz Perspectives* 11, no. 1 (2018): 25–51; Wells, *Between Beats*, 1–32.

[70] Iola Brubeck, Library of Congress, 2008. In the same interview, Iola also considered the difference in appreciation of jazz on college campuses, recalling that in the 1940s, "there was one faculty member at the University of California who was outraged that we were listed in the courses that were offered and said, 'I would rather sleep with a dog than have my name in the same catalog with a jazz musician.'"

audience was white, and though white audiences had listened to jazz for decades, Marek nevertheless believed there was a difference between this audience's engagement with jazz and that of earlier generations. That he portrayed the suburban living room as jazz's new home, writing in a magazine targeting women, suggests that what was especially new about jazz's audience was its gender.

The white, middle-class women in these mid-century living rooms formed a major part of Brubeck's "new" audience. Their engagement with his music demonstrates the extent to which white female audiences accepted Brubeck's jazz as "respectable" enough—white enough—for the white spaces they already occupied as well as the degree to which they increasingly considered jazz to be capable of domestication. Further, these women formed a consumer culture that was often aspirational and predominantly feminine: their purchases, from imported beer to European-branded makeup to records of classical music, could add social value to their family unit. Brubeck increasingly became part of women's aspirational consumerist purchases.

The overwhelming acceptance Brubeck received among white housewives, as they were often described in their own terms and in the press, is evident in the publications in which he appeared. In particular, a piece titled "Grandma and le jazz hot" (1957) shows the broad appeal he had with this group of women.[71] True to the *New York Daily News*'s emphasis on photographs, the article featured four pictures and little accompanying text. The article announced that Brubeck was a guest lecturer in a popular adult course in jazz piano offered in Albany, California. Other guests went unmentioned, and no other well-known musician was photographed with the women. The article noted, "Many of the students are ordinary housewives with time to spare."

The images depict a room full of white women of a variety of ages (they are not all grandmothers); whichever woman is at the piano is foregrounded, and most of the women in the background look on with interest and approval (Fig. 2.3). The women playing the piano are capable performers, their hands poised in the position of pianists with considerable classical training, even if, as the caption to one image suggests, they may now be battling arthritis. Ilene Holmgren (Fig. 2.4), photographed receiving an autograph from Brubeck, had perfect pitch, was an accomplished pianist, earned a degree in music from Washington State University, played in an all-girl band performing in the USO

---

[71] "Grandma and le jazz hot: California Housewives Learn to Beat It Out in Modern Manner," *Sunday News*, September 22, 1957, 38–39.

during World War II, earned a master's degree in music at California State University, Hayward (now California State University, East Bay), and taught piano lessons for over 30 years. [72] The first image printed (Fig. 2.5) showed Brubeck at the keyboard with Mrs. Nettie W. Gallaghan as they performed a four-hand piano composition. Despite their classical training, these women are portrayed in the article not only as consumers of jazz but also as competent scholars of jazz, explaining of one, "Right hand lifted high off keys in concert-stage style doesn't keep Mrs. Ester Rosedale from chopping out jive beat with left." They are described as "hankering for go, girl, go piano technique," and following Brubeck's lecture, the author writes, "Some of the 'girls' squeaked and squealed like ecstatic teenagers while others dug it like supper club sophisticates and took notes for later study." In other words, Brubeck's audience was noted to engage with his music in a variety of ways, all of which

**Figure 2.3.** Dave Brubeck performing during "Dave Teaches Teachers" program, Alameda County, California, 1954. Image from Brubeck Collection, Holt-Atherton Special Collections, University of the Pacific Library. © Dave Brubeck. Photographs by Lonnie Wilson. Permission granted by the photographer's family.

---

[72] Obituary for Ilene Holmgren, *San Francisco Chronicle*, November 18–21, 2015, https://www.legacy.com/us/obituaries/sfgate/name/ilene-holmgren-obituary?pid=176555893.

**Figure 2.4.** Dave Brubeck autographing the cover of *Jazz Goes to College* for Ilene Holmgren of Orinda, California, during "Dave Teaches Teachers" program, Alameda County, California, 1954. Image from Brubeck Collection, Holt-Atherton Special Collections, University of the Pacific Library. © Dave Brubeck. Photographs by Lonnie Wilson. Permission granted by the photographer's family.

could be explained within a feminine sphere of private musical consumption typically reserved for performances of classical music.

Some women who observed Brubeck in such educational settings were inspired to seek out his advice for learning to play jazz piano. For example, Clarine Sigg of Livermore, California, wrote to Brubeck after reading a local newspaper's jazz column, in which he had promoted a course for adult piano students. Sigg, who self-identifies as a thirty-three-year-old "housewife and mother of six lovely children," explains that the column "stirred [her] so much

Professors, Housewives, and Playboys 101

**Figure 2.5.** Dave Brubeck performing with Nettie W. Gallaghan during "Dave Teaches Teachers" program, Alameda County, California, 1954. Image from Brubeck Collection, Holt-Atherton Special Collections, University of the Pacific Library. © Dave Brubeck. Photographs by Lonnie Wilson. Permission granted by the photographer's family.

to sit down for this letter."[73] Sigg describes her musical interest in terms of her passion and distraction from daily troubles and chores: "I sit and play for hours and not having any sense of time passing. Besides having the thrill and satisfaction of playing my troubles and worries go right out of the windows which makes me feel that our world isn't such a bad place to live in at any time." She finishes her letter, highlighting the urgency of her plea: "I have never taken lessons, tho, it's been my heart's desire all my life."

In addition to a general group interest in Brubeck through education, this particular demographic felt comfortable engaging with Brubeck and his music on an individual level, as well. Many wrote fan letters expressing their interest in and support of him, and in these letters, it is clear that the "grandmas" in

---

[73] Personal letter, Clarine Sigg to Dave Brubeck, August 17, 1957, Brubeck Collection, Wilton Library, Wilton, CT.

California were not the only women he inspired to jazz performance. In one, a woman named Jacqueline Storck introduces herself saying, "It's about time you knew there is a housewife and mother of four in KC Mo. who spends her days imitating Brubeck on piano, playing his records, and writing letters to him. (The others weren't mailed)."[74] Storck explains that she had not sent the previous letters because they were "merely an expression of admiration for [Brubeck's] talent," but she now desired advice and help as she considered a turn toward composition. She elaborates,

> An interest in composing, long dormant, has come back to life. I was studying your two piano books of originals, and got inspired by your Two-Part Contention to go to the classics for ideas. I've got a mambo based on Chopin, and another tune pulled from Brahms, but original by now from distortion.

But rather than ask for help from Brubeck, composer to composer, Storck spends the next page of her letter focused on the music business and detailing her (somewhat meager) connections to musicians willing to perform her songs and men in artists and repertoire (A&R) departments. She asks him about the percentage she should split with musicians recording her songs for demos, if Fantasy Records (his old label) has an A&R man to whom she could send demos, and if the music market truly is as tough as they say. For Storck, Brubeck is a man with whom she can make a business connection.[75]

Storck positions herself as different from most women throughout her letter, at once deriding the musical tastes of "mooning teen-agers" and "fat dowager[s] who dabble in music" and establishing herself within a creative realm often reserved for men. Even in the very opening of her letter, she follows her self-identification as a housewife and mother who plays Brubeck's music by explaining, "Though I may not be unique in any other way, I bet the above statement can't be made by many." Anticipating Betty Friedan's *The Feminine Mystique* (1962), Storck urges Brubeck to respond to her letter, writing,

---

[74] Jacqueline Storck to Dave Brubeck, March 24, 1958, Brubeck Collection, Wilton Library, Wilton, CT.

[75] Though there is no record of Brubeck himself responding to Storck (her letter arrived while he was on his US State Department tour), Brubeck's manager, Mort Lewis, did respond with tips on how to break into the music business, including making sure her composition is copyrighted, and that she should talk with any recording artist she can and give the artist her music to play. He suggests that speaking with music publishing firms would be a better recipe for success than record labels, and also writes that Brubeck will likely write her when he is able. Mort Lewis to Mrs. Shelby Storck, April 21, 1958, Brubeck Collection, Wilton Library, Wilton, CT.

> If you could see me neglecting hundreds of domestic chores in favor of struggling over your arrangements of Foggy Day, Alamo, Frenesi, Gone With the Wind, etc., stopping the records and dashing to the piano, then in a rush of guilt, forcing myself to the grocery store and back to cook a meal, waiting for another chance to get back to the piano, I'm sure you would take a few minutes from your own busy life to reply.

Storck's experience reflects what American studies scholar Gavin James Campbell describes regarding women's musical ambitions half a century earlier—as the "tormented struggle between personal ambition and wifely duty."[76] As a housewife, Storck understands the duties society expects her to fulfill—her "domestic chores"—but she also feels alone in her drive to create, even masculinizing her creativity: "I'm just a woman who is plagued with a creative urge (none of my female friends has it)." In such explanations, Storck reinforces the sexist assumptions that granted musical value to fields dominated by men and considered mass culture to be feminine. Further, Storck situates herself within a legacy of gender ideologies that understood the act of musical creation to be distinctly masculine. As Judith Tick writes regarding the gendered ideologies that informed early twentieth-century composer Charles Ives, "Although women were encouraged to study and perform music, the language of creative musical achievement was patriarchal."[77]

Even if Storck felt particularly transgressive in her interest in composing, she was not the only woman to broach the subject with Brubeck. In 1957, Dotti Drummer of Shelburne, Vermont, wrote to Brubeck of her idea to combine jazz with modern dance—an idea she herself could not carry out, as she did not "know that much about composing music."[78] In her letter, Drummer expresses a unique feeling of intimacy with Brubeck, explaining of her idea, "If my husband Jack were here I could splurt it out to him, and seeing as it concerns you, you're the next best thing!" Like Storck, Drummer positions her interest in music within her life as a housewife: she "hopes to study piano, and voice one of these days, in between babies"; she explains to Brubeck that his "music, and compositions have such a wonderful freedom to them, that I can't help but be carried away, and at times forget my motherly duties"; and at the end of her letter, she expresses relief that she has finally shared her idea,

---

[76] Gavin James Campbell, "Classical Music and the Politics of Gender in America, 1900–1925," *American Music* 21, no. 4 (Winter 2003): 447.

[77] Judith Tick, "Charles Ives and Gender Ideology," in *Musicology and Difference: Gender and Sexuality in Music Scholarship*, ed. Ruth A. Solie (Berkeley: University of California Press, 1993), 92.

[78] Personal letter, Dotti Drummer to Dave Brubeck, October 13, 1957, Brubeck Collection, Wilton Library, Wilton, CT.

writing, "I must confess I can once again breath [sic] freely, and get back to my chicken. One that's in the oven. Care to stop over???"

Her enthusiasm nearly leaps off the page through her liberal use of exclamation marks and question marks, and one can only imagine her reaction to Brubeck's response, which validated her interest in composing music for modern dance, and further, his decision just a few years later to compose a ballet titled *Points on Jazz* (1961).

However alone Storck felt, the California grandmas, Sigg, Drummer, and the pervasiveness of cool jazz coverage in mainstream magazines suggest that women in particular found something inviting about Brubeck's music as a representative of jazz music. Brubeck and his promoters took advantage of this audience's willingness to engage with his music in fairly intimate ways by publishing two volumes of transcriptions to accompany the 1956 album *Brubeck Plays Brubeck*, which featured his original compositions. While men and women would have performed these pieces, the parlor piano tradition was gendered female; in other words, Brubeck's publication of his music was part of a sheet music business that, as David Suisman explains with regard to Tin Pan Alley sheet music, was predominantly female.[79]

But there is a signal difference between sheet music culture of the early twentieth century and Brubeck's books: these include not only his compositions but also his improvisations, ostensibly allowing consumers access to his unedited musical stylings (though, of course, they would have almost certainly been edited in the processes of transcription and publication). To play the pieces, Storck, along with the other men and women who purchased the volumes, would have physically embodied Brubeck's particular playing style (a style that is difficult for many men and women's hands). His style had been both praised and criticized by critics; these critics appreciated that his playing was original and that he seemed to be "in it for himself," but they also critiqued his heavy-handed block-chord approach to many of his improvisations and arrangements. Storck's hands would have likely had to stretch to reach the parallel root-fifth-tenth left-hand chords in pieces like "In Your Own Sweet Way." She would have pounded away at her seven-foot Baldwin grand piano (it is likely a coincidence that Brubeck was sponsored by Baldwin), her hands crashing down on the keys of the piano to match the force with which

---

[79] David Suisman, *Selling Sounds: The Commercial Revolution in American Music* (Cambridge, MA: Harvard University Press, 2009), 46. For more on the legacy of gendered musical assumptions for private or at-home musical performance, as well as how those assumptions were part of a broader racist consumer system, see Glenda Goodman, "Bound Together: The Intimacies of Music-Book Collecting in the Early American Republic," *Journal of the Royal Musical Association* 145, no. 1 (2020): 1–35.

Brubeck played (Brubeck often played so loudly in these moments that the microphone would reach its limits, distorting the recorded sound). And as she performed Brubeck's music, Storck began to generate musical ideas of her own, transgressing the gendered hierarchy in which composition was enshrined. Therefore, Storck's living room performances became opportunities to not only replicate Brubeck's music, but to also gently challenge sexist ideologies—even those she herself reinforced—that understood musical consumption to be female and musical creation to be distinctly male.

Whether embodying his performances at the piano, performing with him at the piano bench, or listening to his music in their living rooms, mid-century white women were an active part of Brubeck's audience. Brubeck believed he had converted these "respectable" audiences, and there is a strong case to be made for that; after all, these were women who often represented the very conservative ideal Friedan critiqued and who occupied the conservative suburbs Marek described. Their engagement with him further demonstrates the diverse ways in which women engaged with jazz at mid-century. But despite the fact that Brubeck's archive is littered with letters from women and girls writing of their interest in jazz, the longer letters from self-described housewives often center on one or both of two themes: how interest in Brubeck's music leads these women to shirk their domestic responsibilities, and how each of the women felt alone, or unique, in their interest—that they had few people with whom they could discuss their musical interests. Women's engagement with Brubeck's music depended on an extension of his respectability; in other words, their engagement with his music hinged on his dual positions of authority and respectability, positions made possible by his whiteness, masculinity, and classical background. But these women's letters also reveal that there was some limit to how far Brubeck's respectability could stretch: even if jazz was supposedly newly respectable, being a respectable woman still meant getting the housework done.

## Brubeck in the Penthouse

Given Brubeck's popularity among young, predominantly white housewives and his image as a wholesome family man, his simultaneous collaborations with *Playboy* magazine might have complicated a career built around respectability. Further, his participation in *Playboy* culture, through articles in the magazine, participation in readers' polls and musicians' polls, his and Paul Desmond's joint composition of a song ("Pilgrim's Progress") for *The Playboy Jazz Allstars Vol. 1* album, the quartet's repeated appearances in the Playboy

Jazz Festival, and the quartet's appearance on the television show *Playboy's Penthouse*—all in a span of five years—indicates that Brubeck's interest in *Playboy* was not superficial. Rather, Brubeck seemed to believe that his own association with the playboy image might, like his excursions in the pages of *Vogue* and *Good Housekeeping*, attract "new" audiences to jazz.

Perhaps known by some in the popular imagination today as a naughty magazine, Hugh Hefner founded *Playboy* Magazine in 1953 as a men's lifestyle magazine for indoor entertainment, which included sex among other activities. Such a goal helped Hefner to establish *Playboy* as a legitimate publication, even against those who insisted on *Playboy*'s obscenity (most notably Postmaster General Arthur Summerfield, who in 1954 refused to deliver copies of *Playboy*). According to historian Elizabeth Fraterrigo, *Playboy* magazine's advertisements, articles (often by renowned authors such as Norman Mailer, Ray Bradbury, Jack Kerouac, Margaret Atwood, and Roald Dahl), and interviews (such as with Martin Luther King Jr., Malcolm X, Miles Davis, Frank Sinatra, and Muhammad Ali) in addition to its infamous nude images of playmates, "allowed readers to envision an upscale, masculine identity based on tasteful consumption and sexual pleasure."[80]

Hefner created *Playboy* during what some commentators perceived to be a period of crisis for American masculinity. In a 1958 article for the men's magazine *Esquire*, historian Arthur Schlesinger Jr. addressed this crisis specifically. Far from blaming the influx of women in the workforce and the rights women had achieved throughout the first half of the twentieth century, Schlesinger argued that "something more fundamental is involved in the unmanning of American men than simply the onward rush of American women."[81] The solution to the problem of American masculinity, according to Schlesinger, was to enhance men's spontaneity, releasing them from the confines of "togetherness" into what he theorized as "apartness," in which men could explore their individual masculine identities. Schlesinger's article clearly bears witness to early Cold War anxieties about communism and groupthink, which were shared by Brubeck to some degree. Hefner's approach to *Playboy* offered a masculine image that reconciled what some saw as the feminization of American men by masculinizing consumerism and the home (both of which were typically gendered female). This was a move that allowed men to create an individual identity through consumerism. They could customize purchases—including Brubeck albums—to suit that identity and recapture men's individuality, and

---

[80] Elizabeth Fraterrigo, *Playboy and the Making of the Good Life in Modern America* (Oxford: Oxford University Press, 2009), 3.
[81] Arthur M. Schlesinger Jr., "The Crisis of American Masculinity," *Esquire*, November 1958, 62–63, 183.

in the process, their masculinity. While many commentators saw *Playboy* as an early component of the sexual revolution, historian Barbara Ehrenreich explains that such consumerism marked what was truly revolutionary about *Playboy*: "The new male-centered ensemble of commodities presented in *Playboy* meant that a man could display his status or simply flaunt his earnings without possessing either a house or a wife"—in other words, "a playboy didn't have to be a husband to be a man."[82]

This approach to white masculinity contrasts starkly with that of the mid-1960s. As musicologist Benjamin Piekut writes in *Experimentalism Otherwise: The New York Avant-Garde and Its Limits*, there was a degree of "white-man-as-victim" in post–World War II white masculinity (in which white men became cogs in the "capitalist machine" and were lost in the "incomplete but significant gains of the civil rights struggle, the ascendance of the women's movement and feminism, the collapse of the New Left and rise of 'identity politics,' the failure of the Vietnam War, and the effects of deindustrialization and a major economic downturn in the 1970s").[83] However, *Playboy* offered an alternative approach in the 1950s—one that understood the answer to the so-called crisis of masculinity written about by Schlesinger to be further engagement with consumerism.[84]

In 1955, when *Playboy* Magazine was only two years old, Hefner invited Brubeck to have a conversation with him about jazz, which he then turned into an article (the byline was given to Brubeck). Hefner titled the article "The New Jazz Audience," which allowed him to put forth jazz, as represented by Brubeck, as an appropriate musical outlet for the modern man. In the article, Brubeck emphasized the importance of self-expression and improvisation to jazz, writing that jazz "certainly represents freedom, the right to be different, the right to be an individual."[85] For Brubeck, as for later writers like Schlesinger, the importance of a distinct identity was directly related to Cold War–era politics; he explained here, as he did elsewhere, that jazz was available only in free societies, citing Russia and Hitler's Germany as places in which jazz was prohibited. Brubeck described his own music as being primarily improvisational, a move that established his group's credibility as a jazz ensemble

---

[82] Barbara Ehrenreich, "Playboy Joins the Battle of the Sexes," in *The Hearts of Men: American Dreams and the Flight from Commitment* (Garden City, NJ: Anchor Press/Doubleday, 1983), 49, 51.

[83] Benjamin Piekut, "When Orchestras Attack! John Cage Meets the New York Philharmonic," in *Experimentalism Otherwise: The New York Avant-Garde and Its Limits* (Berkeley: University of California Press, 2011), 49.

[84] Piekut cites literary critic Leslie Fiedler's critique of Beat writers like Jack Kerouac, William Burroughs, and Allen Ginsberg, who wrote that the Beats saw whiteness as "a stigma and symbol of shame." No such shame of whiteness appears to have existed for Brubeck, nor, from available sources, for many of his audiences. Leslie A. Fiedler, "The New Mutants," *Partisan Review* (Fall 1965), 515.

[85] Dave Brubeck, "The New Jazz Audience," *Playboy*, August 1955, 9.

and also implicitly highlighted his group's masculinity. Jazz's emphasis on improvisation, according to Brubeck, "has given us one of the greatest freedoms and challenges ever offered to any musical mind," a statement that inherently connected several discourses of masculinity: (1) freedom of self-expression, as Schlesinger would later argue, was needed for the reclamation of American masculinity; (2) improvisation, as a primary feature of "authentic" jazz, could establish masculinity; and (3) the emphasis on the "musical mind," in addition to the need for self-expression, accessed modes of intellect that were, at mid-century, gendered masculine and raced white.

Further, Brubeck connected the masculine *Playboy* audience to discourses of respectability through his discussion of the "new jazz audience." He announced that a "new kind of jazz is being played in America today. And it is creating a new kind of jazz audience." Like Marek in *Good Housekeeping*, Brubeck presented *Playboy*'s readers with an origin story of jazz based in "honky tonks, brothels, and the lowest sort of dives," explaining, "There was a time when respectable people would have nothing to do with the music. But as jazz grew, so did its audience." He insisted that his music was "complicated and elusive," and in order to understand it, his audience must be up to the intellectual challenge that he and his bandmates faced in each performance. Such a statement in a men's magazine like *Playboy* further suggested that his music was a way for male audiences to access imagination, intelligence, and self-expression. In other words, Brubeck's audience—and *Playboy*'s audience—was respectable *and* masculine.

That Brubeck apparently found no irony in the fact that his "new" and "respectable" audience could be found reading *Playboy* magazine highlights the ways in which white men's overtly sexual interests were considerably downplayed when compared to hypersexualized stereotypes of Black men, and especially Black male jazz musicians. This "new" audience's engagement with jazz seemed to fulfill stereotypes linking jazz with sex that, with the help of Brubeck and Hefner, became newly publicly accessible to the white executive. But significantly, respectability for Brubeck and other mid-century writers seems to have been predicated on *Playboy*'s predominantly white, middle-class male readers, and in particular, its significant proportion of college-aged readers. Hefner emphasized the connection between Brubeck's audience (noting his recent sixty-date college tour) and the *Playboy* audience, explaining that about 25 percent of the *Playboy* audience were college students (which he boasted was the highest percentage of any other magazine).[86] The

---

[86] Hugh Hefner, *Playboy* editor, to Dave Brubeck, May 27, 1955, Brubeck Collection, Wilton Library, Wilton, CT.

target audience for Hefner's brand of masculinity and consumer culture was middle-class and upper-middle-class men—men who aspired to penthouse living and possessed the potential purchasing power to eventually build lives like the *Playboy* ideal. As historian Carrie Pitzulo argues, "While a large portion of the magazine's readership were college-age men who could not yet live up to such a high standard, they could look to *Playboy* as a guide to their future ambitions and imagine that somewhere, men were living such a life."[87] Put simply, *Playboy* marshaled its "bunnies" (playmates), advertisements for particular brands of consumerist goods, and musical recommendations in order to sell a lifestyle—the Playboy lifestyle. As ethnomusicologist Mark Laver argues, "Jazz works in advertising in part because its widely-accepted countercultural status helps obscure the stark realities of consumer capitalism enough to make a patently absurd capitalist narrative seem credible."[88] Instead, jazz consumption, even within a capitalist frame, can appear as a "radical expression of our individuality and our agency."

In his own quest for "new" jazz audiences, Brubeck's marketing strategy continued to rely on his college tours, which not only positioned his quartet to be heard by young audiences who would soon be gainfully employed citizens but also aligned the quartet's image with academia and "intellectual" listeners.[89] That Brubeck was also particularly popular among *Playboy*'s audience is evidenced in the yearly reader's polls; in the first eight years of the poll, Brubeck and Desmond consistently won the top awards for best jazz pianist and alto saxophonist, respectively, and the quartet likewise won for best jazz combo. Dave and Iola Brubeck seemed as proud of these polls as they were the polls in *Down Beat*; on a letter from *Playboy* informing the Brubeck Quartet of their 1958 win and letting them know their silver medallions, rewards for winning, were on their way, Iola Brubeck hand-wrote a message to Mort Lewis, manager of the quartet, asking him to ensure that the medallions were mounted and hung, referencing a similar treatment done with Dave's *Down Beat* medals. Brubeck would go on to cite his success in *Playboy* polls as evidence of his popularity across the South, even when southern universities and colleges refused to allow his then integrated group to perform. Put simply, the partnership between Brubeck and *Playboy* created a relationship between

---

[87] Carrie Pitzulo, *Bachelors and Bunnies: The Sexual Politics of Playboy* (Chicago: University of Chicago Press, 2011), 21.
[88] Mark Laver, *Jazz Sells: Music, Marketing, and Meaning* (New York: Routledge, 2015), 232.
[89] Dave Brubeck, interview with Ted Gioia, NEA Jazz Master interview, Smithsonian National Museum of American History, August 6–7, 2007. Brubeck's college dates grew to be extremely profitable: even as early as 1954, the Brubeck Quartet could receive $1,000 per college concert, plus 50–60 percent privilege in some cases. By 1966, *Variety* reported that colleges were "the most lucrative music venue in the United States." "Hottest B.O. on Campus," *Variety*, March 16, 1966, 55, 58.

masculinity, heterosexuality, and respectability that defined young male audiences from the dorm room to the penthouse, while simultaneously creating yet another way for Brubeck to bring "new" audiences to jazz.

The intersection of race (white), gender (male), and class (middle and upper) in the image of masculinity constructed by Hefner allowed *Playboy*'s readers and viewers to be associated with respectability, even while consuming images of nude and semi-nude women. As Ehrenreich explains, Hefner's early philosophical approach to *Playboy* proposed alternative prerequisites for adult masculinity, attacking conventional expectations of monogamy while simultaneously lauding high-achieving work. Men should still be breadwinners, but they needn't win bread for anyone other than themselves. In particular, Brubeck's affiliation with *Playboy* magazine, *Playboy's Penthouse*, and the Playboy Jazz Festival helped to facilitate what could have otherwise been an uneasy relationship between *Playboy* and respectability. Though Brubeck (and Iola Brubeck and their children) represented the security of monogamy that Hefner at times advocated against, his position as a high-earning jazz musician, with all of the individualism that improvisation entails, balanced respectability with Hefner's philosophical goals (if not his sexual goals).[90]

Perhaps the clearest view of the relationship between Brubeck and the Playboy consumerist model is his appearance on Hefner's short-lived television series, *Playboy's Penthouse* (1959–61). In its two seasons, *Playboy's Penthouse* supported the image of masculinity presented in *Playboy* magazine but made that image even more indelible in the minds of its viewers. The show featured a party in a seemingly typical playboy penthouse hosted by Hefner and attended by "playmates," comedians, intellectuals, actors, and musicians, including Nina Simone, Bob Newhart, Lenny Bruce, Nat "King" Cole, Ella Fitzgerald, Sammy Davis Jr., Josh White, Anita O'Day, and Buddy Rich, to name a few. As Hefner explained, the show was "a sophisticated get-together for people who we dig and who dig us."[91] The show's guests and performers were impeccably dressed in tuxedos and fashionable party dresses, with not a hair astray, and nearly all guests carried a drink in their hands (except for Hefner, who constantly held a pipe). In each episode Hefner accompanied the viewing audience around the penthouse, showing off an urban oasis of intelligent conversation, beautiful women, and the discerning male consumer, who contemplated what style tuxedo to wear and how to make his penthouse

---

[90] Hugh Hefner, "The Playboy Philosophy," *Playboy* January 1963, 41.
[91] Hefner, quoted in Joe Goldberg, *Big Bunny: The Inside Story of Playboy* (New York: Ballantine Books, 1967), 43.

work for his man-about-town lifestyle. *Playboy's Penthouse* was never picked up by a network, though it was syndicated and appeared on stations across the United States. While it operated at a financial loss, Hefner apparently never doubted the show's ultimate success; he explained that *Playboy's Penthouse* was "one of the most valuable things we ever did. It's difficult to pick out any single thing that we've done that's more visible."[92] Hefner's penchant for featuring interracial musical groups and mingling freely with Black performers apparently prevented the show from being aired on any stations across the American South. However, while Hefner's performers were mixed racially, his party guests often were not racially mixed (and when Black guests were shown, they were often somewhat segregated couples), which suggests that while blackness could be consumed, his view of playboy masculinity was particularly white.[93]

Performers featured on *Playboy's Penthouse*, like Brubeck, were presented as examples of the playboy's fascinating life—he knew interesting people and was in touch with only the most modern cultural exponents. When the viewer meets the Brubeck Quartet in an episode from 1960, Hefner's guests are already gathered around the group, sitting casually on stairs, pillows, and sofas, nearly every man with a woman nearby. Hefner introduces Brubeck, announcing Brubeck's "new approach to jazz," and the onstage audience looks on, smiling and applauding. The Brubeck Quartet performs their current hits, "Take Five" and "Blue Rondo à la Turk," and throughout, Brubeck demonstrates clear engagement with the members of his quartet, smiling and shouting at parts of saxophonist Paul Desmond's solo he particularly enjoys, looking back at bassist Eugene Wright as they support Desmond, and turning to focus his attention on drummer Joe Morello's solo.

---

[92] Hefner, quoted in Goldberg, *Big Bunny*, 43–45.
[93] That Hefner's understanding of racial justice went only skin deep is clear in Dizzy Gillespie's 1960 episode, which American studies scholar Robert K. McMichael explores in greater detail. Gillespie attempts to interject a more sophisticated conversation about race, power, and the music industry, stating playfully, "You know that when you hear jazz on the air, it's not being paid for, right?" McMichael describes Hefner's response as half-hearted, but Gillespie presses on, saying, "Jazz musicians don't have no money, so they can't pay off stations to play it." From there, McMichael explains,

"[Gillespie] looks at Hefner and says, 'You've been *embellishing* our art form'. Hefner only responds by putting his hand on Gillespie's shoulder and saying, for the third time (he twice tried but failed to interrupt Gillespie's obviously unscripted remarks), 'Play the *St. Louis* [pronouncing it 'Louie'] *Blues* for us, Diz!'

Hefner's assumption, when booking Gillespie, was based in a particular understanding of how blackness should be represented; the reality of Gillespie's performance belied and subverted such dominant representations of blackness. Instead, Gillespie used his platform on Hefner's nationally syndicated, integrated television show to both position jazz as a uniquely Black American art form and argue to its white fans that jazz was at risk because of payola schemes."

Robert K. McMichael, "'We Insist-Freedom Now!' Black Moral Authority, Jazz, and the Changeable Shape of Whiteness," *American Music* 16, no. 4 (Winter 1998): 375–377.

Viewing Brubeck's performance through the lens of what Nichole Rustin-Paschal refers to as jazzmasculinity demonstrates yet another distinction between "jazz culture" (which Hefner attempted to access through *Playboy*) and mainstream culture. Rustin-Paschal writes, "Within jazz, a cultural sphere that had long defined itself as an exemplar of integration, freedom, and the American democratic ethos, it was the openly emotional man who was seen as most individual, most progressive in thought, and most capable of resisting the trap of conformity."[94] Jazz, Rustin-Paschal argues, could address the concerns of Schlesinger and others surrounding American masculinity by offering an acceptable mode of expression: jazz "allowed men to be emotional and masculine in an era in which the mainstream political and social ideal demanded a 'hard masculine toughness.'" Certainly other performances by jazz musicians on *Playboy's Penthouse* reflect the outward emotion jazzmasculinity encouraged—Sammy Davis Jr., for example, deploys his effortlessly gregarious and open personality, shifting quickly from an exuberant arrangement of "The Lady Is a Tramp" to a suave performance of "All of You" to a heartbreaking rendition of "My Funny Valentine." However, while Brubeck himself believed in jazz as the best representation of, in Rustin-Paschal's words, "integration, freedom, and the American democratic ethos," his own performance on *Playboy's Penthouse* did not reflect the key element of Rustin's analysis of jazzmasculinity: that jazz could re-define masculinity around the open expression of emotion. Brubeck's performance on the show (like Hefner's) is somewhat wooden; he certainly demonstrates excitement, but beyond that, he tends more toward stoic—much like the performances by Cal Tjader and Joe Williams on *Playboy's Penthouse*. Aside from more extroverted performances like Sammy Davis Jr.'s, much of the show's emotional expression related to jazz comes from the mostly white male audience members scattered around the penthouse. They bob their heads to the beat, snap their fingers on the offbeats, and generally give the look of an engaged and knowledgeable audience enjoying themselves. If jazz offered the potential for a re-definition of masculinity around emotional expression for those within jazz culture, it perhaps offered mainstream audiences the opportunity to see and experience a limited embodiment of the emotions of jazz. Jazz thus became a product defined not only by the consumer's relationship to the jazz musician but also by the consumers' relationship to their own embodied expression of the listening experience.

---

[94] Nichole Rustin-Paschal, *The Kind of Man I Am: Jazzmasculinity and the World of Charles Mingus Jr.* (Middletown, CT: Wesleyan University Press, 2017), 318.

Beyond their role as consumerist guides to masculine living, *Playboy* performers also offered access to the women who adorned the penthouse in a way that allowed viewers to consume both the performer and the women. During Brubeck's solo on "Blue Rondo á la Turk," the camera turns, positioning Brubeck in the foreground with a sea of beautiful women looking at Brubeck, and by extension, the camera. Brubeck, though, has his eyes closed and his eyebrows furrowed, seemingly focused intently on his solo and not his surroundings. While the camera appears to focus on Brubeck, the women seated in the front row are put on display for television viewers, who can gaze at them, imagine being with them, all while seeming to focus their attention on Brubeck, who performs with conservative emotional output. In essence, the women are placed as decorative set pieces, offering male viewers a clear and aspirational portrait of American masculinity through a heterosexual lens. This setup replays on many episodes of *Playboy's Penthouse*: Sammy Davis Jr. is more embedded within the audience, but there are similar shots of (nearly all white) women in the background staring at the camera; white pianist Cy Coleman is flanked by women at the piano (at one point, a white woman joins him at the bench); Nat King Cole does not actually sing, but joins a conversation on a couch, and a white woman lounges on a platform above the couch, elegantly laying her legs out long.[95] The pattern is similar for women performers like Ella Fitzgerald and Sarah Vaughan, where one to two women are routinely tucked in the corners of the camera frame. For the *Playboy* audience, it seems Brubeck represented access to the "good life," the jazz life—even if, and perhaps especially if, he himself did not partake. Importantly, white audiences seemed capable of distinguishing between Brubeck and the overt sexuality that surrounded him on the pages and screens of *Playboy* content.

Further, Brubeck's appearance on *Playboy's Penthouse* offered Brubeck the chance to be part of a lifestyle brand that offered men the opportunity to not just seduce women but, as Pitzulo explains, to "chase the American Dream through rampant spending."[96] Audiences need only purchase a Brubeck album to access this particular mode of heterosexual masculinity. On *Playboy's Penthouse*, jazz, whether performed by Black or white musicians, was meant to be both consumed and to mark the consumer as being sophisticated, discerning, and masculine.

---

[95] It is worth noting that while *Playboy's Penthouse* was revolutionary in presenting Black and white performers and audiences, Black musicians were extremely careful about their interactions with white women—for example, Sammy Davis Jr. does not so much as shake the hand of a white woman (though he does physically engage with the one Black woman in the audience). The integrated singing trio Hendricks, Lambert, and Ross offer a notable moment of difference, when it shows white singer Annie Ross pulling Joe Williams (a Black singer for the Count Basie orchestra) up from the couch to join the trio.

[96] Pitzulo, *Bachelors and Bunnies*, 72.

Brubeck, who was not far removed from struggles for success and financial instability, likely attached himself to the *Playboy* brand as a commercial strategy, one that potentially brought a new market of consumers. It is difficult to imagine that he approved of all the images that accompanied his article and record reviews—in interviews and letters, Paul Desmond regularly teases Brubeck's devotion to Iola Brubeck as atypical of the jazz stereotype of loose sexual morals. Likewise, in an interview with Brubeck scholar Keith Hatschek, Brubeck's daughter, Catherine Yaghsizian, recalled Brubeck's "moral streak," which prevented him from accepting money for an interview with *Playboy* magazine (instead, he suggested that Hefner buy the Brubeck children a pony, whom they named Playboy).[97] So how was Brubeck able to be both respectable and to participate so extensively with a lifestyle brand that highlighted non-monogamous sexuality? First, Brubeck's presence offered an answer to the so-called crisis of masculinity facing white men during the Cold War through improvisation. Second, the intersection of Brubeck's heteronormative masculinity and his whiteness enabled him to maintain respectability while adhering to an acceptable sexuality. As a white man, Brubeck was (and is) allowed to be complicated, even contradictory, in ways Black men (and women generally) typically were and are not. Ultimately, Brubeck's ability to maintain his respectability while simultaneously becoming more and more involved with the *Playboy* brand, complete with centerfolds and playmates, highlights the ways in which white middle- and upper-class men's overtly sexual interests were considerably downplayed when compared to hypersexualized stereotypes of Black men, and especially Black male jazz musicians.

But maybe they read *Playboy* for the articles. I have heard that argument from a few people, largely women who insisted that they would not have read their husbands' subscriptions if the magazine was truly "naughty." Historian Marjorie Lee Bryer argues as much, writing that *Playboy*'s well-known interviews with major proponents and opponents of the civil rights movement across the 1960s and subsequent letters from readers demonstrate how the magazine "provided a forum for discussing racial politics."[98] Still, the line often acts as a familiar throw-away joke—a joke that regardless of its level of truth reinforces the unique privilege *Playboy* audiences had and have in both separating their identity from their sexuality and in constructing an "acceptable" sexuality. For these audiences, *Playboy* sexuality—including its objectification of women and focus on male heterosexual fantasy and pleasure—was

---

[97] Qtd. in Keith Hatschek, *The Real Ambassadors: Dave and Iola Brubeck and Louis Armstrong Challenge Segregation* (Jackson: University of Mississippi Press, 2022), 245.

[98] Marjorie Lee Bryer, "Representing the Nation: Pinups, Playboy, Pageants and Racial Politics, 1945–1966," PhD diss., University of Minnesota, 2003, 111.

somehow different from the racist stereotypes of presumed hypersexualized and primitive Black jazz musicians. *Playboy* sexuality, as presented by Hefner and demonstrated by Brubeck, was cultivated, cultured, and refined; it was as selective as the man improvising a masculine identity through consumerism. It was, in a word, respectable.

## Conclusion: Cooking with Iola

In "making converts" of new and "respectable" audiences, Brubeck relied on the intersection of his whiteness and heteronormative masculinity. The image he presented, and upon which his promoters subsequently capitalized, was distinct from previous stereotypes of past jazz musicians, white or Black; Brubeck had the ability to represent white middle-class ideals of a nuclear family unit in which a man provides for a woman and their children, resulting in the dream of upward social mobility. Such an image not only drew new, mainstream, white audiences to his music but also encouraged them to engage with jazz music in ways that were new to them: they heard Brubeck's music in nightclubs like Storyville, learned from him, performed his music, and were even inspired to compose like him. While Brubeck's masculinity was at times overtly questioned within the field of jazz, "mainstream" popular music audiences could be satisfied that he represented a conservative ideal of white, upper-middle class, heteronormativity, an example of an American Dream that at mid-century was almost entirely white.

Dave Brubeck's image, and specifically his ability to appeal to mainstream audiences, was in many ways created, reinforced, and supported by his wife, Iola Brubeck. It was Iola who arranged the first college tours both to bring jazz to younger audiences unable to go to clubs and to find an audience that might appreciate the Octet's difficult music (the Associated Booking Corporation would continue these tours *after* Dave signed with them), who often responded to fan mail (Dave would sign the letters later), wrote (and in some cases, delivered) Dave's lectures on jazz, managed his early career and their household of six children, and was present in nearly every feature on Dave, from *Time* to the *Bethlehem Steel* advertisement to the glint of his wedding band in the lipstick advertisement. She was a fixture in his coverage: as Harris wrote in Dave Brubeck's *Time* magazine article, "While itinerant musicians are apt to dally with the belles along the way, Dave is happily married and has four children (a fifth is on the way)."[99] Iola Brubeck not only helped to create

---

[99] T. George Harris, "The Man on Cloud No. 7," *Time*, November 8, 1954, 73.

Dave's image, but she was a crucial element of his commercial appeal to "respectable" audiences.

Further, Iola Brubeck was perhaps Dave's first jazz convert. She explained in 2008 that Dave Brubeck introduced her to jazz, and she "sort of became a crusader along with him."[100] For Iola Brubeck, new to jazz (she explains that she grew up with very little music at all in her home), jazz had importance because it was capable of moving beyond entertainment and could express individuality. In her work as a jazz crusader, however, there was an emphasis on uplifting the genre from what had come before; she explains, "I think often that [expression] was hidden because people like Louis Armstrong, Fats Waller especially in that period knew that in order to reach an audience they had to entertain, and there is nothing wrong with entertaining, I think that it is necessary, but they also were doing something far more than that, which not everybody picked up or understood."[101] Iola carefully points out that the representations of jazz as presented by Armstrong and Waller had by 1950 become increasingly uncomfortable (Dizzy Gillespie, Miles Davis, and others would similarly express discomfort with such stereotypes), placing the primary fault for misrepresentation in the hands of the audiences who would not have welcomed jazz into their homes. But implicit within her narrative is the need to move jazz beyond what canonic figures like Armstrong and Waller could—toward a new, respectable jazz, with her husband at the forefront.

In 1959, reporter Kay Wahl of the *Oakland Tribune* published a piece on Iola Brubeck titled "She Also Cooks . . ." that included a recipe for a "simply supreme" cheese cake, and was accompanied by an illustration of a woman in the kitchen surrounded by a saxophone, clarinet, bass, and drums, with children hovering expectantly in the doorway.[102] The article itself is an interesting portrait of a woman who mostly worked behind the scenes, exerting far more power and agency over Dave's career than many audiences could know, while at the very same time, like Storck, still adhering to many of the stereotypical gender roles of a 1950s housewife. As Robin D. G. Kelley wrote in the *New York Times* in 2002, the wives of jazz musicians "became a significant social and economic force in the jazz world."[103] Iola Brubeck explained that her roles included both "a lot of the apron strings and getting dinner on the table," and the management of Dave Brubeck's career, which included bookkeeping (salaries and taxes), program notes, travel booking, and generally keeping track of where the quartet was and where they were supposed to go

[100] Iola Brubeck, Library of Congress, 2008.
[101] Ibid.
[102] Kay Wahl, "She Also Cooks..." *Oakland Tribune*, March 8, 1959.
[103] Robin D. G. Kelley, "The Jazz Wife: Muse and Manager," *New York Times*, July 21, 2002.

(and how); in her role as manager, she joked that "they called me central intelligence."[104] She mingled housework with Dave's work, referring to setting up the Brubeck Quartet's college tours as "kitchen table work": "I sat down and wrote to every college up and down the west coast that I thought was within driving distance of where we lived in San Francisco." Jazz wives' labors have largely been relegated to anecdotes that often serve to praise their husbands for their unwavering devotion to their craft, and Wahl's article is no exception (though Dave Brubeck and their children would routinely acknowledge Iola Brubeck's labors).

However, the title of Wahl's piece also highlights a crucial difference in how Dave Brubeck's music was received in mainstream publications, like the *Oakland Tribune*, as opposed to jazz publications. "She Also Cooks . . ." was likely meant as a witty reference to the notion that just as her husband cooks on the stage in a jazz sense, so too does Iola in the kitchen in a culinary sense. While mainstream writers and audiences seemed to have no trouble hearing Dave as an authentic jazz musician—one who swings or "cooks"—jazz magazines saw and heard him as an outsider to jazz. For these critics, Dave's overwhelming whiteness and commercial appeal was not only part of his visual image but part of his sound. Thus, critics wrote whiteness into descriptions of the sounds he performed. "She Also Cooks . . ." reveals the challenge Dave Brubeck faced in performing an image of whiteness to convert predominantly white audiences to jazz, a genre that had historically given space to Black musicians who were typically unable to be as easily accepted in mainstream society. Within jazz, he did not "cook," a term that by Iola's 1959 interview had been established as a sonic descriptor for the predominantly Black genre hard bop. "Cookin'" was left to musicians such as Miles Davis (*Cookin'*, 1957 Prestige), Horace Silver ("Cookin' at the Continental," *Finger Poppin' with the Horace Silver Quintet*, 1959 Blue Note), and Jimmy Smith (*Home Cookin'*, 1959 Blue Note). As Gennari writes, "The mainstreaming of [jazz's] image was racially rigged: in the 1950s American popular mind, jazz was represented not by Lee Morgan's jamming at black neighborhood bars, but by Dave Brubeck's concerts at white colleges, genteel affairs attended by lots of earnest students in plaid shirts and khakis."[105]

While Dave Brubeck claimed to be able to "make converts" of respectable audiences, those audiences did not necessarily hear his place within a broader

---

[104] Iola Brubeck with Denise Gallo, "Jazz Conversation: Lyricist Iola Brubeck," Library of Congress, April 10, 2008, https://www.loc.gov/item/webcast-4797/. Elsewhere in the interview, Iola describes how she created the Brubeck Quartet's college tours, her work as a lyricist with Dave, as well as her work collecting and documenting archival material for the Brubeck Collection.

[105] Gennari, *Blowin' Hot and Cool*, 214.

field of Black musical creation—a fact that jazz critics were quick to point out (see chapter 1). Instead, mainstream audiences overwhelmingly recognized and appreciated jazz through white musicians such as Dave Brubeck. They believed that his music was uniquely intellectual and that by their ability to listen "seriously" to his music, they, too, were "intellectual," and his respectability ensured their own respectability. In other words, Brubeck's mainstream audience privileged the modes of whiteness they recognized in his music and presentation, and his placement in the publications they consumed—from *Time*, to *Good Housekeeping*, to *Vogue*, to *Playboy*—facilitated their acceptance of his jazz in their homes.

# 3
# (In)Visible Men

## White Recognition and Trust

In 1954 Dave Brubeck received a particular kind of mainstream honor rarely bestowed upon jazz musicians during any point in the genre's long history: he was featured on the cover of *Time* magazine. Only three other jazz musicians were so featured at mid-century: Louis Armstrong (1949), Duke Ellington (1956), and Thelonious Monk (1964) (Wynton Marsalis became the fifth and most recent jazz cover in 1990). Though he began the Brubeck Quartet in relative obscurity in 1951, Brubeck's appearance on *Time*'s cover reflects the steep rise in popularity he experienced in the early 1950s. His success, of course, came in part from the capital his "new" audience had to spend on Brubeck's performances—his "new" audience was "serious" and had previously been put off by jazz's supposedly low-brow, low-class associations (see chapter 2).[1] However, his media portrayals did not only enhance his visibility—something jazz's most famous exponents could also boast. Brubeck's particular brand of visibility went further and reveals another mode of whiteness: that of recognition, in this case between Brubeck and his fans.

In perhaps the best-known passage from Ralph Ellison's 1952 novel *Invisible Man*, Ellison's nameless narrator attempts to describe his invisibility to the whites he encounters day after day:

> I am an invisible man. No, I am not a spook like those who haunted Edgar Allan Poe; nor am I one of your Hollywood-movie ectoplasms. I am a man of substance, of flesh and bone, fiber and liquids—and I might even be said to possess a mind. I am invisible, understand, simply because people refuse to see me.... When they approach me they see only my surroundings, themselves, or figments of their imagination—indeed, everything and anything except me.[2]

---

[1] Nat Hentoff, Review of Jazz at Oberlin, by Dave Brubeck, *Down Beat*, December 2, 1953, 14–S; Dave Brubeck, "The New Jazz Audience," *Playboy*, August 1955, 9, 14; Ralph J. Gleason, "Brubeck: 'I Did Do Some Things First,'" *Down Beat*, September 5, 1957, 14–16, 35; C. H. Garrigues, "Brubeck's Fans Learned About Jazz in College," *San Francisco Examiner*, November 3, 1957; "Jazz Climbs Up the Social Ladder—With a Mighty Shove from Dave Brubeck," *New York National Enquirer*, March 16, 1958.

[2] Ralph Ellison, *Invisible Man* (1952; repr., New York: Vintage International, 1995), 3.

He distinguishes himself from the "spooks" or "ectoplasms" of popular white imagining, such as the title character of the 1933 movie *Invisible Man* based on H. G. Wells's 1897 science fiction novel of the same name (as well as its sequels and remakes of the 1940s). Instead, the narrator's invisibility is tied to his blackness. In this passage, Ellison's narrator highlights three important characteristics of his invisibility as a Black man. First, being invisible is a negative construction, for although the narrator has a mind and body, invisibility is defined by what he does not have, which the reader learns at the end of the prologue is recognition from mainstream (white) society. Second, invisibility is a denial of personhood, for to be unseen, to not be recognized, is to not count as human. Because the invisible man asserts that he is a "man of substance" and therefore some kind of physical being, it is clear that for him human identity does not rest in the visibility or presence of the body alone. His lack of human identity necessarily puts the invisible man at odds with the visible, or recognized, society. Finally, invisibility is outwardly constructed; the invisible man's invisibility is defined by those within the norms of humanity, by which Ellison means white Americans. Ellison's focus on invisibility and the inability to be recognized thus offers his readers a critique on the idea that whiteness, a race white people have often defined by its invisibility, is "normal."

In her 2004 book *Undoing Gender*, philosopher and gender theorist Judith Butler, commenting on psychoanalyst Jessica Benjamin's work, defines recognition as "the condition under which the human subject achieves psychic self-understanding and acceptance."[3] However, Butler explains that recognition is not a simple "seeing" of another person: "It is, rather, a process that is engaged when subject and Other understand themselves to be reflected in one another, but where this reflection does not result in a collapse of the one into the Other . . . or a projection that annihilates the alterity of the Other." Recognition, then, requires a mutual active engagement between two parties who admit and accept both similarities and differences.

Likewise, Ellison's definition of invisibility does not rely on a simple inability to see the Other but on lack of recognition of and responsibility to the Other. At the end of the prologue, Ellison writes, "Irresponsibility is part of my invisibility. . . . Responsibility rests on recognition, and recognition is a form of agreement."[4] This follows a story in which the protagonist accidentally bumps a white man, who then calls the narrator a name. The narrator responds aggressively, grabbing at the white man's coat lapels, head butting him and kicking him, before the narrator realizes that the man had not seen

---

[3] Judith Butler, *Undoing Gender* (New York: Routledge, 2004), 131.
[4] Ellison, *Invisible Man*, 14.

him precisely because he is invisible. As the narrator exclaims at the end of the prologue, "*He* bumped *me, he* insulted *me*. Shouldn't he, for his own personal safety, have recognized my hysteria, my 'danger potential'?" But the white man did not recognize Ellison's narrator. The white man took no responsibility for his own behavior, and thus, neither did Ellison's narrator. With a lack of recognition comes a lack of responsibility—for oneself and for others—among both parties. However, because it is the white man who controls his own "dream world," in which the narrator is an invisible phantom, only the narrator is invisible; he can "see" the white man, while the white man cannot see him. Indeed, seeing the white man is part and parcel of the narrator's survival as a Black man.

This chapter focuses on Dave Brubeck's 1954 appearance on the cover of *Time* magazine and the ways in which *Time*'s mainstream, predominantly white audience recognized him. In order to interrogate the shifting levels of power between invisibility, visibility, and recognition, as well as their relationship to race, I pay particular attention to the differences between Brubeck's portrayal and those of the three other jazz musicians featured at mid-century (Armstrong, Ellington, and Monk). While previous chapters have focused on the invisibility of whiteness, deconstructing and revealing modes of white privilege, this chapter examines how the invisible norms of whiteness render even the most seemingly visible Black jazz musicians invisible. Whereas Louis Armstrong, Duke Ellington, and Thelonious Monk illustrate Ellison's concept of invisibility, Brubeck epitomizes the visibility of a white musician in the same field to mainstream audiences. Further, Brubeck illustrates the degree to which mid-century white mainstream audiences were capable of recognizing the full personhood of white musicians over the personhood of Black musicians. Put simply, Brubeck's whiteness renders him visible as human, even as his whiteness, and its modes of privilege, remains invisible.

## Recognition and Invisibility in *Time* Magazine and Mainstream Audiences

By the 1950s, *Time* magazine's guiding philosophy had changed little since its founding in 1923 by Henry Luce, who ran the publication based on the notion that "Names make news. . . . People are interested in People."[5] The purpose of the magazine was not to make arguments but rather to give readers the sense

---

[5] James L. Baughman, *Henry R. Luce and the Rise of the American News Media* (Boston: Twayne, 1987), 171.

of being "in the know." Luce's image of his prospective readers largely reflected his own interests, and he believed that what interested him would ultimately sell magazines:

> "I am a Protestant, a Republican and a free enterpriser," [Luce] declared. "I am biased in favor of God, Eisenhower and the stockholders of Time Inc.—and if anybody who objects doesn't know this by now, why the hell are they still spending 35 cents for the magazine?"[6]

While Luce may have thought that such an approach was an effective marketing strategy, social critic Dwight MacDonald believed that *Time* magazine and publications like it, notably *Life*, perpetuated a middle-brow approach to culture. Of Luce, MacDonald wrote, "A journalistic entrepreneur like Henry Luce—by no means the worst—has the same kind of idle curiosity about the Facts and the same kind of gee-whiz excitement about rather elementary ideas . . . as his millions of readers have."[7] Essentially, MacDonald's description of Luce was an indictment of *Time*'s approach to news that suggested that Luce pandered to his audience.

However, Luce would have likely argued that he was simply in tune with the desires of mass culture audiences. Luce made no political or ideological compromise in order to increase his readership, and his writers targeted Luce's conception of the everyman: himself. Luce was part of a system in which Black Americans were thought to be invisible, and his conception shaped the portrayal of Black jazz musicians in his magazines. *Time*'s images of Black jazz musicians, both written and on the cover, reflect a set of idiosyncratic behaviors and rituals that further perpetuated their invisibility. Such portrayals highlighted these musicians' blackness and confined them to racial stereotypes that prevented the extent to which each musician was visible to *Time*'s mainstream audience. *Time*'s portrayals of Black jazz musicians (and other notable Black figures appearing on its cover) are thus part of what musicologist Matthew Morrison refers to as "Blacksound," or blackface minstrelsy's legacies (sonic, embodied, and visual) that have shaped and continue to shape popular entertainment, culture, and identity in America and beyond.[8]

---

[6] Baughman, quoting Luce, *Henry R. Luce*, 173.
[7] Dwight MacDonald, "Masscult & Midcult," in *Essays Against the American Grain*, ed. John Summers (New York: New York Review of Books, 2011), 33.
[8] Matthew D. Morrison, "Race, Blacksound, and the (Re)Making of Musicological Discourse," *Journal of the American Musicological Society* 72, no. 3 (2019): 781–823; Matthew D. Morrison, "The Sound(s) of Subjection: Constructing American Popular Music and Racial Identity Through Blacksound," *Women & Performance: A Journal of Feminist Theory* 27, no. 1 (2017): 13–24.

Prior to the 1950s, mainstream news sources largely considered jazz musicians and audiences through sensationalized and racist stereotypes of deviant, drug-addicted musicians. Historian Burton Peretti notes that although such associations existed in earlier periods of jazz, by 1940, the stereotypical "hipster" figure, complete with sunglasses, beret, and drug and alcohol addictions, reigned in the popular imagination's understanding of jazz musicians—and increasingly, their audience.[9] In fact, as ethnomusicologist Patrick Burke explains, jazz audiences of the late 1930s were actually quite diverse—even if the press did not always acknowledge that fact.[10] They included Black and white audiences of a range of ages, both men and women, some of whom were in college, and others who were well out of college but had stoked their interest in jazz there. And just as Burke found with white, college-educated audiences in the 1930s and 1940s, 1950s jazz critics likewise recognized early on that college audiences could lend the commercial success necessary to "make or break" jazz groups.[11]

But even when the mainstream press acknowledged audiences' broader engagement with jazz in the 1930s, there remained a signal difference between how Black and white audiences were represented. To illustrate the distinction, historian Benjamin Cawthra draws on two *Life* magazine articles on jazz, each of which highlighted the audience.[12] The first, published in 1936, featured audiences at the Savoy Ballroom, a predominantly (though not entirely) Black venue in Harlem (unlike many nightclubs, the Savoy had a non-discrimination policy).[13] This audience, *Life* proclaimed, was filled with "happy extroverts"; the article went on to describe their dancing as "a jungle dance in its wilder manifestations," and further, noted the seemingly oversexualized behavior of the dancing couples: "As unselfconscious in their kissing as in their dancing, Savoy customers seek no secluded corners for their fun." The following year, in 1937, *Life* described a Benny Goodman performance at the Madhattan Room in Pennsylvania.[14] Unlike the primarily Black Savoy audience, Goodman's all-white audience was portrayed in the article as quietly restrained; the article noted that "intermittent dancing is subordinated to the almost scholarly pleasure of listening to Benny," and "standing and listening is what most Goodman fans do for more than half of a typical Madhattan Room evening."

---

[9] Burton Peretti, *The Creation of Jazz: Music, Race, and Culture in Urban America* (Urbana: University of Illinois Press, 1992), 120–144.

[10] Patrick Burke, *Come in and Hear the Truth: Jazz and Race on 52nd Street* (Chicago: University of Chicago Press, 2008), 127.

[11] Jack Egan, "'Stuff' Smith Does His Stuff at Onyx Club," *Down Beat* 3, no. 3 (March 1936): 4.

[12] Benjamin Cawthra, *Blue Notes in Black and White: Photography and Jazz* (Chicago: University of Chicago Press), 20–25.

[13] "*Life* Goes to a Party: At the Savoy with the Boys and Girls of Harlem," *Life*, December 14, 1936, 64–68.

[14] "*Life* Goes to a Party: To Listen to Benny Goodman and His Swing Band," *Life*, November 1, 1937, 126.

Such narratives reflect those written for Boston's Storyville; as Cawthra writes, "*Life*'s characterization of Goodman's Madhattan Room audience"—particularly in contrast with its characterization of the Savoy Ballroom—"used swing to revise the traditional jazz narrative of disreputable nonconformity into one of cultural uplift."[15]

Such distinctions in how white and Black musicians were portrayed in mainstream sources like *Time* and understood by its readership reflect Ralph Ellison's descriptions of invisibility and recognition. Because a lack of recognition defines invisibility, to be invisible also means to exist outside the norms of humanity. As Butler writes, "If there are norms of recognition by which the 'human' is constituted, and these norms encode operations of power, then it follows that the contest over the future of the 'human' will be a contest over the power that works in and through such norms."[16] In other words, those with power, like the white man from Ellison's narrator's anecdote, control the norms of recognition, which in turn control *who* is defined as human and *how* that definition is represented. Black jazz musicians fell outside these norms of recognition and were thus not recognized as human by the system of white supremacy that controlled mainstream media. For Ellison's narrator, invisibility "gives one a slightly different sense of time, you're never quite on the beat. Sometimes you're ahead and sometimes behind. Instead of the swift and imperceptible flowing of time, you are aware of its nodes, those points where time stands still or from which it leaps ahead."[17] Invisibility, Ellison writes, is something that enhances the difference of life between Black and white Americans, but not something that aids in understanding that difference for the visible.

Ellison's protagonist calls people like the man he bumped into ("*He* bumped *me*, *he* insulted *me*") sleepwalkers, or dreamers, because they are unaware of their place among others in the world. Indeed, it is possible that, short of an encounter like that between the narrator and the white man, these dreamers could go through life without seeing a Black body, without acknowledging their own place within a broader racial world. Race could

---

[15] Cawthra, *Blue Notes*, 25.
Jazz magazines, however, often offered somewhat different portrayals of Black jazz musicians. The shift in visibility of Black jazz musicians on the cover of *Down Beat*, a jazz magazine that nevertheless had a predominantly white readership, between 1950 and 1967 demonstrates the distinction between the jazz and mainstream presses' approaches to race and representation. Ingrid Monson charts the frequency with which white and Black musicians appeared on the cover of *Down Beat* between 1950 and 1967. She found that in 1950, twenty-two out of twenty-six of the covers featured white musicians, while in 1967, seventeen covers featured Black musicians and nine featured white musicians. Ingrid Monson, *Freedom Sounds: Civil Rights Call Out to Jazz and Africa* (Oxford: Oxford University Press, 2007), 68–69.
[16] Butler, *Undoing Gender*, 13.
[17] Ellison, *Invisible Man*, 8.

be invisible to them because Black humanity was invisible. In fact, the invisibility of whiteness required the simultaneous visibility of blackness and invisibility of Black bodies. In other words, though whiteness had already defined itself around particular traits, white supremacy needed (and still needs) an overarching Black identity—a stereotype—defining "them" as Other while maintaining a selfhood that applied to individual whites. In this way, Black musicians on view for white audiences could not attain recognition beyond their blackness.

Ellison's narrator is quick to clarify that his invisibility is not defined by how others judge his actions and statements. Instead, his invisibility stems from outward perceptions and stereotypes—pre-judgments that have nothing to do with his particular self. He writes,

> That invisibility to which I refer occurs because of a peculiar disposition of the eyes of those with whom I come in contact. A matter of the construction of their *inner* eyes, those eyes with which they look through their physical eyes upon reality.[18]

Ellison blames mainstream depictions of African Americans found in movies and literature for this "construction" of inner eyes. By highlighting the act of constructing race-based perceptions of people, Ellison's account differs from a similar description written by James Baldwin in 1955: "I learned . . . that to be a Negro, one was never looked at but was simply at the mercy of the reflexes the color of one's skin caused in other people."[19] For Baldwin, invisibility stems from a passive reflex, caused simply by the sight of Black bodies. Ellison's description, on the other hand, implies that the white gaze *actively creates* the invisibility of Black Americans. Elsewhere, Ellison recognizes that such images have their root in stereotypes derived from minstrelsy, calling the minstrelsy characters a mask whose "function it was to veil the humanity of Negroes thus reduced to a sign, and to repress the white audience's awareness of its moral identification with its own acts and with the human ambiguities pushed behind the mask."[20] The mask of minstrelsy therefore aided in de-humanizing African Americans, ultimately making them unrecognizable as individuals—invisible.

In the mid-twentieth century, the legacy of racist minstrelsy stereotypes initiated as a nineteenth-century form of entertainment manifested itself in music, movies, and literature, in which, Ellison argued, "too often what is

---

[18] Ibid., 3.
[19] James Baldwin, "Notes of a Native Son," *Notes of a Native Son* (Boston: Beacon Press, 1984 [1955]), 93.
[20] Ralph Ellison, "Change the Joke and Slip the Yoke," in *Shadow and Act* (1964; repr., New York: Vintage International, 1995), 49.

presented as the American Negro (a most complex example of Western man) emerges an oversimplified clown, a beast or an angel."[21] These caricatures of African Americans flatten the complexities of human life into a limited number of figures whose personalities remain unchanged, no matter the book or movie. While Black Americans were made identifiable through these stereotypes, these images rendered their human identities invisible. Ellison stresses that the proliferation of such stereotypes in Hollywood in the twentieth century implicitly ties Black Americans to such stereotypes in the white imagination: "The anti-Negro image is thus a ritual object of which Hollywood is not the creator, but the manipulator. Its role has been that of justifying the widely held myth of Negro inhumanness and inferiority by offering entertaining rituals through which that myth could be reaffirmed."[22] Ellison argues that such simplistic depictions of African Americans as subservient members of society encourages white audience members to create their own stereotypes "by reading into situations involving Negroes those stock meanings which justify [whites'] emotional and economic means."[23] Put more plainly, Ellison explained that mainstream outlets, such as books and movies, that perpetuate such stereotypes "are not *about* Negroes at all; they are about what whites think and feel about Negroes."[24]

For Brubeck and many of his mainstream followers, jazz no longer required membership in a so-called deviant subculture but could be accessed by broader audiences, even as those audiences maintained the stereotypical assumptions regarding Black musicians that had created that subculture in the first place. In other words, even if by the 1950s jazz's audience was no longer only a deviant subculture, that remained the stereotype in the minds of some mainstream, *Time* magazine audiences. And in their portrayals of Black and white jazz musicians, *Time* fulfilled such assumptions, thus rendering the most visible Black jazz musicians invisible.

## Louis Armstrong (1949)

While Louis Armstrong continues to be known as an innovator who initiated jazz's emphasis on virtuosic improvised solos, this in large part derives from recordings from the first two decades of his career, the 1920s and

---

[21] Ralph Ellison, "Twentieth-Century Fiction and the Black Mask of Humanity," in *Shadow and Act* (1964; repr., New York: Vintage International, 1995), 25.

[22] Ralph Ellison, "The Shadow and the Act," in *Shadow and Act* (1964; repr., New York: Vintage International, 1995), 277.

[23] Ellison, "Twentieth-Century Fiction," 28.

[24] Ellison, "Shadow and Act," 277.

1930s.²⁵ By 1949, when he appeared on the cover of *Time*, jazz audiences were conflicted about Armstrong's stage behavior. Despite his musical legacy, his showy antics and wide smile were, for some members of his audience, an uncomfortable real-life image of Black stereotypes rooted in the blackface minstrelsy tradition. Jazz critic George T. Simon described Armstrong's supposed "mugging" in 1949: "At Bop City he was mugging like mad, putting on the personality, bowing, scraping and generally lowering himself as a human being in the eyes of his worshippers."²⁶ In 1956, when Harold Lovette, Miles Davis's business manager and lawyer, criticized Armstrong's own criticism of bop music, he directly related Armstrong to derogatory minstrel terms, explaining that "'Uncle' Louis" did not believe that musicians performing music Armstrong could not understand (i.e., bebop) were creative or experienced: "It is elementary that to understand contemporary jazz you either must be a musician of certain caliber or your appreciation must be developed jazz-wise. Louis has not had the time to do either, he has been too busy being a 'Tom.'"²⁷ The fact that Simon was a white critic and Lovette was a Black critic demonstrates that it was not simply white or Black listeners who were growing uncomfortable with Armstrong's performance style.²⁸

By the late 1940s, other jazz musicians had become wary of Armstrong's presentation of jazz. In his autobiography, Dizzy Gillespie writes, "I criticized Louis for other things, such as his 'plantation image.' We didn't appreciate that about Louis Armstrong, and if anybody asked me about a certain public image of him, handkerchief over his head, grinning in the face of white racism, I never hesitated to say I didn't like it. I didn't want the white man to expect me to allow the same things Louis Armstrong did."²⁹ However, reflecting back on Armstrong years later, Gillespie contextualized Armstrong's image within a lineage of Black performers:

> Every generation of blacks since slavery has had to develop its own way of Tomming, of accommodating itself to a basically unjust situation. . . . Later on, I began to

---

²⁵ Many scholars and critics point to Armstrong's Hot Five and Hot Seven Recordings of 1925–1928. Louis Armstrong, *Hot Fives and Sevens [complete collection]*, including Kid Ory, Johnny Dodds, Johnny St. Cyr, Lil Hardin Armstrong, Earl Hines, © 2000 by JSP Records.
²⁶ George T. Simon, "Armstrong, Commercialism, and Music," *Metronome*, October 1949, 38.
²⁷ Harold Lovette, "Louis Armstrong: Is He an Immature Jazz Fan?" *Metronome*, August 1956, 11.
²⁸ Future Supreme Court Justice Thurgood Marshall further underscored this integrated response to Armstrong's 1950s performances. Commenting just after Armstrong publicly decried President Eisenhower's inaction in the Little Rock Nine scene playing out in Arkansas in 1957, Marshall explained the benefit of Armstrong's statements to journalist Mike Wallace: "I do know the Negroes in New York all still say what Satchmo says. They were so happy about Satchmo's outburst—because he's the No. 1 Uncle Tom! The worst in the U.S.!" Mike Wallace, "Mike Wallace Asks Thurgood Marshall," *New York Post*, September 30, 1957.
²⁹ Dizzy Gillespie, *To Be or Not to . . . Bop* ([1979]; Minneapolis: University of Minnesota Press, 2009), 295.

recognize what I had considered Pops's grinning in the face of racism as his absolute refusal to let anything, even anger about racism, steal the joy from his life and erase his fantastic smile. Coming from a younger generation, I misjudged him.[30]

Likewise, Miles Davis at times criticized Armstrong's public persona, relating it to a broader issue of Black mainstream representation: "Those talk shows would take a black man on a television back then only if he grinned, became a clown, like Louis Armstrong did. . . . Man, I just hated when I saw him doing that, because Louis was hip, had a consciousness about black people, was a real nice man. But the only image people have of him is that grinning image off TV."[31] However, like Gillespie, he also recognized that Armstrong was of a different generation of jazz musicians, which required different methods of performance. Jazz critic Dan Morgenstern later recalled being seated next to Miles Davis at Basin Street East, both watching Louis Armstrong perform. He writes, "Davis was accompanied by his then lawyer Harold Lovette, a loquacious man. Louis's set had begun, but Lovette was still talking. Without taking his eyes off Louis, Miles said: 'Shut *up*, man! I want to hear Pops!'"[32] Though Gillespie and Davis both expressed discomfort with Armstrong's mode of self-presentation and felt that Armstrong potentially limited the extent to which audiences would accept their own public personae, they also recognized Armstrong as an autonomous individual making decisions to survive and thrive in an unjustly white-dominated music industry.

For someone unfamiliar with Ellison's notion of invisibility, it might appear as though Armstrong was very visible; his records appeared on *Billboard* charts like those of other popular stars, he appeared in mainstream magazines and movies, and he was perhaps more of a household name than any other jazz musician. Nevertheless, because Armstrong's showmanship reflected certain white conceptions, rooted in minstrelsy, of how a Black performer was supposed to behave, including so-called mugging, tomming, and putting on the personality, he remained invisible as an artist, successful precisely because he appeared to fulfill mainstream (i.e., white) expectations.[33] Some critics believed that Armstrong's "putting on the personality" was an intentional

---

[30] Ibid., 296.
[31] Miles Davis, with Quincy Troupe, *Miles* (New York: Simon & Schuster, 1989), 313.
[32] Dan Morgenstern, *Living with Jazz: A Reader* (New York: Pantheon Books, 2004).
[33] Images of Armstrong as "primitive" were prevalent from the very beginning of his film career. See in particular the short film *Rhapsody in Black and Blue* (1932) in which Armstrong wears a faux-leopard skin and growls throughout his performance, and a Betty Boop cartoon (1932), in which Armstrong performs the title song "I'll Be Glad When You're Dead You Rascal You." In this cartoon, Armstrong appears as the leader of a band of "savage" Africans who kidnap Betty Boop.

construction of an identity that would be commercially appealing to white audiences (which it was); Marshall Stearns mused that Armstrong was adept at "embroidering beautifully on the stereotyped mask, and enjoying the whole affair hugely. In a word: he is the master—not of just the music but also of a complex and ironic attitude."[34] For Ralph Ellison, Armstrong symbolized the "Invisible Man," making "poetry out of being invisible," and potentially "unaware that he *is* invisible."[35] In suggesting that Armstrong is unaware of his invisibility, Ellison argues that Armstrong's invisibility cannot be distinguished from any conception of Armstrong's "true" self, for Armstrong's invisibility constantly informed his "authentic" self, and vice versa. Of course, Armstrong could very well have been playing into these white stereotypes in an act of passive resistance, accessing a certain degree of visibility otherwise inaccessible to many Black performers.

Whether or not he was aware of his own invisibility, Armstrong himself understandably bristled at any accusation of "clowning" or "Tomming." Personal tapes he recorded at home reflect his anger and bitterness at such accusations; in one tape from the late 1950s, Armstrong's frustration and pain are clear in the tone and timbre of his voice as he reacts to a journalist who called him an Uncle Tom—"And that motherfucker called *me* an 'Uncle Tom!' Shit. Them son-of-a-bitches, wait til they come to my dance or concert and act a damn fool."[36] When a British reporter asked him about such critiques in 1959, Armstrong's response clearly denied any negative connotation of clowning while also suggesting that what he did was something different. He explained, "I know, but I mean, people enjoy the *clown*ing, you know, you see the ma*jo*rity rules in *my* playing, you know, that's what *I* go by."[37] Armstrong positions his music and his performance approach as being modern rather than those taken by musicians like the Modern Jazz Quartet or Miles Davis, who took on a more "serious" performance persona: "I suppose I could stand up there like Mozart, all I'm playing is *music*, you know. This is a modern *age*, now, you put a little *sauce* on it, you know." He closed by asserting his stature in the jazz community, stating, "Clowning is when you can't play nothing. . . . I don't think that's such a cute phrase. You don't play 45 years and hit notes

---

[34] Marshall Stearns, *The Story of Jazz* (Oxford: Oxford University Press, 1956), 318–319.
[35] Ellison, *Invisible Man*, 8.
[36] Louis Armstrong, personal recording, late 1950s, LAHM 1987.3.281, quoted in Ricky Riccardi, "'I'm Still Louis Armstrong—Colored': Louis Armstrong and the Civil Rights Era," *That's My Home: Louis Armstrong House Museum Virtual Exhibits*, May 11, 2020, https://virtualexhibits.louisarmstronghouse.org/2020/05/11/im-still-louis-armstrong-colored-louis-armstrong-and-the-civil-rights-era/?fbclid=IwAR2CgI7Woqzrrmo__uDWkbz9QLeRLbU_ewHP0kZzb9AxpamNGrryyZSsuNg, accessed May 12, 2020.
[37] Louis Armstrong, radio interview, 1959, LAHM 1987.3.525, quoted in Riccardi, "I'm Still Louis Armstrong."

and do things nobody else can *do*. You're not slippin'. Whatever it is, can't nobody do what I do. Now, I'm egotistical to say that, because I feel that if they can try to get a laugh, I'll get one, too." Taken together, Armstrong's responses suggest that he simultaneously *is* recognized (in terms of his abilities) and is *not* recognized by his audiences (that they had forgotten or perhaps no longer valued his virtuosity, as well as his authority to perform in whatever manner he desired). Indeed, the tapes Armstrong recorded of his private life suggest a greater degree of control over his image—which was, of course, among the most successful and well-known images in jazz of the twentieth century. Some critics, however, believed that the damage done to Armstrong's representation was not a product of Armstrong's personality, self-presentation, or authority, but of the audience's misconceptions—an interpretation that mirrors Ellison's invisible narrator's experience encountering people who see "everything and anything except me." As critic Ralph Gleason asserted, "I think if you look at Louis and have a comic image in your mind, you're doing the man a great injustice. And I also think you're indicating something about yourself."[38]

In his *Time* cover illustration of Armstrong, illustrator Boris Artzybasheff, a regular among *Time*'s cover artists, depicted Armstrong as exactly that showman that many jazz musicians, critics, and even audiences wanted to leave behind, wide toothy grin and all (Fig. 3.1). Everything in the image

**Figure 3.1.** Louis Armstrong on *TIME* magazine cover, 1949. Artist: Boris Artzybasheff © TIME.

[38] Ralph Gleason, in "A Jazz Summit Meeting," in *Keeping Time: Readings in Jazz History*, ed. Robert Walser (Oxford: Oxford University Press, 2014), 255. Quoted from "The Playboy Panel: Jazz—Today and Tomorrow," *Playboy*, February 1964, 29–31, 34–38, 56, 58, 139–141.

is slightly off-center, from the tilt of Armstrong's head, to his crown, to his placement in the frame, as if to further emphasize Armstrong's own personal marginality. Artzybasheff depicted Armstrong in a subservient pose, despite his crown, looking up at a musical note, rather than down at his musical subjects.

The story accompanying the cover image continued to portray Armstrong through familiar Black stereotypes, as he took his place as King of the Zulus in the annual Zulu parade for Mardi Gras in New Orleans. A *Billboard* article chronicling the event described Armstrong's dress for the parade as king: "Armstrong was dressed in a royal garb which included white paint circling his eyes, a big cigar in his mouth, a red tunic trimmed with gold sequins, a wide gold waist band, black tights and high gold shoes that reached halfway to his knees."[39] *Time* explained further, "Among Negro intellectuals, the Zulus and all their doings are considered offensive vestiges of the minstrel-show, Sambo-type Negro. To Armstrong such touchiness seems absurd, and no one who knows easygoing, nonintellectual Louis will doubt his sincerity."[40] Political scientist and jazz historian Charles Hersch argues that Armstrong had the potential to transform minstrel material, using the persona as a "weapon when he chose to do so."[41] But while the Zulu parade could be read ironically, as a minstrelsy satire, the *Time* article and cover image miss this potential interpretation—and indeed, many of his Black audiences likewise interpreted the "King of the Zulu" image as more damaging than ironic, as cultural historian Gerald Early writes.[42] By unequivocally positioning Armstrong against the "Negro intellectuals" who objected to the Zulu caricature, *Time* made it clear that it was not Armstrong, the jazz innovator of the 1920s and 1930s, but rather Armstrong, the popular performer, who found a place in the American mainstream. Additionally, *Time*'s assertion implied that Black intellectuals were too sensitive with regard to the "Sambo-type Negro," a description that managed to insult both Armstrong and Black intellectuals. Needless to say, *Time*'s stereotyped visual image of Armstrong, both through its words and art, was one for which the bebop generation had no use, but that fulfilled *Time*'s mainstream expectations of Black musicians.

---

[39] "'Satchmo' Hailed as King of Zulus at N.O. Mardi Gras," *Billboard*, March 12, 1949, 23.
[40] "Louis the First," *Time*, February 21, 1949, 52.
[41] Charles Hersch, "Poisoning Their Coffee: Louis Armstrong and Civil Rights," *Polity* 34, no. 3 (Spring 2002): 388.
[42] Gerald Early, *Tuxedo Junction: Essays on American Culture* (Hopewell, NJ: Ecco Press, 1989), 296.

## Duke Ellington (1956)

If *Time* portrayed Armstrong as a simple Sambo or Uncle Tom to its audience, the magazine exchanged Armstrong's gregarious stage presence for a sophisticated and even ostentatious appearance in its cover article on Duke Ellington. Even Ellington's nickname, *Time* explained, originated from "the dandified dress he wore when he was a schoolboy in Washington."[43] Carter Harman's *Time* article highlighted details of Ellington's oddities and superstitions that implicitly linked Ellington to stereotypically primitivist discourses of blackness. This was most evident in the following passage, which detailed Ellington's "Fickle Tricks":

> In his pleasant Harlem apartment or in his dressing room, he usually goes about in his shorts, possibly to preserve the creases in his 100-plus suits of clothes. His public personality resembles his public appearance, which is fastidious to the point of frivolity; few are the people who get a glimpse of the man beneath this polished exterior. . . . Often, his efforts to avoid unpleasantness take the form of hypochondria—as he puts it, 'I'm a doctor freak.'[44]

Harman focused on details revolving around Ellington's obsession with appearance and well-made suits, and his fear of illness was described as being so intense and peculiar as to qualify as a disease, albeit a psychological ailment that might also befall a sensitive artist.

However, as Burton Peretti notes, Ellington's superstitions—such as "a fear of losing a button or finding one on a piano keyboard, or of receiving gifts of shoes or socks"—were typical of Black folk beliefs, particularly for southern Black Americans (Ellington was only one generation removed from small-town North Carolina).[45] Such phobias, Peretti explains, were often exploited by northern commentators as representative of the stereotype of the superstitious "primitive." By highlighting such "Fickle Tricks" without explaining that they could be typical to those of other southern African Americans, Harman linked Ellington to primitivist discourses that rejected recognition for simplistic assumptions.

Harman's depiction of Ellington largely differed from Peter Hurd's cover illustration for the same issue (Fig. 3.2). Hurd created an artistic image of

---

[43] "Why Duke Ellington Avoided Music Schools," *PM*, December 9, 1945, in *The Duke Ellington Reader*, ed. Mark Tucker (Oxford: Oxford University Press, 1993), 252.
[44] Carter Harman, "Mood Indigo & Beyond," *Time*, August 20, 1956, 54–55.
[45] Burton Peretti, *The Creation of Jazz: Music, Race and Culture in Urban America* (Urbana: University of Illinois Press, 1992), 65.

**Figure 3.2.** Duke Ellington on *TIME* magazine cover, 1956. Artist: Peter Hurd © TIME.

Ellington performing alone onstage in the background, dressed in a tuxedo, his arms in the midst of a virtuosic musical flourish. If the viewer did not know Ellington, it would be impossible to know that the image portrayed a jazz musician. The foregrounded bust of Ellington further complicated Harman's easy stereotypes. Ellington's face is pulled into a look of amusement, eyebrows raised and lips slightly pursed. For those acquainted with Ellington's image, it was a familiar look. Ellison refers to it in his 1969 "Homage to Duke Ellington on His Birthday" as an "enigmatic smile," which served to mask Ellington's true feelings to those unfamiliar with him.[46] For Ellison, Ellington's "enigmatic smile" was evidence of an "aura of mockery" found in both Ellington's work and personality: "He is one of the most handsome of men, and to many his stage manners are so suave and gracious as to appear a put-on—which quite often they are."[47] Harman suggests that he was able to see behind the mask when he explains that "few are the people who get a glimpse of the man beneath this polished exterior." Such an implication would have no doubt guaranteed his *Time* readers that they were getting the true, unvarnished, and novel truth about Ellington—even as Harman continued to place Ellington neatly within a white frame of understanding, denying him

---

[46] Ralph Ellison, "Homage to Duke Ellington on His Birthday," in *Living with Music: Ralph Ellison's Jazz Writings*, ed. Robert G. O'Meally (New York: Modern Library, 2002), 83. Indeed, Krin Gabbard notes that Ellington "always wore a mask in public," even when biographer Stanley Dance attempted to interview him. Krin Gabbard, "How Many Miles? Alternate Takes on the Jazz Life," in *Thriving on a Riff: Jazz and Blues Influences in African American Literature and Film*, ed. Graham Lock and David Murray (Oxford: Oxford University Press, 2009), 188.

[47] Ellison, "Homage to Duke Ellington on His Birthday," 85.

any true recognition. Hurd's image, on the other hand, offered a recognition of Ellington's private and public lives while still portraying him as a suave and sophisticated artist, a performing identity Ellington had cultivated for decades.

Ellington's smile was a subtle example of Signifyin(g), in that it both represented what the audience expected from a Black performer and allowed Ellington some agency in critiquing such stereotypes. Historian Henry Louis Gates explains that Signifyin(g) is "black double-voicedness" and represents a "technique of indirect argument." Such indirectness was likewise used by enslaved Black Americans as a way of expressing themselves while avoiding violence from white slave owners.[48] As musicologist Douglas Malcolm writes, "African Americans employed signifying because it was fundamental to Black culture and an effective way of subverting the white supremacist ideology and the harsh social conditions it imposed."[49] Recall Gillespie's acknowledgment that "every generation of Black slaves since slavery has had to develop its own way of Tomming, of accommodating itself to a basically unjust situation": Ellington's strategy was "double-voicedness."[50] As Ellington put it, "What we could not say openly, we expressed in music, and what we know as 'jazz' is something more than just dance music."[51]

For Ellison, Ellington was capable of both pointing out the falsity of Black stereotypes and presenting a new image. However, if *Time*'s audience could not look at Ellington and recognize him, all that remained was an "enigmatic smile" whose mockery was not visible.[52] Part of Signifyin(g) relies on a misreading. As Malcolm explains, "Irony . . . is often a social discourse involving several individuals in which the members of the group or audience who understand only the surface meaning of the ironic communication are often the target of the irony."[53] For Ellison, Ellington's smile represented this

---

[48] Henry Louis Gates Jr., *The Signifying Monkey: A Theory of Afro-American Literary Criticism* (Oxford: Oxford University Press, 1988), 51, 54.

[49] Douglas Malcolm, "'Myriad Subtleties': Subverting Racism Through Irony in the Music of Duke Ellington and Dizzy Gillespie," *Black Music Research Journal* 35, no. 2 (2015), 189.

[50] Gillespie, *To Be or Not to . . . Bop*, 296.

[51] Duke Ellington, "The Duke Steps Out" (1931), in *The Duke Ellington Reader*, ed. Mark Tucker (Oxford: Oxford University Press, 1993), 49.

[52] To be clear, I am not arguing that Ellington went along with primitivist portrayals. Indeed, Ellington made his opinion of such stereotypes clear as early as 1940s in an interview in which he explained the impetus for his musical *Jump for Joy*: "'Jump for Joy' provided quite a few problems. There was the first and greatest problem of trying to give an American audience entertainment without compromising the dignity of the Negro people. Needless to say, this is the problem every Negro artist faces. He runs afoul of offensive stereotypes, instilled in the American mind by whole centuries of ridicule and derogation. The American audience has been taught to expect a Negro on the stage to clown and 'Uncle Tom,' that is, to enact the role of a servile, yet lovable, inferior." Interviewer John Pittman wrote more directly: "Another way of putting it is to say that the Duke is no Uncle Tom. He abhors 'Uncle Tomism.'" John Pittman, "The Duke Will Stay on Top!," unidentified clipping, probably San Francisco, August or September 1941, in *The Duke Ellington Reader*, ed. Mark Tucker (Oxford: Oxford University Press, 1993), 148.

[53] Malcolm, "'Myriad Subtleties,'" 190.

same expectation of "misreading" from *Time*'s audience. Through his smile, Ellington signified upon his audience, presenting an exteriority that could be interpreted by *Time*'s predominantly white audience as the smiling Black entertainer while safely and secretly maintaining what Ellison referred to as an "aura of mockery" that simultaneously asserted his agency and concealed his visibility.

## Thelonious Monk (1964)

In his biography of Thelonious Monk, Robin D. G. Kelley begins his discussion of the Monk *Time* article with a question: "It was his [Monk's] image, all right, but was it his story?"[54] Like Harman's *Time* article on Ellington, Barry Farrell's *Time* article featuring Thelonious Monk described Monk in terms of his particularities, beginning with his penchant for strange hats (including an episode in Finland in which Monk had to stop at a hat store before his performance), continuing through his use of drugs (Farrell explains that "every day is a brand-new pharmaceutical event for Monk"), and highlighting his "Monkish" dance routine.[55] Many of these descriptions fell into already recognizable assumptions about Monk and his approach to music; as Kelley writes, "For well over half a century, the press and the critics have portrayed Monk as 'eccentric,' 'mad,' 'childlike,' 'brooding,' 'naïve,' intuitive,' 'primitive,' even 'taciturn.'"[56] This image started with a 1949 press release by Blue Note Records' Lorraine Lion, who dubbed Monk the "High Priest of Bebop" and framed him as "elusive, mysterious, strange, eccentric, weird, genius." As Kelley writes, "Monk's behavior was weird and made good copy."[57] Ethnomusicologist Gabriel Solis likewise documents the lens of white fascination with Black men's physical masculinity that dominated jazz critics' descriptions of Monk in the 1950s and 1960s and rendered Monk as a "man-child." Solis argues that recognition of Monk would include "hearing the playful side of his expressive palette," while simultaneously setting aside the racist baggage that too often

---

[54] Robin D. G. Kelley, *Thelonious Monk: The Life and Times of an American Original* (New York: Free Press, 2009), 354.

[55] Kelley notes that prior to 1959, Monk almost always performed without a hat. Writing of Monk's 1959 performance at the Newport Jazz Festival, Kelley explains, "Whether it was vanity [he was losing his hair] or the climate [when asked, Monk said he was cold], an element of Monk's trademark style was born that evening." Kelley, *Thelonious Monk*, 270.

[56] Ibid., iv.

[57] Ibid., 132. Thelonious Monk press release (ca. February 1948) Blue Note Archives, Capitol Records (qtd. in Kelley, *Thelonious Monk*, 130–132).

equated playfulness with childishness—a distinction utterly missed by Farrell and other mid-century critics.[58]

Farrell's portrayal of Monk's performance was another example of *Time*'s writers viewing Black jazz musicians through preconceptions, thus reifying their invisibility. For example, Farrell created the following image of Monk's dancing:

> Then he would rise from the piano to perform his Monkish dance. It is always the same. His feet stir in a soft shuffle, spinning him slowly in small circles. His head rolls back until hat brim meets collar, while with both hands he twists his goatee into a sharp black scabbard. His eyes are hooded with an abstract sleepiness, his lips are pursed in a meditative O. His cultists may crowd the room, but when he moves among them, no one risks speaking: he is absorbed in a fragile trance, and his three sidemen play on while he dances alone in the darkness. At the last cry of the saxophone, he dashes to the piano and his hands strike the keys in a cat's pounce.[59]

Farrell's account includes all of the elements of an early anthropologist observing an exotic "primitive" ritual at some distance. Monk dances, he seems to be meditating, and his followers are cultists, devoted to their leader. Farrell's description of Monk's performance focused intensely on his peculiar actions rather than his music.

Similarly, in his article on Ellington, Harman's opening description of Ellington's performance at the 1956 Newport Jazz Festival focused more on the audience's physical reaction to the music than the musical performance:

> At that magic moment Ellington's Paul Gonsalves was ripping off a fast but insinuating solo on his tenor saxophone, his fancies dandied by a bounding beat on bass and drums. . . . The Duke himself tweaked an occasional fragment on the high piano. Gradually, the beat began to ricochet from the audience as more and more fans began to clap hands on the offbeats until the crowd was one vast, rhythmic chorus, yelling its approval. There were howls of "More! More" and there was dancing in the aisles. One young woman broke loose from her escort and rioted solo around the field, while a young man encouraged her by shouting, "Go, go, go!"[60]

---

[58] Gabriel Solis, *Monk's Music: Thelonious Monk and Jazz History in the Making* (Berkeley: University of California Press, 2008), 56.
[59] Barry Farrell, "The Loneliest Monk," *Time*, February 28, 1964, 85.
[60] Harman, "Mood Indigo," 54.

Despite the difference in musical style between Ellington and Monk, both *Time* articles emphasized forms of ritualized movement. The *Time* writers' frequent association of Black musicians with the physical ignores the realities of each musician's performative style (both sonic and visual) and reinforces these musicians' invisibility by employing preconceived notions of primitivism and bodily engagement.[61]

At the end of the article, seemingly out of nowhere, Farrell inserts Monk directly into the fray of race and jazz, by suggesting that one of Monk's merits, and one of the things that makes him the "Loneliest Monk," includes not being part of the "racial woes [that] are at the heart of much bad behavior in jazz."[62] Farrell dedicates a strange amount of space to musicians he accuses of instigating these "Crow Jim" racial woes (including Sonny Rollins, Charles Mingus, John Coltrane, and especially Miles Davis)—Black musicians who, by pointing out racially discriminatory hiring, promotional, and other practices across the music industry, frequently received a backlash from white critics and musicians who felt personally attacked. As Kelley explains, "Like most white liberals uncomfortable with rising black militancy, Farrell felt betrayed by the strident racial politics of Max Roach's *Freedom Now Suite* or the 'angry' sounds of the 'New Thing.' Monk, much to Farrell's relief, was above the fray."[63] Essentially, for Farrell and for some readers, Monk's seeming lack of interest in politics was more evidence of a "childlike" approach to the world than a deliberate decision regarding his political image. Kelley notes that both Theodore Pontiflet, writing for the socialist magazine *The Liberator*, and Ralph de Toledano, writing for the right-wing *National Review*, "treated Monk as a kind of idiot savant, unaware of the world around him, and they both believed he embodied their political position."[64] However, as Ingrid Monson points out, Monk was among several jazz musicians who, though they were not politically outspoken, lent their musical abilities to fund-raising events for various civil rights causes on many occasions.[65] Such shrewd management of his

---

[61] In chapter 1, I discuss the relationship between blackness, "authenticity," physicality, and primitivism in more detail, as do Kofi Agawu, "The Invention of 'African Rhythm,'" *Representing African Music* (New York: Routledge Press, 2003), 55–70; Simon Frith, "Rhythm: Race, Sex, and the Body," in *Performing Rites: On the Value of Popular Music* (Cambridge, MA: Harvard University Press, 1996): 123–144; Ted Gioia, "Jazz and the Primitivist Myth," in *The Imperfect Art* (New York: Oxford University Press, 1988); Ingrid Monson, "The Problem with White Hipness: Race, Gender, and Culture Conceptions in Jazz Historical Discourse," *Journal of the American Musicological Society* 48, no. 3 (Autumn 1995), 396–422.

[62] Farrell, "The Lonelist Monk," 87.

[63] Kelley, *Thelonious Monk*, 354.

[64] Ibid., 355. Theodore H. Pontiflet, "The American Way," *Liberator* 4, no. 6 (June 1965), 8–9; Ralph de Toledano, "Thelonious Monk and Some Others," *National Review*, October 19, 1965, 940–941.

[65] Ingrid Monson, *Freedom Sounds: Civil Rights Call Out to Jazz and Africa* (Oxford: Oxford University Press), 199–206.

image, business, and politics suggests a much more complicated and knowing portrait of Monk, particularly when it came to 1960s racial politics.

While Farrell's story on Monk emphasized the peculiarities of his personality and the physical aspects of his performance, cover artist Boris Chaliapin's representation of Monk resisted many obvious idiosyncrasies (Fig. 3.3). Monk is depicted in one of his trademark hats, and his goatee is somewhat scraggly, but Chaliapin did not provide any imagery in the background, opting instead to illuminate Monk with *Time*'s iconic red coloring as the only backdrop. Without the text on the page, "Jazz: Bebop and Beyond" and "Jazzman Thelonious Monk," it could be impossible to know that this is a jazz musician, just as with Ellington's cover portrait. One reading of the cover is that its simplicity ultimately enhances the inexplicability of Monk. While Chaliapin's cover does not highlight Monk's specific eccentricities, the lack of any defining imagery and positioning of Monk in half profile, almost looking at the viewer but instead looking just beyond, creates an unknowable image of an "Other." Another reading, however, could assert that Chaliapin's naturalistic depiction removes Monk from more primitivist tropes and styles. Ultimately, the simplicity of the cover yields multiple interpretations or active engagement between the viewer and Monk's image, allowing some recognition—or at least acknowledgment for the possibility of recognition—where Farrell's article did not.

**Figure 3.3.** Thelonious Monk on *TIME* magazine cover, 1964. Artist: Boris Chaliapin © TIME.

Unlike Armstrong and Ellington's articles, Monk's appearance on *Time* rankled members of the jazz press, many of whom believed that the benefit of showcasing Monk, a decidedly non-mainstream musician whom they believed was worthy of attention, did not outweigh the danger of reinscribing racist stereotypes on jazz musicians in the mainstream press. Ralph Gleason called the article "revolting," and even "libelous to jazz."[66] Leonard Feather wondered if the article should have been written at all, arguing that "for white readers with little knowledge of the racial components that shaped the background of the story, the damage can be twofold; here we are dealing with an image that has suffered not decades but centuries of damage."[67] Feather pondered further if *Time* had chosen Monk to focus on because of the easy connections made between Monk and drugs, alcohol, dancing, and hats, which Feather argued mindfully misrepresented musicians in order to fulfill "*Time*'s idea of a rich, full, adventurous, newsworthy life." Though Monk deserved commercial exposure and its financial benefits, Feather believed Monk's portrayal within primitivist stereotypes could only harm images of Black jazz musicians for mainstream audiences:

> In crucially sensitive times like these, there are extramusical factors to be taken into consideration—factors that could have been weighed more seriously before a jazzman was explained away to millions of Luce-minded readers as a lovable, dignified, jive-talking, honest, odd-hatted, unselfish weirdo.

Likewise, Amiri Baraka wondered why *Time* chose to feature Monk, though he agreed that Monk had "paid his dues" and deserved the cover. For Baraka, Monk, unlike most musicians, found commercial success without losing himself, which ultimately made his *Time* story a success in ways Armstrong's and Ellington's were not. Much like Ellison, Baraka instead suggested that Monk's audience was the root of any "oddities" or "weirdness" in Monk's performances and argued that Monk's musical interpretation was made manifest in his "Monkish dance":

> The quick dips, half-whirls, and deep pivoting jerks that Monk gets into behind the piano are part of the music, too. Many musicians have mentioned how they could get further into the music by watching Monk dance, following the jerks and starts, having dug that that was the emphasis Monk wanted on the tune.[68]

---

[66] Ralph J. Gleason, "Monk Puts on a Magazine," *San Francisco Chronicle*, March 2, 1964.
[67] Leonard Feather, "Feather's Nest," *Down Beat*, April 23, 1964, 39.
[68] Amiri Baraka [LeRoi Jones], "The Acceptance of Monk," *Down Beat*, February 27, 1964, 22.

Monk's dancing thus demonstrated the complex rhythmic understanding musicians already knew he possessed, enhancing their own musical knowledge. Still, even with Baraka's translation, Monk's depiction can hardly be claimed as an example of visibility within the mainstream press, as even Baraka acknowledged the discrepancy between *Time*'s sensationalistic portrayal of Monk's dancing and Monk's own musical understanding of the same activity.

## Dave Brubeck (1954)

As with the other *Time* features of jazz musicians, T. George Harris, the author of the Brubeck article, also approached his research on Brubeck with certain preconceived notions of jazz musicians, whether Black or white. Brubeck's saxophonist, Paul Desmond, later called Harris "one of the most disillusioned journalists" he had ever met. Apparently, on the first day he was with the quartet, Harris ordered bourbon, but the bourbon went untouched, and the bucket of ice in which it sat "melted away kind of pathetically." Apparently disabused of the notion that all jazz musicians smoked, drank alcohol, and fooled around with women, a confused Harris commented to Desmond, "Is this for real? . . . This is supposed to be a story about a typical jazz musician. Nobody will ever believe it."[69]

The difference between how Harris dealt with his assumptions about Brubeck and how *Time*'s reporters on Armstrong, Ellington, and Monk dealt with theirs demonstrates the privileged recognition granted to Brubeck. While Armstrong, Ellington, and Monk were each presented as performers with fetishistic behaviors that seemed to a middlebrow public to suit both a Black 'Other' and a jazz musician, Harris normalized Brubeck, while further Othering the rest of the field of jazz musicians:

> Brubeck is as untypical in the jazz field as a harp in a Dixieland combo. In a business that has known more than its share of dope and liquor, Brubeck rarely drinks, and, after seriously and philosophically considering the possible value of mescaline, rejected the whole idea. While itinerant musicians are apt to dally with the belles along the way, Dave is happily married and has four children (a fifth is on the way). Although a shady background was once almost essential to the seasoning of

---

[69] Paul Desmond to unnamed, December 12, 1960, in file 1.18, coll. 309, Paul Desmond Papers, Holt-Atherton Special Collections, University of the Pacific Library, Stockton, CA.

a real-life jazzman, Dave spent his youth playing nursemaid to heifers and earned his first money ($1 a Sunday) playing hymns in school.[70]

As jazz studies scholar Eric Porter writes, Brubeck's *Time* cover article "employed a discourse of respectability as it celebrated Brubeck and his contemporaries while marginalizing the contributions and experiences of Black musicians. The article associated blackness and immorality in jazz and saw the new 'mainstream' jazz as a step forward from an unhealthy past."[71] Indeed, Harris normalized Brubeck to *Time*'s readership by distancing him from other jazz musicians. While Farrell emphasized Monk's dancing over his music and Harman focused on the dancing of the audience over Ellington's music, Harris described a performance of Brubeck's in detailed musical terms. Using such words from the European concert tradition as "passacaglia," "polyphonic," "sonata," and "contrapuntal," Harris's description confers an importance and high-art status to Brubeck's music that is absent from the other *Time* profiles of jazz musicians. Harris also distanced Brubeck's "cool" jazz from dance, instead explicitly aligning it with intellect and the mind: "[Brubeck's music] evokes neither swinging hips nor hip flasks. It goes to the head and the heart more than to the feet."[72]

As a performer, Brubeck, like Armstrong, Ellington, and Monk, was subject to critics' narratives. However, the narrative critics wrote for Brubeck was one that relied heavily on his white heterosexual masculine normativity, a narrative imbued with a power and agency that Black performers were rarely recognized as possessing. In 1958, Leonard Feather described the Brubeck Quartet's image in terms of Brubeck and Desmond's appeal to white audiences, explaining,

> In addition to their talents, their rapport and Brubeck's compositional ability, Brubeck and Desmond have an 'all-American boy' quality, combined with just enough of the academic approach, to provide them with a visual and aural appeal that came just at the right time, when a new postwar generation of young jazz fans sought for a more intellectual avenue toward jazz.[73]

On top of the multiple references to European classical music, academia, and intellectuals that critics often made regarding Brubeck, it seems unlikely

---

[70] T. George Harris, "Man on Cloud No. 7," *Time*, November 8, 1954, 70, 73.
[71] Eric Porter, *What Is This Thing Called Jazz?: African American Musicians as Artists, Critics, and Activists* (Berkeley: University of California Press, 2002), 120.
[72] Harris, "Man on Cloud No. 7," 67.
[73] Leonard Feather, *Jazz: An Exciting Story of Jazz Today* (Los Angeles, CA: Trend Books, [1958]), 42.

**Figure 3.4.** Dave Brubeck on *TIME* magazine cover, 1954. Artist: Boris Artzybasheff © TIME.

that any of *Time*'s writers would have used the phrase "all-American boy" to describe the other performers discussed in this chapter. As Ingrid Monson writes, "The *Time* magazine article was racially coded. . . . Brubeck's popularity with college students across the country seemed to promise a jazz that would be more upscale, less interested in social protest, and whiter."[74]

Another of the primary differences in visibility between Brubeck and Armstrong, Ellington, and Monk is in the depiction of the gaze on these *Time* covers. Artzybasheff's portrayal makes it impossible to see this image without seeing Brubeck, confronting him just as Harris was forced to do in writing his article (Fig. 3.4). Brubeck stares straight out of the image, his brow slightly furrowed. His black shirt and the disembodied white hands and instruments framing him draw attention to his face; his eyes are the focal point of the image. As the only musician whose gaze can be met by the viewer, Brubeck represents the difference between white and Black subjects. If, as Ellison and Butler argue, true visibility is only reached through *mutual* recognition, Brubeck attained greater visibility by fulfilling this role of the stereotypical white man—a man whose gaze *Time*'s audience could feel comfortable enough to meet.

Judith Butler's definition of "recognition" requires an engagement between parties, in which both parties receive acceptance while maintaining their

[74] Monson, *Freedom Sounds*, 94.

differences. Brubeck's outward gaze forces the audience's engagement. Unlike when they view the portrayals of Black jazzmen, the audience cannot simply gaze *at* Brubeck; they must instead *meet* Brubeck's outward gaze. By staring back, Brubeck obtains power in a move that cultural historian Benjamin Cawthra notes would have "spelled trouble for black males."[75] Only three African Americans featured on the cover of *Time* magazine between 1949 and 1964 were depicted as staring directly out of the frame as Brubeck does: Sugar Ray Robinson (1951), Althea Gibson (1957), and James Baldwin (1963). In contrast, white figures are portrayed looking in any number of directions, including directly out of the image, which reflects the greater number of representational options available to white subjects. Philosopher George Yancy writes that within the power of the white gaze, "only whites have the capacity of making valid moral judgments," for as bell hooks notes, "to look directly was an assertion of subjectivity, equality."[76] By depicting Black jazz musicians as not returning the viewer's gaze, *Time*'s illustrators pacified the anxiety their mid-century white viewers might have felt in looking at a Black man who returned their gaze.[77] Such control over the Black gaze was not new to the editors and illustrators of *Time* magazine; as hooks writes, "An effective strategy of white supremacist terror and dehumanization during slavery centered on white control of the black gaze."

*Time* editor Otto Fuerbringer highlighted the power implicit in his position as a white viewer when he wrote to illustrator Peter Hurd, describing his reaction to Ellington's cover: "I kept looking at it, seeing more and more nuances in his face, imagining more and more explosive expressions emanating from his mouth."[78] Fuerbringer, unencumbered by having to meet Ellington's gaze on the cover, was able to repeatedly survey the image, viewing every detail that Hurd painted. Furthermore, Fuerbringer "imagines" Ellington's behavior and speech from the image. In reality, however, Ellington was a sophisticated, mild-mannered performer, whose mouth would rarely emit the "explosive" expressions Fuerbringer imagined. Fuerbringer's comment to Hurd demonstrated his inability to truly see and hear Ellington beyond the stereotypes surrounding him. Ellington, like Armstrong and Monk, remained nothing more than a figment of the *Time* imagination, while Brubeck was able to break away

---

[75] Cawthra, *Blue Notes*, 155.
[76] George Yancy, "Walking While Black," *New York Times*, September 1, 2013, 4; bell hooks, "Representing Whiteness in the Black Imagination," in *Displacing Whiteness: Essays in Social and Cultural Criticism*, ed. Ruth Frankenberg (Durham, NC: Duke University Press, 1997), 168.
[77] Catherine A. Lutz and Jane L. Collins, *Reading National Geographic* (Chicago: University of Chicago Press, 1993), 190.
[78] Fuerbringer qtd. in Charles Waters, "Anatomy of a Cover: The Story of Duke Ellington's Appearance on the Cover of *Time* Magazine," *Annual Review of Jazz Studies* 6 (1993), 23.

from stereotypical portrayals of mid-century jazz musicians and become visible to *Time*'s audience. Essentially, his visibility afforded him a greater range of believable representations—which *could* include white musicians aspiring to blackness (i.e., Norman Mailer or Mezz Mezzrow), but which did not have to.

By denying the gaze of notable Black figures featured on *Time*'s cover, the editors and artists at *Time* magazine became part of what hooks describes as a system of white supremacy that "cultivated the practice of denying the subjectivity of Blacks (the better to dehumanize and oppress), of relegating them to the realm of the invisible."[79] In other words, while Armstrong, Ellington, and Monk were made visible by *Time*'s cover, *Time*'s control of these musicians' gaze and depictions denied each the individual subjectivity Brubeck received, rendering them invisible. Ultimately, it was the invisibility of whiteness—the refusal to recognize it—that made Brubeck visible—recognizable—as human.

## Brubeck's "New" Audience and Recognition

A deeply felt recognition between audience and performer, relying on responsibility to one another, was crucial to Brubeck's musical approach. He explained to Gene Lees in 1961,

> There's a certain trust that you try to get from an audience, and you want to get it as soon as possible—making them know that you're not going to bore them, that you are capable, that you are a good group. Because once they trust you, you can do anything.[80]

Brubeck's emphasis on trust can be understood through Julie Dawn Smith and Ellen Waterman's concept of "listening trust," which they define as "a pact among performers and listeners that they will listen and be listened to, an agreement to engage in an 'empathetic communication across time' and to employ an 'ethics of respect' for the performative journey with which and in which they engage."[81] In other words, "listening trust" is a kind of aural recognition, requiring mutual respect and empathy in the listening process. Brubeck's ability to facilitate recognition among his audiences—particularly

---

[79] hooks, "Representing Whiteness," 158.
[80] Gene Lees, "About This Man Brubeck... Part 2," *Down Beat*, July 20, 1961, 17.
[81] Julie Dawn Smith and Ellen Waterman, "Listening Trust: The Everyday Politics of George Lewis's 'Dream Team,'" *People Get Ready: The Future of Jazz Is Now!*, ed. Ajay Heble and Rob Wallace (Durham, NC: Duke University Press, 2013), 84–85.

among white, suburban audiences who were not primarily jazz listeners—was undoubtedly aided by his public image as a "serious" performer. Brubeck's mass media image was in large part based on his ability to bring "respectability" to jazz and his fulfillment of heteronormative ideals of white, educated, upper-middle class masculinity—an image in which Brubeck's *Time* and *Vogue* audience saw themselves reflected. This was a crucial element of white audiences' willingness to recognize Brubeck.

Brubeck also believed that an ideal musical performance was one in which the audience feels with the performer, and this was a similarly crucial part of his relationship with mainstream audiences in particular. In 1954 Brubeck explained what it meant to become one with his audience in a listening community, stating, "When I'm playing my best I can feel the audience going with me."[82] Brubeck continued in greater detail, illustrating what he meant when he said he could "feel the audience":

> It's almost like a ritual and sometimes the audience and ourselves get into a frenzy. I get myself involved in a tough spot in improvisation.... I don't know how I'm going to get out of it... probably the audience doesn't.... I can feel the tension in the audience, and the relief, the release at the end when I finally work my way out.

Brubeck's statement highlights two important ways in which Brubeck distinguished his performances from those in the European classical art music discourse. First, Brubeck's description was based in movement, imagined in part in primitivist terms, such as "frenzy" and "ritual." Brubeck believed that audience participation, particularly participation through dance, was ideal to creating "good jazz": "The sense of participation [jazz] offers to audience as well as performer is the most important thing about [jazz]. It still is an art. It's still folk music. But I think it should be danced to, as well as heard, and we should go back to that."[83]

Second, Brubeck's image of his ideal jazz performance captured the beginnings of the breakdown of the hierarchical division between performer and listener. Rather than treat the audience, performer, and composer as distinct elements, capable of being removed from the artwork, Brubeck argued that it was in the mutual relationship between audience and performer that works of art were composed—a relationship in which each member maintained a distinct identity, and one did not collapse into the another. In doing so, Brubeck upended a power structure that would have held him, as

[82] John Wm. Riley, "Brubeck's Key to Jazz: Improvise, Let Audience In," *Boston Globe*, January 21, 1954.
[83] Riley, "Brubeck's Key to Jazz."

composer/performer, as having power over his audience. Such a move may have invited his audience to use their commercial power to support their recognition of each other.

Finally, Brubeck demonstrated a certain responsibility for his audiences' musical experience, thereby further facilitating recognition with his audiences. In 1962, Iola Brubeck expanded on Dave Brubeck's approach to feeling with his audience, writing, "There is an *art* in *capturing* the imagination of the public [original emphasis]."[84] According to Iola Brubeck, Dave Brubeck's original and best promoter, his approach to jazz was in understanding the audience as a community of listeners. She reiterated Dave Brubeck's earlier statements, "If the artist performs his best, out of love for his art, and for those who perform and receive it, an audience *will be reached*," further specifying that the audience is reached on an emotional level—specifically, love. Together, the Brubecks made known that the audience played an important role; as Iola wrote, "There is an *art* to approaching music and people with respect and dignity [original emphasis]." Love, dignity, and respect for every member of the audience was necessary for the Brubecks' creation of a listening community, and further, for mutual recognition between audience and performer.

## Commercial Success and Jazz Distress

Brubeck's recognition by the mainstream juggernaut *Time* magazine may have offered him recognition from mainstream audiences, but it also alienated him from the jazz press, who chafed at the idea that Brubeck, a relatively new arrival to the jazz scene in 1954, had landed on *Time*'s cover before others who had paid their dues and who tended not to appreciate the "new" audiences Brubeck attracted to jazz—audiences many critics believed lacked the ability to put prejudice aside and listen to Black jazz musicians. Importantly, Brubeck also believed that he had appeared on *Time* too soon, explaining his own mortification when, while on tour with Duke Ellington, Ellington delivered an issue of Brubeck's *Time* cover to Brubeck's hotel room: "It was the worst and the best moment possible, all mixed up, because I didn't want to have my story come first. I was so hoping that they would do Duke first, because I idolized him. He was so much more important than I was. . . . [H]e deserved to be first."[85]

---

[84] Iola Brubeck, "The Significance of Dave Brubeck," *Crescendo*, November 1962, 3.
[85] "PBS: Rediscovering Dave Brubeck with Hedrick Smith," originally broadcast on December 16, 2001, http://www.pbs.org/brubeck/theMan/classicBrubeckQuartet.htm, accessed June 22, 2020.

In 1955, jazz critic Nat Hentoff excoriated the mainstream press and intellectuals whom he felt had not only neglected jazz but, driven by their racial prejudice, were now solely interested in the music of white jazz musicians like Brubeck. According to Hentoff, mainstream presses, and their mainstream audiences by extension, typically gave jazz little attention, but when they did, "the newspapers and wire services are indeed quick to use the handy caricatures of the jazz musician in their leads if a jazzman ever does get into trouble, but their writers have neither knowledge of nor respect for jazz."[86] Hentoff went on to criticize white intellectuals, whose interest in jazz he believed was entirely motivated out of racial fear: "Our intellectuals are still largely ambivalent toward the Negro creator in our society.... It [intellectuals' guilt and fear] frequently exists not only in the intellectuals' relationship to jazz, but also in their daily relationship with Negroes."

For Hentoff, Brubeck's appearance on *Time*'s cover was perhaps the best example of the media's eagerness to participate in what Hentoff believed to be an inauthentic form of jazz. He juxtaposed bebop alto saxophonist Charlie Parker, who had passed away just months earlier and whom many in the jazz press considered to be under-appreciated by audiences outside jazz, with Brubeck, opining that "Parker, the most important modern jazz influence in many years, was ignored when *Time* finally decided to 'recognize' jazz. *Time*, instead, gave its cover story to Dave Brubeck, a highly individualized modern jazz pianist of considerable resources but at some distance from Parker's jazz attainments." By noting Brubeck's individuality and resources, Hentoff distanced the pianist from the narratives of authentic jazz occupied by Parker. Further, Hentoff's sneer quotes suggest that he did not believe that the recognition jazz received through Brubeck's appearance on *Time*'s cover was meaningful to the broader field of jazz. For Hentoff, *Time*'s inability to recognize jazz as performed by a Black jazz musician like Parker demonstrated that "the concept of an American Negro musical innovator of Parker's freshness, originality, and complex power was quite beyond the knowledge or imagination of *Time*'s music editor—as it is beyond the ken of most American intellectuals."

Parker, a prominent representative of bebop, could not be recognized by the audience of *Time* magazine; for that audience to have recognized Parker would have required them to view him beyond the stereotypes of bebop musicians that were well entrenched by 1954. Indeed, some of the founding tenets of bebop—that it was virtuosically complex, that musicians not make overt efforts to appeal to audiences—and the characteristics by which bebop

---

[86] Nat Hentoff, "Jazz and the Intellectuals: Somebody Goofed," *Chicago Review* 9, no. 3 (Fall 1955): 114.

musicians were described—as Monson describes, "their unorthodox clothing, their refusal to speak in mainstream English to mixed crowds, and their refusal to play at mainstream dance tempos"—were an often mindfully direct contradiction to the *Time* audience.[87] As Dizzy Gillespie would come to acknowledge, though such stereotypes created publicity bebop musicians were initially glad to receive, he eventually "found it disturbing to have modern jazz musicians and their followers characterized in a way that was often sinister and downright vicious.... I wondered whether all the 'weird' publicity actually drew some of these way-out elements to us and did the music more harm than good."[88] That many bebop musicians claimed bebop as a particularly Black genre that reclaimed jazz from Swing's commercialized clutches made the relationship between blackness, bebop stereotypes, and lack of recognition all too clear. In other words, though beboppers like Parker gained publicity, or a kind of visibility from white mainstream audiences, they, like Armstrong and Ellington, were not recognized beyond the stereotypes that defined Black musicians at mid-century.

## "Commercial Is Not a Bad Word..."

While Brubeck's placement in magazines such as *Vogue* and *Good Housekeeping*, in lipstick advertisements, and in venues of higher education may have been somewhat unusual for mid-century jazz musicians, it was not unheard of. Nevertheless, critics and Brubeck seemed convinced that Brubeck, his image and his music, could create interest in jazz among a wider (whiter) population to an extent that other jazz musicians had thus far not attained. Ultimately, the difference lay in the ability of Brubeck's mainstream audience to see him beyond stereotypes, allowing a mutual relationship to develop in which audience and performer recognize one another. Brubeck facilitated this recognition by breaking down typical hierarchical divisions between performer and audience, and communicating the role of the audience in his performances.

However, such a relationship was inaccessible to popular Black jazz musicians at mid-century, who remained defined by primitivist stereotypes that reflected the lack of responsibility *Time* felt toward Black musicians. Though Brubeck, as a white man, could be looked on by white audiences and

---

[87] Ingrid Monson, "The Problem with White Hipness: Race, Gender, and Cultural Conceptions in Jazz Historical Discourse," *Journal of the American Musicological Society* 48, no. 3 (Autumn, 1995): 411.
[88] Gillespie, *To Be Or Not to... Bop*, 278.

look back, recognition between Armstrong, Ellington, or Monk and their audiences, a relationship in which a white audience would gaze at a Black musician, *and he would gaze back*, threatened to challenge societal norms that formed the basis of power structures in the United States at mid-century.

Brubeck's visibility and success with predominantly white mainstream audiences ultimately made him a target for jazz critics and musicians, who maintained that jazz was a place for those who remained outside the broader society (who, as Ellison explained, were "nowhere").[89] If Brubeck had found recognition in society, they must have wondered, how could he still claim a place in a genre they considered to be a liminal space, a space considered to be for musicians who could not receive recognition elsewhere? In all likelihood, Brubeck's ability to be recognized by his audience was to some degree part of an effective promotional strategy that understood Brubeck's whiteness and his "serious" approach to music as having commercial value with an apparently untapped mainstream audience. As Brubeck told Larry King in 1964, "Commercial is not a bad word. . . . Commercial meaning that people would like to hear it."[90] His appearances in mainstream advertisements and features allowed this "new" audience to envision a place for themselves within the field of jazz performance. They now possessed a sense of belonging in a musical genre that had formerly been reduced to stereotypical images, and in which they could not, and indeed would not, see themselves reflected in jazz's mostly Black performers. And Brubeck, too, could find a place among an audience demographic that Ellison argues frequently left Black Americans in a state of invisibility, carefully stepping around the sleepers and dreamers.

But in doing so, *Time* contributed to the construction of whiteness as invisible that resulted in both the hyper visibility of blackness and the invisibility of Black individuals, a legacy that continues to be fought today. In his 2015 *Between the World and Me*, Ta-Nehisi Coates connected the 1960s civil rights movement to protests for social justice in the wake of Michael Brown's killing, writing, "Perhaps that was, is, the hope of the movement: to awaken the Dreamers, to rouse them to the facts of what their need to be white, to talk like they are white, to think that they are white, which is to think that they are beyond the design flaws of humanity, has done to the world."[91]

---

[89] Ralph Ellison, "Harlem Is Nowhere," in *Shadow and Act* (1964; repr., New York: Vintage International, 1995), 297.
[90] Dave Brubeck, interview with Larry King, *Larry King Show* WIOD, February 6, 1964. Brubeck Collection, Wilton Library, Wilton, CT.
[91] Ta-Nehisi Coates, *Between the World and Me* (New York: Spiegel and Grau, 2015), 146.

## Conclusion

Did Brubeck recognize his own whiteness? If recognition of another person is a process of mutual, active engagement, in which each is seen, understood, and responsible to the other, recognition of whiteness is likewise a process of active engagement, in which whiteness is seen, its privileges understood, and the viewer becomes responsible for their whiteness. As with Ellison's *Invisible Man*, recognition of whiteness disrupts its invisibility, revealing inequalities and privileges based in race.

When he appeared on *Time*'s cover, Brubeck had not yet had that moment of encounter with his own racial experience—his whiteness and all its privileges and benefits were invisible to him, even as they grew increasingly visible to many Black musicians and to some members of the jazz press. By the mid-1950s, Brubeck continued to maintain the colorblind, meritocracy-oriented approach that had informed his 1950 *Down Beat* column describing the evolution of jazz as having been inspired by the "uprooting" and "transplanting" of both Africans and Europeans to a new continent (see chapter 1).[92] However, Brubeck's platform had changed significantly: since his cover feature on *Time* magazine, Brubeck had not only expanded his white audience, but he had also begun to be criticized by jazz critics who were dismayed that Brubeck, a white pianist at the beginning of his career, had been featured on *Time* before musicians such as Duke Ellington and Charlie Parker, and they suggested that Brubeck's success was at least in part a result of his whiteness. In response to such critiques, and even though he himself wished Ellington had appeared on *Time* magazine first, Brubeck resorted to a version of grievance politics. Despite attempts by critics such as Leonard Feather to explain how Brubeck's whiteness benefited him, Brubeck continued to highlight the ways in which the field of jazz performance was challenging to break into for everyone, regardless of race. He opined to a *Down Beat* critic, "And they say 'Brubeck never struggled.' Never struggled? They should have seen me in 1946—living in a one-room apartment in a housing project. Do the critics think all of this came easy?"[93] Brubeck's comments, which were rooted in several years' worth of financial hardship as he launched his career in the Bay Area, reveal the extent to which his colorblind and meritocratic musical beliefs extended from a perspective in which empathy, too, could be blind to color.

---

[92] Dave Brubeck, "Jazz' Evolvement as Art Form," *Down Beat*, January 27, 1950, 12.
[93] Don Freeman, "Dave Brubeck Answers His Critics: A Lot of Them Are Being Unfair, Insists Jazz' Controversial Pianist," *Down Beat*, August 10, 1955, 7.

However, Brubeck's approach shifted in 1958, four years after his *Time* cover. Before that year, Brubeck had engaged in very little of what could be called early civil rights activism. But in January 1958 Brubeck made a change to his quartet's personnel that would have a lasting impact on Brubeck's involvement. The Brubeck quartet was about to embark on a United States State Department–sponsored tour of several of the countries bordering the Iron Curtain. White bassist Norman Bates quit the quartet, wanting to stay in California with his family. To replace him, Brubeck hired Black bassist Eugene Wright in January 1958 to prepare for the quartet's trip in March. Though Brubeck had performed with Black bassists before, including Wyatt "Bull" Ruther, Freddie Dutton, and Joe Benjamin, he had not, as a well-known entity, toured extensively with an interracial quartet.[94] The night before the quartet departed for the State Department tour, they were scheduled to perform at East Carolina College (now East Carolina University); however, as I document in more detail in chapter 4, a policy forbidding integrated performing groups very nearly prevented the performance from taking place. This moment was one of the first in which racism had a clear and direct impact on Brubeck and his quartet, and his incredulity at both the incident and its timing was clear in his later reflections to Ralph Gleason: "The next morning we were to leave for Europe sponsored by the State Department to represent this country and one of the best things we could do was to show that prejudice was not everywhere in the United States, as we were a mixed group. And they [East Carolina College] wanted to do this to us the night before!"[95]

Brubeck's State Department tour is one of the most well-documented periods of his career. The Quartet began with a European tour before traveling to Poland, Turkey, India, Sri Lanka, Bangladesh, Pakistan, Afghanistan, Iran, and Iraq—a literal ring around the Iron Curtain. As Penny von Eschen documents, the tour was chaotic, the band members' health was compromised on more than one occasion, and the Quartet was often not told of the delicate

---

[94] While it may be easy to assume that the US State Department specifically chose the Brubeck Quartet because it was interracial, in order to counter Russian propaganda about American racism, this actually was not the case. As Stephen Crist notes, one of the appeals of the Brubeck Quartet for the State Department was the fact that State Department officials believed the group was all white. The Quartet was not intended to promote an image of interracial equality to confront Russian propaganda about American racism, but rather was meant to sidestep the issue of race altogether. Communications between Czechoslovakia and Secretary of State John Foster Dulles include the following telegram: "for U.S. purposes white jazz group preferable, as this side-steps regime propaganda linking jazz to oppression [of] Negroes in America." So although other jazz groups, like Dizzy Gillespie's band, had been sent abroad specifically to show America's so-called progressive racial attitude, this was never the intent for the Brubeck Quartet. Department of State, Prague, incoming telegram, #279, to Secretary of State, November 7, 1957; General Records of the Department of State, Record Group 59, as quoted in Stephen Crist, "Jazz as Democracy? Dave Brubeck and Cold War Politics," *Journal of Musicology* 26, no. 2 (Spring 2009): 149.

[95] Ralph Gleason, "Brubeck Cancels South Africa Because of Negro Artist Ban," *Daily Boston Globe*, October 19, 1958, 61.

political circumstances in which they were placed.[96] Nevertheless, Brubeck would later insist that this tour was among the most rewarding experiences of his life, in large part due to the opportunities he had to perform with musicians from each country he visited.

Others have noted the important musical changes to the quartet after the tour, primarily through Brubeck and Morello's increased experiments with meter and rhythm on the resulting album *Time Out* (1959), and on the album *Jazz Impressions of Eurasia* (1958).[97] But I argue that the tour also resulted in a change in what Brubeck considered to be his place within the broader world of musicking. Immediately following the tour, Brubeck tempered his focus on counterpoint and the complexities of European harmony and melody over "primitive" rhythms, and walked away from comments positioning music as a universal language. As he elaborated in a 1961 interview with Walter Cronkite,

Walter Cronkite: Is music an international language?

Dave Brubeck: Well, I *know* it's not an international language. I left on this State Department tour thinking that it was, and I became educated in the middle of India when I played for two hours to an audience that had absolutely no response for this. There was no communication. This is when you'll know for sure that music is not an international language. But what I did learn on this tour—that rhythm is an international language. Not harmony and melody, but rhythm. Maybe the thing that binds humanity together is the heartbeat. And it might be the one pulse, the thing in life that binds all of us together.[98]

In this interview, recorded several years after the fact, Brubeck returns to the State Department tour as an impactful musical moment of revelation: no longer did he believe that harmony and melody were the locus of musical development and complexity, and nor was rhythm primarily primitive. Through encounters abroad, and importantly, with non-white audiences and musicians, Brubeck learned enough about diverse musical systems through the tour's real and meaningful opportunities for cultural exchange

---

[96] Penny von Eschen, *Satchmo Blows Up the World: Jazz Ambassadors Play the Cold War* (Cambridge, MA: Harvard University Press, 2004). See also Stephen Crist, "Jazz as Democracy? Dave Brubeck and Cold War Politics," *Journal of Musicology* 26 (2009), 133–174; Keith Hatschek, "The Impact of American Jazz Diplomacy in Poland During the Cold War," *Jazz Perspectives* 4, no. 3 (2010), 253–300; Ilse Storb, *Dave Brubeck: Improvisations and Compositions—The Idea of Cultural Exchange* (New York: Peter Lang, 1994).

[97] Stephen A. Crist, *Dave Brubeck's* Time Out (Oxford: Oxford University Press, 2019).

[98] Dave Brubeck, interviewed by Walter Cronkite, "The Jazz of Dave Brubeck," on *The Twentieth Century*, CBS (August 15, 1961).

to understand that each musical tradition had complex and differing musical priorities worth respecting.

A shift in his approach to musical systems prompted Brubeck's further rhythmic and meter experimentations for which he would ultimately become primarily known. For example, Brubeck's "Blue Rondo à la Turk" was built on a metrical division of 2 + 2 + 2 + 3, stemming from the Turkish aksak, a rhythmic system that juxtaposes binary and ternary cells. Decades later, he explained that he had heard street musicians playing the aksak. He pressed them on the rhythm, and as they played, he observed that, "boy, this is a rhythm that really works. . . . So I put a melody to the rhythm and called it 'Blue Rondo à la Turk.'"[99] These musical changes, which would come to define Brubeck's career, were based on Brubeck's overriding priority in performance, which was to engage *with his audiences* in the act of performing. For example, he explained in 1953 that he considered "the audience as important a fact as the guys on the stand," and in 1955 that "a musician needs people—he needs the spark only an audience can give him." He believed that the audience was as important in the musical process as the performers, and his goal in performance was to gain the audience's trust, "because once they trust you, you can do anything."[100] As Brubeck explained to Cronkite, an unresponsive audience hindered the effectiveness of his performances during the State Department tour. In other words, Brubeck extended the same expectations he gave to his audiences at home, Black and white, and received a different response on his tour abroad. In finding new ways of communicating with diverse audiences and in motivating them to respond to him musically, Brubeck's musical beliefs changed, making room for new priorities and ways of experiencing music that could be equal to his own.

In an interview with white critic Ralph Gleason several months after the tour, Brubeck explained the effect his 1958 State Department tour of the Iron Curtain had had on his understanding of racial prejudice as detrimental to American foreign interests within a Cold War context: "Prejudice is indescribable. To me, it is the reason we would lose the world. I have been through Asia and India and the Middle East and we have to realize how many brown-skinned people there are in this world. Prejudice here or in South Africa is setting up our world for one terrible let down."[101] For Brubeck, it was not

---

[99] Dave Brubeck, "A Long Partnership in Life and Music," an oral history conducted in 1999 and 2001 by Caroline C. Crawford, Regional Oral History Office, Bancroft Library, University of California, Berkeley, 2006; February 17, 1999, interview, p. 55. In Crist, *Dave Brubeck's* Time Out.

[100] Gene Lees, "About This Man Brubeck . . . Part 2," *Down Beat*, July 20, 1961, 17.

[101] Ralph Gleason, "Brubeck Cancels South Africa Because of Negro Artist Ban," *Daily Boston Globe*, October 19, 1958, 61.

just his encounter with different musical systems but his interactions with audiences and performers of color. He and Iola Brubeck (along with other jazz ambassadors like Dizzy Gillespie and Louis Armstrong) describe receiving a lot of criticism of and questions about American racial injustice throughout their tour. While abroad, Brubeck struggled to justify his unflappable, Cold War–based belief in the values and principles of American democracy—an American democracy that simultaneously subjugated non-white peoples in his own country; his recognition of his international audiences, of their musical experiences, ultimately amplified their experiences with racism, rendering both them and Brubeck's whiteness visible.

But Brubeck's story of recognition offers one last lesson: that recognition of whiteness alone cannot reveal white privilege and white supremacy. For that, white people must also recognize people of color. Brubeck's responsibility as a cultural diplomat facilitated some of this deep, true recognition. Following his tour, Brubeck recognized his responsibility to audiences of color at home and abroad, and, as I discuss in chapter 4, he became responsible for Eugene Wright. Wright's presence in the quartet coincided with the rise of strictly enforced segregationist policies across the American South and would ultimately nudge Brubeck from his colorblind dream. Once awakened, Brubeck began to confront race and racism in the public sphere, using his whiteness as a tool to both attract southern audiences (another "new" audience) and dismantle segregation across the South.

For Brubeck, as for many white Americans, whiteness did not become visible easily or quickly—there was no one moment that catalyzed his shift away from musical colorblindness, and indeed, though he no longer held music to a universal harmonic ideal, his racial colorblindness was more challenging to disengage.[102] He altered his original view of jazz as equally white and Black to acknowledge its roots in Black American musical culture, explaining in a February 1964 *Playboy* Summit that jazz began as "the expression of the American Negro." Even so, he also maintained in a June 1964 *Crescendo* interview that "jazz is essentially *European*," and that Black contributions to jazz were based more in the "spirit" of jazz than a particular musical contribution.[103] It took sustained contact, repeated encounters, and continued labor,

---

[102] In a *New York Times* article he wrote on his return from the State Department tour, Brubeck proclaimed, "Jazz is colorblind," explaining that when audiences around the world saw his integrated quartet performing together, "a lot of the bad taste of Little Rock is apt to be washed from [the audiences'] mouth." Dave Brubeck, "The Beat Heard 'Round the World," *New York Times*, June 15, 1958, SM14.

[103] Dave Brubeck, in "A Jazz Summit Meeting," in *Keeping Time: Readings in Jazz History*, ed. Robert Walser (Oxford: Oxford University Press, 2014), 244. Quoted from "The Playboy Panel: Jazz—Today and Tomorrow," *Playboy*, February 1964, 29–31, 34–38, 56, 58, 139–41; Les Tomkins, "Jazz? It's as Much European as African, Claims Dave Brubeck," *Crescendo*, February 1964, 18.

and still, Brubeck could easily revert to colorblind rhetoric depending on the situation. But for many listeners over the past sixty years, Brubeck's experience sharing responsibility and empathy across color lines, and putting aside privilege in exchange for recognition of others, would ultimately result in one of jazz's most enduring and popular records: *Time Out* (1959).

# 4
# "We Want to Play in the South"
## Brubeck's Southern Strategy

In January 1960, Brubeck made headlines after twenty-two colleges and universities across the American South refused to allow his interracial quartet to perform.[1] Initially, eleven of the schools backed out of their contracts with Brubeck on learning that he and two other white musicians, saxophonist Paul Desmond and drummer Joe Morello, would be performing with African American bassist Eugene Wright, who had joined the quartet two years earlier, in 1958. After Brubeck informed the remaining fourteen schools of Wright's presence in his quartet, eleven more insisted Brubeck replace Wright with a white bassist, leaving only three willing to allow the integrated combo to perform (The University of the South, Sewanee, Tennessee; Vanderbilt University, Nashville, Tennessee; and Jacksonville University, Jacksonville, Florida). Brubeck refused to replace Wright, foregoing the $40,000 in revenue (worth over $400,000 today) he would have received had he instead performed with a white bassist. Representatives of the various schools insisted, one after the other, that their cancelations of Brubeck's contracts were not based in prejudice, but on principle and policy. For the schools and their administrators, Brubeck broke his contract; for Brubeck, contracts requiring segregation had no legal or moral basis.[2]

Taken together, these cancelations became a defining moment in Brubeck's career. Jazz and entertainment newspapers, such as *Down Beat* and *Variety*, and Black newspapers, including the *New York Amsterdam News*, *Pittsburgh Courier*, *Baltimore Afro-American*, *Los Angeles Sentinel*, and *Chicago Daily Defender*, covered the event extensively, and nearly all positioned Brubeck as a kind of civil rights hero.[3] After his death, many of Brubeck's obituaries

---

[1] Portions of this chapter previously appeared as Kelsey A. K. Klotz, "Dave Brubeck's Southern Strategy," *Dædalus* 148, no. 2, special issue "Jazz Still Matters," ed. Ingrid Monson and Gerald Early (Spring 2019): 52–66. Reproduced here with the permission of MIT Press.

[2] Ralph J. Gleason, "An Appeal from Dave Brubeck," *Down Beat*, February 18, 1960, 12–13.

[3] One exception was Norman Granz, who, as founder of Jazz at the Philharmonic, had been canceling concerts at venues with segregated audiences since the 1940s. For Granz, Brubeck's insistence on performing in an integrated ensemble had not gone far enough—by 1960, Brubeck should have insisted that the audiences be integrated. Norman Granz, "The Brubeck Stand: Divergent View by Norman Granz," *Down Beat*, July 21, 1960, 24; Ingrid Monson, *Freedom Sounds: Civil Rights Call Out to Jazz and Africa* (Oxford: Oxford University Press, 2007), 63–64.

remembered him as having stood up for civil rights when he refused to replace Wright in the segregated South. Combined with his work in the Wolf Pack (an integrated World War II army band), refusal to play segregated audience venues, performances with Black musicians prior to Eugene Wright, performances at concerts benefiting civil rights organizations, composition of the musical *The Real Ambassadors* (1962), and willingness to face race-based hate in southern performances, the 1960 tour cancelation marks one big moment among others in which Brubeck worked toward racial justice at mid-century.

By his 1960 southern tour, Brubeck had long been considered a "respectable" jazz musician—a racially coded term indicating that he was an acceptable choice for college campuses and concert halls and could bring "new" (i.e., white) audiences to jazz. In addition to his media image, critics and audiences also closely linked his sound to sonic signifiers of whiteness. Critics and audiences were simply more likely to accept Brubeck as an intellectual, to accept his music as "cerebral," to view him as having credentials within the sphere of classical music, and to consider him as respectable because he was white. This facilitated his entrance to spaces (including colleges around the country and segregated institutions in the South) and audiences to which, as a jazz musician, he otherwise might not have had access. However, the same relationship to "respectability" and intellect that came with Brubeck's whiteness may have also had the side effect of making his protest all the more surprising to southern universities and their administrators.

Brubeck began quietly engaging with early civil rights–era protests before the 1960 tour. Eventually, he began to leverage his whiteness to support integration efforts, even as he continued to benefit from a racial capitalist system that privileged his voice over those for whom he advocated. While Brubeck has been hailed as a civil-rights advocate simply for refusing to appear without Wright, his activism also inspired him to adopt a new musical and promotional strategy that married commercial interest with political ideology. Still, Brubeck's story also shares similarities with other "white heroes" of jazz (e.g., Benny Goodman, who performed in an integrated combo in 1936 and integrated his band with the addition of Lionel Hampton in 1938; Artie Shaw, who toured with an integrated band in the 1940s; and Norman Granz, who refused to perform in venues with segregated audiences with his Jazz at the Philharmonic). As jazz scholar Reva Marin explains, "While many white jazz musicians, including the leading white bandleaders of the Swing Era—Benny Goodman, Artie Shaw, and Charlie Barnet—took important steps when they integrated their bands and initiated interracial recording sessions and public performances, they had established sufficient leverage in the music world when they did so to withstand any serious backlash against their actions."[4] Put differently, white bandleaders, even when well-meaning, often were ultimately blind to racial politics, power dynamics, and broader systems of white supremacy, and their careers, images, and legacies were the ultimate beneficiaries of their decisions to advocate racial justice through incremental change.

## Brubeck Begins to Protest

## Dallas, Texas, 1957

By 1957, Brubeck, like many musicians, had made no public announcement or action against racial prejudice or segregation. The civil rights movement was just beginning to take root, spurred by the 1954 *Brown v. Board of Education* decision, which declared segregation in schools to be illegal; the 1955 murder of Emmett Till; and the 1955–56 Montgomery bus boycott. Many jazz musicians began engaging in the civil rights movement in response to the 1957 Little Rock integration crisis. On September 4, nine African American students attempted to enter the formerly all-white Little Rock Central High School; however, Arkansas governor Orval Faubus ordered the Arkansas National Guard to the high school to bar the students' entrance. It was not until September 23, when President Dwight D. Eisenhower federalized the Arkansas National Guard, thereby shifting their purpose from preventing to facilitating integration, that the students were allowed entrance.

While Louis Armstrong, Charles Mingus, and their supporters openly decried the Little Rock integration crisis, Brubeck mounted his own private protest, even as he maintained his public silence. On September 10, small regional papers around Texas began to report that he and white jazz impresario Norman Granz had canceled their upcoming concert dates at the State Fair Park auditorium in Dallas, Texas. Brubeck and his quartet were scheduled to perform on September 29, and Granz's Jazz at the Philharmonic was to perform on October 1. As Ingrid Monson explains, Granz had been canceling Jazz at the Philharmonic concert dates at segregated venues like the State Fair Park since the late 1940s, and according to newspaper reports, had canceled this date for that reason as well.[5]

---

[4] Reva Marin, *Outside and Inside: Race and Identity in White Jazz Autobiography* (Jackson: University of Mississippi, 2020), xxx.

[5] Monson, *Freedom Sounds*, 63–64. The Dallas State Fair Park was a site of frequent protest for Black activists fighting segregation on the grounds. In addition to the segregation of many of the rides and food establishments within the park, the State Fair held a "Negro Achievement Day," the only day when Black

But Brubeck neglected to explain why he canceled the date; all newspaper accounts simply write that "Brubeck sent word only that his mixed group would be unavailable"—an unusual statement, given that at that time, he was regularly performing with white bassist Norman Bates and would not begin performing with Wright until late January 1958.[6] Brubeck's cancelation of the date was mentioned only briefly in regional papers in Texas, Arizona, and southern California; major newspapers such as the *New York Times* and *Los Angeles Times* and Black newspapers including the *Chicago Defender*, *Daily Defender*, and *New York Amsterdam News* mention nothing about the concert. Brubeck's September 29 concert, whose cancelation was announced just one week after the beginning of the Little Rock crisis, is an unstudied moment in his performance history that reveals a nearly inaudible moment in his move toward race activism.

By all accounts, the reason for Brubeck's cancelation of this single concert was ambiguous—any publicly stated views on social justice and racial prejudice were nonexistent. However, a fan letter written to him a few weeks after the cancelation suggests that three years prior to his failed $40,000 tour of the South, Brubeck was already protesting segregation, however quietly. In the letter, dated October 22, 1957, Betty Jean Furgerson, a Black woman from Waterloo, Iowa, thanked him for canceling the Dallas concert "because of the policy of segregated seating."[7]

---

patrons could fully participate in the State Fair. Martin Herman Kuhlman, "The Civil Rights Movement in Texas: Desegregation of Public Accommodations, 1950–1964," PhD diss., Texas Tech University, 1994; Donald Payton, "Timeline: A Concise History: Black Dallas Since 1842," *D Magazine*, June 1998, accessed January 15, 2016, http://www.dmagazine.com/publications/d-magazine/1998/june/timeline-a-concise-history; Kathryn Siefker, "NAACP Youth Council Picket Line, 1955 Texas State Fair," *Bullock Texas State History Museum*, https://www.thestoryoftexas.com/discover/artifacts/naacp-state-fair-spotlight-012315.

[6] "Brubeck Cancels Dallas Booking," *Daily Journal*, Commerce, TX, September 10, 1957, 1; "Brubeck Band Cancels Out Dallas Date," *The Times*, San Mateo, CA, September 10, 1957, 17; "Jazz Combos Cancel Dallas Bookings," *Tucson Daily Citizen*, September 10, 1957, 5; "Jazz Groups Skip Trips over South," *Corsicana Daily Sun*, September 12, 1957, 4; "Jazz Concerts Cancelled over Racial Issue," *Galveston Daily News*, September 12, 1957, 21. Bassist Joe Benjamin began recording with the Brubeck Quartet in 1958.

[7] Personal Letter, B. J. Furgerson to Dave Brubeck, October 22, 1957, Brubeck Collection, Wilton Library, Wilton, CT. Quotations used by permission of the Furgerson family. Betty Jean (B. J.) Furgerson, born 1927, was the daughter of Lee Burton Furgerson, a doctor and active member of the NAACP, and Lily Furgerson, the first African American teacher in the Waterloo, Iowa, school district. In a 2006 oral history interview, Furgerson explained that her family frequently took trips to national NAACP conventions and met with high-ranking members such as Thurgood Marshall, Walter White, Roy Wilkins, and Mary McLeod Bethune. Furgerson graduated from Iowa State Teachers College (now the University of Northern Iowa) with a BA in secondary education, and earned her master's degree in social work from the University of Kansas in 1972. Beginning in 1974, Furgerson served as director of the Waterloo Human Rights Commission. She also served on the Legislative Higher Education Task Force and the Excellence in Education Task Force as well as the Regional Executive Council on Civil Rights; she was an original member of the Iowa Department of Education's Multicultural, Nonsexist Curriculum Committee (now called the Educational Equity Committee). In addition, she was a member of the Iowa State Board of Regents and served as president of the Iowa Public Broadcasting Board. In 1990, Furgerson was inducted into the Iowa Women's Hall of Fame, and in 2013, she was inducted into the Iowa African American Hall of Fame. She passed away in 2018.

Furgerson's relationship with Brubeck went beyond that of a simple fan who had once asked him for an autograph. Her family had close connections with members of the Duke Ellington orchestra, with whom Brubeck had toured, and frequently hosted jazz musicians in their home in the 1950s, feeding them and offering them relaxation.[8] As Furgerson later remembered, "I learned they came to those dinners because we only had family members other than band members. They knew they did not have to be on stage and/or talk or be the entertainment. They could relax!"[9] Iowa musician Roger Maxwell recalled meeting Brubeck at Furgerson's family's house in the 1950s, explaining, "It isn't everyday that you can walk into a friend's kitchen and see an internationally renowned musician sitting in a breakfast nook. Mrs. Furgerson greeted me and Betty Jean said, 'Roger, have you met Dave?'"[10] Even though Brubeck had not told the press why he canceled the concert, Furgerson's account connected his actions to a conversation the two had in the privacy of her family home. As she explained, "I know from talking with you that you have deep feelings about such practices."

Throughout her letter, Furgerson demonstrated remarkable empathy and charity toward southern segregationists, drawing on her own experiences and challenges to explain their seeming inability to abolish segregation. She wrote, "I deeply sympathize with those persons who are honestly struggling with their consciences to resolve their conflicts between practicing democratic ideals or maintaining regional beliefs and customs." Furgerson explained that, like southern segregationists, she was torn between acting as an individual and for the country: "I want to act as an individual and citizen in good conscience and not as part of a minority voting bloc." Furgerson clearly agonized

---

[8] Prior to the 1950s, the Furgerson family hosted well-known NAACP members and Mahalia Jackson. The Ellington Orchestra's frequent stops at the house were likely due in some part to policies of segregation and discrimination in the area. Even though Iowa passed one of the first state statutes banning discrimination in the 1880s, the statute was not enforced in the 1950s, and many restaurants, cafes, and hotels in Waterloo—one of the state's most segregated cities, then and now—denied service to Blacks and other minority citizens. Rebecca Furgerson Sloan, Betty Jean Furgerson's sister, recalled that her mother offered hospitality to famous Black travelers because of racism in the region, explaining that while their home never appeared in *The Green Book*, it could have in intent and frequency of guests. Bruce Fehn, "The Only Hope We Had: United Packinghouse Workers Local 46 and the Struggle for Racial Equality in Waterloo, Iowa, 1948–1960," *Annals of Iowa* 54, no. 3 (Summer 1995): 185–216; Kyle Munson, "Black Iowa: Waterloo Rallies to Combat Violence, Racial Divides," *Des Moines Register*, July 13, 2015, accessed November 28, 2015, http://dmreg.co/1IRVhIe; Theresa E. Shirey, "Common Patterns in an Uncommon Place: The Civil Rights Movement and Persistence of Racial Inequality in Waterloo, Iowa," Honors Project, Bowdoin College, 2014; Rebecca Furgerson Sloan, email message to author, January 26, 2021.

[9] Betty Jean Furgerson, "Jazz in Iowa: Betty Jean (BJ) Furgerson's Memories," *Iowa Public Television*, accessed October 31, 2015, site inactive on 18 April 2022, http://www.iptv.org/jazz/bj_furgerson.cfm.

[10] Roger Maxwell, "Jazz in Iowa: Backstage Conversations, Impressions & Remembrances, My Experiences with Popular & Jazz Artists," *Iowa Public Television*, accessed October 31, 2015, site inactive on 18 April 2022, http://www.iptv.org/jazz/backstage.cfm#brubeck.

over representing herself and her race: though she firmly believed it was the democratic duty of an American citizen to represent herself as an individual, she also believed it was her duty to vote for politicians supporting civil rights. She wrote of a "human family," across which lines should not be drawn to exclude certain groups; democracy, she explained, worked for the majority and the minority through consensus.

Furgerson's October 1957 letter, likely written one year after Brubeck had stood in her kitchen, is remarkable for its empathy and calm clarity, even as she negotiates the complexities of her feelings: "It seems I swing between feelings of great hope and deep bitterness. I am definitely angered. I may care and feel too deeply. I hope I never become calloused to the fate and well-being of my fellow humans. This would be a great wrong—indifferentness is a great evil."[11] Reading her letter alongside Brubeck's actions demonstrates the extent to which musical and political meaning was made at the level of the individual; that his cancelation was meaningful to Furgerson was enough for her, even if it was an underpublicized, ambiguous, or invisible act to most of the country. For Furgerson, it was an affirmation of what she had discussed with Brubeck at her mother's kitchen table. As she explained,

> All this is to thank you for acting like a decent, feeling human being. You can never know how much it means to me to know that there are people [who] react positively to injustices. Too many of us give lip service to it. It's much easier and less convenient and more comfortable. It is a terrible thing to have to deny people the beauty of your music because they fear unintelligently.

Furgerson's words speak to struggles for racial equality across the century, and in her final sentence, she links Brubeck's music, his live performances in particular, to a broader political effort to disrupt segregationist practices. Further, her letter offers an intimate view of some of the conversations in which Brubeck was involved in the early years of the civil rights movement.

As she wrote her letter, however, Furgerson did not know that at the same moment Brubeck seemed to be motivated by the events in Little Rock to oppose segregation, he was simultaneously advising restraint to one of Governor Faubus's most vocal opponents: Louis Armstrong, whose criticism of President Eisenhower (who he said had "no guts" and was "two-faced") and Governor Faubus (whom he referred to as an "uneducated plow boy")

---

[11] Personal Letter, B. J. Furgerson to Dave Brubeck, October 22, 1957, Brubeck Collection. Quotations used by permission of the Furgerson family.

made national news on September 19.[12] In the midst of the Little Rock crisis, Armstrong explained to an audience in Grand Forks, North Dakota, that "the way they are treating my people in the South, the government can go to hell."[13] When Armstrong's road manager, Pierre Tallerie, attempted to walk back his statements, Armstrong's reply was pointed: "I wouldn't take back a thing I've said. I've had a beautiful life over 40 years in music, but I feel the downtrodden situation the same as any other Negro.... Tallerie and no prejudiced newspaper can make me change it. What I've said is me." Such statements were particularly surprising to the Black press and perhaps to some of Armstrong's Black audiences; as the *Pittsburgh Courier* pointed out, "The Armstrong statements also shocked many of his critics who have long put him in the ranks of the 'Uncle Toms' because of his willingness to play before segregated audiences in the South."[14]

While many jazz musicians praised Armstrong for his strong stand, Brubeck apparently did not agree with the form of protest Armstrong chose to initiate. According to musicologist Stephen Crist, a letter to Brubeck written from Armstrong's white manager, Joe Glaser, who also performed a managing role for Brubeck, suggests that within one week of Armstrong's statements, Brubeck had rushed to write to Glaser to recommend Armstrong take a more moderate approach toward Little Rock. Glaser wrote on September 25,

> I appreciate the way you express yourself about Louis and I assure you Dave that Louis has already done exactly what you say he should as no doubt you have heard the various stories on the air and seen the press stories ... in sending Pres. Eisenhower a personal wire and I assure you I am going along with the thoughts that you have expressed.[15]

It is impossible to know exactly what Brubeck advised, but one day after Glaser wrote to Brubeck, Armstrong announced to Iowa audiences that "this is the greatest country," "things are looking a lot better than they did before," and Eisenhower's action was "just wonderful."[16] Further, Armstrong announced that he had sent Eisenhower a telegram, telling him, "If you decide to walk into the schools with the colored kids, take me along, daddy. God bless you."

---

[12] "Louis Armstrong, Barring Soviet Tour, Denounces Eisenhower and Gov. Faubus," *New York Times*, September 19, 1957, 23.

[13] "'I Won't Take Back a Thing I've Said!' 'Satchmo' Tells Off Ike, U.S.!" *Pittsburgh Courier*, September 28, 1957, 33.

[14] Ibid.

[15] Joe Glaser to Dave Brubeck, personal letter, September 25, 1957, Brubeck Collection; published in Stephen Crist, *Dave Brubeck's* Time Out (Oxford: Oxford University Press, 2019), 31–32.

[16] "Musician Backs Move: Armstrong Lauds Eisenhower for Little Rock Action," *New York Times*, September 26, 1957, 12.

Whether or not Glaser and Armstrong followed Brubeck's advice exactly, or if the pair had already made plans to walk back Armstrong's stronger statements, Glaser credits Brubeck with having Armstrong's best interests at heart.

As Crist writes, given the little evidence that exists pertaining to Armstrong's perspective, this is a challenging scene to understand—not least because by this point, Dave and Iola Brubeck had already begun drafting the musical *The Real Ambassadors*, which was ultimately a pointed critique of racial injustice that they wanted Armstrong to star in.[17] Based on the advice he appears to have given Armstrong, Brubeck's muted reaction to the Little Rock crisis seems to reflect what he believed to be the appropriate response by artists to political events at that time. However, Brubeck's typically colorblind outlook toward racial difference may have resulted in a blind spot: as Monson notes, Black critics and audiences expected much more political engagement from Black musicians than from white musicians, even when in many situations, white musicians faced less risk (both from violence and financial impact) in their political protests.[18] Armstrong in particular had frequently been criticized by the Black press for his reticence to object to racial injustice as well as his continued performances for segregated audience. Essentially, though Brubeck's silent method of protest worked for him, a white artist, it simply did not work for Black artists like Armstrong, a fact that neither Brubeck nor Glaser seemed to have recognized.

There is another reason Brubeck's Dallas protest may not have been what it seemed to Furgerson or to the papers that covered it. Although the announcement of Brubeck's cancelation at the segregated Dallas State Fair Park auditorium came just after the Little Rock Crisis began, and though Furgerson's letter clearly places Brubeck's decision to cancel within the context of protests about race and integration, records from the Brubeck Collection suggest a different series of events. Within the financial record of this story lies a mystery: not only is there no contract for a Dallas concert on September 29 (not in and of itself unusual, as the collection contains few unfulfilled contracts), but there is a fulfilled contract for a multi-day gig at the Red Hill Inn in Camden, New Jersey, a venue at which Brubeck performed frequently, for September 27, 28, and 29. The contract was signed July 11, 1957—two months before the Little Rock crisis began and two months before newspapers began to report

---

[17] The musical was recorded in late 1961, and performed live at the 1962 Monterey Jazz Festival. Keith Hatschek, *The Real Ambassadors: Dave and Iola Brubeck and Louis Armstrong Challenge Segregation* (Jackson: University Press of Mississippi, 2022).

[18] As Monson writes, "If in the mid-1940s playing with a mixed band was taken as a sign of a progressive racial attitude, by the mid-1950s a performer had to refuse to play to segregated audiences to meet the rising moral standards of the civil rights movement" (Monson, *Freedom Sounds*, 61).

Brubeck's Dallas cancelation for September 29. This suggests that if Brubeck had canceled the concert, he had likely done so well before the Little Rock episode. Regardless of when he canceled the concert, the timing of the announcement understandably gave the impression that Brubeck was part of a broader fight against segregation (and indeed, Brubeck would later refuse to perform at segregated performing venues). Further, the announcement signaled a potential and small move toward race activism—even if reality begs the question of whether or not Brubeck stood to benefit from announcing the cancelation when he did and if that benefit outweighed the support his subtle announcement lent to integration efforts. Indeed, the balance between Brubeck's career and security and his race activism would shift back and forth in the years to come.

## South Africa, 1958

With the arrival of Eugene Wright to the quartet in 1958, Brubeck's protests became significantly more direct by necessity. On October 19, 1958, jazz critic Ralph Gleason reported that Brubeck had turned down a tour of South Africa worth $17,000 (over $170,000 today) because the apartheid-era South African government would refuse to allow Eugene Wright to enter the country, let alone perform with the group. Gleason's article in the *Daily Boston Globe*, which was subsequently covered in the *Los Angeles Sentinel* and the *Philadelphia Tribune*, both Black newspapers, focused on an interview with Brubeck regarding the cancelation. In it, Brubeck explained the effect his 1958 State Department tour of the Iron Curtain had on his understanding of racial prejudice as detrimental to American foreign interests within a Cold War context: "Prejudice is indescribable. To me, it is the reason we would lose the world. I have been through Asia and India and the Middle East and we have to realize how many brown-skinned people there are in this world. Prejudice here or in South Africa is setting up our world for one terrible let down."[19] These words were later reprinted, without the explicit reference to South Africa, to explain why Brubeck had refused to appear without Wright in the South in 1960. Though Brubeck's cancelation of the South Africa tour was an explicit foreign policy message from a former US State Department–sponsored cultural ambassador, coverage was again nonexistent in mainstream papers like the *New York Times* and jazz magazines like *Down Beat*. In

---

[19] Ralph Gleason, "Brubeck Cancels South Africa Because of Negro Artist Ban," *Daily Boston Globe*, October 19, 1958, 61.

other words, Brubeck's comments, which reflect a particular concern with the responsibility white Americans had to act against racism in the United States, were directed largely toward white Americans, but primarily read by Black Americans.

Like the concert cancelation in Dallas, it is unclear how much of a plan for the Brubeck Quartet's potential tour of South Africa existed. On May 5, 1958, South African promoter L. M. Steinberg wrote to Brubeck to inquire about the possibility of a tour, which would pay $10,000 excluding expenses. Steinberg noted that the American musicians Bob Cooper, Bud Shank, June Christy, and the Claude Williamson Trio had "just completed a highly successful tour" of South Africa and that because Brubeck's name was particularly well-known among jazz fans, he anticipated that Brubeck's tour would be similarly successful.[20] Brubeck's manager, Mort Lewis, replied with great interest on June 10, providing a number of main points on which Brubeck insisted. In addition to inquiring about the locations for the performances (concerts or clubs) and potential dates, insisting on a minimum of $12,000 (excluding expenses), and outlining the expenses that would need to be paid for (including transportation), Lewis's first inquiry was about Wright. Lewis suggested that he was unfamiliar with South African laws, asking if there was any law prohibiting an integrated group from performing together.[21] According to Brubeck, the promoter responded, informing Lewis not only of an ordinance prohibiting integrated groups, but that Wright would not be allowed in the country at all, "and therefore the tour would have to be made without him."[22] In all likelihood, the potential for a South African tour lasted only three letters between Steinberg and Lewis. Nevertheless, Brubeck's decision to forgo a tour that would have excluded Wright both garnered him a sort of activist credential among many jazz and Black audiences and is an important precursor to the failed 1960 southern tour.

## East Carolina College, Greenville, North Carolina, 1958

While Brubeck's cancelation of the South African tour is notable, its coverage revealed an earlier near-cancelation of a Brubeck performance at East Carolina College (now East Carolina University). This event offers a glimpse into the goals Brubeck had for his southern performances with Wright as well

---

[20] L. M. Steinberg to Dave Brubeck, personal letter, May 5, 1958, Brubeck Collection.
[21] Mort Lewis to L. M. Steinberg, personal letter, June 10, 1958, Brubeck Collection.
[22] Ralph Gleason, "Brubeck Cancels South Africa Because of Negro Artist Ban," *Daily Boston Globe*, October 19, 1958, 61.

as the confidence he might have gained from a successful college protest. On February 5, 1958, the Brubeck quartet was preparing to go onstage in Wright Auditorium when they were stopped by the dean of student affairs for East Carolina College, James Tucker. Tucker informed Brubeck that the school's policy would not allow Eugene Wright to perform. Brubeck's account of the event centered on his experiences with his upcoming State Department tour abroad; he reported to Gleason that he told Tucker "that the next morning we were to leave for Europe sponsored by the State Department to represent this country and one of the best things we could do was to show that prejudice was not everywhere in the United States, as we were a mixed group. And they wanted to do this to us the night before!"

A retrospective by East Carolina University demonstrates the levels of bureaucracy the college went through to allow Brubeck to perform without losing state funding: the president of the college, John Messick, telephoned North Carolina governor Luther Hodges, who apparently reminded Messick that "because the school had signed a contract for the performance, it would have to pay the band whether they played or not."[23] Brubeck claimed it was his own argument that swayed the dean, who announced to the audience that the Brubeck Quartet would appear after all; Tucker told the waiting crowd that "Mr. Brubeck and his quartet leave tomorrow for a State Department tour of Europe and we want them to tell the world that North Carolina is not Little Rock."[24] Brubeck's near-miss resulted in institutional change at East Carolina College: later that month, the board of trustees enacted a new policy, one that no longer banned Black performers outright, and placed the issue of campus performances by Black musicians at the discretion of the administration, essentially (though not officially) allowing Black musicians to perform on campus.[25]

In his recollections of the East Carolina College concert, Brubeck frequently noted that based on cheers, clapping, and foot stomping from the crowd, the students clearly wanted the group to perform—an assertion he would repeat regarding the 1960 southern tour. In a 1981 interview with Kerry Frumkin, Brubeck recalled asking President Messick, "Well, why were we hired?" Messick apparently responded, "The *students* hired you, not me."[26] Throughout his career, Brubeck used this episode as proof of his audiences' positive intent with regard to racial prejudice, arguing that his audiences did not care whether the group was integrated, but were only interested in

[23] Steve Tuttle, "When Music Broke the Color Barrier," *East* 12, no. 1 (2013): 14.
[24] Gleason, "Brubeck Cancels South Africa."
[25] Tuttle, "When Music Broke the Color Barrier," 14.
[26] Dave Brubeck, interview with Kerry Frumkin, October 17, 1981, WFMT, Brubeck Collection.

the music the group performed—an argument that matched Brubeck's own colorblind ideology.[27] As he explained to journalist Hedrick Smith decades later, in 2001, "So here's the reason you fight is for the truth to come out and people to look at it. Nobody was against the Quartet's black bass player. They cheered him like he was the greatest thing that ever happened for the students. Everybody was happy."[28]

Within the context of the civil rights movement, Brubeck's 1957 cancelation in Texas and 1958 near-miss in North Carolina may seem small—after all, it was only Furgerson's insider knowledge that allowed her to recognize his cancelation as an act of protest, not any public statement from Brubeck himself, and the few papers that covered the incidents at East Carolina College did so many months after the fact. However, though three years is a short period historically, the difference between the racial politics and activism of 1957 and 1960 is vast. This was the period when the first lunch counter sit-ins began in Wichita, Kansas (1958); Oklahoma City, Oklahoma (1958); and Greensboro, North Carolina (1960). Then they spread across the South in 1960 to Richmond, Virginia; Nashville, Tennessee; and Atlanta, Georgia, to name a few high-profile protests, and then to northern locations, including Waterloo, Iowa, where Furgerson lived.[29] The visibility of Brubeck's protests likewise shifted during this time period. As he continued to tour across the South, and with the permanent addition of Eugene Wright to his quartet, Brubeck made public his commitment to combating racial prejudice.

## Athens, Georgia, 1959

Five months after news of the South Africa tour broke, the Brubeck Quartet was scheduled to perform at the University of Georgia (UGA) in Athens, Georgia, on March 4, 1959. Shortly before the concert, Stuart Woods, a senior sociology major and the head of UGA's brand new Jazz Society, received publicity photos for the quartet that included Wright, and he immediately knew there would be a problem. Two years earlier, in 1957, UGA had instituted a policy banning integrated entertainment groups from performing on campus; similar policies were implemented in schools across the South following the

---

[27] Dave Brubeck, "Brubeck Oral History Project," interview by Shan Sutton, 2007, Brubeck Collection; Dave Brubeck, "Talking with Dave," interview by Hedrick Smith, 2001, from *Rediscovering Dave Brubeck*, PBS; Gleason, "Brubeck Cancels South Africa"; Gleason, "An Appeal from Dave Brubeck," *Down Beat*, February 18, 1960, 13.

[28] "PBS: Rediscovering Dave Brubeck with Hedrick Smith," originally broadcast on December 16, 2001, https://www.pbs.org/brubeck/talking/daveOnRacial.htm, accessed January 5, 2021.

[29] Fehn, "The Only Hope We Had," 213.

*Brown v. Board of Education* decision and the crisis in Little Rock in attempts to formally institute segregationist policies that had previously been standard practice. Stuart Woods had seen the Brubeck Quartet in 1957, when white bassist Norman Bates was a regular member and therefore had not anticipated any problems.[30] With the addition of Wright to the quartet and UGA's new policies, however, UGA's administration gave Woods no choice but to cancel the performance.[31]

In press reports, Brubeck called the school's move to cancel the concert "unconstitutional and ridiculous," and he insisted that he would not perform with a white bassist "for a million dollars."[32] Instead, *Variety* reported that Brubeck played a concert at Atlanta's Magnolia Ballroom, a Black venue that became an integral staging ground for civil rights meetings.[33] Reports in the *Daily Defender*, the *Atlanta Daily World*, and *Variety* added that Brubeck's manager, Mort Lewis, had recently turned down a national television show on Brubeck's behalf because it would have required Brubeck to substitute a white bassist for Wright.[34] That the *New York Times*'s story did not include this information reflects the ways in which the Black press and occasionally sympathetic entertainment papers made connections between similar modes of institutional racism that the mainstream press did not, or would not, recognize.[35]

Brubeck's canceled concert reverberated across the UGA campus as students took sides debating integration and musical performance. The ensuing conversations make clear the complexity of the student body's feelings toward integration in an era and place that tended to simplify them. Woods immediately began a petition to repeal the university's policy requiring only segregated performing groups; but by April it was clear that his petition had failed. Though the UGA Student Council denied his request for the body to

---

[30] Woods told the *New York Post*, "I didn't realize Brubeck's group was mixed until I saw Wright's picture.... I think, personally, it would have been all right to have a mixed group but the school officials felt it was pretty touchy. We are a state school and I think they realized the type of reaction the politicians would have had. It's unfortunate when a man can't play on a stage with another man just because of his color." "Why Brubeck's Band Won't Play in Georgia," *New York Post*, February 24, 1959.

[31] In a 2015 interview with Stephen Crist, Woods explained that when he objected to the segregated performance policy, the institution threatened future jazz concerts and organizations; he was told by the director of student activities, based on a directive the from board of regents, "If you can't accept that, then you won't be producing these concerts, and you won't have an organization either" (Crist, *Dave Brubeck's* Time Out, 60).

[32] John Keasler, "Jazz Society Cancels Brubeck Appearance for Campus Concert," *Red and Black*, February 26, 1959, 1.

[33] "U. Of Ga. Nixes Brubeck (Bassist a Negro) but OK at Atlanta 'Race' Spot," *Variety*, March 4, 1959, 49.

[34] "Cancel Brubeck's Ga. Date Because of Negro Bassist," *Daily Defender*, February 25, 1959, 2; "Halt Brubeck Show; Negro Playing Bass," *Atlanta Daily World*, February 25, 1959, 1.

[35] "Jazz Unit Rebuffed: Racial Policy Cancels Brubeck Quartet Show at Georgia U." *New York Times*, February 25, 1959, 63.

sponsor a campus-wide poll to ascertain student opinion on the policy, the Student Council also denied a counter-motion that asked the group to make public its support of the policy.[36] Students wrote editorials in the newspaper, *The Red and Black*, both in support of Brubeck and in support of the policy preventing Brubeck's appearance. Students in favor of the Brubeck concert argued that the quartet and other musical groups should be allowed to play on the basis of skill and musical worth (a version of the "let's keep politics out of music" argument), or that students should be allowed more autonomy to set their own policies (a riff on states' rights rhetoric frequently used by states in the South to fight against civil rights laws at the federal level). These written responses supporting Brubeck's performance reflect the somewhat colorblind comfort level of what Martin Luther King Jr. would later call "white moderates" more interested in keeping order (and perhaps seeing a Brubeck concert) than extending justice to all.[37] As philosopher Shannon Sullivan writes, "White liberalism generally doesn't aim to end white domination. Quite the opposite: it aims to render it more tolerable, both to its beneficiaries and its victims."[38]

For students and administrators against Brubeck's concert, the near-performance at UGA ignited what historian Carol Anderson refers to as "white rage." As Anderson explains,

> White rage is not about visible violence, but rather it works its way through the courts, the legislatures, and a range of government bureaucracies.... White rage doesn't have to wear sheets, burn crosses, or take to the streets. Working the halls of power, it can achieve its ends far more effectively, far more destructively.[39]

White rage, Anderson argues, is often triggered by Black advancement: "It is not the mere presence of black people that is the problem; rather, it is blackness with ambition, with drive, with purpose, with aspirations, and with demands for full and equal citizenship." In other words, those protesting Wright's presence in the quartet objected to the notion that Brubeck could not find a white musician who could equal Wright's musical ability, and administrators used segregationist policies to prevent his performance.

---

[36] "Council Discusses Jazz Club Petition," *Red and Black*, April 16, 1959, 1.
[37] Martin Luther King Jr., "Letter from a Birmingham Jail," The Martin Luther King, Jr. Research and Education Institute, April 16, 1963, https://kinginstitute.stanford.edu/king-papers/documents/address-freedom-rally-cobo-hall.
[38] Shannon Sullivan, *Good White People* (Albany: State University of New York Press, 2014), 4.
[39] Carol Anderson, *White Rage: The Unspoken Truth of Our Racial Divide* (New York: Bloomsbury, 2016), 3.

But white rage operates in both subtle and visceral ways. For example, one UGA student suggested that all of Brubeck's records be broken, explaining that UGA should not accept or appreciate Black musicians' skills, "not even for the sake of art," because it risked a "giant step toward integration."[40] As he continued, his rage was palpable, even on the page, as he advocated disbanding the Jazz Club (which he referred to as the "Athens Integration Society") and running its members "out of town on a rail for having the audacity to even suggest such an outrage." He ended with a warning, suggesting that the Brubeck concert would have meant "contamination of the campus and riots in the streets." While some on UGA's campus would have accepted Wright's skill as proof of his worth to be included on UGA's otherwise white-dominated campus, such a meritocratic vision of racial harmony was unconvincing to others.

In fact, Brubeck's bass position was a notoriously difficult role to fill to Brubeck's satisfaction, as a 1954 document titled "Aims and Principles of the DBQ" makes plain.[41] In it, Brubeck instructs then bass player Bob Bates against common jazz bass decisions such as substitutions or outlining different chords, noting that the bass note mistakes happened when "the bass man deviates from the agreed on changes." Later, Brubeck instructs Bates specifically (no longer "the bass man") to learn Bach inventions and review Bach chorales as a solid model for bass lines. Brubeck's penchant for playing bass lines, even with a bassist, along with his interest in out harmonies (using unexpected substitutions and extensions, or visiting other key areas) likely resulted in his pickiness for bassists. Bob Bates was one in a line of bassists that lasted only one year or so with the quartet; after Bob, Norman Bates (Bob's brother), played two years with Brubeck before Wright was hired. Wright remained the Brubeck Quartet's bassist until its dissolution in 1967, which suggests that Brubeck truly meant it when he said he could not replace Wright musically.

UGA's policy banning integrated performing groups received wide support across campus, and this should not be surprising. After all, as many in the Black press would point out, the policy was only two years old. In other words, it was enacted in the same year as the Little Rock integration crisis—the same year a student editorial ran in *The Black and Red* warning that the pain of integration felt in Little Rock could undoubtedly come to Athens.[42] Fear, however unfounded, fueled the rage that ultimately prompted Brubeck's own struggle against UGA's segregationist policies—and further, policies across the South.

---

[40] Robert Ingram, "Letters to the Editor, *The Red and Black*, 26 Feb. 1959, 4.
[41] "Principles and Aims of the DBQ," [1954], Brubeck Collection.
[42] Earl Leonard, "Tyranny Fought Nobly," *Red and Black*, October 4, 1957, 4.

## Brubeck's "Southern Strategy": An Integrationist Approach to Marketing

Brubeck's experience with UGA set the stage for his 1960 southern tour. In the lead up to the 1960 concert cancelations, he mounted a direct campaign for southern audiences that included two albums full of southern songs: *Gone With the Wind*, recorded in April 1959 and released in August, and *Southern Scene*, recorded in September and October 1959 and released in the spring of 1960. *Gone With the Wind*, recorded less than two months after the UGA cancelation and meant as a commercial and financial safeguard against the experimental (and ultimately wildly popular) *Time Out* (1959), paid particular tribute to the state of Georgia through the inclusion of both its title track and "Georgia on My Mind." As Brubeck explained to jazz columnist Ralph Gleason after schools had canceled his 1960 tour, "Let me reiterate: we want to play in the south.... Therefore, we appeal to them to help us."[43]

Brubeck's plan was to motivate southern audiences to accept his integrated group through performances of popular southern songs; in doing so, he again banked on his ability to attract "new" audiences to jazz. Across these albums, Brubeck's visual and musical choices reflect what Karl Hagstrom Miller describes as a northern approach to the South: as both a "land of potential consumers and an object of northern fantasy—the exotic, pastoral region depicted in countless popular songs."[44] Brubeck, Desmond, Morello, and Wright each specifically chose popular southern songs, including well-known minstrel and parlor songs by Stephen Foster ("Swanee River," "Camptown Races," "Oh Susanna," and "Jeanie with the Light Brown Hair"), jazz standards ("Gone With the Wind," "When It's Sleepy Time Down South," and "Basin Street Blues"), mainstream hits ("Little Rock Getaway," "Georgia on My Mind," and "Deep in the Heart of Texas"), nineteenth-century spirituals and plantation songs ("Nobody Knows the Trouble I've Seen" and "Short'nin Bread"), and popular songs written by white composers from the perspective of Black musicians ("The Lonesome Road," "Ol' Man River," and "Darling Nellie Gray"). Nearly all of the songs across both albums had been performed by popular musicians, such as Bing Crosby, Ray Charles, Julie London, and Frank Sinatra, and well-known jazz musicians like Louis Armstrong, Ella Fitzgerald, Sarah Vaughan, and Miles Davis. The diverse mix of original composers and subsequent performers in part indicates Brubeck's interest

---

[43] Ralph Gleason, "An Appeal from Dave Brubeck," *Down Beat*, February 18, 1960, 13.
[44] Karl Hagstrom Miller, *Segregating Sound: Inventing Folk and Pop Music in the Age of Jim Crow* (Durham, NC: Duke University Press, 2010), 3.

in promoting musical integration to the widest possible audience. Indeed, music had been an arena in which many Black Americans hoped that white enthusiasm for Black music like rhythm and blues might either reflect or inspire change in white racial attitudes, as Brian Ward writes in *Just My Soul Responding: Rhythm and Blues, Black Consciousness, and Race Relations*. However, Ward continues, "Historically, whites had always been capable of admiring black culture and acknowledging the skill, even genius, of individual blacks in certain areas of endeavor . . . without necessarily conceding the full humanity of blacks as a race, let alone supporting their bid for genuine equality of opportunity in America."[45] In other words, whether composed by, performed by, or performed about Black people, music alone could not hope to challenge intractable racial beliefs. Nevertheless, these albums became part of Brubeck's strategy as an advocate for integration, a strategy that was particularly directed at the South.

Brubeck's song choices were not the only positive messages of integration across these two albums. Whereas Brubeck's image and music had been described and promoted as decidedly "white" in his early career, with *Gone With the Wind* and *Southern Scene* Brubeck explicitly advanced an integrated visual image by making Wright especially visible on both album covers. *Gone With the Wind*'s cover artwork depicts a southern pastoral fantasy (Fig. 4.1). The Brubeck quartet stands on a covered pavilion surrounded by lush green trees, whose grandiose archways and pillars evoke a massive southern plantation. Brubeck and Desmond, the group's more well-known members, are foregrounded, with Morello and Wright standing at a pillar in the background. The color photo could not be more clear: this is an integrated quartet. The cover of the later *Southern Scene* asserts the group's integration even more plainly (Fig. 4.2). Amid illustrations of stereotypical scenes of the South (a plantation home and a steamboat) is a photo of the quartet in the shade of a tree on the bank of a river. Desmond, Wright, and Morello are seated together, wearing identical black suits, while Brubeck, in his gray leader's suit, leans over them, hand on Morello's shoulder. All four men are looking at the camera and smiling, and Wright, surrounded by his three white bandmates, is at the center of the image. The fact that apparently no one either objected to or noticed Wright's presence on *Gone With the Wind* prior to the 1960 tour suggests that Brubeck's image had previously been established as sufficiently white to render such an inclusion invisible—particularly to school administrators who may not have followed the quartet closely. However, the

---

[45] Brian Ward, *Just My Soul Responding: Rhythm and Blues, Black Consciousness, and Race Relations* (Berkeley: University of California Press, 1998), 232.

**Figure 4.1.** *Gone with the Wind* album cover. © 1959 Sony Music Entertainment. Courtesy of Sony Music Entertainment.

later *Southern Scene* image, released after the publicity of the southern tour had died down, made the quartet's racial makeup unavoidable; for audiences who supported integration, it would have served as a clear reminder of Brubeck's southern protest, while for audiences who supported segregation, it would have shown an ideological misalignment.

Throughout the 1950s, Brubeck's bassists were typically the least frequently featured members of the quartet. Therefore, his decision to feature Wright prominently on these albums, particularly on "Ol' Man River" and "Happy Times" (composed by Wright), is remarkable—and represents his most explicit attempt to highlight Wright's musical contribution within the quartet directly to southern audiences. For those "in the know," these songs represented moments of sonic integration; for those less informed, the album demonstrated Brubeck's colorblind approach to music, in which white and Black musicians could freely cross what sound studies scholar Jennifer Lynn

**Figure 4.2.** *Southern Scene* album cover. © 1960 Sony Music Entertainment. Courtesy of Sony Music Entertainment.

Stoever calls the "sonic color line."[46] Simultaneously, Brubeck attempted to demonstrate why Wright was essential to his quartet's performances—and further, that he not only *would* not replace Wright, but he *could* not replace Wright, lest the quartet's music suffer. (And, as Stephen Crist suggests, Desmond made his own feelings about the Georgia debacle known on the bridge of "Georgia on My Mind," when he slipped in a quote of Artie Shaw's theme song, "Nightmare.")[47]

According to Brubeck's autobiographer Fred Hall and liner notes for *Gone With the Wind* written by Teo Macero, Wright chose to perform "Ol' Man River."[48] The Brubeck quartet's version is a bass feature (Desmond sits

---

[46] Jennifer Lynn Stoever, *The Sonic Color Line: Race and the Cultural Politics of Listening* (New York: New York University Press, 2016).
[47] Crist, *Dave Brubeck's* Time Out, 61.
[48] Fred M. Hall, *It's About Time: The Dave Brubeck Story* (Fayetteville: University of Arkansas Press, 1996), 63; Teo Macero, liner notes, *Gone With the Wind* (Columbia Records, 1959).

this one out) that begins in a quick tempo. Wright performs the melody line alone, accompanied by harmonic and rhythmic interjections from Brubeck and Morello. After a full statement of the head melody, the group transitions suddenly to a half time, bluesy bass solo. The song ends in a sudden and unaccompanied cadenza that tapers off to a seemingly incomplete conclusion as Wright descends in register, as if his solo, like the Mississippi River, will "just keep rollin' along." As musicologist Todd Decker writes, "Ol' Man River" is "at its core—about the experience of being black in a segregated America."[49] The Brubeck version maintained the primacy of Wright's experience in performing a song that had, in its more than thirty-year history, been used as both a song of protest and a song of southern nostalgia. In doing so, the quartet forced unwitting southern segregationists to hear a song about southern Black experiences from a Black man, supported by his white bandmates as they insisted on Wright's integral musical position within the quartet. That they did so in an album packaged for commercial audiences simultaneously cushioned the quartet from any overt retaliation from segregationists and allowed Brubeck to advance his own subtle political ideology.

Brubeck not only highlighted Wright's musical contributions but also emphasized the qualities of his personality that anyone, even audiences outside the music business, would understand as valuable character traits. According to liner notes written by Brubeck for "Happy Times," a Wright original and feature on *Southern Scene*, the song offered listeners a chance not only to hear Wright's composition but to get to know Wright:

> "Happy Times," an original by Gene Wright, is typical of the relaxed happy sound which has been the antidote to the history of trouble expressed in 'Nobody Knows the Trouble I've Seen' [the previous track]. I think Gene's bass solo expressed the Wright attitude toward life—amiable, relaxed and smiling.[50]

In these notes, Brubeck maps the easygoing and upbeat theme of "Happy Times" onto Wright's personality, and indeed, the reliance of the melody line on the roots of chords does result in a strong feeling of stability. Brubeck associates both "Nobody Knows the Trouble I've Seen" and "Happy Times" with a common history of Black musical production, albeit with a notable distinction in mood: the former song represents a troubled history of racial prejudice, whereas the latter represents Wright's hopeful, optimistic present. To hear "Happy Times" is essentially to enter into conversation with Wright: the

---

[49] Todd Decker, *Who Should Sing "Ol' Man River"?* (Oxford: Oxford University Press, 2015), 14.
[50] Dave Brubeck, liner notes, *Southern Scene* (Columbia, 1960).

arrangement chosen by the quartet makes it difficult for listeners to engage with any of the other musicians, as Brubeck and Morello perform subdued accompanying roles to Wright's solo and Desmond lays out on this piece. This allows Wright's voice, performed through his bass, to become the auditory focal point. On the other hand, "Nobody Knows the Trouble I've Seen" features solos by Brubeck and Desmond, whose performances narrate Black history in a particularly upbeat and optimistic version of the song.

*Southern Scene* also features a duet between Brubeck and Wright—a moment that perhaps underscored Brubeck's personal support of Wright. According to the liner notes, Brubeck had planned a quartet version of "At the Darktown Strutters' Ball," a popular vaudevillian song written in 1917 by Shelton Brooks, a Black Canadian American; however, what ended up on the LP was what Brubeck referred to as a "happy twosome" featuring himself and Wright. Brubeck's description of how the duet came to be once again reinforces Wright's positive and obliging work ethic:

> Gene had arrived at the studio a half hour early, as is his habit, and we had started to play to get warmed up for the session. Teo Macero, producer of our date, had never heard Gene and me play in this style, and had decided to himself that it might make an interesting release.

What resulted is an old-time jazz feel, with sonic resonances of ragtime, featuring Wright's steady bass line and Brubeck's typically heavy block chords in both hands. Crucially, this recording offers a sonic representation of Wright's position within the quartet—and provides one potential reason why Brubeck valued him as a bass player. Midway through the song, Brubeck's left hand plays strong offbeat chords that nearly obscure the actual beat, and toward the end, he adds a stride left hand that rushes wildly ahead. The steadiness of Wright's bass line grounds both Brubeck and the listener, providing a reliable home base in the coveted "pocket" (the sweet, center spot of the tempo). It is not Wright who threatens to upend the balance or the tempo, but Brubeck; Wright provides stability while simultaneously making space for Brubeck's added bass line, demonstrating a particularly valuable talent in accompaniment. Regardless of whether Brubeck intended to musically underscore his flattery of Wright's personality, as observed throughout the liner notes, this recording nevertheless offers sonic evidence of Wright's strengths within the Brubeck Quartet as well as the partnership between the integrated twosome.

Brubeck does mention the other members of the quartet in the liner notes, but these primarily focus on Desmond's reactions to a certain take or a technique used by Morello, offering little in the way of information about their personalities, and in particular, do not focus on positive traits in as direct a manner as with Wright. However, though Brubeck described Wright only in complimentary terms, the descriptions also adhered closely to negative stereotypes of Black men as harmless to the point of subservience—an "Uncle Tom" stereotype represented solely through Brubeck's descriptions (not from any interview or quote from Wright) that nevertheless may have worked to Brubeck and Wright's advantage with southern audiences ranging from squeamish to enraged at the thought of the quartet's integration. Regardless, in these liner notes, written just months after the University of Georgia had canceled its concert over Wright's presence in the quartet, Brubeck made the case that Wright was a crucial member of the group, essentially marketing integration to southern audiences.

Both albums sold well, despite middling reviews by jazz critics and the albums' utter eclipse by *Time Out* (1959). However, critics were quick to pick up on and promote Brubeck's attempts to champion integration, and their reviews likewise commended the ease with which the men performed together as a musically integrated unit, rather than focusing on each as a soloist, marking a slight departure from earlier reviews. For example, Gleason chose *Gone With the Wind* as his "Album of the Week" in the *Daily Boston Globe*, commenting that "Gene Wright, Joe Morello, Paul Desmond and Dave individually and collectively contribute delightfully swinging jazz performances."[51] The *Down Beat* review of *Gone With the Wind* likewise remarked on the high level of "rapport" demonstrated on the album, concluding by stating, "This is a happy, swingin' LP lacking in pretentiousness and played by a group of men who obviously enjoy their work and each other."[52] Don DeMichael's review of *Southern Scene*, released six months after the canceled southern tour, focused on Wright's essential, albeit background, role within the quartet: "Supporting all the others is Wright, a quiet and unassuming but indispensable part of the whole."[53] For these critics, compliments for the quartet's musical integration seemed to thinly veil compliments for the group's racial integration. The reception of these albums suggests that Brubeck's attempts to market integration, particularly in demonstrating the essential role Wright fulfilled in the quartet, may have been to some degree successful—at least to already sympathetic audiences.

What makes Brubeck's decisions particularly notable—to release two albums full of "southern songs" and to subsequently forgo the 1960 southern

---

[51] Ralph J. Gleason, "Album of the Week," *Daily Boston Globe*, September 20, 1959, 81.
[52] Review, *Gone With the Wind*, *Down Beat*, October 1, 1959, 27.
[53] Don DeMichael, Review of *Southern Scene*, *Down Beat*, June 23, 1960, 30.

tour—is the approach to integration that he both advocates and models. In 1954, *Brown v. Board of Education* ruled that within the public educational system, separate was not equal. The highest court in the land proclaimed segregation to have ended, even though battles over segregation were in many ways just beginning, as southern states rapidly adopted additional segregationist policies in *Brown*'s wake. However, the method of that integration focused primarily on integrating Black and brown bodies into white spaces, which were understood to be superior, and not on integrating white bodies into Black and brown spaces. Chief Justice Earl Warren's opinion explicitly highlighted who would benefit most from integration: "To separate [colored children] from others of similar age and qualifications solely because of their race generates a feeling of inferiority as to their status in the community that may affect their hearts and minds in a way unlikely ever to be undone. . . . Segregation of white and colored children in public schools has a detrimental effect upon the colored children."[54] As writer and historian Ibram X. Kendi explains, "After *Brown*, the integrated white space came to define the ideal integrated space where inferior non-White bodies could be developed."[55] Black spaces remained raced, while white spaces could be considered "nonracial," "neutral and objective."[56] By focusing on the "feeling of inferiority" among Black students stemming from separation, Kendi argues, rather than the fact that Black schools received significantly less funding and resources than white schools, Justice Warren made the implicit argument that (in Kendi's words), "Integration (into Whiteness) became racial progress."[57] Put simply, school integration was and is built on the belief that Black minds were inferior to white minds, and further, that proximity to white minds would allow Black minds to "rise" to a supposed white standard of excellence. Integration was not primarily initiated on the belief that white schools have historically been better supported than Black schools, nor did it include an argument that would suggest that white students could improve or benefit through entrance into Black spaces. The decision thus further entrenched solutions to racism within a sphere of individual choices and prejudices, rather than addressing centuries of systemic oppression.

However, Brubeck's inclusion and advocacy of Wright within his quartet offers another approach to integration. Whether at East Carolina College,

---

[54] *Brown v. Board of Education*, 347 U.S. 483, 493 (1954).
[55] Ibram X. Kendi, *How to Be an Antiracist* (New York: One World, 2019), 178.
[56] Barack Obama, *Dreams from My Father: A Story of Race and Inheritance* (New York: Crown, 2007), 99–100.
[57] Kendi, *How to Be an Antiracist*, 178.

the University of Georgia, or on *Gone With the Wind* and *Southern Scene*, Brubeck's argument was not that his quartet or those schools should be integrated because it was good for Wright but because it was good for the white members of the Dave Brubeck Quartet and the white students for whom they would perform. In other words, Brubeck's approach to integration suggested that white people—not just Black people—could also benefit from racial integration. Such an approach still focuses on the integration of Black bodies into white spaces—and only Black bodies deemed "worthy" through some demonstrable skill or talent. And indeed, this approach still very much centers white folks (especially as it resonates uncomfortably with the weak rationales for diversity initiatives in institutions and programs across the country).[58] However, it was a progressive approach to integration not taken by many white Americans at the beginning of the civil rights movement and indeed, it was an untenable approach for the southern institutions Brubeck attempted to access in 1960.

## The 1960 Tour and Its Aftermath

Shortly after the release of *Gone With the Wind* in fall 1959, Associated Booking Corporation (ABC) booking agent Bob Bundy began to solidify plans for a southern tour of the Dave Brubeck Quartet. Whether southern tour dates were the result of a request by Brubeck or not is unclear, though the albums he was working on certainly suggest a particular interest in southern audiences. Bundy wrote to Brubeck on October 6, warning him that the chairman for the organization sponsoring the southern tour "wanted to know if you had any colored boys in your group."[59] Bundy continued, telling

---

[58] Sara Ahmed, *On Being Included: Racism and Diversity in Institutional Life* (Durham, NC: Duke University Press, 2012).

[59] Bob Bundy to Dave Brubeck, October 6, 1959, Brubeck Collection; also qtd. in Crist, *Dave Brubeck's Time Out*, 229. The organization to which Bundy refers is likely the Southern Universities Student Government Association (SUSGA), which formed in 1959 as a southern alternative to the National Student Association (NSA) and by 1960 had a membership of twenty-two southern colleges and universities (the same number of schools that canceled their contracts with Brubeck). Though the NSA was a fairly moderate organization, its creation of a Southern Student Human Relations Project, which promoted "interracial understanding among students in the south," and the failure of a pro-segregation resolution in 1958 left many southern universities with the impression that the NSA was promoting integration, despite the objections of southern schools. The SUSGA, on the other hand, touted its support of local student governments and their own unique needs. The SUSGA also employed block booking, a practice in which many institutions join together to attract entertainment acts at a lower price—a particular benefit of their more regional organization. Buzz Hoagland, "An Explanation of SUSGA and What It Means to USC," *Gamecock*, May 6, 1960, 2; Bud Kirkpatrick, "Block Booking in Dixie," *Billboard*, March 27, 1965, 46; Henry H. Lesesne, *A History of the University of South Carolina: 1940–2000* (Columbia: University of South Carolina Press, 2001), 132.

Brubeck, "My purpose in writing you is to see if you could arrange to have an all-white group to play these colleges and universities, because they will not accept you as a mixed group." Even though Brubeck had made clear that he would not replace Wright in incidents that same year at UGA, one year earlier with the failed tour of apartheid-era South Africa, and two years earlier at East Carolina College, Bundy apparently felt that this opportunity warranted re-considering the group's racial makeup. Bundy continued, emphasizing to Brubeck that "25 dates for $1500 per concert are not to be sneezed at," and that "This should be considered seriously, as college concerts are the backbone of your income." Bundy's letters to Brubeck often read as if they are the most crucial letters Brubeck could possibly ever read, but this had an even more urgent tone than most, as he concluded the letter with a hand-written note at the bottom: "You need this."

Bundy was not exaggerating when he wrote that $1,500 per concert was a significant sum of money for Brubeck—as well as for the Associated Booking Corporation (ABC). In late 1958, Brubeck's typical single college dates offered between $1,000 and $1,500 (not including transportation), and tours, which included transportation, often paid only $860 per concert. The southern tour dates were also organized to minimize travel as much as possible, making it an easier and more appealing nightly arrangement. Furthermore, with a regular nightly rate of $1,500, Brubeck's agents could potentially raise his fees for subsequent performances. While it is hard to imagine Brubeck ever considering replacing Wright, it is equally difficult to imagine any booking agent letting such an offer pass by. So it seems that Brubeck, armed with his recent album, *Gone With the Wind*, and with *Southern Scene* in the works, proceeded with plans for the tour, despite possibly knowing that the sponsors of his tour would refuse an integrated ensemble. On December 26, 1959, just one month before the southern tour, Brubeck's wife, Iola Brubeck, wrote to Eugene Wright regarding quartet rehearsals, accommodations, the upcoming schedule, and his paycheck.[60] In her letter, she confirmed that the southern tour was still scheduled to last from January 28 to February 20, suggesting that the tour was still on for all members of the quartet, including Wright.

In going along with the tour with no intention of replacing Wright, it seems that Brubeck, his booking agents, probably Iola, and possibly the entire quartet knew that the southern schools might cancel; unlike earlier concerts, they do not seem to have stumbled into this protest. It is almost as if Brubeck

---

[60] Iola Brubeck to Eugene Wright, personal letter, December 26, 1959, Brubeck Collection.

and his team decided to simply proceed and see what would happen—a fairly cavalier decision given that at the time, integration was a matter of life and death in some of the areas in which they planned to travel. When they canceled the concerts, the twenty-two schools insisted that Brubeck had broken his contract; but given that Brubeck's standard contract at the time (which he usually used for organized tours) mentioned nothing about race, it seems unlikely that Brubeck officially violated the terms of his contracts. However, he certainly seems to have broken some sort of agreement made between booking agent Bob Bundy and the southern organization sponsoring the tour.

As we now know, the tour fell apart.[61] Some time between December 26, when Iola Brubeck wrote to Wright, and January 6, when an ABC booking agent sent a new, reduced itinerary for Brubeck's southern tour, eleven colleges canceled Brubeck Quartet concerts, citing the fact that his group was integrated.[62] According to Brubeck, after he told the remaining schools that the quartet was integrated, only three schools remained on the itinerary, and ABC scrambled to fill his lost February income. Between January 6 and January 22, a team of booking agents, including Joe Glaser, Bob Bundy, Larry Bennett, Fred Williamson, Paul Bannister, Hugh Hooks, Bobby Phillips, and Jack Archer, urgently sought dates, often reaching deals with club owners or colleges only to have them interfere with another booking agent's tentative plans. Dates in St. Paul, Minnesota; Washington, DC; and a tour of Colorado were all suggested, only for surprised agents to discover that those dates had already been filled within a day's time. When all was said and done, Brubeck's agents managed to replace his $40,000 southern tour, which included travel costs, with just $18,250 worth of dates at colleges and clubs, which did not include travel costs (Table 4.1). Brubeck felt the loss keenly; in his in-depth report of the tour, Ralph Gleason noted that Brubeck had stated "wistfully," "It was a hard tour to lose."[63]

Brubeck was quick to publicly excuse his fans from any racist or segregationist agendas held by the schools, organizations, and states that refused to allow his integrated quartet to perform. For Brubeck, there were many audiences across the South that were simply interested in the quartet's music, no matter the race of its members—which, for Brubeck, meant that those

---

[61] Louis Armstrong also had a southern tour canceled in 1960 because he was touring with an integrated band. Michael Meckna, *Satchmo: The Louis Armstrong Encyclopedia* (Westport, CT: Greenwood Press, 2004), 47.

[62] I have not found a full accounting in either Brubeck's records or press releases of the schools that canceled.

[63] Ralph Gleason, "Brubeck Sorry for Southerners," *San Francisco Chronicle*, February 8, 1960.

Table 4.1. Revised Itinerary for the Brubeck Quartet, February 1960

| February (date) | Venue | Location | Payment | % Privilege Gross Receipts |
|---|---|---|---|---|
| 1 | Jacksonville University | Jacksonville, FL | 1500,00 US$ | |
| 2 | | | | |
| 3 | Vanderbilt University | Nashville, TN | 1500,00 US$ | |
| 4 | University of the South | Sewanee, TN | 1500,00 US$ | |
| 5 | | | | |
| 6 | Northwestern University | Evanston, IL | 2000,00 US$ | |
| 7 | | | | |
| 8 | Eastern Illinois University | Charleston, IL | 1250,00 US$ | 60 % |
| 9 | Whitefish Bay High School | Whitefish Bay, OH | 1750,00 US$ | 60 % |
| 10 | Wittenberg College | Springfield, OH | 1500 US$ | |
| 11 | Basin Street | New York City | $5000/week (est.) | |
| 12 | Basin Street | New York City | | |
| 13 | Basin Street | New York City | | |
| 14 | Basin Street | New York City | | |
| 15 | Basin Street | New York City | | |
| 16 | Basin Street | New York City | | |
| 17 | Basin Street | New York City | | |
| 18 | | | | |
| 19 | City Auditorium | Colorado Springs, CO | 1000,00 US$ | 50 % |
| 20 | Auditorium Theatre | Denver, CO | 1250,00 US$ | 50 % |

audiences did not support the schools' segregation policies. As he explained to Gleason,

> I've talked to students at those schools and they wish we could stay there. We wish we could, too, and as soon as they will accept us as we are, we'll be glad to [go] down there.[64]

Perhaps Brubeck attempted to bluff southern schools into integration in 1960, as he had in North Carolina in 1958. Maybe it was simply an oversight. But for possibly the first time, he found that his whiteness—his intellect, respectability, and recognition—was not enough to gain entrance into the white spaces of southern universities and colleges. To enter those spaces required a

---

[64] Gleason, "Brubeck Sorry for Southerners," 1960.

white supremacist ideology, or at the very least, a willingness to go along with such an ideology. This was untenable for Brubeck; in a letter to Charles Jones, a composition teacher at the Juilliard School of Music, written in the middle of the scramble to replace the southern tour dates, Brubeck matter-of-factly stated that the tour was "scuttled by the 'white supremacists.'"[65] Brubeck's ability to understand his "new" jazz audience, an ability that had garnered him so much fame so fast, had met its match in the segregationist policies that restricted his quartet from performing.

As segregationist policies eventually fell across the South in the early to mid-1960s, the Brubeck Quartet quickly returned to schools that had once forbade them, at times becoming the first integrated group to perform at previously all-white institutions.[66] But despite earlier protests and a clear dedication to social justice, Brubeck remained a major part of a larger musical industry that included Columbia Records and the Associated Booking Corporation—a musical industry that still overwhelming privileged whiteness.

Correspondence between Brubeck and his booking agents at ABC after 1960 suggest that everyone involved in his career was shocked by the southern schools' decision to forgo Brubeck in favor of segregation, and they were not eager to repeat the loss of revenue. Going forward, Dave and Iola Brubeck, along with manager Mort Lewis, carefully confirmed with booking agents that parties involved in all existing contracts were aware that the quartet was racially mixed.[67] Subsequent contracts issued anywhere there might conceivably be an issue with the integrated quartet included a race clause. This usually took the form of, "It is mutually agreed and understood between all parties concerned that the Artist or Artists have the prerogative of cancelling this contract, if in any instance an audience is segregated because of color or race," or, less frequently, "It is understood that Dave Brubeck carries an integrated group." Sometimes, such notes were handwritten onto the contract, but usually agents used a stamp. While the race clause was included on contracts in the South, such as in Arkadelphia, Arkansas (1962) and Lexington, Kentucky (1962), some agents seemed eager to include the clause on any venue in their region (booking agent Paul Bannister, for example, included the clause on

---

[65] Dave Brubeck to Charles Jones, January 18, 1960, Brubeck Collection. Also qtd. in Crist, *Dave Brubeck's* Time Out, 231.

[66] By 1962, Brubeck referenced twenty colleges in which he had been the first to cross the color line. Allison Murray, "He Left the Steers for Stravinsky," *Newington Town Crier*, May 313, 1962, 10.

[67] Stephen Crist writes that booking agent Jack Archer assured Brubeck that the promoters of a Virginia Beach concert in July 1960 were aware that the group was integrated, and further, that "Eugene Wright will be received with the proper respect as a member of your group." Crist, *Dave Brubeck's* Time Out, 233; Mort Lewis to Jack Archer, April 21, 1960, Brubeck Collection; Jack Archer to Dave Brubeck, April 25, 1960, Brubeck Collection.

Midwestern contracts in 1962 for Des Moines, Iowa; Rock Island, Illinois; Platteville, Wisconsin; Chicago, Illinois; and Omaha, Nebraska).

Brubeck also demonstrated significantly more caution in the years following the 1960 tour, sometimes writing to booking agents to ensure that a particular school was integrated. For example, Brubeck wrote to booking agent Bob Bundy in 1963 to confirm details about a contract with the Georgia Institute of Technology. Brubeck directly questioned Bundy on potential issues, essentially re-instructing him that he was not to initiate contracts with segregated schools (Georgia Tech had actually integrated on August 30, 1961, over two years before Brubeck performed there on February 1, 1964).[68]

As ABC's southern booking agent, Bundy seemed to have been especially eager for Brubeck, one of ABC's best-known performing artists, to return to his geographic sphere. He deployed a booking strategy that was potentially as aggressive as it was risky—even life-threatening, for Eugene Wright—by placing the Brubeck quartet in southern universities that had only been forcibly integrated months earlier (in later interviews, Brubeck would recall being escorted by police to various southern performances).[69] Take, for example, Brubeck's performance at the University of Alabama (UA) in 1964. In a letter written just before the contract for the performance was signed, Bundy reassured Brubeck about his upcoming performance at UA, explaining that Brubeck need not worry.[70]

However, Bundy left out crucial details of UA's integration: namely, that it had happened in the previous summer, just four months before Bundy had drawn the contracts.[71] Integration at UA, as at many institutions across the South in this period, was the result of federal intervention; in this case, in May 1963, a federal district judge told the University of Alabama it must admit two Black students that had applied to UA. On June 3, after Governor George Wallace threatened to personally bar the students' admittance to the university, the Justice Department asked a federal court to urge Wallace not to

---

[68] Dave Brubeck to Bob Bundy, November 8, 1963, Brubeck Collection.

[69] Crist, *Dave Brubeck's* Time Out, 234. Stephen Crist explains Brubeck's experience with hotels following the 1960 southern tour debacle. Crist details a night the quartet spent in segregated hotels following a performance at the University of Oklahoma. The following night, Crist writes, "all four members of the Quartet were accommodated at the Holiday Motel in Tulsa," and Brubeck noted in his daytimer that they "should make more future reservations nationwide with them." Brubeck followed up on his idea to support an integrated hotel chain, writing to an organizer for a concert in West Virginia to inform them that the quartet would prefer to stay in a hotel or motel that would accommodate all members, and specifying, "If there is a member of the Holiday Motel chain in Wheeling, I have found them to be excellent motels for us because of their interracial policy." "Executary, May [1960]," entry for May 17, Brubeck Collection; Dave Brubeck to Thomas G. Slokan (Oglebay Institute, Wheeling, West Virginia), June 8, 1960, Brubeck Collection, qtd. in Crist, *Dave Brubeck's* Time Out.

[70] Bob Bundy to Dave Brubeck, October 14, 1963, Brubeck Collection.

[71] UA was integrated on June 11, 1963; Brubeck's performance was on February 16, 1964, and the contracts for the performance were signed on October 15, 1963.

interfere with integration at UA. To comply with federal orders, UA proceeded with plans to admit two Black students, Vivian Malone and James Hood, to its Tuscaloosa campus on June 10. On June 8, Wallace sealed the UA campus with 400 state troopers, revenue agents, and game wardens, along with 600 Alabama National Guardsmen—all of whom Wallace claimed were necessary to preserve the peace. According to the *Crimson-White*, UA's student newspaper, the university enforced a 10:00 PM to 6:00 AM curfew, along with rules barring bicycles and unauthorized vehicles, requiring everyone on campus to present ID cards on request, and prohibiting students from working for news agencies or clustering in groups greater than three people.[72]

As he had threatened, Wallace physically blocked entry to UA's Foster Auditorium on June 10—the same auditorium where the integrated Brubeck Quartet would perform eight months later. Malone, Hood, and the spectators waited hours until the newly federalized national guard arrived to replace the state police. Wallace, having made his point that the federal government was unlawfully intervening in a state matter and having avoided violence, left the steps of the auditorium, and Malone and Hood were allowed to enroll. The *Crimson-White*, UA's student newspaper, reported that Wallace left to "loud applause for his stand," suggesting that although Tuscaloosa citizens would not interfere, that did not reflect a shift in their views on segregation.

Student coverage of the Brubeck Quartet concert eight months later carefully avoided any mention of race, integration, or segregation. The announcement of the concert one week prior mentioned only Brubeck, Desmond, and Morello, entirely leaving out any mention of Wright (or the presence of a bass at all) in the quartet. Though that article did so under the guise of noting only the members of the Brubeck Quartet named to the Playboy All-Star Band (which included all but Wright), the author essentially rendered Wright's Black body invisible.[73] Similarly, in an article after the concert, *Crimson-White* managing editor Dee Merrill included excerpts of an interview with Brubeck, and in the process managed not to list a single other member of the quartet.[74] However, a concert review by Frank Gilson in the same paper specifically referred to Wright's performance as "A-number-one."[75] This acknowledgment of Wright's musicianship offered him a personhood denied by the pointed absences in the previous articles.

---

[72] Lonnie Falk, "All-Out Peace Effort Sees Campus Guarded," *Crimson-White*, June 9, 1963, 1.

[73] "Brubeck, Combo Here Sunday in Foster," *Crimson-White*, February 13, 1964, 1, 3.

[74] Dee Merrill, "Take Five with Dave Brubeck, the Gray Flannel Jazz Pianist," *Crimson-White*, February 20, 1964, 1, 8.

[75] Frank Gilson, "Dave Swings in His Own Realm at Foster, but the Audience . . ." *Crimson-White*, February 20, 1964, 8;

Brubeck's performance was the first integrated performance for the first integrated audience held at the university, a fact confirmed by the head of the department of music at UA, Wilbur Rowand, several years later, in 1967. As Rowand explained to Brubeck,

> The Sunday afternoon program presented by you and your musicians was the first time that the box office at our main auditorium had been integrated. We had a number of colored people at that program in spite of the fact that there was considerable threat on the outside by representatives of the KKK. I am pleased to report to you that we have had no unpleasant incident since that day and all of our concerts, lectures and public attractions have been integrated.[76]

Rowand continued, offering an appraisal of Brubeck's performance and the audience's reception, "In my opinion, the reception given you and your trio, including the Negro musician, was so enthusiastic that it took the minds of the worried few off the problem of admitting for the first time Negro patrons." The letter, though written from the naive perspective of a white administrator, nevertheless offered Brubeck proof of his positive impact on integration at UA—even while it simultaneously acknowledged a very real and present threat to the Quartet and its audience. Brubeck responded to Rowand in kind, ignoring any threat of danger or continued inequities and praising the steps made by Tuscaloosa: "Some of our smug New England towns have a lesson to learn from Tuscaloosa."[77] The exchange between Rowand and Brubeck is a familiar one in which such acknowledgments of "extremism from both sides" seems, at least to them, a small price to pay for the victory of integration over white supremacy.

## Performing Within Racial Capitalism

Though segregation in public schools had been made illegal in 1954 with *Brown v. Board of Education*, it took years to untangle the mess of official and unofficial policies protecting segregated spaces in American society. Within the music industry, eventual enforcement of desegregation laws simply represented a shift in how white supremacy operated within the marketplace.

---

[76] Wilbur H. Rowand to Dave Brubeck, February 27, 1967, Brubeck Collection. Contents of the letter are also cited here: Madison Underwood, "Jazz Great Dave Brubeck Helped Integrate University of Alabama with 1964 Concert, According to Letter," *AL.com* December 6, 2012, https://www.al.com/spotnews/2012/12/dave_brubeck_integration_unive.html.

[77] Dave Brubeck to Wilbur H. Rowand, April 7, 1967, Brubeck Collection.

As George Lipsitz explains, "White Americans are encouraged to invest in whiteness, to remain true to an identity that provides them with resources, power, and opportunity."[78] Brubeck was clearly willing to perform at universities across the South as they integrated, but he was not the sole decision maker when it came to his southern return. Rather, his return was arranged by Bob Bundy. As a booking agent, Bundy received compensation based on the performances he arranged, and as one of the highest paid musicians in the country, Brubeck was likely a boon to booking agents like Bundy. However, if Bundy was located primarily in the segregated South, and Brubeck had an integrated quartet, Bundy must have had the most to lose from Brubeck's inability to tour across that region. Considering how quickly Brubeck performed at recently integrated southern schools (eight months after integration at UA and four months after integration at Mississippi State University), it seems that Bundy jumped at the chance to once again earn commissions on Brubeck's performances. Paired with Bundy's message to Brubeck, exhorting him to consider taking an all-white quartet on the 1960 southern tour and urgently scribbling "You need this" on the letter, it seems Brubeck's moral scruples had cost Bundy as much as anyone else. Put simply, before the emergence of a victory narrative for the civil rights movement, Bundy was not willing to lose financially simply because the southern schools required a segregated performing group.

Like Brubeck, Bundy represents one small part of the broader commercial music industry. It can be tempting to delve into his thoughts regarding racial justice, segregation, and integration to understand how his individual beliefs impacted his actions and decisions, and further, impacted Brubeck's actions and performances. However, not only would it be virtually impossible to uncover Bundy's personal racial ideologies in the early 1960s, to do so would obscure a more pressing issue; namely, that within the commercial music industry, personal beliefs can directly support white supremacist systems—but they do not have to for such systems to thrive. As jazz historian John Gennari writes, "Personal friendships and individual virtue can help dissolve the color line, [but] they can't quite as easily dismantle the power of systemic, institutional racism in a culture that was founded on white supremacy."[79] Brubeck did not create the notion that intellect, respectability, or recognition denoted particular modes of white performance (and neither did his critics, fans, and

---

[78] George Lipsitz, *The Possessive Investment in Whiteness* (Philadelphia, PA: Temple University Press, 2006 [1998]), xvii.

[79] John Gennari, *Blowin' Hot and Cool: Jazz and Its Critics* (Chicago: University of Chicago Press, 2006), 384.

industry representatives), nor did he necessarily recognize such modes as being particularly white. Rather, this was a collective effort, supported and sustained by white people (and some non-white people) in and outside the music industry across centuries in varying degrees of invisibility. In short, what I have described is a system of white supremacy, in which whiteness is defined through legal, social, cultural, and political distinctions between the ambiguous racial Other and the white self.

An ideological system like white supremacy shapes the actions, statements, and beliefs of every individual within that system, but it does not depend on those individuals' good or bad intentions; as cultural theorist Stuart Hall writes, "We formulate our intentions *within ideology* [emphasis in the original]."[80] The ideologies within which individuals formulate intentions also shape how individuals theorize and construct structures like capitalism. Political theorist Cedric J. Robinson calls this confluence "racial capitalism," arguing, "The development, organization, and expansion of capitalist society pursued essentially racial directions, so too did social ideology."[81] Robinson continues by explaining how individuals theorize and build structures like capitalism within ideology: "As a material force, then, it could be expected that racialism would inevitably permeate the social structures emergent from capitalism." Robinson argues that because capitalism emerged from a feudal society already organized around race, capitalism was already and always entwined with racialism. As historian Robin D. G. Kelley explains, "Capitalism and racism, in other words, did not break from the old order but rather evolved from it to produce a modern world system of 'racial capitalism' dependent on slavery, violence, imperialism, and genocide."[82] In such valuations, capitalism operates not only as its own cultural system but also one that both supports and is intertwined with white supremacy; Ta-Nehisi Coates makes plain the historic relationship between ownership and racism when he writes that "the heritage of white supremacy was not so much birthed by hate as by the *impulse towards plunder* [emphasis mine]."[83] As others, such as historian Walter Johnson, have shown, racialism/racism and capitalism grew and evolved together; what served as racial capitalism in one century (for example, slavery) was altered in another (share cropping, FHA loans,

---

[80] Stuart Hall, "Whites of Their Eyes," in *Gender, Race and Class in Media: A Text Reader*, ed. Gail Dines and Jean M. Humez (Thousand Oaks, CA: Sage, 1995), 19.

[81] Cedric J. Robinson, *Black Marxism: The Making of the Black Radical Tradition* (Durham, NC: University of North Carolina Press, 2000 [1983]), 2.

[82] Robin D. G. Kelley, "Foreword," in *Black Marxism: The Making of the Black Radical Tradition* ([1983]; Durham, NC: University of North Carolina Press, 2000), xiii.

[83] Ta-Nehisi Coates, "Take Down the Confederate Flag—Now," *The Atlantic*, June 18, 2015, https://www.theatlantic.com/politics/archive/2015/06/take-down-the-confederate-flag-now/396290/.

gentrification).⁸⁴ Political activist and Black feminist Angela Davis explains further, "While it is important to acknowledge the pivotal part slavery played in the historical consolidation of capitalism, more recent developments linked to global capitalism cannot be adequately comprehended if the racial dimension of capitalism is ignored."⁸⁵

In other words, white supremacy is so sprawling, so embedded in European and European American conceptions of personhood, that it is inextricably tied to other key cultural systems like capitalism.⁸⁶ Brubeck's return to the South offers a crucial look at how the music industry's role in upholding white supremacy was rewarded by capitalism: ABC was happy to entertain a tour sponsored by an organization requiring a segregated musical group and segregated audiences. ABC likely did not think of this as a political decision but rather a financial decision that would ultimately be rewarded within a capitalist system of competition and profit. Put simply, within the capitalist system in which ABC, Bundy, and Brubeck operated, profit and mass consumption were considered to be more valuable than integration efforts—until a mass of consumer interest in integration could be identified. As Kelley explains, "Racial capitalism is not merely a *type* of capitalism, say, as opposed to non-racist capitalism. We don't have non-racist capitalism. . . . The term [racial capitalism] simply signals that capitalism developed and operates within a racist system or a racial regime."⁸⁷ In other words, capitalism shares the racial ideology of the society in which it exists.

Black jazz musicians across the twentieth century repeatedly made plain the connections between racism, white supremacy, and the music industry through record companies, television spots, hotels, and restaurants during tours, advertising, and the press. Nevertheless, the relationship between race (and specifically white supremacy) and capitalism remained largely invisible not only to Brubeck, but to many white musicians and critics in the 1960s. In a 1964 panel discussion on jazz for *Playboy* magazine, moderator Nat Hentoff

---

⁸⁴ Walter Johnson, *The Broken Heart of America: St. Louis and the Violent History of the United States* (New York: Basic Books, 2020).

⁸⁵ Angela Davis, interview with Gaye Tehreas Johnson and Alex Lubin, "Angela Davis: An Interview on the Futures of Black Radicalism," *Verso Books*, October 11, 2017, https://www.versobooks.com/blogs/3421-angela-davis-an-interview-on-the-futures-of-black-radicalism.

⁸⁶ Ingrid Monson notes many of the ways in which the 1960s music business was "astonishingly segregated," including the consolidation of recording and broadcast industries and the emergence of major labels and national radio networks; the copyright system, which Monson notes rewards songwriters and publishers, not performers; the "standard contracts [that] all but ensured that most [artists] would never see a royalty check"; and the segregated locals of the American Federation of Musicians, which "controlled access to the highest paying gigs in the music industry." Monson, *Freedom Sounds*, 29–30.

⁸⁷ Robin D. G. Kelley, "What Is Racial Capitalism and Why Does It Matter?" Lecture, University of Washington Simpson Center for the Humanities, November 18, 2017, https://www.youtube.com/watch?v=--gim7W_jQQ&t=3s, accessed June 15, 2020.

asked the participants, a mix of Black and white jazz musicians and white critics, if Jim Crow still existed in bookings.[88] Dizzy Gillespie and Gunther Schuller affirmed that yes, it still exists, though in different, perhaps more subtle ways. Cannonball Adderley attempted to explain the feeling of double consciousness, the persistent feeling of subordination and need to reckon with a racist white society, stating, "You're always conscious of the fact that you're Negro."[89] Hentoff, perhaps feeling that there was a relationship between business and race, pushed the panelists for more specifics in the "business end of jazz." (One might point out the potential difficulty in asking some of the highest paid and best-known jazz musicians in the field, who likely draw some of the widest audiences, about racism in business practices.) Brubeck's rather short-sighted responses focused on individual successful Black jazz musicians, as well as his struggles as the leader of an integrated group: "I always figured that the charge of Jim Crow in jazz was a fairy tale, because I played for years during which one Negro soloist would be making more than my entire quartet" and "I know that I lost the highest paying job I was ever offered in my life because my group was mixed. An all-Negro group took it. And that was on nationwide television."

But critic Ralph Gleason's response offers a more specific picture of how Jim Crow operated visibly, and how it operated invisibly, at least to some white jazz musicians and critics. Gleason acknowledged that there were bookings Black jazz musicians did not get due to racial prejudice, and he explained that Jim Crow was present in the southern towns in which Black musicians were allowed to perform but not stay in the segregated hotels and motels they were barred from—but he argued that racism did not exist in the majority of the jazz business itself: "But the way in which the major booking agencies function, as far as I can tell from where I stand, is not Jim Crow. All *they're* interested in doing is making money, and they're not interested any more than any other money-making machine is in the color of the person who makes the money for them."[90] Such an analysis misses the connections between capitalism and racism: when booking agencies pursued contracts with colleges and universities requiring all-white groups, Black musicians lost potential jobs, potential revenue, potential audiences, and further, potential recording contracts by studios looking for groups with bigger audiences and "broader"

---

[88] Participants included Cannonball Adderley, Dizzy Gillespie, Charles Mingus, George Russell, Ralph Gleason, Nat Hentoff, Dave Brubeck, Stan Kenton, Gerry Mulligan, and Gunther Schuller.
[89] Cannonball Adderley in "A Jazz Summit Meeting," in *Keeping Time: Readings in Jazz History*, ed. Robert Walser (Oxford: Oxford University Press, 2014), 261; quoted from "The Playboy Panel: Jazz—Today and Tomorrow," *Playboy*, February 1964, 29–31, 34–38, 56, 58, 139–141.
[90] Ralph Gleason in "A Jazz Summit Meeting," 262.

appeal—symbols that define success within capitalism. Therefore, ostensibly non-political business decisions, such as performing in segregated venues, directly benefited white musicians in the name of meritocracy and capitalism-derived definitions of success. On the panel, Cannonball Adderley attempted to explain such a relationship, saying, "We've played clubs where a club owner will very frankly say, 'You draw a lot of white business. You know, most Negro groups don't draw a lot of white business. So I can afford to pay you more because you draw Negroes and whites.'" That such decisions repeatedly replayed across the music industry demonstrates how the system of white supremacy automatically reproduces itself through other cultural systems—in this case, capitalism.

The mid-century music industry of course operated within capitalism—but it also operated within a white racial frame.[91] Various stakeholders within the music industry repeatedly made "business" decisions, arguing that those decisions had nothing to do with race—even as the financial bottom line repeatedly favored artists who demonstrated caution toward racial justice movements. As cornetist Rex Stewart told Nat Hentoff in the 1970s, "Where the control is, the money is. Do you see any of us [Black musicians] running any record companies, booking agencies, radio stations, music magazines?"[92] Charles Mingus made the matter even more plain by drawing a contrast between the terms "Jim Crow" and "Crow Jim" in the same panel with Hentoff, Gleason, Gillespie, Adderley, and Brubeck, cited above: "Until we start lynching white people, there is no word that can mean the same as Jim Crow means. Until we own Bethlehem Steel and RCA Victor, plus Columbia Records and several other industries, the term Crow Jim has no meaning."[93] Even earlier, Langston Hughes's poem "White Man" (1936) clearly linked whiteness and capitalism. Referencing Louis Armstrong's recordings and the question of who owned the copyright, Hughes ends the poem asking white readers, "Is your name spelled / C-A-P-I-T-A-L-I-S-T?"[94] In other words, Black scholars, artists, poets, and musicians described the effects of racial capitalism long before white jazz critics ever began to even deny the relationship.

Many conversations surrounding the effects of white privilege and its revelation for white people are framed around individual agency. However, though highly visible musicians like Brubeck made decisions to resist, they

---

[91] Joe R. Feagin, *The White Racial Frame: Centuries of Racial Framing and Counter-Framing*, 3rd ed. (New York: Routledge, 2020).
[92] Qtd. in Nat Hentoff, *Jazz Is* (New York: Random House, 1976), 276.
[93] "A Jazz Summit Meeting," 289.
[94] Langston Hughes, "White Man," in *New Masses*, December 1936, qtd. in *Black on White: Black Writers on What It Means to Be White*, ed. David R. Roediger (New York: Schocken Books, 1998), 124–125.

did so within the context of a broader commercial music industry—an industry that included booking agents like Bundy and others, whose influence remains largely unknown, and an industry that often demonstrated little interest in musicians' ostensibly "risky" political opinions. Further, musician-allies like Brubeck remained tied to systems of racial capitalism outside the music industry. As Evelyn Nakano Glenn writes, "A white person in America enjoys privileges and a higher standard of living by virtue of the subordination and lower standard of living of people of color, *even if that particular white person is not exploiting or taking advantage of a person of color* [emphasis mine]."[95]

## Conclusion

As Brubeck navigated early civil rights protests, he worked to find an approach that suited his image and career, which he and his wife, managers, record producers, and advertisers had cultivated for nearly a decade. The result was a new musical and promotional approach for Brubeck, one that leveraged his whiteness to support integration efforts in the South. With the growing visibility of his concert cancelations, Brubeck became emboldened, and his indignation with policymakers at southern colleges and universities met the white rage of the segregationists protesting his performances. As Wynton Marsalis, trumpeter and artistic director for Jazz at Lincoln Center, once said, "[Brubeck] is important because he stood up for Civil Rights, when many of us—sat down."[96] As a white man, Brubeck was able to simultaneously voice his anger and maintain a nonthreatening image in ways that, as Marsalis implies, Black protesters typically could not. Ultimately, this period in Brubeck's career is important because it allows deep consideration of his privilege as an activist, particularly regarding who he spoke for and who he spoke over, who listened, and for whom his actions as a civil rights advocate were meaningful.

Certainly, the first person for whom Brubeck spoke was Wright, for whom Brubeck canceled the South Africa tour, UGA concert, and 1960 southern

---

[95] Evelyn Nakano Glenn, *Unequal Freedom: How Race and Gender Shaped American Citizenship and Labor* (Cambridge, MA: Harvard University Press, 2002), 14. As Christi Jay Wells writes of bandleader Paul Whiteman, white musicians "[do] not need to be redeemed nor exonerated." Christopher J. Wells, "'The Ace of His Race': Paul Whiteman's Early Critical Reception in the Black Press," *Jazz & Culture* 1 (2018): 97.

[96] Wynton Marsalis, "The Life and Music of Dave Brubeck," concert featuring the Jazz at Lincoln Center Orchestra, April 12, 2014, Rose Theater, Jazz at Lincoln Center, New York. https://youtu.be/PQ-yXQItCGg, accessed October 30, 2015. As for Brubeck, he firmly believed that jazz had "always been an example set to the world of true integration." "Editorial," *San Francisco Chronicle*, n.d., ca. 1960, Brubeck Collection.

tour. But while Brubeck received glowing praise for doing so, Wright largely stayed quiet. In fact, Brubeck seemed to have shone a spotlight on issues that Wright, a Chicago native, would rather not define him. A 1960 article in the *Pittsburgh Courier* by George Pitts quotes Wright as explaining, "Whatever Dave does is okey [sic] by me." He continued, "If he wants to make the trip without me, it would be okey. I know he's all right, and I know if Brubeck decides to do something it will not be because of any feeling of his own on race."[97] Wright's comments display considerable trust in Brubeck's decisions, but they did not have the impact many Black journalists, including Pitts, desired. While Brubeck was lauded for his actions, Wright's experience with the press was more closely related to the criticisms faced by Nat King Cole, Duke Ellington, and Louis Armstrong when they failed to live up to the expectations Black communities held for highly visible Black men—expectations that, as Ingrid Monson explains, were significantly higher for Black musicians than for white musicians.[98] Wright was subtly criticized by the Black press for his comments. Pitts explained Wright's apparently unsatisfying statements: "Wright finally found an opportunity to express his feelings, but all Americans knew his expression would be that of most Negroes who long have tasted the slurs of the Southland."[99] The Baltimore *Afro-American* referred to Wright, a fairly dark-skinned man, as a "tan bassist," which suggests that the writer meant to criticize Wright for not being supportive enough of racial justice causes.[100] Despite such criticism, Wright maintained his diplomatic stance in an interview decades later, as he recounted the story of a school that had initially refused to allow him to perform: "I won't say the name—that way nobody'll get hurt."[101] When asked how he thought Wright felt about the quartet's entry into the civil rights movement, Brubeck explained that Wright had the "greatest attitude":

He made it a point not to be political or to side in with any of the organizations that would ask him to join their group and protest and all that. He said, "The way

[97] George E. Pitts, "Give Brubeck Credit for a Slap at Bias," *Pittsburgh Courier*, February 12, 1960, 12.
[98] Ingrid Monson, *Freedom Sounds*, 59–65.
[99] Pitts, "Give Brubeck Credit for a Slap at Bias," 12.
[100] "Tan Bassist Given OK in Memphis," *Afro-American*, January 23, 1960, 16. This may have been an implicit form of reverse colorism. While colorism typically would privilege light-skinned Black people (and therefore is, as Ibram X. Kendi writes, "A collection of racist policies that cause inequities between Light people and Dark people, and these inequities are substantiated by racist ideas about Light and Dark people"), this statement suggests that Wright was acting too "light," or had assimilated too much to white ideals and behaviors. Ibram X. Kendi, *How to Be an Antiracist* (New York: One World, 2019), 110.
[101] Fred Hall, *It's About Time: The Dave Brubeck Story* (Fayetteville: University of Arkansas Press, 1996), 87. Likewise, in an interview with Keith Hatschek, Wright recalled that at one concert in the "Deep South," the FBI sent additional security, but that nothing came of the threats. Hatschek, *The Real Ambassadors*, 39.

I can do a lot of good is doing just what I'm doing. And we're integrating a lot of places."[102]

But while for Wright, performing in an integrated quartet and performing in segregated schools across the South was an important means of disrupting white supremacy, it seems that Pitts and some other Black audiences may have expected a different form of protest (as they did from musicians like Louis Armstrong and Nat King Cole).

Indeed, it seems as if, at least initially, Wright had little say in Brubeck's move toward race activism—even when Brubeck's protests positioned Wright as an implicit activist as well. For example, in a 1981 interview, Brubeck spoke about the concert at East Carolina College, admitting that Wright had not known that the school was segregated and did not want to allow him to play—the school had approached Brubeck alone.[103] Further, Wright had not known that part of the compromise in allowing the quartet to perform at East Carolina College was that Wright stay in the background—so when Brubeck called him to the front of the group for a solo, Wright went. This reflects an unawareness faced by many white liberals attempting anti-racist actions, in which, as Sullivan writes, "their ignorance [of living their racial identities] often poses as knowledge, making it all the more insidious."[104] Throughout that night, and in the years that followed, Brubeck made anti-racist decisions that positioned both him and Wright as race activists; as he explained to journalist Hedrick Smith,

> And we've had a lot of terrible things happen to us while we're fighting to have equality—police escorts from the airport to the university, or where I wouldn't go on [stage] until the black audience could come in or [until they] didn't have to sit in the balcony. I wouldn't play until they were in the front row.[105]

Brubeck's decisions are remarkable, especially for a white musician in the early 1960s; however, he made them without seeming to understand the difference

---

[102] Dave Brubeck, "A Long Partnership in Life and Music," an oral history conducted in 1999 and 2001 by Caroline C. Crawford, Regional Oral History Office, Bancroft Library, University of California, Berkeley, 2006.

[103] Dave Brubeck, interview with Kerry Frumkin, WFMT Chicago, October 17, 1981, Brubeck Collection.

[104] Sullivan, *Good White People*, 3.

[105] "PBS: Rediscovering Dave Brubeck with Hedrick Smith," originally broadcast on December 16, 2001, https://www.pbs.org/brubeck/talking/daveOnRacial.htm, accessed January 5, 2021. Iola Brubeck also recalled threats of violence in an interview with Keith Hatschek, though she commented that nothing came of them. While much attention has been paid to the Brubecks' southern civil rights activism, both commented on the prejudice they experienced in northern states, like their home of Connecticut. For example, after they had moved to Weston, Connecticut, Iola Brubeck described receiving "one of those nasty name-calling phone calls" after Eugene Wright had been to the house to rehearse, and possibly stayed the night. Hatschek, *The Real Ambassadors*, 39.

between what it meant for a white man to protest racial injustice in front of a white audience in the South, and what it meant for a Black man to do so.[106]

Wright had the potential to be the focus of this story, and it certainly seems as if some audiences wanted him to be. But the fact that it was Brubeck at the center, with Wright in the limelight, demonstrates the privilege Brubeck had in potentially pushing Wright into a protest toward which he felt at best publicly ambivalent.[107] Brubeck's centrality to the story, however, also offered a unique challenge to audiences unused to hearing a white man explicitly position a Black man as an integral part of his own career. Within the context of the early civil rights era, Brubeck's voice—as a bandleader, as an established musician, and as a white man whose career and image had been constructed around implicit norms of whiteness for over a decade—ultimately weighed more than Wright's for many Black and white audiences, members of the music industry, and southern audiences. Further, Brubeck benefited from the lower standard to which these audiences held him, as a white performer, on civil rights issues. William Pollard of the *Los Angeles Sentinel*, a Black newspaper, commended Brubeck, arguing that "the majority race needs to lead the way in this respect," and emphasizing that "the perpetuation of racial discrimination is of their making."[108] At the same time, Pollard criticized unnamed Black artists who performed in segregated establishments "in order to receive the fabulous salaries each week." He continued, "It is good that Dave Brubeck and others of the majority race are willing to lead the way in this fight to have a man accepted based upon his ability. But, it is a sad story indeed, when these crusaders for equality find the Negro artist doing little or nothing to supplement their efforts." In other words, while it may have been Brubeck's responsibility to protest racial prejudice and segregation, the response to his actions reflected his privilege.

There lies an uneasy tension, then, between Brubeck's outspoken support of integration and Wright's relative silence, whether chosen or not. That tension

---

[106] In a 2007 interview with Shan Sutton, Brubeck suggests that he took a different approach on his 1976 tour of South Africa. He explains that Iola Brubeck had received death threats against Dave Brubeck and his sons if Dave Brubeck's integrated group performed for an integrated crowd in Johannesburg (he was touring with Black South African bass player Victor Ntoni). He explains that he told Ntoni, "You don't have to go on and go through with this. But we'll go on." Ntoni responded that he would go on—that in fact, his brother had been killed in Soweto, and that Brubeck should not be afraid because, "They won't do anything. They'll be afraid to do anything to you." "Brubeck Oral History Project," interview by Shan Sutton, 2007, Brubeck Collection, https://scholarlycommons.pacific.edu/bohp/27/.

[107] That Wright could handle such matters privately seems clear from a story he told Keith Hatschek in a 2008 interview. While in India on the 1958 US State Department tour, Wright was confronted by a man who asked "how he [Wright] could support his government as a jazz ambassador," given the discrimination Black Americans like him faced at home. Wright apparently asked the man "what business he had asking me about that, when his own country [India] had a much longer history of discrimination." The man simply walked away. Hatschek, *The Real Ambassadors*, 30.

[108] William F. Pollard, "Labor's Side," *Los Angeles Sentinel*, January 28, 1960, A7.

highlights a primary issue in white advocacy for racial justice causes—namely, that in supporting those whose voices have been systematically silenced throughout history, it can be easy to speak over the very voices that advocates intend to amplify. Brubeck's actions and rhetoric were meaningful to countless fans and organizations, including the California chapter of the NAACP, who wrote to *Down Beat* and Brubeck, thanking him for taking a visible stand against prejudice. And clearly Wright supported Brubeck's decisions as bandleader. However, for Wright, Brubeck did not need to take the steps he did. Had Brubeck been true to Wright's voice, he might not have canceled any concerts; as Wright's comments above suggest, he knew Brubeck was "alright."

But though Wright was the reason for Brubeck's advocacy, Brubeck ultimately did not make his stand only for Wright but also for people like Betty Jean Furgerson, whose letter to Brubeck made clear her belief that his actions could support and amplify her perspective. He spoke directly to his own southern supporters, appealing to their musical tastes and making the case for musical integration. He inspired white students like Stuart Woods, who attempted to reverse UGA's segregationist policy, and institutions like East Carolina College, which reconsidered discriminatory policies that prevented Black musicians from performing. His protest influenced audiences around the nation, including Barbara Bruff, a student at the University of California at Berkeley, who wrote to tell Brubeck that his actions had helped to "ease the cynicism that [she] was beginning to acquire"; Robert S. Willis, an airman stationed at Malstrom Air Force Base in Great Falls, Montana, who wrote to *Down Beat* in support of Brubeck; and Ginger Kugle of East Texas who, though she did not like Brubeck's music, felt compelled by his actions to write to thank him for his stand.[109]

And, ultimately, Brubeck took this stand for himself, and, importantly, for his belief in the supremacy of an American democratic system—a belief shared among many white Americans within the context of the Cold War at mid-century. Consider again Brubeck's words on his return from his US State Department Tour: "Prejudice is indescribable. To me, it is the reason we would lose the world. I have been through Asia and India and the Middle East and we have to realize how many brown-skinned people there are in this world. Prejudice here or in South Africa is setting up our world for one terrible let down."[110] Brubeck's recognition of racism, and perhaps of his own whiteness,

---

[109] Barbara Bruff to Dave Brubeck, personal letter, January 14, 1960, Brubeck Collection; Robert S. Willis, Letter to the Editor, *Down Beat*, July 21, 1960; Ginger Kugle to Dave Brubeck, personal letter, ca. 1960, Brubeck Collection.

[110] Ralph Gleason, "Brubeck Cancels South Africa Because of Negro Artist Ban," *Daily Boston Globe*, October 19, 1958, 61.

was motivated by a dedication to American exceptionalism. That dedication was accompanied by a realization that continued American racism left that exceptionalism unfulfilled and was ultimately unconvincing for people of color outside American borders. In other words, a key selling point of fighting prejudice (primarily, in Brubeck's case, through integration) was the imagery of American racism, how it might be viewed by people of color around the world, and how that would impact America's performance in the Cold War. For Brubeck, and for other mid-century white progressives, solving racism (by insisting on integration) could fulfill the promise Brubeck defended in World War II: that American democracy could provide a moral and political model for the world.

In interviews looking back on this period, Brubeck's indignation at justice unfulfilled is clear. Though it is hard to imagine Brubeck facing any consequences had he decided to replace Wright for the tour, his fear for his own livelihood is also apparent, both as he crept toward a more public engagement with the civil rights movement and in his hesitance to return to the South afterward. But even if he believed he could have lost his career by directly confronting segregation, Brubeck's image and legacy as bandleader ultimately benefited from his decisions to support integration (and benefited more than other members of the quartet).[111] As with other white bandleaders at mid-century, Brubeck's assumed heroism within the context of the civil rights movement reflects the cultural capital granted to white anti-racists of the period—a cultural capital that did not demand measurable outcomes or policy changes, and that bestowed a privilege of heroism not granted to Black musicians. At the same time, Brubeck's advocacy relied on his power and privilege within the mainstream music industry to craft albums and marketing approaches that amplified the music and beliefs of the African Americans with whom he had grown close. In doing so, he harnessed his white image in order to once again bring new audiences to jazz—and to his own music—in the segregationist South.[112]

---

[111] Bandleader Stan Kenton's legacy, for example, has never quite been able to shake either the 1953 *Jet Magazine* article in which he is quoted as saying, "The harmonic structure of Negro jazz was not enough to satisfy Europeans. Their ears are accustomed to more complex harmony and melody," or the telegram he sent to *Down Beat* magazine in response to the 1956 critics' poll, protesting on behalf of "a new minority group, 'white jazz musicians.' The only thing I gained from studying the opinions of your literary geniuses of jazz is complete and total disgust." "Stan Kenton Attacked for Slur on Negro Jazz," *Jet Magazine*, December 24, 1953; telegram qtd. in Leonard Feather, *The Jazz Years: Earwitness to an Era* (New York: Da Capo Press, 1987), 122.

[112] Brubeck continued to protest racial inequality and social justice throughout the 1960s. The quartet performed in benefit concerts for the Southern Christian Leadership Conference (SCLC), the National Association for the Advancement of Colored People (NAACP), the Student Nonviolent Coordinating Committee (SNCC), and the Congress of Racial Equality (CORE). He also found compositional avenues to share his own personal beliefs regarding racial equality, such as the musical *The Real Ambassadors* (1960), the oratorio *The Light in the Wilderness* (1968), and the cantata *The Gates of Justice* (1969).

# 5
# Negotiating Jewish Identity in *The Gates of Justice*

In 1968, Rabbi Charles D. Mintz commissioned a Jewish cantata from Dave Brubeck, a white, non-Jewish jazz musician and newly minted composer of large-scale works.[1] *The Gates of Justice* premiered in 1969 at the dedication of the new Rockdale Temple in Cincinnati, Ohio, following the Temple's move from a predominantly Black neighborhood in the city to an overwhelmingly white suburb. The cantata's second performance took place at the 1969 Biennial Convention of the Union of American Hebrew Congregations (UAHC), the congregational wing of American Reform Judaism (today known as the Union for Reform Judaism).

The work was intended to mend the growing divide in Black-Jewish relations in the late 1960s by addressing themes many Reform Jewish communities understood as central to this relationship: (1) that both communities had experienced shared histories of suffering and oppression; and (2) that Jews had a moral imperative to become involved in the civil rights movement. However, the cantata's texts and themes (the cantata blends texts from the Bible; the Jewish sage, Hillel; Martin Luther King Jr.; spirituals; and new text by Iola Brubeck), Brubeck's wide-ranging musical references and ensemble decisions (including a tenor soloist singing in Jewish cantorial style and, according to the program note, a "Negro baritone"), and its premiere at Rockdale Temple's new, suburban location, also reveal aspects of Black-Jewish relations during the civil rights movement that some Black activists found to be increasingly problematic; according to Black writers like James Baldwin, Richard Wright, and Julius Lester, these included race and class privilege, gradual white assimilation, white flight, and unequal partnerships.

At the same time, the cantata offered another chance for Brubeck to make an unambiguous statement affirming his continued commitment to the civil

---

[1] Portions of this chapter previously appeared as Kelsey Klotz, "Negotiating Jewish Identity in Dave Brubeck's *The Gates of Justice*," Milken Archive of Jewish Music, December 2020, https://www.milkenarchive.org/articles/view/negotiating-jewish-identity-in-dave-brubecks-the-gates-of-justice/. Reproduced here with the permission of the Milken Archive of Jewish Music.

rights movement through musical action (following the 1960 tour, this included his composition of the musical *The Real Ambassadors*, and numerous concerts benefiting civil rights organizations).[2] With the violence of the assassinations of Martin Luther King Jr. and Robert Kennedy, continued civil rights struggles, and escalations in and protests against the Vietnam War, Brubeck seemed interested in finding new and more direct ways to address the turmoil of the late 1960s. In 1969 a journalist for the *Washington Post* asked Brubeck if he had "taken part in any of the peace demonstrations related to the war in Vietnam."[3] Brubeck responded, "Everything I write is part of taking part." He continued, telling the reporter that his recent shift from jazz to classical was made in part because "I think I can reach more people with what I think is important now—at this time in my life and at this time in our history through this medium." In another interview from 1969, Brubeck explained that he quit the quartet at its financial peak out of an urgent need to do whatever he could to save the United States, essentially highlighting the need for highly paid artists like himself to put their money where their mouth was: "I don't think any group ever commanded the fees we did. But civilization is in a crisis. If people don't get in and do something—do whatever they can in their own way—we're lost. We must face what we're up against."[4]

*The Gates of Justice* commission provided Brubeck a chance to once again engage in the civil rights movement, making a clear musical statement in a religious context that was meaningful to him. While Brubeck and Rabbi Mintz intended *The Gates of Justice* to be an intervention that would strengthen a strained Black-Jewish relationship, it also serves as musical documentation of both that relationship and the relationship between Jewish communities and mid-century American whiteness. Once considered by some to be useful allies in a postwar climate celebrating democracy and equal opportunities for all, by the late 1960s, Jewish and Black civil rights leaders were often engaged in increasingly bitter and increasingly public struggles over leadership in civil rights organizations and key issues, including who should define the movement's goals and methods. As some Black leaders sought to assert independence from allyships with whites, Jewish communities responded to growing anti-Semitic attacks with waning support for civil rights causes. The cantata's premiere at the dedication of Rockdale Temple's new synagogue building in the Cincinnati suburb of Amberley Village, its second

---

[2] For more on The Real Ambassadors, see Keith Hatschek, *The Real Ambassadors: Dave and Iola Brubeck and Louis Armstrong Challenge Segregation* (Jackson: University of Mississippi Press, 2022).

[3] "Brubeck Becomes Serious," *Washington Post*, February 23, 1969, H1–2.

[4] Tom Mackin, "Brubeck Work Debuts," *Evening News* (Newark, NJ), April 4, 1969. The article is about the Easter television premiere of Brubeck's oratorio *The Light in the Wilderness* (1968) on CBS.

performance at the 1969 Biennial Convention of the UAHC, and its subsequent performances were primarily aimed at Jewish audiences.[5] Therefore, while the goal of the cantata was to address the relationship between two diverse communities, it seems to have done so almost entirely through Jewish congregants. As they imagined multicultural solutions to the civil rights movement, both Brubeck and the Reform Jewish audiences targeted in the commission used the cantata as they negotiated their places within, outside, and against the American Black/white racial binary.

## *The Gates of Justice* Commission

After the Brubeck Quartet's final concert in December 1967, Brubeck shifted his focus from jazz to classical composition with the choral and orchestral premieres of the oratorio *The Light in the Wilderness*.[6] This was not Brubeck's first "classical" composition (even beyond his compositions as a student of Darius Milhaud at Mills College), nor his first composition in which he marshaled large instrumental forces in a classical style (such as *Elementals*, 1963), nor even his first composition that had a particularly strong social message (*The Real Ambassadors*, 1961); nevertheless, it marked a significant departure from his work with the quartet and defined a new phase in his career. He was finally making good on a promise he made to *Down Beat* readers in 1953: that one day, he would return to classical composition full-time.

*The Light in the Wilderness* was Brubeck's first attempt to marry classical and jazz-tinged music with a clear social commentary that combined religious themes with democratic action. The oratorio is based on the biblical story of Jesus's forty days in the desert and musically interprets the Devil's temptations as universal temptations for humanity. For Brubeck, the contemporary message of this oratorio was clear; as he told Leonard Feather, the oratorio was the start of an ideology of reconciliation guided by love:

> "Man cannot live by bread alone" has an odd double meaning for jazz musicians, who call money bread. We've given more aid to the world than any country in the

---

[5] *The Gates of Justice* was well received in its first performances, which were among predominantly Jewish audiences (there were multiple mentions in Jewish newspapers of an "overwhelming response" from the audience and "sharp and impassioned" audience enthusiasm). William D. Miranda, "Dave Brubeck's 'Gates of Justice' Presented," *Jewish Advocate*, December 31, 1970, 17; Monroe Levin, "Notes on Music," *Jewish Exponent*, May 8, 1970, 82.

[6] The choral premiere (for piano and choir) took place in January in Chapel Hill, North Carolina, and the orchestral premiere was presented in February with the Cincinnati Symphony Orchestra and the Miami University A Cappella Singers as part of an ecumenical service.

history of civilization. It hasn't done much good, because along with it must go love and understanding. This is the only real weapon that can save humanity. If I can express this feeling in words and music I'll feel I have really accomplished something.[7]

Brubeck critiques financial and economic support as not enough to "save humanity," arguing that empathy and love must accompany charity. Not only that, but love should be harnessed as a weapon in the United States' arsenal as it pursued its agenda abroad. In this statement, Brubeck asserted that his oratorio joined the efforts of activists who championed civil rights issues as a matter of national security.

Inspired by the oratorio's ideological focus on loving enemies, Rabbi Charles D. Mintz, on behalf of the UAHC, and with the College Conservatory of Music at the University of Cincinnati (CCM), commissioned Brubeck's next composition. The result was *The Gates of Justice* (commissioned in 1968, premiered in 1969). As Brubeck explained in an interview years later, Mintz approached Brubeck after the premiere of *The Light in the Wilderness* at Cincinnati's second annual Ecumenical Concert and told him he wanted "equal time."[8] The Brubecks, Mintz, and three other rabbis met at Brubeck's home to discuss the themes on which the composition might focus.[9] Mintz's account of that conversation implies that Brubeck was the first to suggest a composition that might directly address tensions between Jewish and African American communities:

Throughout all of our preliminary discussions, wherein we explored the possibility of his writing on a Jewish theme, Mr. Brubeck again and again alluded to the parallel between the historical experiences of the Jewish people and those of the black men in contemporary America. . . . The Hebrew Bible and most particularly the prophetic writings with their passion for social justice represent for him the essence of religious thought.[10]

---

[7] Leonard Feather, ". . . And All That Jazz," *Milwaukee Journal*, April 30, 1966.
[8] Dave Brubeck, interview with Howard Reich, "Summer Music Interview," *Moment* Magazine, July–August 2010, https://www.momentmag.com/summer-music-interview/.
[9] In later interviews, neither Mintz nor Brubeck name the other rabbis. At the time, Rockdale Temple had experienced unprecedented turnover in the position of senior rabbi. Until 1962, only four men had served as senior rabbi in the congregation's entire 139-year history. Rabbi Murray Blackman became senior rabbi in 1962 and resigned in 1967; then, Rabbi David Hachen became senior rabbi until 1969, at which point Rabbi Harold Hahn became senior rabbi. Hachen would have been senior rabbi when the commission was made, while Hahn was the senior rabbi when the cantata premiered. Jonathan D. Sarna and Karla Goldman, "From Synagogue-Community to Citadel of Reform: The History of K. K. Bene Israel (Rockdale Temple) in Cincinnati, Ohio," in *American Congregations*, vol. 1, ed. James P. Wind and James W. Lewis (Chicago: University of Chicago Press, 1998), 201–207.
[10] Nels Nelson, "Brubeck: From Jazz to Cantatas," *Philadelphia Daily News* April 24, 1970, A29.

While Mintz places responsibility for the composition's messaging on Brubeck, Brubeck's later recollections suggest that Mintz and his fellow rabbis requested the topic specifically. When asked why he thought Mintz chose him for the commission, Brubeck explains,

> They thought that with my background in jazz I could create something to heal the rift between the African-American community and the Jewish community that had at one time been so closely allied. At this time there were many cities in the U.S. that were being destroyed, suffering from riots in the aftermath of the assassinations of Martin Luther King, Jr. and Robert Kennedy. I thought by showing the similarities in the history of both peoples—slavery, the diaspora, rejection—I could contribute to a mutual understanding that would help everyone to act together in the cause of social justice.[11]

That the topic had been requested by Mintz and three other rabbis remained a consistent refrain in interviews with both Dave and Iola Brubeck.[12]

What might Mintz and the other rabbis have had to gain by insisting that it was the Brubecks who recognized what Mintz referred to as the "parallel experiences" of Black and Jewish histories of oppression? I argue that choosing Brubeck as the creative arbiter for the future of Black-Jewish relations allowed Mintz, Rockdale Temple, and the UAHC to walk a fine line between whiteness and Blackness while simultaneously appealing to a multi-generational audience.[13] As anthropologist Karen Brodkin explains, several prominent Jewish intellectuals (i.e., Lionel Trilling and Norman Mailer, to which we might add Nat Hentoff and Leonard Bernstein) became "interpreters of white America in the 1950s": "Being able to write and speak as white, and for non-Jews to accept Jews as white like them, was an important experience of Jewish maleness in the 1950s."[14] In this case, the reverse seems likely: if a white, non-Jew like Brubeck, a musician who publicly supported the civil rights movement,

---

[11] Brubeck, interview with Howard Reich.
[12] Dave Brubeck, interview with Eugenia Zukerman, "Dave and Iola Brubeck: The Gates of Justice," *Milken Archive of Jewish Music* September 23, 2003, https://www.milkenarchive.org/oral-history/category/audio/dave-and-iola-brubeck; Dave and Iola Brubeck, interview with Shan Sutton, "Dave and Iola Brubeck on *The Gates of Justice*," Brubeck Oral History Project, University of the Pacific Library, 2007. https://scholarlycommons.pacific.edu/bohp/29/, accessed August 1, 2019.
[13] Mintz could have selected Brubeck as a representative of a "hipper" musical genre in an attempt to communicate the ideals of the Reform movement to young people who were becoming increasingly disenchanted with Reform Jewish leaders; as critic Monroe Levin wrote in an early review of the work, "Rabbi Mintz's conviction that this type of art can be a religious force of attraction on young people was supported by the vocal response of the many students present." Monroe Levin, "Notes on Music," *Jewish Exponent*, May 8, 1970, 82.
[14] Karen Brodkin, *How Jews Became White Folks: And What That Says About Race in America* (New Brunswick, NJ: Rutgers University Press, 1994), 143.

recognized a unique relationship between Black and Jewish communities, then surely that could be an important signal to the cantata's Jewish audiences of what many Reform Jews understood to be the emotional and historical connections between Black and Jewish communities.

That the cantata was a commission outside his own religion did not seem to be much of an issue to Brubeck, at least publicly; at that point, Brubeck was a proud nondenominational Christian (it also clearly was not a problem for Mintz). Before becoming Catholic in 1980, Brubeck often explained that he did not follow an organized religion, but that he was "reared as a Presbyterian by a Christian Scientist mother who attended a Methodist Church."[15] He went on to explain that such flexibility regarding religious institutions was important to his spiritual approach: "I would rather go to the teachings of the religious leaders than to the churches that say they represent them. That way, I feel I can get closer to them." In other statements, he might add that though *The Light in the Wilderness* was "written with the theological counsel of a Vedanta leader, a Unitarian minister, an Episcopalian bishop and several Jesuit priests, I am not affiliated with any church."[16] Citing the influence of three Jewish teachers (Irving Coleman, Darius Milhaud, and Jesus), Brubeck rooted himself within a broader Judeo-Christian religious sphere.[17] In another account, he explains that in addition to his mother's religious flexibility, his father had told him "not to join anything."[18]

The story Brubeck told (and told often) about his religion in the 1950s and 1960s was ambiguous, but not ambivalent. It was a story that allowed him to use his broadly Christian background to take principled stances while not alienating particular sects. By commenting on the influence of Jewish teachers just before *The Gates of Justice* premiered, Brubeck also made an

---

[15] Tom Mackin, "Brubeck Work Debuts," *Evening News* (Newark, NJ), April 4, 1969.

[16] "Dave Brubeck Writes Church Music After 10-Year Pause," *Livermore Herald and News* (Livermore, CA), April 6, 1969.

[17] Though any mention of Brubeck's 1940s composition teacher was left out of the cantata's reception, it is impossible not to consider Milhaud's influence on the commission. John Salmon has traced the myriad ways Milhaud influenced Brubeck's compositional style through counterpoint, polytonality, and a multicultural approach to music, as well as Milhaud's importance to Brubeck's early career. Milhaud's postwar stature, as not only a French composer but increasingly also as a Jewish composer, may have lent Brubeck further credibility. Musicologist Erin K. Maher explains that though in his early career Milhaud carefully positioned himself as part of the French musical tradition, and not within a more marginalized Jewish musical tradition, Milhaud's Jewish identity became central to more of his compositions by the 1960s, and by the time *The Gates of Justice* premiered, Maher explains Milhaud's general American reception thus: "At a time when Milhaud's music—particularly his late works—was considered a tiresome anachronism by many, it was as a Jewish composer that his name still commanded significant prestige in the United States." John Salmon, "What Brubeck Got From Milhaud," *American Music Teacher*, February/March 1992, 26–29, 76; Erin K. Maher, "Darius Milhaud in the United States, 1940–71: Transatlantic Constructions of Musical Identity," PhD diss., University of North Carolina at Chapel Hill, 2016, 140.

[18] Nelson, "Brubeck."

argument for why his approach to religion, spirituality, and faith, an approach that recognizes common ground between Jewish and Christian (Protestant and Catholic) faiths, might be appropriate in a Jewish temple. Decades later, Brubeck reaffirmed this common ground approach, explaining that although he and Iola were not Jewish, "it seemed that our [the Brubecks' and the rabbis'] thoughts were very compatible."[19]

Brubeck's faith could thus act as a mirror to that of his Judeo-Christian audience members: he could reflect ostensibly universal points of agreement, while masking any denominationally specific theological disagreements.[20] His broadly defined Christianity, specifically Protestantism, intersected with his white, male heterosexuality, representing another facet of unmarked white privilege and connection to or compatibility with religious institutions with a history of supporting white supremacy that was invisible to him.[21] Notably, Brubeck expressed frustration about what Martin Luther King Jr. referred to as the most segregated hour of Christian America, 11:00 AM on Sunday, similarly protesting, "And think of the ridiculousness of how we operate segregated churches."[22] Nevertheless, the ease with which Brubeck crossed religious boundaries is in some ways similar to his racial colorblindness: as with race, he understood there to be essential, universal experiences shared among people of different identities. However, as with colorblindness, his faith-blind approach flattened the experiences of adherents to those various religions and ultimately obscured the privilege granted to Protestantism as another marker of whiteness at mid-century.[23] By suggesting a certain universality between Judeo-Christian religions in his own religious story, Brubeck also potentially, and unintentionally, associated Jewishness with whiteness, which was a fraught connection at best at mid-century.

---

[19] Brubeck, interview with Howard Reich.
[20] Even before Brubeck explicitly turned to religious compositions, some of his fans understood him to possess what they considered to be a unique relationship with religion, and especially Christianity, and wrote to express their own religious experiences of his music (see chapter 2). After *The Light in the Wilderness* and *The Gates of Justice*, fans of various Christian denominations wrote to Brubeck, revealing that they had been spiritually moved, that the compositions represented intelligent and sensitive philosophies, and that Brubeck himself might be a musical prophet.
[21] For more on the relationship between Christianity and white supremacy, see Robert P. Jones, *White Too Long: The Legacy of White Supremacy in American Christianity* (New York: Simon & Schuster, 2020).
[22] Kathleen Morner, "Jazzman's Church Music: Sermon by Brubeck," *Chicago Sun Times*, April 28, 1968.
[23] Brubeck had been somewhat privately investigating Catholicism as early as the mid-1950s. In a letter from the famed "jazz priest" Father Norman J. O'Connor, O'Connor first expresses surprise at Brubeck's interest, noting that the list of books Brubeck apparently sent him demonstrates an avid interest in Catholicism. O'Connor's parting words offer further insight into Brubeck's self-conception as a religious person; in essence, O'Connor wrote to Brubeck that he should not be embarrassed for being a "free-thinking art appreciating soul" (the quotations suggest that this was how Brubeck had described himself to O'Connor). Brubeck became Catholic in 1980, shortly after completing the Mass *To Hope*.

## The Role of *The Gates of Justice* at the UAHC and Rockdale Temple

Brubeck's history of support for the civil rights movement largely matched that of the Union of American Hebrew Congregations (UAHC), on whose behalf Mintz had in part commissioned the work. The UAHC had been consistent and vocal in its support of the civil rights movement and racial and economic justice throughout the 1960s. These resolutions began in the 1950s, but as the civil rights movement gained steam, the UAHC's resolutions on civil rights became both more specific and more pointed. Often, the resolutions demanded self-reflection on the part of Jewish congregations, asking them to do more to combat prejudice in their own localities. For example, in 1961, the UAHC issued a resolution titled "Achieving Equality Under the Law," reaffirming their consistent opposition to racial segregation and appealing to their members and congregations to "redouble their efforts" and to "strive unceasingly to complete the mission of equal rights and full opportunities under the law."[24] In a 1965 resolution on "Discrimination in Housing," the UAHC combined racial and economic justice issues, urging President Lyndon B. Johnson, all congregants, and governors to end housing discrimination. In doing so, the UAHC simultaneously explained why Jewish congregants should be so closely aligned with racial injustice:

> Shocking incidents of racial conflict in American cities have demonstrated again that the racial ghetto is the key to the pattern of segregated living which pervades and vitiates almost every phase of Negro life and Negro-white relationships. Jewish history has a special sensitivity to the horror of the ghetto, and Judaism is an affirmation of the God-given right of every man to equality and justice.[25]

In 1969, at the Biennial Convention of the UAHC (at which *The Gates of Justice* was performed), the UAHC reaffirmed their commitment to racial justice in a resolution that recognized oppression of Black communities and the particular obligation the Reform movement had to address injustice, in addition to offering concrete action items for congregants. In their emphasis on brotherhood, the indefatigable belief in American moral exceptionalism tied to religious imperative, and the inability to reconcile equality with discrimination,

---

[24] Union for Reform Judaism, "Achieving Equality Under the Law," 1961, https://urj.org/what-we-believe/resolutions/achieving-equality-under-law, accessed June 21, 2020.

[25] Union for Reform Judaism, "Discrimination in Housing," 1965, https://urj.org/what-we-believe/resolutions/discrimination-housing, accessed June 21, 2020.

many of the UAHC's resolutions matched Brubeck's own approach to integration and racial justice.

Despite the UAHC's clear racial justice goals and calls to action, local Jewish communities at times operated differently, depending on their own specific "on-the-ground" racial politics. However, the joint commission of *The Gates of Justice* for both the dedication of Cincinnati's new Rockdale Temple building and the UAHC Biennial Conference suggests an agreement on the cantata's message among many in the Reform Jewish community.

## Rockdale Temple

When the cantata premiered at Rockdale Temple, the congregation had just moved to the Cincinnati suburb of Amberley Village following periods of significant civil unrest in Cincinnati. During the "Long Hot Summer of 1967," windows in Rockdale Temple's previous building were broken; the city sustained roughly $2,000,000 in damages. In an apparent attempt to maintain congregants' interest in supporting the civil rights movement despite the damage, an article in the *American Israelite*, a weekly Jewish newspaper based in Cincinnati, reported that less than 1 percent of the Black population was involved. The article further insisted that "no Cincinnatian can close his eyes to the fact that many members of both races have long recognized the inequalities under which members of the Negro race have labored."[26]

The civil unrest following King's assassination in 1968 caused even more damage. Congregants Philip and Helene Cohen recounted the aftermath: "They came in and overnight the whole temple was destroyed. They came in and they pulled out every fixture, every piece of brass, all the beautiful lights were pulled down.... All the pews were broken and turned over, and the place was just ramshackled."[27] Construction of the new Rockdale Temple had already started, but the congregation was not yet ready to move. Temple leadership put in place a plan that both limited use of the temple by Jewish congregants and invited Black community groups to use the temple's facilities free of charge.[28] In exchange, Cohen explained, Rockdale Temple received protection from the Black community until the congregation officially moved to the new facilities.[29]

---

[26] *American Israelite*, June 22, 1967, in Jonathan D. Sarna and Karla Goldman, *The Jews of Cincinnati* (Teaneck, NJ: Holmes & Meier, 1986), 174.
[27] Philip T. Cohen and Helene Cohen, interview, in Sarna and Goldman, *The Jews of Cincinnati*, 174.
[28] Sarna and Goldman, "From Synagogue-Community to Citadel of Reform," 205.
[29] Philip T. Cohen, "Our History," Rockdale Temple, July 14, 2017, https://www.rockdaletemple.org/our-history.html, accessed June 21, 2020.

Cincinnati was one of nearly 200 cities across the United States that experienced civil unrest in the wake of Martin Luther King Jr.'s assassination on April 4, 1968. The turmoil, social unrest, and violence of those evenings were very clearly on Brubeck's mind as he wrote *The Gates of Justice*, and given the timing of the commission, could have inspired Mintz's request. Movement IV, "Except the Lord Build the House," features text from Psalm 127:1: "Except the Lord build the house, they labour in vain that build it; except the Lord keep the city, the watchman taketh but in vain." In the program note for movement IV, Brubeck explains, "Many of our beleaguered cities were riot-torn when I began to set the text.... I wished there was some way to engrave this warning into the mind of every policy-maker, on every level from national defense systems to police enforcement."[30] In an interview with the *Jewish Advocate* just before the cantata's premiere, Brubeck spoke even more plainly about what he felt was the primary problem: "We spend millions to guard the walls of our cities and pennies to improve the quality of life within."[31] For congregants at Rockdale Temple, seated in a new temple less than one year after the old temple had been damaged in what many referred to as race riots, this text must have had particular resonance. As members of the Reform movement, which was particularly engaged in civil rights activism, the Rockdale Temple congregation could likely have heard "Except the Lord Build the House" as a reminder to continue the work of the civil rights movement.

Brubeck underscores this goal in Movement IV of the cantata through the bass line, harmonic motion, and melodies. The movement has three short sections: tenor solo with choir, baritone solo with choir, and tenor and baritone duet with choir. The tenor soloist enters with the choir, singing his line ("Except the Lord build the house, they labor in vain that build it") first. The tenor melody is accompanied by a bass pedal on C and suspended harmonies that avoid any thirds, whether major or minor. The result is very little harmonic movement. When the baritone soloist enters, the bass and harmonies change. Instead of harmonic stasis, the bass ascends a minor scale from C to G (including the Gb blue note) over four measures; the tenor line matches the bass ascent, but the soprano and alto lines descend, creating a sense of collapse. The second half of the baritone solo reverses course, creating a sense of expansion: the bass line descends over an octave to a low F over the course of six measures, and the soprano, alto, and tenor lines ascend to a fortissimo climax. The tenor solo re-enters in the third section of the movement, engaging in a duet with the baritone, each singing their texts in their distinct

---

[30] Dave Brubeck, program note, *The Gates of Justice*.
[31] "Premiere in Fall for Jewish Cantata by Dave Brubeck," *Jewish Advocate*, August 21, 1969, A7.

musical styles (the tenor sings in a Jewish cantorial style, the baritone sings in a more blues-inflected style). The harmony shifts again, this time to recognizable progressions, moving from Cm7 to F7 to Bb13 to Eb13 to Fm to Cm—essentially, moving in ii-V-I substitutions until the final minor "Amen" cadence (iv-i). As the harmonies progress from open fourths to triads moving by half step to functional harmonies, movement IV seems to suggest that if the soloists act alone, neither the Jewish nor Black communities can progress, whereas if they work together, they can achieve a more harmonious and productive end result.

Beyond the civil unrest following King's death, Mintz and Rockdale Temple's rabbis had yet another reason to remind the congregation to continue to be involved in civil rights efforts—the move of the temple itself. Rockdale Temple's move from Rockdale Drive in Cincinnati's Avondale neighborhood to the northern suburb of Amberley Village reflected Cincinnati's broader white flight at mid-century. The congregation was formally organized in 1824, and the first temple was consecrated at Sixth and Broadway in 1836. In 1869 the congregation dedicated a new temple at 8th Street and Mound Street. In 1906 the congregation dedicated a new temple in what was then Cincinnati's Avondale and Walnut Hill suburbs. Located on Rockdale Drive, the temple was named Rockdale Temple. The congregation moved again in 1969, this time to the Amberley Village suburb, but kept the name Rockdale Temple. It was this temple's dedication that *The Gates of Justice* was meant to celebrate.

Census data for both the Avondale Rockdale Temple and the Amberley Village Rockdale Temple in 1960 and 1970 show that these neighborhoods were experiencing massive population shifts at mid-century. Nestled in the boundaries of census tract 67, the demographics of the Rockdale Temple's Avondale neighborhood changed significantly between 1950 and 1970. In 1950, the total population of tract 67 was 6,024; 76 percent (4,584) of the residents were white, and 23 pecent (1,440) were non-white (mostly Black, or "negro"). By 1960, tract 67 had grown to a total population of 6,924; only 7.8 percent (537) of the residents were white, and 92 percent (6,374) of the residents were "negro." The massive shift in racial demographics of Rockdale Temple's Avondale neighborhood continued into the 1960s. The total population in 1970 decreased to 4,714 residents, but the percentage of "negro," or Black, residents increased to 98.5 percent (4,643 Black residents total; 57 white residents total).

Rockdale Temple's new neighborhood in Amberley Village was nearly entirely white. In 1960, Amberley Village was 99 percent white (the total population was 3,680, the white population was 3,649, and "negro," or Black, population was 31). While the population ballooned in 1970 to 5,574, the

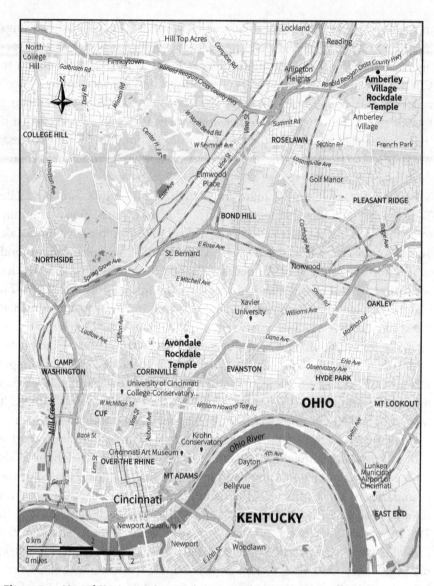

**Figure 5.1.** Map of Cincinnati showing locations of the Rockdale Temple in the Avondale neighborhood and its suburban Amberley Village location.
Note: Map uses present-day landmarks.

percentage of white residents remained the same, at 99 percent. Put another way, the Rockdale Temple moved from a neighborhood that in 1960 was 92 percent Black to a neighborhood that in 1970 was 99 percent white.

The temple's relocation was reflective of the broader shifts in population across Cincinnati and its suburbs during this period. As historian Charles Casey-Leininger documents, the Walnut Hills and Avondale neighborhoods "became a nucleus of the second black ghetto" after World War II.[32] In the same period, the total suburban population of Cincinnati increased from 219,954 to 361,550. Of that suburban population, only 2 percent was Black. When the congregants of Rockdale Temple made the decision to move to the overwhelmingly white suburb of Amberley Village in the mid-1960s, their Avondale location had undergone a massive population shift from white to Black—one that the congregants themselves were no doubt part of. As Greenberg explains, "With concerns now couched in class rather than racial terms, most Jews fled to suburbs almost as quickly as white Christians to avoid what they perceived as the deterioration of their schools and neighborhoods. They pointed to riots as evidence of civil rights agendas run amok."[33]

Some Jewish leaders recognized that the movement of synagogues from cities to suburbs mimicked other signs of white flight, and further, that such changes in location signified Jews' success at white assimilation and threatened relationships between Jewish and Black communities. Albert Vorspan, a leader of Reform Judaism, explained what he saw as the growing challenges Jews faced in identifying with Black oppression:

> The chief hang-up of Jewish liberalism is that Jews do not really know Black people as human beings. We know them as symbols, as headlines, as problems, as statistics. As Jews have flooded to suburbia (and racial feelings are only one small explanation of this thrust), Jews have settled into white, mostly segregated, often Jewish self-segregated (separate but better) communities. Hundreds of synagogues have torn up their roots in the center cities (almost invariably selling the old structure to Negro Baptists) and, on the backs of the mobile congregants, chugged to the cotton-candy nirvana of suburbia.... One gets the feeling that Jews are on a conveyer belt that draws them en masse farther and farther from the center cities.[34]

---

[32] Charles F. Casey-Leininger, "Making the Second Ghetto in Cincinnati: Avondale, 1925–1970," in *Race and the City: Work, Community, and Protest in Cincinnati*, ed. Henry Louis Taylor Jr. (Urbana: University of Illinois Press, 1993), 235, 243.

[33] Cheryl Lynn Greenberg, *Troubling the Waters: Black-Jewish Relations in the American Century* (Princeton, NJ: Princeton University Press, 2006), 206. Importantly, Jews sometimes remained restricted in terms of the neighborhoods in which they could safely reside.

[34] Albert Vorspan, "Blacks and Jews," in *Black Anti-Semitism and Jewish Racism* (New York: Richard W. Baron, 1969), 209–210.

In premiering *The Gates of Justice* at the dedication of the new Rockdale Temple, Mintz and the other rabbis responsible for the cantata's messaging drew a clear connection between the new temple and the old, perhaps reminding congregants that though they may be in a new neighborhood, at greater distance physically and psychologically from areas most affected by the civil unrest, their imperative as Reform movement Jews had not changed: despite their pain, congregants needed to recall their theological and historical mandate to identify with the oppressed in their community. This reminder must have seemed all the more important to Mintz and the Cincinnati rabbis as the congregation moved from a nearly all-Black neighborhood to a nearly all-white one, while simultaneously struggling against the notion that as Jews, they did not believe they had assimilated into white America and white supremacy. In other words, even as Rockdale Temple distanced itself geographically from Cincinnati's growing Black inner city, both the temple's leadership and leaders in the Reform movement more generally continued to publicly acknowledge what they saw as Judaism's scriptural imperative to engage in civil rights.

## "Simultaneously Immersed and Watchfully Apart"

In 1969, many Jews would have debated the extent to which they could be considered white, or whether they had indeed been granted any institutional privileges of whiteness after World War II.[35] Even so, historian Matthew Frye Jacobson explains that for all intents and purposes, "from 1790 onward Jews were indeed 'white' by the most significant measures of that appellation: they could enter the country and become naturalized citizens."[36] Both the post–World War II prosperity and beginning of the Cold War helped to "speed the alchemy by which Hebrews became Caucasian."[37] Citing the GI bill, and FHA and VA mortgages, Brodkin explains, "The myth that Jews pulled themselves up by their own bootstraps ignores the fact that it took federal programs to create the conditions whereby the abilities of Jews and other European immigrants could be recognized and rewarded rather than denigrated and denied."[38] Nevertheless, as historian Cheryl Greenberg writes, "Jews have

---

[35] Brodkin, *How Jews Became White Folks*, 3.
[36] Matthew Frye Jacobson, *Whiteness of a Different Color: European Immigrants and the Alchemy of Race* (Cambridge, MA: Harvard University Press, 1999), 176.
[37] Ibid., 188.
[38] Brodkin, *How Jews Became White Folks*, 50.

moved to the inside in a society that still has an outside. Yet most Jews still perceive themselves as at least partly outside."[39]

Indeed, Jews had and have an ambivalent place in the American Black/white racial binary, and anti-Semitism remains at the core of white supremacist language and violence.[40] Jewish jazz musicians' negotiations around racial and ethnic identity, particularly in the 1920s and 1930s, have been well documented.[41] For example, clarinetist and bandleader Artie Shaw (1910–2004) explained that he changed his name early in his career from Arthur Arshawsky ("obviously a Jewish kid, or at any rate some kind of a 'foreigner'") to Artie Shaw ("doesn't *sound* very 'foreign' . . . an American kid—may as well let it go at that") in an attempt to "pass" as white.[42] Other jazz musicians attempted to distance themselves from whiteness: as literary scholar Maria Damon writes of blackface performances like Al Jolson's in *The Jazz Singer* (1927), "a number of Jews found in African American culture the resources for resisting absorption into dominant culture they found stultifying, hierarchic, unjust, unaesthetic, and un-Jewish."[43]

By the mid-1960s, historian Eric Goldstein argues that Jews had successfully integrated into white, middle-class society.[44] As historian Marc Dollinger explains further, "With access to professional jobs, suburban homes, and the nation's top colleges and universities, Jews, according to this interpretation, became 'white' and formed political opinions based more on what George Lipsitz described as their 'possessive investment in whiteness' than on their history as an oppressed minority group."[45] Jews could increasingly benefit

---

[39] Cheryl Lynn Greenberg, *Troubling the Waters: Black-Jewish Relations in the American Century* (Princeton, NJ: Princeton University Press, 2006), 252.

[40] Deborah Lipstadt, "Anti-Semitism Is Thriving in America," *The Atlantic*, May 3, 2019, https://www.theatlantic.com/ideas/archive/2019/05/poway-shooting-shows-anti-semitism-flourishing/588649/, accessed April 29, 2020. Reva Marin, "Representations of Identity in Jewish Jazz Autobiography," *Outside and Inside: Race and Identity in White Jazz Autobiography* (Jackson: University of Mississippi Press, 2020), 82–121.

[41] For more on how Jewish jazz musicians conceived of their relationships between whiteness and blackness, see Reva Marin, "Representations of Identity in Jewish Jazz Autobiography," *Outside and Inside: Race and Identity in White Jazz Autobiography* (Jackson: University of Mississippi Press, 2020), 82–121. For more on Jewish jazz musicians, see Charles Hersch, *Jews and Jazz: Improvising Ethnicity* (New York: Routledge, 2017); Charles Hersch, *Subversive Sounds: Race and the Birth of Jazz in New Orleans* (Chicago: University of Chicago Press, 2007).

[42] Artie Shaw, *The Trouble with Cinderella: An Outline of Identity* (1952, Farrar, Straus, and Young; McKinleyville, CA: Fithian Press, 1991), 92.

[43] Maria Damon, *Postliterary America: From Bagel Shop Jazz to Micropoetries* (Iowa City: University of Iowa Press, 2011), 44.

[44] Eric L. Goldstein, *The Price of Whiteness: Jews, Race, and American Identity* (Princeton, NJ: Princeton University Press, 2006), 212.

[45] Marc Dollinger, *Black Power, Jewish Politics: Reinventing the Alliance in the 1960s* (Waltham, MA: Brandeis University Press, 2018), 65. Historian Andrew Heinze argues that Jewish immigrants had to some extent desired the privileges that integration into white American society might afford: Andrew R. Heinze, *Adapting to Abundance: Jewish Immigrants, Mass Consumption, and the Search for American Identity* (New York: Columbia University Press, 1990).

from some privileges reserved for white Americans, and they acted on that privilege. As Greenberg explains, "Most Jews were white people and held white people's attitudes to a greater or lesser extent. That meant not only a certain amount of Jewish racism but also an unwillingness to dismantle existing social structures that conferred special benefits on those with white skin, whether they recognized those benefits or not."[46]

For those who did recognize those benefits, the gap between self-identification as a Jewish person and identification from others as a white person was difficult to reconcile. For example, in 1969 Nat Hentoff expressed discomfort (though not disbelief) with being considered, as he put it, "*goyim*," or a white gentile. Hentoff, who was Jewish, noted that though his "roots are only American," he had "always been both participant and skeptic, simultaneously immersed and watchfully apart."[47] As Michael Lerner, editor of the progressive Jewish and interfaith magazine *Tikkun*, asserted in 1993, "Jews can only be deemed 'white' if there is massive amnesia on the part of non-Jews about the monumental history of anti-Semitism."[48]

By the late 1960s, the civil rights movement had resulted in some notable successes, including the Civil Rights Act of 1964; the Voting Rights Act of 1965; Executive Order 11246, which enforced affirmative action in federal employment; *Loving v. Virginia* (1967), which ruled that prohibiting interracial marriage was unconstitutional; the appointment of Thurgood Marshall to the Supreme Court (1967); and the Fair Housing Act (1968). In the midst of what some saw as growing assimilation into whiteness, combined with the growing narrative that civil rights had been achieved, some Jewish leaders believed their communities needed strong reminders to remain vigilant in the civil rights movement—hence the repeated UAHC resolutions that confirmed the movement's continued support of anti-discrimination efforts across the 1950s and 1960s. To do so not only re-affirmed their particular moral imperative but also re-asserted their outsider status as Jews by aligning themselves with the needs of Black communities. *The Gates of Justice*, then, needed to offer a sonic model that both attempted to mend relationships between Black and Jewish communities perceived to be growing apart and re-asserted Jewish identity as distinct from whiteness.

---

[46] Greenberg, *Troubling the Waters*, 119.
[47] Nat Hentoff, "Introduction," in *Black Anti-Semitism and Jewish Racism* (New York: Richard W. Baron, 1969), ix.
[48] Michael Lerner, "Jews Are Not White," *Village Voice*, May 18, 1993, 33.

## Locating *The Gates of Justice* in Both Sound and Black-Jewish Relations

From the beginning of the program notes, Brubeck made the purpose of *The Gates of Justice* clear: "to bring together—and back together—the Jewish people and American blacks."[49] Brubeck illustrated the two communities primarily through two soloists: a tenor described as singing in Jewish cantorial style, and a baritone (referred to in the program note as a "Negro baritone") singing blues and spiritual-influenced melodies. That the soloists are meant to represent the relationship between American Black and Jewish communities is clear in the racially essentialist musical styles in which they often (though not always) sing. The tenor maintains a cantorial style, mostly through a melody based on minor modes, an emphasis on half-note relationships, particularly on downbeats, and embellished augmented seconds (noting the influence of the Jewish mode, Freygish scale, or Phrygian dominant scale). The baritone sings in a vaguely Black musical aesthetic, signaled primarily through the frequent flatted fifth scale degree in the melody—the blue note. In a 2003 interview with Eugenia Zukerman for the Milken Archive of Jewish Music, Dave and Iola Brubeck recall past performances that have featured different compositions of soloists in locations where a suitably talented Black baritone or Jewish tenor could not be found (i.e., a white baritone, Black tenor, female tenor). When pressed as to whether the cantata achieved its goal in these alternate performance settings, both insisted that it did work; Iola Brubeck added that "I think the words are the power"—a statement that seemingly subverts the musical juxtapositions throughout the composition. However, given that Dave and Iola Brubeck presented other performance identities as alternatives, only used in cases where necessary, it seems clear that they believed the initial racial identities of the soloists are important to the performance.[50]

The soloists are accompanied by a choir, small wind ensemble (with the option to be replaced by organ), and optional improvising jazz rhythm section (keyboard, bass, and percussion). While the soloists reflect clear-cut musical depictions of racial difference, the choir typically sings in a western art style that is racially unmarked; however, as Nina Eidsheim argues, this art style has long been understood to sound white, though typically racially unmarked.[51] In a few movements, the choir takes on musical characteristics outside white American and European styles—these are clearly marked in the

---

[49] Brubeck, liner notes, *The Gates of Justice*.
[50] Dave Brubeck, interview with Eugenia Zukerman, 2003.
[51] Nina Sun Eidsheim, *The Race of Sound: Listening, Timbre & Vocality in African American Music* (Durham, NC: Duke University Press, 2019).

score (this is most obvious in Movement X, discussed below). Race and ethnicity are marked implicitly (white) and explicitly (Black, Jewish, and others) throughout the score, reflecting Brubeck's own performance of whiteness as an unmarked western classical composer.

Brubeck locates the cantata within a more typically Jewish soundscape from the beginning. The first movement in particular makes clear the cantata's primary intention to be heard by and to be meaningful to Jewish audiences. The first sound heard in the cantata is the shofar, or ram's horn (the score calls for "quasi rams horn," no doubt to make the piece more easily translatable across performing forces).[52] The shofar performs an ascending perfect fifth interval—an interval recognizable to many audiences as a battle call. But for Jewish audiences, the shofar would certainly have had a more specific connotation based in Jewish traditions. The shofar is used for signaling; in *The Jewish Encyclopedia*, a twelve-volume text published in 1906 still renowned for its extensive scholarship, Francis L. Cohen explains that the shofar had a wide variety of purposes and signals, including celebration, repentance, alarm, excommunication, and calls to prayer.[53] *The Jewish Encyclopedia* notates some common shofar calls in both the Sephardic and Ashkenazi traditions, including the *Teruah*, which features the root in staccato sixteenth notes and ascending a perfect fifth to a longer note value; the *Shevarim*, in which the root is a short note and the fifth is a dotted note (this pattern is repeated three times); and the *Tekiyah*, in which both the root and the fifth are performed in long tones just once.[54] Example 5.1a represents these calls as published in *The Jewish Encyclopedia*, and example 5.1b shows how Brubeck inserted these

**Ex. 5.1a.** Shofar call, *The Jewish Encyclopedia* (New York: Funk & Wagnall's, 1906).

---

[52] As Brubeck later explained, the shofar is a challenging instrument to control: "It was safer to have a French horn do the call. And that's what I did many of the times. But sometimes there would be a great shofar player that you could trust. Not too often!" Dave Brubeck, interview with Eugenia Zukerman, 2003.

[53] Cyrus Adler, Francis L. Cohen, Abraham De Harkavy, and Judah David Eisenstein, "Shofar," *The Jewish Encyclopedia* (New York: Funk & Wagnalls, 1906), http://www.jewishencyclopedia.com/articles/13602-shofar. Like the shofar, the text of the first movement clearly positions the cantata within the context of its Rockdale Temple commission. The tenor sings text from King Solomon's prayer at the dedication of the temple in Jerusalem (1 Kings 8:27–30, 41–43).

[54] Ibid.

Ex. 5.1b. Mvt. I, Horn introduction, mm. 1–8. Copyright © 1970; St. Francis Music Company and Malcolm Music, Ltd.; International Copyrights Secured; All Rights Reserved.

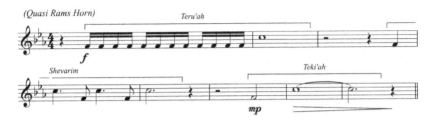

into the introduction to movement I of *The Gates of Justice*. The sonic representation of the shofar's call shifts to brass instruments and is interspersed in the accompaniment throughout the tenor solo. Despite Brubeck's apparent adherence to the calls as notated in *The Jewish Encyclopedia* (indeed, he has replicated them nearly note for note), this notation provides a generic overview of the sounds and notes the shofar might blow.[55] In other words, while Jewish audiences would have recognized the sounds and notes of the shofar as written by Brubeck, the shofar here is divorced from the specific and deeply symbolic arrangements used on High Holidays within Jewish synagogues. Rather than having a particular resonance in the ears of Jewish congregants, the shofar would have been heard as a generic sonic indicator of Jewishness.

In both message and sound, Brubeck makes clear the importance of continued civil rights activism for the Jewish audience in attendance from the very beginning of the cantata. The shofar indicates that the first movement is, as Brubeck puts it, "a call to battle or to conscience."[56] He explains that the cantata expresses both of these purposes by addressing "the battle for the survival of mankind, and the recognition of what humanity should be." Following the shofar, the movement operates primarily as a tenor solo. In interviews and the program notes, Brubeck frequently positioned the cantata in universal terms, but the melodic content of the tenor solo, which is filled with half steps, augmented seconds, minor scales, and improvisatory embellished melismas, also emphatically situates the tenor within a Jewish cantorial style recognizable to both Jewish and non-Jewish audiences (see examples 5.2a and 5.2b).[57]

---

[55] Many thanks to Judah Cohen for his thoughtful comments and advice on this and other portions of this chapter.

[56] Dave Brubeck, program notes, *The Gates of Justice*, 1969.

[57] In speaking with Eugenia Zukerman, Brubeck insisted that the modal quality of the cantor's melodies was a coincidence, claiming that when Mintz heard the piece, he commented that Brubeck must have been familiar with Jewish modes. Brubeck replied that he was not, to which Mintz reiterated that it sounded like he *was*, in fact, familiar with the modes. Brubeck considered it to be luck that he managed to capture the

**Ex. 5.2a.** Mvt. I, Tenor line, mm. 9–16. Copyright © 1970; St. Francis Music Company and Malcolm Music, Ltd.; International Copyrights Secured; All Rights Reserved.

**Ex. 5.2b.** Mvt. I, Tenor line, mm. 30–34. Copyright © 1970; St. Francis Music Company and Malcolm Music, Ltd.; International Copyrights Secured; All Rights Reserved.

However, like the shofar, the sounds marking the cantor as "Jewish" are general, and do not represent the specific modes used within Jewish synagogues.

## Shared History and Jewish Moral Imperative

Within this soundscape, Brubeck attended to the two primary themes that motivated Jewish support of the civil rights movement: a religious imperative and a sense of shared history of oppression. In the program notes for the cantata, Brubeck made the relationship clear, highlighting a shared history of suffering, hate, and alienation, writing, "It is impossible to concern oneself with the history and tradition of either without feeling overwhelmed by the inequities and injustices which have pervaded all strata of society."[58]

cantorial sound, even as he asserted the influence of Darius Milhaud's *Service Sacré* (1948). Earlier Jewish jazz musicians had also remarked on the similarities they heard between jazz and Jewish religious music. Clarinetist Mezz Mezzrow (1899–1972) recalled a Jewish celebration he was asked to perform in while in prison (according to Mezzrow, the Jewish inmates asked him to lead the celebration as a "colored guy"): "I find out once more how music of different oppressed peoples blends together. Jewish or Hebrew religious music mostly minor, in a simple form, full of wailing and lament. When I add Negro inflections to it they fit so perfect, it thrills me. . . . They [Jewish inmates] can't understand how come a colored guy digs the spirit of their music so good." Though trumpeter Max Kaminsky (1908–1994) offers a more complicated reflection on the relationship among Jewishness, whiteness, and blackness, he likewise says that Torah singing allowed him to hear Charlie Parker more easily: "When I first started to improvise on the trumpet as a kid I used to go off into those atonal intervals that I had heard in the temple chants simply because they were so familiar to me and so easy to do." Dave Brubeck, interview with Eugenia Zukerman, 2003; Mezz Mezzrow and Bernard Wolfe, *Really the Blues* (1946; New York: Random House; repr. New York: New York Review of Books, 1974), 333; Max Kaminsky and V. E. Hughes, *Jazz Band: My Life in Jazz* (1963; repr. New York: Da Capo Press, 1981), 193.

[58] Dave Brubeck, program notes, *The Gates of Justice*, 1969.

This theme ran throughout Jewish civil rights activism. As Reform Rabbi Arthur Lelyveld explained in the *Congress Bi-Weekly*, a publication of the American Jewish Congress,

> The Jewish people by reason of its very warrant to exist cannot be indifferent to persecution or to discrimination or to any force or attitude that denies dignity to the human person. . . . It does not diminish our dignity as Jews when we seek to achieve the precious ability to feel *empathy* with Negro bitterness and frustration. The command that we do so comes to us directly out of the Torah: *V'atem y'datem et nefesh hager*—"You should be able to know the *very being* of the stranger for you were strangers in the land of Egypt." And not only in Egypt 3,000 years ago: we were there yesterday! We learned in our experience that ghetto and degradation, poverty and filth, inevitably go together. Some of us are able to recollect, even personally, the dirt and over-crowding in Jewish slums, the stench of tenements with inadequate sanitary facilities.[59]

In other words, Jewish people knew what suffering, oppression, and slavery meant, both in a historical context (Egypt) and in a more recent context (including both anti-Semitism and discrimination in America, as well as the Holocaust). Because of that history, for some liberal Jews, Jewish theology also mandated a heightened commitment to racial justice issues.[60] However, as historian James Loeffler argues, some post–World War II American Jews in particular dedicated themselves to human rights causes not primarily because of the horrors of the Holocaust but rather the "dreams and dilemmas of Jewish nationhood."[61] Involvement in the civil rights movement could include a number of different activities, including participating in marches or protests like the 1964 Freedom Summer, donations to African American organizations like the NAACP or SNCC, or ensuring integration and equality in Jewish-owned businesses. As Greenberg writes, throughout

---

[59] Arthur J. Lelyveld, "Negro and Jewish Relationships," *Congress Bi-Weekly* 33, no. 10 (1966): 9.

[60] Lelyveld makes mention of *L'takayn olam*, Hebrew for "to improve the world until it reflects God's Kingship." While not a prominent part of Jewish theology in the 1960s civil rights movement (nor well-defined), the imperative to repair the world, or *tikkun olam*, would be cited more often beginning in the 1970s, particularly among those in the Reform movement. Jonathan Krasner, "The Place of Tikkun Olam in American Jewish Life," *Jewish Political Studies Review* 25, no. 3 & 4 (November 1, 2014); Elliott N. Dorff, *The Way into Tikkun Olam: Repairing the World* (Woodstock, VT: Jewish Lights Publishing, 2005), 12.

Musicologist Naomi Graber further describes the varying ways in which Jews approached a relationship or kinship with African Americans, depending on background and denomination in the early twentieth century: Naomi Graber, "Colliding Diasporas: Kurt Weill's *Ulysses Africanus* and Black-Jewish Relations During the Great Depression," *Musical Quarterly* 99 (2017): 329.

[61] James Loeffler, *Rooted Cosmopolitans: Jews and Human Rights in the Twentieth Century* (New Haven, CT: Yale University Press, 2018), xiii.

the civil rights movement, "Jews as a group committed themselves to the cause of Black equality more fully and for a longer time than any other white community."[62]

In movement VI, "Ye Shall Be Holy," Brubeck reminds Jewish listeners of their historical obligation to engage in civil rights activism by invoking Egypt. The baritone soloist sings Leviticus 19:34, "If a stranger dwell with thee in your land, ye shall not do him wrong." The tenor joins the baritone for the next phrase, "And thou shalt love him as thyself." Until this point, the choir has been chanting variations on the text, "Ye shall be holy for God is holy," but the choir joins the soloists to finish the phrase, "For ye were strangers in the land of Egypt." The abrupt change of harmony and rhythm in the choir at this point is notable. Prior to the "land of Egypt" line, the choir's chanting is rhythmically slow, using mostly dotted half notes, and is harmonically static and polytonal. As shown in example 5.3a, the tenor and bass sing a G-flat major triad, while the soprano and alto sing a C major triad; all parts are a tritone apart, performing what classical listeners might hear as Stravinsky's "Petrushka chord," or what jazz listeners might hear as a tritone substitution.[63] When the soloists enter, their melodic lines follow a G-flat major scale. As the parts begin to sing "strangers in the land of Egypt," the choir and soloists perform shorter note values (quarter notes and eighth notes), and the harmony revolves primarily around consonant major chords (Ex. 5.3b). The dynamic marking also shifts

**Ex. 5.3a.** Mvt. VI, choir, mm. 1–6. Copyright © 1970; St. Francis Music Company and Malcolm Music, Ltd.; International Copyrights Secured; All Rights Reserved.

[62] Greenberg, *Troubling the Waters*, 119.
[63] Critics and musicians often found Brubeck's harmonic language to be complicated, reflecting modern classical composers like Stravinsky, Ravel, Gershwin, and, unsurprisingly, Milhaud.

**Ex. 5.3b.** Mvt. VI, choir and soloists, mm. 35–42. Copyright © 1970; St. Francis Music Company and Malcolm Music, Ltd.; International Copyrights Secured; All Rights Reserved.

**Ex. 5.3b.** Continued

from piano to fortissimo. The effect draws the listener's attention to this final portion of text, essentially highlighting the legacy of Jewish suffering and oppression as a way to draw similarities with Black Americans' suffering and oppression, and reminding the congregation that because of that past, they now possess a moral imperative to stand with the oppressed.

## The Imperative of the "Unheard Millions"

For Brubeck, the choir performs a crucial role throughout the cantata in speaking to Jewish audiences. He describes the chorus as "the voice of the people who have been pawns of history" and as "unheard millions"—in other words, something similar to a Greek chorus with a clear political message. As a large group of unknown performing forces, Brubeck deploys the choir as a weapon, "battering at the man-made barriers which have separated men from each other, and consequently from knowing the nature of God."[64] Throughout, he offers a musical model for the congregations listening to the cantata: one must break down the barriers that separate each other in order

---

[64] Dave Brubeck, program note, *The Gates of Justice*, by Dave Brubeck, 1969.

to achieve justice for all, and ultimately, more truly know God. In doing so, Brubeck reiterates that civil rights activism has a personal benefit to everyone involved.

Movement IIIa, "Open the Gates," perhaps best demonstrates Brubeck's choral "battering" effect, and how, in moving from dissonance to consonance, Brubeck modeled effective social relationships. He names this movement the "heart of the cantata," calling the cry "Open the gates of justice!" a plea, a demand, and an exhortation. The movement starts with the choir singing in chords a tritone apart (the same "Petrushka" chord used in the sixth movement, described above), suggesting that the distance between each community is unholy (ex. 5.4a). The choir repeats the text "open the gates" as the baritone solo enters, expanding the text to include the full verse ("Open to me the gates of justice, I will enter them and give thanks to the Lord"). The alto, tenor, and bass descend by half step in parallel fourths, while the soprano stands apart, maintaining an upper pedal C (ex. 5.4b). The choir joins together in contracting cluster and suspended chords on the text "throw wide the gates," increasing its dynamic level from mezzo piano to mezzo forte. After this moment of heightened dissonance, the tenor soloist enters, the text returns to "open the gates," and the harmonies simplify to open fifths, before the soprano, alto, and tenor sing on C an octave apart (ex. 5.4c). The bass also sings on C but is now rhythmically displaced from the other parts by one measure. The dissonance returns to the soprano, alto, and tenor, and the bass line becomes rhythmically agitated, introducing a sixteenth-note motive (ex. 5.4d). As both tenor and baritone soloists enter in a duet, the choral parts continue to expand and contract, simplify and complicate, unify and separate. Eventually, the full choir returns to the bass's rhythmic agitation motive,

**Ex. 5.4a.** Mvt. IIIa, choir, mm. 1–2. Copyright © 1970; St. Francis Music Company and Malcolm Music, Ltd.; International Copyrights Secured; All Rights Reserved.

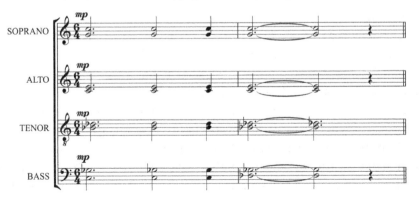

**Ex. 5.4b.** Mvt. IIIa, choir and soloists, mm. 5–10. Copyright © 1970; St. Francis Music Company and Malcolm Music, Ltd.; International Copyrights Secured; All Rights Reserved.

singing the sixteenth-note pattern together for four measures (ex. 5.4e). There is a small pause in the music, before the choir amasses together on the text "Go thro'!," as if the gate has been broken down by their insistent pounding. After a brief "optional improvisation" section, the choir continues jubilantly; the tempo increases as the sixteenth note agitation motive transforms around the text "out of the way, out of the way, out of the way, out of the way of the people!" The choir insistently repeats this text. Eventually, each part embarks on its own path (ex. 5.4f): as the tenor and bass repeat the sixteenth-note agitation motive, the soprano line outlines a C major triad in short, syncopated rhythms, and the alto line repeats the line "take up the stumbling block" in

Ex. 5.4c. Mvt. IIIa, choir and tenor soloist, mm. 17–20. Copyright © 1970; St. Francis Music Company and Malcolm Music, Ltd.; International Copyrights Secured; All Rights Reserved.

an ascending C minor scale in quarter-note triplets. Then, the tenor and soprano lines unite in a new syncopated exclamation on the text "clear the way," but their minor-7th interval cuts through the alto and bass. The soprano line shouts "Make way! Cast up the highway" on a high G-flat, its dissonance ringing out across the other parts, before all are finally reunited once more, demanding "out of the way of the people!" together again.

Throughout the shifts and movements across the choral parts, as the text repeats, it is as if each individual part is examining its own place within the full choir. Each line experiments with its own unique rhythm or dissonance at some point within the piece, and in the insistent chaos, a common rhythm eventually emerges. Brubeck's message to the audience, who, like the choir, represent the "unheard millions," is clear: just like this choir, each person must find how their part fits into the whole of the civil rights movement. Throughout the third movement, the relationships between each musical part are not perfect, do not always result in functional harmonies, and there is often no clear path from dissonance to harmony—there are steps backward along the way. But by the end of movement IIIa, the individual parts forge a working whole.

Movement IIIa leads into movement IIIb, "Open the Gates chorale." It may seem odd for Brubeck to rely on the quintessentially Protestant Bach in a composition designed around Jewish identity. However, for Brubeck, who insisted on his indebtedness to Bach throughout his career, there was

**Ex. 5.4d.** Mvt. IIIa, choir, mm. 21–25. Copyright © 1970; St. Francis Music Company and Malcolm Music, Ltd.; International Copyrights Secured; All Rights Reserved.

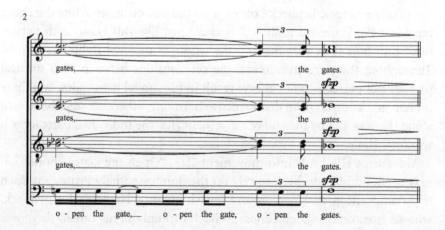

**Ex. 5.4e.** Mvt. IIIa, choir, mm. 43–51. Copyright © 1970; St. Francis Music Company and Malcolm Music, Ltd.; International Copyrights Secured; All Rights Reserved.

perhaps no clearer way to demonstrate the potential of a group of "unheard millions" to unite than to have the chaos and dissonance of Movement IIIa dissolve into a Bach-style chorale, following (some of) Bach's part-writing rules. When musicologist Stephen Crist asked Brubeck what he found appealing about chorales, Brubeck responded, "It must be a combination of the emotional sound of the chorale and the emotional sound of voices.... The thing that move[s] me the most [are] the chorales, *a cappella*. That's what I love the most.... Just that sound, and no instruments, and the human voice, and just what it's conveying from the choir."[65] Example 5.5a shows the

---

[65] Stephen Crist, "The Role and Meaning of the Bach Chorale in the Music of Dave Brubeck," in *Bach Perspectives: Bach in America*, vol. 5 (Champaign: University of Illinois Press, 2002), 212.

**Ex. 5.4e.** Continued

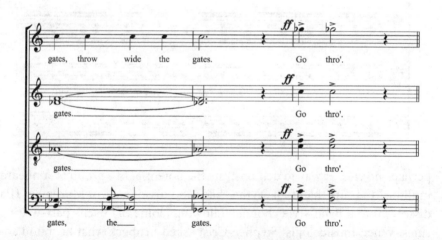

first eight measures of the chorale. Essentially, Brubeck suggests that when each of the parts has worked out their role, they can reach the apparent pinnacle of complex harmony in western music—a Bach chorale. In the program note, Brubeck explains that congregations will know when justice has been delivered, because when God is asked, "Where is God?" according to Brubeck, "It will be self-evident: 'HERE I AM!'" The choir and soloists offer

**Ex. 5.4f.** Mvt. IIIa, choir, mm. 69–80. Copyright © 1970; St. Francis Music Company and Malcolm Music, Ltd.; International Copyrights Secured; All Rights Reserved.

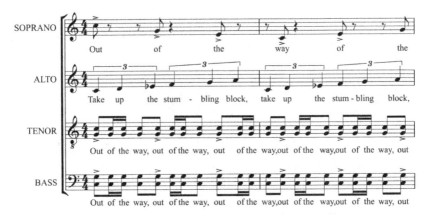

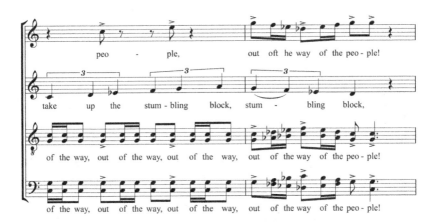

that response in Movement IIIb, on a fortississimo, accented, perfect octave on G (ex. 5.5b).

But this moment, "HERE I AM!," happens in the middle of the movement rather than as an exultant conclusion. To conclude, the movement dispenses with the chorale, returning to the frenetic "out of the way, out of the way, out of the way of the people" line from Movement IIIa, suggesting that the chorale, which had culminated in a great, "Here I am!," was simply an aspiration—an image of what could be but not what had already been achieved. The baritone soloist further underscores this point; as the choir and tenor soloist repeat "Open the gates!" the baritone twice adds "*When will* you open the gates?" The first phrase, sung in a descending line, is

**Ex. 5.4f.** Continued

nearly lost in the fortississimo choral chords, but the second is unmistakable. Sung in the baritone's upper range, ascending a G melodic minor scale, ending on an F-sharp, the line clashes strongly against the choir and tenor soloist's triumphant C major chord (ex. 5.5c). In other words, Brubeck inserts harmonic ambiguity into a moment that would have otherwise sounded unmistakably triumphant. There is yet more work to be done by the "unheard millions."

**Ex. 5.4f.** Continued

Movement IIIb reminds the congregation of a moral duty to assist the oppressed by linking to a shared history between Jewish and Black communities. As the choir sings "open the gates," this time softly and on long tones in consonant harmonies, the baritone and tenor solos offer scriptural reminders of why the audience should work to "open the gates of justice." The tenor sings in an embellished and Jewish mode melody, "Is not this the fast that I have

**Ex. 5.5a.** Mvt. IIIb, choir, mm. 1–8. Copyright © 1970; St. Francis Music Company and Malcolm Music, Ltd.; International Copyrights Secured; All Rights Reserved.

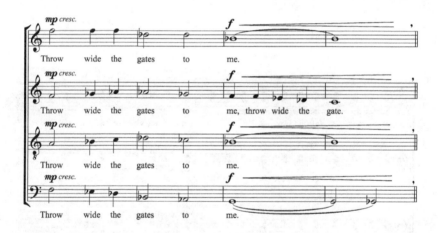

chosen to loose the fetters of wickedness; to undo the bands of the yoke; and to let the oppressed go free?," to which the baritone adds (blue notes and all), "Open the doors to bring the poor that are cast out to thy house, when thou see the naked thou shalt cover him." Moments like these were likely meant to solidify the relationship between Jewish and Black communities by empathetically appealing to the religious and moral beliefs of the (initially) primarily Jewish audience, thus fulfilling one of Rabbi Mintz's goals for the cantata: to help bring Black and Jewish communities back together. Such a goal suggested that, at least among some Jewish civil rights allies, the once robust "golden age" of Black-Jewish relations was past.

**Ex. 5.5b.** Mvt. IIIb, choir and soloists, mm. 49–56. Copyright © 1970; St. Francis Music Company and Malcolm Music, Ltd.; International Copyrights Secured; All Rights Reserved.

**Ex. 5.5c.** Mvt. IIIb, choir and soloists, mm. 81–86. Copyright © 1970; St. Francis Music Company and Malcolm Music, Ltd.; International Copyrights Secured; All Rights Reserved.

## Triggering Empathy: The Role of the Black Baritone

For Brubeck, the baritone performed a key role in arguing the cantata's relevance to modern-day audiences. In the program notes and preceding interviews, Brubeck was painfully clear in explaining that the baritone soloist needed to be a "Negro." The baritone was also racially marked sonically, as most of the solo lines feature blue notes and were meant to evoke the sound of a number of Black musical genres, including spirituals, the blues, and gospel music. Prior to the performance, the *Jewish Advocate* advertised the relationship between the tenor and baritone soloists: "Tenor soloist will be a cantor who will sing the teachings of Judaism while a Negro baritone will question their relevance to his life."[66] The baritone's questioning was intended to evoke empathetic introspection and reflection within the audience and ultimately, to remind Jewish audiences of the stakes of inaction. The first question, from Movement IIIb, is "When will you open the gates?" The next is from Movement V, "Lord, Lord," a mournful lament in which the baritone asks, "Lord, how can I face this day?" and "Lord, when will the ill winds change?" as the choir repeats around each solo, "What will tomorrow bring?" In Movement VII, "Shout Unto the Lord," the baritone begins with questions from Isaiah 50:8, "Who will contend with me? Who is my adversary?" He then combines questions from the Jewish sage, Hillel, and Martin Luther King Jr. Hillel wrote, "If I am not for myself, then who will be for me? And if I am only for myself, then what am I? And if not now, when?" The baritone links this sentiment with King's "fierce urgency of now," asking, "If the time for action is not now, when is it?" Movement VIII presents an extended interrogation from Psalm 8 in the baritone's voice: "What is man, that Thou art mindful of him? And the son of man, that Thou thinkest of him, yet Thou hast made him but little lower than the angels, and hast crowned him with glory and honor?"

The baritone performs a critical role not only from a performance standpoint but also within the realm of social justice in which Brubeck places him. While the chorus of "unheard millions" unites to eliminate barriers and the cantor sings familiar messages from the Jewish tradition in a recognizable style to an audience of shared faith, the baritone, likely to have been one of the few Black performers on stage (later performances also featured Black conductor Everett Lee), quite literally stands alone, prodding white and Jewish audiences into activism. Iola Brubeck explained that the baritone's text was intended to express the impact of racism to a non-Black audience: "It tells the experience of walking down the street and feeling at peace, and then something happening

---

[66] "Premiere for Brubeck 'Jewish Cantata,'" *Jewish Advocate*, July 17, 1969, 4.

on the street that makes you realize that you are marginalized in this society."[67] Her text recalls somewhat philosopher Frantz Fanon's essay on the embodied experience of a Black man, "oblivious of the moment when his inferiority is determined by the Other [whites]," until "an unusual weight descended"—a moment of encounter, such as a child, who upon meeting Fanon on the street announces to their mother, "Look! A Negro! . . . I'm scared!"[68] The baritone is the face of Black suffering, whose trauma should trigger empathy among a Jewish congregation that would likely have had similar experiences with anti-Semitism. The baritone alone represents the modern potential of a historic religion, Judaism, that as James Baldwin writes, "is part of the moral history of the world."[69]

Today, over fifty years after the premiere, there is a discomfort inherent to the baritone solo, and the tenor, for that matter. Put plainly, *The Gates of Justice* relies on a racial essentialist argument that understands different races to create inherently different musical sounds. Brubeck writes race into the score, both by requiring a Jewish cantor-style tenor and "Negro" baritone, and also in the cantor-style embellishments, minor scales, and blue notes that pervade the respective melodic lines. In a 2003 oral history interview with Dave and Iola Brubeck, Eugenia Zukerman made this musical racial distinction plain, pointedly asking about the need for the baritone to sing both operatic and blues styles: "And yet you use operatic bass/baritones, I mean, highly trained classical voices. These are not blues singers. Why did you want them to have that, the purity of operatic voices?" Dave seems taken off-guard by the question, responding, "Good Question. Uh . . . I would hope that they would have the operatic voice, but would have listened to the blues." Dave, Iola, and Zukerman laugh together, as Zukerman brushes over the potential racial discomfort Dave might have revealed, saying, "I think we hope that of opera singers always."[70] This interaction, thirty years after the premiere, suggests an assumption that even an operatically trained Black bass/baritone would have a more natural connection with the blues and spirituals, an old convention present in Broadway musicals like *Porgy and Bess* and which impacted the careers and receptions of Black western classical musicians like Marian Anderson, Paul Robeson, and Leontyne Price. It also reflects Zukerman's assumption that singers trained in an operatic style—a European classical style whose

---

[67] Iola Brubeck with Denise Gallo, "Jazz Conversation: Lyricist Iola Brubeck," Library of Congress, April 10, 2008, https://www.loc.gov/item/webcast-4797/.

[68] Frantz Fanon, *Black Skin, White Masks*, trans. Richard Philcox (1952; New York: Grove Press, 1967), 90–91.

[69] James Baldwin, "Negroes Are Anti-Semitic Because They're Anti-white," *New York Times*, April 9, 1967.

[70] Dave Brubeck, interview with Eugenia Zukerman, 2003.

implicitly white racial coding is made explicit by Zukerman's description of its "purity"—would not have a particular relationship with Black musical genres.[71] Needless to say, neither of the musically based racial essentialisms ages comfortably.

But the discomfort with the baritone solo goes further, to a lack of Black representation in the cantata's creation and selection of texts. For the bulk of the lyrics, Dave and Iola Brubeck, Charles Mintz, and other unnamed rabbis collaborated on at least some of the selected biblical passages as well as excerpts from texts by Hillel and some that Iola wrote herself. Years later, Iola described the process of determining the texts, which involved meeting with rabbis who "told me about various texts that expressed what they wanted to express," from which she selected the cantata's lyrics.[72] She continued, explaining that she believed that further texts were needed to "express more the African American experience," so she added some of those. Those texts, she adds, were what she was "most proud of," because of the ways in which they seemed to naturally fit within the context of the piece, even if the publishers were less convinced: "The publishers at the time said, 'Well, all this other text comes, you know, from the Old Testament or from the scriptures of some sort and now you are throwing in an element that is a little different.' And I said, 'Well, that's exactly what we want, an element that is a little different, that shows the African American experience.'" For Iola Brubeck, it was important that the Black and Jewish experiences presented not be exactly the same, but publishers seemed to bristle at her addition. The publishers then apparently turned to Dave Brubeck for the last word, and he decided to keep those texts. Though Dave Brubeck suggests that the message of the cantata grew to transcend the particular arguments to present a more universal message, the intention throughout the cantata's promotion, reception, and program notes is clear: This is a message coming from a Black man, intended to directly represent the (singular) Black community in 1969. However, some amount of discomfort remains in that that message has been curated and crafted by non-Black architects, and ultimately reflects a particularly Jewish point of view through its texts, themes, and arguments.

### A "Golden Age"?

Whose message does the baritone sing? Whether or not there had ever been a "golden age" of relationships between Black and Jewish communities, by

---

[71] Nina Sun Eidsheim, "Marian Anderson and 'Sonic Blackness' in American Opera," in *Sound Clash: Listening to American Studies*, ed. Kara Keeling and Josh Kun (Baltimore, MD: Johns Hopkins University Press, 2012), 197–227.

[72] Iola Brubeck with Denise Gallo, "Jazz Conversation."

the 1960s it became increasingly clear that a more public rift was forming between Black and Jewish activists, as Black activists began to voice their growing frustrations with white and Jewish "partners." Historian Leonard Dinnerstein charts a buildup in tensions between African Americans and American Jews beginning in 1966 at a school board meeting on desegregation in Mt. Vernon, New York that quickly grew heated (at one point, an official from CORE shouted, "Hitler made a mistake when he didn't kill enough of you").[73] In 1968 and 1969, a series of incidents on the East Coast "convinced Jews that Blacks were becoming more antisemitic" and those same incidents further convinced Blacks that "Jews controlled the media and other power points in American society."[74] This period also saw civil rights organizations like the Student Non-Violent Coordinating Committee (SNCC) shift tactics and political goals, at times opting for an increased militant approach, Black leadership (and the eventual and fraught expulsion of white members from SNCC), and standing against Israel.[75] As impactful as these events were, Greenberg understands these moments as "symptoms, not causes, of the fraying of the coalition."[76]

White and Jewish civil rights activists understood the relationship between Jewish and Black Americans to have declined across the 1960s, but Black writers across the twentieth century suggested that these relations were often tense prior to the 1960s. Black communities were just as likely as white communities to hold anti-Semitic views; both were, after all, part of a broader American culture in which Jews were often discriminated against.[77] Dinnerstein's history of Black anti-Semitism begins with Booker T. Washington, who, he explained, seems "to have thought of Jews as exploitative shopkeepers and usurious creditors and from time to time differentiated between the Jew and the white man."[78] In his 1945 memoir *Black Boy*,

---

[73] Leonard Dinnerstein, *Anti-Semitism in America* (Oxford: Oxford University Press, 1995), 211. Dinnerstein notes that the incident resulted in a rapid drop in financial donations to the Congress of Racial Equality (CORE).

[74] Ibid., 213. These incidents include the Ocean Hill-Brownsville school board's firing of a large number of Jewish teachers (which was done in an effort to increase Black control of schooling); John Hatchett's appointment as director of New York University's Afro-American Center in 1968 (Hatchett had accused Jews of controlling the New York City school system, and was soon fired for calling Hubert H. Humphrey and Richard Nixon "racist bastards"); radio host Julius Lester's invitation for an African American teacher to read an anti-Semitic poem by a student on air; and the opening of an exhibit titled "Harlem on My Mind" at the Metropolitan Museum of Art (the catalogue included lines by a fifteen-year-old student attributing the exploitation of Blacks in Harlem to Jewish shopkeepers).

[75] Clayborne Carson, "Blacks and Jews in the Civil Rights Movement: The Case of SNCC," in *Bridges and Boundaries: African Americans and American Jews*, ed. Jack Salzman (New York: George Braziller, 1992), 36–40.

[76] Greenberg, *Troubling the Waters*, 206.

[77] As James Baldwin wrote in 1945, "When the Negro hates the Jew as a Jew he does so partly because the nation does and in much the same painful fashion that he hates himself." James Baldwin, "From the American Scene: The Harlem Ghetto: Winter 1948," *Commentary*, February 1948.

[78] Dinnerstein, *Anti-Semitism in America*, 200.

author Richard Wright documented the cruel taunts he would sing to the Jewish people in his neighborhood, with each taunt tailored to children, adult women, redheaded Jewish children, and a Jewish store owner. He explained, "All of us black people who lived in the neighborhood hated Jews, not because they exploited us, but because we had been taught at home and in Sunday school that Jews were 'Christ killers.'"[79] He explained that such antagonism "was not merely racial prejudice, it was part of our cultural heritage."[80] Such feelings stemmed in some measure from religious views, but they also grew from interactions: in urban Black neighborhoods, like Harlem, there were many Jewish landlords and shop owners. As Martin Luther King Jr. explained to the Rabbinical Assembly in March 1968, "[The Negro] confronts the Jew as the owner of the store around the corner where he pays more for what he gets. . . . The fact is that the Jewish storekeeper or landlord is not operating on the basis of Jewish ethics; he is operating simply as a marginal businessman."[81]

While some Black civil rights leaders frequently noted the importance of Jewish support (notably Martin Luther King Jr.), others refuted the notion that American Jews and Black Americans shared similar histories of oppression, and further, they understood the mythos of a "shared history" to be at the heart of the troubled relationship. For them, the experiences of American Jews and Black Americans in the mid-twentieth century could not have been more different, no matter the history. As historian David Biale explains, the two groups were "fundamentally different: despite the mythic memory of enslavement in Egypt, the more recent history of the Jews in Europe was not commensurate with the African American experience of slavery. . . . Whether they liked it or not (and usually they did), the Jews in postwar America had become white."[82] Historian Harold Cruse explained his own skepticism of any shared Black-Jewish experiences, writing, "During the late 1940's and early 1950's, nothing provoked my enmity toward Jews more than hearing a Jew tell me, 'I know how you feel because I, too, am discriminated against. I am a Jew.'"[83] For Cruse, the distinction in experience resided chiefly in white (gentile) America's ability to see potential in Jews that they were unable to see in Black people. Similarly, historian and activist Julius Lester, who was Black and who converted to Judaism in 1982, acknowledged the many similarities in

---

[79] Richard Wright, *Black Boy* (New York: Harper & Brothers, 1945), 52.
[80] Ibid., 53.
[81] "Conversation with Martin Luther King," *Conservative Judaism* 22, no. 3 (Rabbinical Assembly, 1968): 10.
[82] David Biale, "The Melting Pot and Beyond: Jews and the Politics of American Identity," in *Insider/Outsider: American Jews and Multiculturalism* (Berkeley: University of California Press, 1998), 28.
[83] Harold Cruse, "My Jewish Problem and Theirs," in *Black Anti-Semitism and Jewish Racism* (New York: Richard W. Baron, 1969), 173.

historical experiences shared between Jewish people and Black people, but he ultimately insisted on a distinction, explaining that "a similarity of experience is not the same as a *shared* experience."[84] Lester, like Cruse, distinguishes between the experience of European Jews as victims, from that of American Jews, as success stories. As Dollinger argues, "Postwar Jewish integration into white America undermined a key premise of the black-Jewish alliance; the two communities did not share a similar sociological reality."[85]

In an oft-cited 1967 *New York Times* essay, James Baldwin made a clearer distinction between Jewish experiences of suffering and Black oppression: that is, that Jewish suffering "is recognized as part of the moral history of the world and the Jew is recognized as a contributor to the world's history: this is not true for the blacks."[86] He cites American Jews' relative success in achieving safety and prosperity for future generations, both in terms of income and neighborhood. He compares narratives of the Warsaw Ghetto Uprising and the Harlem and Watts riots of 1964 and 1965, respectively, explaining, "The Jew is a white man, and when white men rise up against oppression, they are heroes: when black men rise, they have reverted to their native savagery." Another distinction between Jewish suffering and Black oppression, for Baldwin, is the location of suffering; as he writes, "It contradicts the American dream to suggest that any gratuitous, unregenerate horror can happen here. We make our mistakes, we like to think, but we are getting better all the time." For Baldwin, the distinction between Jewish and Black oppressions is based in the essential myths on which America was built: that white men can overcome an oppressive ruling class (as in the Revolutionary War); that white men's children can be promised a better life (as with the American Dream); that white men safeguard America's moral values (such as the promise of equality); and that white men make history (whether in the Bible or across America's political history). Importantly for Baldwin, these myths had, by 1967, all become associated with American Jews but continued to be denied to the vast majority of Black Americans. Undergirding each of Baldwin's arguments was the explicit assumption that by the 1960s, Jews had become part of the white supremacist system under which Black Americans suffered.

Baldwin's frank assessment of what some considered to be a special relationship elicited many responses, particularly from Jewish writers. While some in the Jewish community faulted African Americans entirely for any bad relationship, others sought to distance the Jewish community from a

---

[84] Julius Lester, "The Lives People Live," in *Blacks and Jews: Alliances and Arguments*, ed. Paul Berman (New York: Delacorte Press, 1994), 168.
[85] Dollinger, *Black Power*, 63.
[86] Baldwin, "Negroes Are Anti-Semitic Because They're Anti-White."

full assimilation into white society.[87] Despite his insistence that Jewish theology required civil rights activism, Rabbi Lelyveld also maintained that Jews faced double discrimination from Black Americans, writing, "It is not true that Jews are 'just white men' to Negroes and are therefore resented in equal measure with other whites. We are 'whites' (without pride or finality) and we are Jews."[88] As if anticipating Baldwin's argument, S. Andhil Fineberg of the American Jewish Committee wrote in 1963, "I am in no mood to protect any slumlord who is a Jew. All people have a right to hate them. My only concern is that their activity be not catalogued as Jews."[89]

In the absence of Black voices in the formation of *The Gates of Justice*, these tensions are not explicitly addressed; instead, the cantata focuses on a history of shared suffering and oppression that many Black communities did not fully accept. Nevertheless, there are moments in which these tensions sound in the background, such as in movement XI, "His Truth is a Shield." Beginning with a jubilant brass feature and option for improvisation, the movement leads into the final solos of the cantata; the baritone enters first, and the tenor concludes the movement. Despite the score marking that the baritone line be sung in "blues style," this solo is particularly straight; there are few blue notes or swung rhythms. Thus, the sonic signifiers of blackness Brubeck used in the earlier movements are missing from the baritone line (the prominent rhythm section and piano improvisation nevertheless offer a link to jazz). However, the bass line in this movement features a unique and crucial link to the essential "Black musical style" Brubeck seems keen to project. The bass line shares a remarkable resemblance to the bass line from Dizzy Gillespie, Chano Pozo, and Gil Fuller's 1947 tune, "Manteca." Example 5.6 illustrates the rhythmic and intervallic similarities in terms of note lengths, order of notes, and intervals between the notes, even given the differing time signatures. One of Gillespie's best-known songs, he later added a lyric to the bass line: "I'll never go back to Georgia."[90] If Brubeck intended to make that reference, it potentially reminds very attentive listeners of the real-world, brutal impacts of ignoring the cantata's message of nonviolence. Yet at a moment when some civil rights organizations were increasingly considering the use of force in protests, this reference reflects a major tension in Black-Jewish partnerships: who was allowed to set the terms for *how* activists protested?

---

[87] Robert Gordis, "Negroes Are Anti-Semitic Because They Want a Scapegoat," *New York Times Magazine* April 23, 1967, 235.
[88] Lelyveld, "Negro and Jewish Relationships," 9.
[89] S. Andhil Fineberg, qtd. in Greenberg, *Troubling the Waters*, 223.
[90] The lyric was included on a 1961 live album recorded at Carnegie Hall.
Dizzy Gillespie, *Carnegie Hall Concert*, The Dizzy Gillespie Big Band, Verve V8423, 1961.

**Ex. 5.6.** Mvt. XI, bass line, mm. 30–33. X's denote where the bass lines up melodically and rhythmically with the bass line from "Manteca" (the "Manteca" bass line is in 4/4).

## An Unequal Partnership

In the face of this question, Brubeck seems to use the cantata to model effective partnerships moving forward. For example, though Movement VII, "Shout unto the Lord," is meant to feature the choir, it also presents a brief moment of ideal partnership between the tenor and baritone soloists. In the program notes, Brubeck explains that while this movement is primarily a celebration, it also presents a reminder that even joy requires us all to work together: "It expresses the ecstasy and release of communal joy. However, at its core is the sobering message from Martin Luther King, Jr., our contemporary prophet: 'If we don't live together as brothers, we will die together as fools.'" This message also formed the basis of many descriptions of the piece by both Brubeck and Mintz. Mintz solidified Brubeck's social justice credentials by invoking the message, "Like Martin Luther King, Dave Brubeck is convinced that we must learn to live together as brothers or die together as fools."[91] Forty years later, Brubeck explained, as if still in lockstep with Mintz, "Martin Luther King, Jr.'s quote, 'We either live together as brothers or die together as fools,' sums up the central idea of the piece."[92]

For Brubeck, as for Mintz, this line is an important moment in the cantata. It comes in the middle, and the movement begins with an excerpt from King's "I Have a Dream" speech, in which King explains the strength of the faith he has in his dream; it is this faith which will allow the nation "to stand up for freedom together, knowing that we will be free one day."[93] As shown in example 5.7, the baritone soloist begins his phrase with this excerpt, shifting

---

[91] Nelson, "Brubeck."

[92] Dave Brubeck, interview with Howard Reich, 2010. In an interview with Herb Wong, Brubeck explained that he had heard this passage in a speech given by King to a college attended by Darius Milhaud (probably Wesleyan University), and that when he heard it, he had wanted to set it to music, calling it the "meat" of the piece." Dave Brubeck, interview with Herb Wong at the Monterey Jazz Fest 2002, *Jazz on My Mind: Liner Notes, Anecdotes and Conversations from the 1940s to the 2000s* (Jefferson, NC: McFarland, 2016), 170. Brubeck had long been interested in using the theme of brotherhood as a way of addressing racial justice issues. In 1959 he described the theme of *The Real Ambassadors*: "The theme is that he that loveth his God, loveth his brother also, obviously the racial question." Chuck Wheat, "Sermon in Jazz May Help Man Love His Brother," *Tulsa Daily World*, November 11, 1959.

[93] Martin Luther King Jr., "'I Have a Dream,' address delivered at the March on Washington for Jobs and Freedom," August 28, 1963, Washington, DC. In Clayborne Carson and Kris Shepard, ed., *A Call to Conscience: The Landmark Speeches of Dr. Martin Luther King, Jr.* (New York: Grand Central Publishing, 2001), 75–88. Brubeck paraphrases the text slightly: "We must stand for freedom together, knowing that one day we will be free."

**Ex. 5.7a.** Mvt. VII, baritone and tenor solos, mm. 100–115. Copyright © 1970; St. Francis Music Company and Malcolm Music, Ltd.; International Copyrights Secured; All Rights Reserved.

fluidly to another speech by King to sing, "If we don't live together as brothers." The tenor joins the baritone to sing, "We will die." The parts begin a ninth apart, and as the tenor sings a descending line and the baritone an ascending line, they meet at a perfect fifth interval, as if working out their differences to reach a more perfect union. As they finish the line, "together as fools," both parts ascend together in thirds, offering a clear sense of harmonic agreement (ex. 5.7a). The parts continue, rising in thirds to a climax featuring text from the end of King's "I Have a Dream" speech: "Free at last, I'm free at last! Thank God Almighty, we're free at last! I'm free!" As the soloists descend, they continue in thirds until the last note (sung on "free"), on which they finally perform in unison (ex. 5.7b).

However, the soloists are not ready to return the musical reins to the choir of "unheard millions." In a passage that mingles texts from Isaiah, King, and Hillel, the tenor and baritone leave the comfort of their parallel thirds in favor of a back and forth. The tenor enters, singing the line from Isaiah 50:8, "Who will contend with me?," and the baritone follows, singing the same text and melody; they again end in unison. Then, the tenor repeats a phrase from King's "I Have a Dream" speech, "Let us stand up together," with text painting clear in the ascent on the word "up." The baritone re-enters with more text

**Ex. 5.7b.** Mvt. VII, baritone and tenor solos, mm. 121–130. Copyright © 1970; St. Francis Music Company and Malcolm Music, Ltd.; International Copyrights Secured; All Rights Reserved.

from Isaiah 50:8, singing in a descending melodic line, "Who is my adversary?" The tenor continues this descent in the passage from Isaiah, inviting the baritone's adversary to "come near" to the tenor ("Let him come near to me"). The baritone then invokes Hillel, asking, "If the time for action is not now, when is it?" (ex. 5.7c).

Movement VII is largely a choral movement, but Brubeck highlights the text from Isaiah, King, and Hillel by adding the soloists in this section. The parts begin with a dissonant interval, before reaching harmonic thirds, and eventually, unison. But just as peace does not require sameness, Brubeck demonstrates how the soloists' paths can diverge and still support one another; just as the tenor supports the baritone by completing his phrase, speaking the words of Martin Luther King Jr. and inviting attack upon himself, and the baritone relies on the wisdom of the Jewish sage to explain his position.

While Brubeck's musical interpretation of an ideal partnership among Black and Jewish activists seems clear, this was a much more complex issue than he presents. The question of who was able to define the relationship, and furthermore, what the path forward might look like was extremely contested. By the late 1960s, Black civil rights activists were increasingly criticizing Jewish activists for what they understood to be patronizing and colonial

**Ex. 5.7c.** Mvt. VII, baritone and tenor solos, mm. 133–146. Copyright © 1970; St. Francis Music Company and Malcolm Music, Ltd.; International Copyrights Secured; All Rights Reserved.

attitudes. As Dinnerstein writes, "Jewish leaders assumed the role of senior partner because they believed that they had the necessary know-how to take charge."[94] Put simply, from the perspective of many Black activists, Jews had by and large transcended much of the discrimination they had previously faced in the United States and had "made it" to the middle class—and therefore, had also achieved at least some of the benefits of whiteness. Greenberg describes the relationship as somewhat paternalistic, arguing that such paternalism was born out of an impulse to act on Judaism's historical and moral obligations: "Jewish groups, in other words, may have acted paternalistically (likely out of an unawareness of the power dynamics inherent in the relationship), but they did recognize their obligation not only as discrimination's victims but also its beneficiaries, to act rather than leave it to others."[95]

To change the balance of the relationship would require a re-thinking of the role of white and Jewish people within the civil rights movement, and indeed, determining whether there was a role for them at all. As psychologist and civil rights activist Kenneth Clark explained in 1957, "Jews who help Negroes in the

---

[94] Dinnerstein, *Anti-Semitism in America*, 208.
[95] Greenberg, *Troubling the Waters*, 159.

struggle for equality do so from a position of unquestioned economic and political superiority. It may require a restructuring of the total pattern of this relationship ... when and if the Negro attains the position where he no longer requires or desires the help of benefactors."[96] Albert Vorspan, one of the leaders responsible for the focus of Reform Jews on social justice issues, later explained that the relationship between Jewish and Black activists was "kind and benevolent, but it was also colonial." Like Clark, and unlike some other Jewish allies, Vorspan understood that leadership roles needed to shift from Jewish activists to Black activists and defended Black Power, but he maintained that Jews still had an important role as allies:

> Black Power is, first and foremost, a drive for self-respect, autonomy, self-determination, manhood. I do not believe that the black man, by himself, can bring about the needed social revolution in America. He will need allies in the white community, including Jews, because the ultimate arena is political. But no longer will blacks be dependents, supplicants, mere symbols of injustice, or objects of our efforts.[97]

Furthermore, while some Jewish activists were willing to put their lives on the line for civil rights (notably Michael Schwerner and Andrew Goodman, who, with Black Mississippi resident James Chaney, were killed by members of the KKK in response to their work with CORE's Freedom Summer campaign), some Black activists saw Jewish and other white allies as fairweather friends who could assimilate into American whiteness whenever the benefits suited them.[98]

---

[96] Kenneth Clark, "A Positive Transition," *ADL Bulletin*, December 1957, 6.

[97] Vorspan, "Blacks and Jews," 209. As the executive director of the Philadelphia chapter of the American Jewish Congress, Murray Friedman, explained, "There was an alliance, but side by side much tension which Jews tended to ignore but Blacks clearly recognized." Murray Friedman, qtd. in Dinnerstein, *Antisemitism in America*, 208.

[98] Black activists sometimes accused Jews who had stepped away from allyship of trading in on these benefits. As Julius Lester wrote, "If there are Jews and other white people out there who understand, never was there a more opportune time for them to let their voices be heard. All I hear is silence, and if that's all there's going to be, then so be it." However, Jewish voice-raising was often complicated, as made clear in a *New York Magazine* article by Tom Wolfe about a party by Leonard Bernstein. Wolfe describes a party hosted by Leonard and Felicia Bernstein benefiting the Panther 21 (21 Black Panther members arrested for planning attacks on police officers). The event featured appetizers, drinks, and a glittering array of famous and wealthy attendees (i.e., Otto Preminger, Julie Belafonte, and Barbara Walters), along with the invited guests, who were members of the Black Panthers (Leon Quat and Don Cox). When a journalist later wrote about the party, the Bernsteins were accused of "elegant slumming," and of "mock[ing] the memory of Martin Luther King Jr." Further, some of the hate mail the Bernsteins received was from other Jews; namely, the chairman of the Jewish Defense League "blasted Lenny publicly for joining a 'trend in liberal and intellectual circles to lionize the Black Panthers.'" Excoriated by the mainstream press and by Jewish organizations, the Bernsteins eventually walked back the event, calling it a meeting, not a party, insisting on the Black Panthers' democratic rights, but also opposing their philosophies. The Bernstein party ultimately made clear some of the risks of Jewish voice-raising, as sympathetic Jews began to distance themselves from the Black Panther Party. Julius Lester, "A Response," in *Black Anti-Semitism and Jewish Racism* (New York: Richard W. Baron, 1969), 237; Tom Wolfe, "Radical Chic: That Party at Lenny's," *New York Magazine*, June 8, 1970, http://nymag.com/news/features/46170/.

## Particularism and Universalism in a Multicultural Soundscape

In the face of growing assumptions of whiteness and white privilege, some Jewish communities sought to mitigate feelings of partial assimilation by re-asserting their Jewishness. Brodkin suggests that "Embracing the privileges of whiteness seemed to cost them the loss of a meaningful Jewish cultural identity."[99] Many emphasized their Jewishness through activity in the civil rights movement, positioning their moral obligation to act against discrimination as both part of post–World War II American moral exceptionalism and also specific to their experience as Jews. As Dollinger argues, "Although Jews may have perceived themselves as becoming more Jewish, their [1960s civil rights] activism actually reflected a new identity-based *Americanist* credo. In what seems an ironic twist, Jews became more American by acting more Jewish."[100] In other words, Jews could claim a solid place as white Americans by participating in post–World War II American moral superiority that understood racism and bigotry as un-American—much like Brubeck's own approach.[101] At the same time, by asserting that their Jewish faith undergirded their civil rights activism, Jews could maintain a particular tie to Jewishness without risking the loss of privilege being seen as white now granted them. As Goldstein writes, "Jews often looked to racial liberalism as a surrogate for expressing ethnic distinctiveness, since it allowed them to identify as part of the white mainstream's political culture without making them feel as if they had abandoned their legacy as a persecuted minority group."[102]

Historian James Loeffler refers to this constant negotiation of mainstream white political culture and minority group sympathy as a delicate balance between particularism and universalism.[103] Though often considered to be dichotomous, Loeffler argues that throughout Jewish history, particularism and universalism have never been mutually exclusive; instead, it has been Jews' interest in the particular (Jewish politics) that has inspired involvement

---

[99] Brodkin, *How Jews Became White Folks*, 183.
[100] Dollinger, *Black Power*, 17.
[101] Goldstein, *The Price of Whiteness*, 195.
[102] Ibid., 212. Likewise, Loeffler details the work of Jewish human rights activist and president of the American Jewish Committee Jacob Blaustein (d. 1970), who believed that "to survive in the postwar world . . . Jews needed to define themselves as an apolitical religious faith rather than as a quarrelsome national minority." Such an approach, Loeffler explains, would "deflect attention from the ethnic and political aspects of Jewish advocacy," instead pointing toward a "triple melting pot" of Judeo-Christian beliefs encompassing Judaism, Catholicism, and Protestantism (*Rooted Cosmopolitans*, 86). However, as Loeffler also points out, not all Jews and Jewish organizations felt this way; this "colorblind" approach to Jewish activism was particularly challenged by Zionists like Rabbi Abraham Heller, who advocated "maintain[ing] and foster[ing] their group identity" (110).
[103] Loeffler, *Rooted Cosmopolitans*, 296–299.

in the universal, or a more worldwide concept of human rights (including the American civil rights movement). As Loeffler writes, citing philosopher Hannah Arendt, "The phrase '[to] be human as a Jew' reads like an oxymoron today. It smacks of special pleading or relativism. Human rights are supposed to transcend difference, not affirm it. Yet this is not the only way to define human rights. The Jewish political tradition... recognized national politics as a precondition of international justice. To survive as a minority required political self-definition, which in turn meant collective politics."[104]

In *The Gates of Justice*, Brubeck espouses a similar identity-focused approach to racial harmony; in his vision, a nation is strongest when people of different races, ethnicities, and religious traditions maintain their specific group identities. It is essentially a multicultural approach in which difference is celebrated and assimilation is avoided; the seeming universal commonalities between each particular tradition are likewise celebrated. This is particularly evident in his treatment of the tenor and baritone soloists, who frequently maintain their particular style (either the Jewish cantor-style or the gospel/blues style). But Brubeck's identity-focused approach is perhaps nowhere more clear than in Movement X, "The Lord Is Good," which he describes as the "climactic section" of the entire cantata. The movement represents a "collage of sound" and includes "texts from Isaiah, Martin Luther King, Hillel, and the Psalms, and music from The Beatles, Chopin, Israeli, Mexican, and Russian folk songs, Simon & Garfunkel, improvised jazz and rock."[105]

This movement uses juxtaposition as a compositional tool to heighten the sonic contrasts between a variety of musical traditions. Table 5.1 notes each of these stylistic changes; some are explicitly noted in the score or program notes while others are referenced through the musical style, added text, and performing forces. For many of these, the referenced style is made so obviously as to nearly reflect a caricature. Example 5.8 depicts measures 63–71, or the "Mexican" and "classical" sections. The so-called Mexican section is a version of *Jarabe Tapatío*, often referred to as the Mexican hat dance: the sopranos move in parallel thirds, and the altos exclaim "Olé!"[106] While the choice of the Mexican hat dance may seem either hackneyed or ironic, Brubeck chose similarly stereotypical musical representations of other countries in these short sections. His goal seems to have been to quickly (within 3–5 measures) insert

---

[104] Ibid., 296. Arendt wrote in 1942, "A Jew can preserve his human dignity only if he can be human as a Jew." Hannah Arendt, "A Way Toward the Reconciliation of Peoples," in *Hannah Arendt: The Jewish Writings*, ed. Jerome Kohn and Ron Feldman (New York: Schocken Books, 2007), 261.

[105] Dave Brubeck, program note, *The Gates of Justice*, 1969.

[106] *Jarabe Tapatío* was originally a courtship dance from the nineteenth century. While it was popular throughout Mexico, becoming part of Mexico's cultural identity, the tune became particularly popular in the United States through the *Speedy Gonzalez* cartoons of the 1950s.

**Table 5.1.** Styles in Movement X, "The Lord Is Good," *The Gates of Justice*

| Measures | Genre/style* | Changes in performing forces and other notes |
|---|---|---|
| 1–23 | | Choir, both soloists |
| 24–27 | Israeli folk song | Tenor soloist; cymbal/temple blocks |
| 28–31 | Gospel* (baritone)/Rock* (Choir and accompaniment) | Baritone soloist; African tree or gourd |
| 32–35 | Israeli folk song | Tenor soloist; cymbal/temple blocks |
| 36–39 | Gospel/Rock | Baritone soloist; African tree or gourd |
| 40–47 | Transition | |
| 48–50 | Israeli folk song | Tenor soloist; cymbal/temple blocks |
| 51–54 | Swing* | Baritone soloist; maracas, tambourine, cowbell |
| 55–56 | Israeli folk song | Tenor soloist; cymbal/temple blocks |
| 57–62 | Swing | Baritone soloist; maracas, tambourine, cowbell |
| 63–67 | Spanish/Mexican | Choir; castanets<br>text: "olé" |
| 68–71 | Classical (Baroque) | Choir; triangle<br>direction: "strict" |
| 72–75 | Russian folk | Choir; Zither<br>Beatles reference (text: "all the lonely people") |
| 75–80 | "Oriental sing–song style"* | Choir; cymbal tree<br>Simon and Garfunkel reference (text: "sound of silence") |
| 81–97 | Spiritual* (baritone)/Gospel sound* (choir) | Baritone soloist<br>Text: "hah!": "a forceable expulsion of breath on any pitch, as in a worksong" |
| 98–127 | Blues* | Tenor soloist |
| 128–139 (end) | | Choir, both soloists |

*indicates description as noted in score (style markings without asterisk come from the program notes)

a musical style with recognizably different countries of origin. In the "classical" section, the alto part is an exact transcription of the subject of J. S. Bach's C minor fugue. The choir's "gospel sound" in measure 81 is driven primarily by the tenor's "hah!," which Brubeck describes in the score as "a forceable expulsion of breath on any pitch, as in a worksong." The "gospel singer style" of the baritone soloist seems to be most apparent in blue notes, and the tenor soloist's augmented second embellishments seem to drive the "Israeli folk song" references. By the end of the movement, all of the stylistic differences melt away as the choir and soloists sing text adapted from Psalm 91:4: "He will give you refuge, under His wings, refuge for all when we are one, all generations, when we are one." Thus, a movement that relied primarily on musical differences concludes as the baritone and tenor sing in unison, "When we are one!"

Through such juxtapositions, Movement X explicitly highlights musical and racial difference. Both Dave and Iola Brubeck had been grappling with this philosophical theme in their compositions and lyrics for nearly a decade. In the program notes to *The Gates of Justice*, Dave Brubeck asks, "Have we not all one Father? If God created man in His image and likeness, surely He accepts all men in their diversity." Similarly, in 1961, Dave Brubeck recorded *The Real Ambassadors*, a musical critiquing the hypocrisy of the US State Department's use of Black jazz musicians to portray the United States as having achieved racial harmony, even as Black citizens across the country continued to face discrimination and extreme acts of racial violence. Iola Brubeck also wrote the lyrics for *The Real Ambassadors*. The musical featured Louis Armstrong, the cultural ambassador, as the "real" ambassador.

In a feature song, Armstrong ponders the discrepancy between biblical passages presenting humans as having been created in the image of God, and the lived experience of discrimination and oppression faced by African Americans. Responding to the title lyrics of the song, "They say I look like God," Armstrong asks, "Could God be black? My God!"[107] The piece was originally written as a more comedic number ("to show how ridiculous it [segregation] was," according to Brubeck), and the lyrics that followed suggest a wry humor: "If all are made in the image of Thee, could Thou perchance a Zebra be?" But according to Brubeck, Armstrong transformed the number in their live performance at the Monterey Jazz Festival: "Louis had tears in his eyes. He didn't go for a laugh, and the audience followed him away from our original intentions. And all through the night, he took those lines that were supposed to get a laugh and went the other way with it. And at the record session he cried."[108] The story Brubeck shares about "They Say I Look Like God" again reflects Brubeck's belief that he and Iola Brubeck could (unintentionally, even) produce believable Black experiences in their work. Crafting a narrative that would move Louis Armstrong to tears is therefore a testament to their own authenticity and authorial power. However, the product—the recording—preserves Armstrong's approach to the song, and not Brubeck's, which simultaneously demonstrates Brubeck's willingness to give up some authorial control over the messaging of *The Real Ambassadors*, allowing Armstrong the

---

[107] Louis Armstrong, "They Say I Look Like God," *The Real Ambassadors*, lyrics by Iola Brubeck, Columbia OL 5850, 1962.

[108] Brubeck, qtd. in Penny von Eschen, *Satchmo Blows Up the World: Jazz Ambassadors Play the Cold War* (Cambridge, MA: Harvard University Press, 2009), 89.

space to express his own experiences, both as a musician and as an unofficial cultural ambassador.

In struggling with this concept—that all people reflect God's image—Brubeck eventually shifts from a colorblind conception of race to a more multicultural understanding. Brubeck's colorblindness had previously played a key role in his activism; throughout the 1950s, Brubeck seemed to remain committed to the belief that racism came from noticing racial differences. Therefore, if he claimed to not see race, he could treat all people equally. But his colorblindness missed a central element of racism: racism does not result from simply *observing* racial difference, but rather *discriminating* based on racial difference. Ignoring race also meant ignoring the power dynamics that, for example, allowed him to perform in places Eugene Wright could not, or that allowed him to purchase a home in neighborhoods less likely to be available to Wright, or that allowed him to protest on Wright's behalf at East Carolina College without informing Wright there was an issue. While the multicultural approach of *The Gates of Justice* allows distinctions in race to be noticed, and indeed celebrated, it still does not require a recognition of systemic discriminations.

In Movement X of *The Gates of Justice*, listeners witness abrupt juxtapositions between diverse musical styles. The musical contrasts could not be greater, and it is clear that Brubeck is relying on those musical contrasts to invoke racial contrasts. This is particularly clear in mm. 28–31 and 36–39,

**Ex. 5.8.** Mvt. X, choir and percussion, mm. 63–71. Copyright © 1970; St. Francis Music Company and Malcolm Music, Ltd.; International Copyrights Secured; All Rights Reserved.

Ex. 5.8. Continued

in which the Black baritone soloist is directed to sing in "gospel" style, a historically Black musical genre, and the choir is directed to sing in "rock" style, a genre historically assumed to be white, as opposed to R&B or gospel; at no other point in the movement does Brubeck ask the choir and soloists to sing in different styles. In Movement X, he presents musical evidence of the strengths of non-assimilation: by maintaining unique group identities, and loving each other for those differences, relationships can be stronger, and all people can truly unite as one. In doing so, he demonstrates an understanding of racism as focused predominantly on individual expressions of hate rather than systems of oppression that operate often regardless of intent.

## Conclusion

By reminding audience members of the historic ties that bound Black and Jewish communities (both in Cincinnati and elsewhere), relying heavily on a Black baritone to inspire an empathetic return to the Jewish moral imperative to end oppression of others, and reinforcing an identity-based approach to racial and ethnic difference, *The Gates of Justice* attempts to re-assert Jewishness as an identity set apart from whiteness. However, Black leaders and activists diverged from Jewish leaders and activists on a number of key issues throughout the 1960s—issues Jewish leaders continued to believe were important motivators for continued activism on the part of Jewish congregations, and issues that were foundational themes in the cantata. While the cantata was meant to bridge the perceived growing gap between Jewish and Black communities, it did so from a distinctly Jewish perspective—that is, the cantata does not seem to have been particularly meant for Black audiences, both in terms of who it spoke for and who it spoke to. The cantata thus granted both its Jewish audiences and Brubeck the authorial privilege of imagining a new relationship between the communities.

Perhaps unsurprisingly, the cantata's reception in Black newspapers seems to reflect an ambivalence about the composition. While the *Chicago Defender*, *Los Angeles Sentinel*, and *New York Amsterdam News* announced regional premieres of the work, each focused less on the message (providing mostly a cursory overview) and more on the performance's inclusion of a Black soloist and later, a Black conductor. The *New York Amsterdam News* and *Chicago Daily Defender* each published articles featuring bass-baritone soloist McHenry Boatwright's background almost exclusively.[109] The *Chicago Daily Defender* published a subsequent article detailing conductor Everett Lee's background and struggles for acceptance within the overwhelmingly white American orchestral world.[110] In his review of the Chicago performance, Earl Calloway noted that Brubeck's improvisations "clearly communicat[ed] the deep and stirring emotions of a race surviving against the odds," but responsibility for the performance's success went exclusively to Lee, about whom

---

[109] Perdita Duncan, "Music in Review: McHenry Boatwright, Bass-Baritone," *New York Amsterdam News*, October 4, 1969, 18; "Baritone Sings Brubeck's Cantata," *Chicago Daily Defender*, August 17, 1971, 10.
[110] Earl Calloway, "Everett Lee Conducts 'Gates of Justice' Premiere," *Chicago Daily Defender*, August 21, 1971, 16.

Calloway writes, "It is difficult to believe that any other living conductor could provide such eloquence, such expressiveness in fashioning Brubeck's 'The Gates of Justice' into such a magnificent example of universalism within an artistic musical concept."[111] The relative disinterest in *The Gates of Justice* on the part of the Black press likely reflected the growing disinterest among Black audiences for records by white artists: as American studies scholar Brian Ward documents, peak interest among Black audiences in albums by white artists coincided with the hopefulness of the early years of the civil rights movement (1957–1964). As disillusionment in and disappointment with the movement grew in the mid to late 1960s, Black interest in white records likewise began to wane.[112]

Ethnomusicologist Judah Cohen describes such juxtapositions of dissimilar experiences (i.e., between Jewishness and blackness) as "facing," a concept from Diaspora studies.[113] As Cohen explains, facing inevitably brings up "questions of intention, collaboration, and dynamic interaction," as successful facing requires carefully curated spaces.[114] Mintz and the Brubecks carefully curated the message of *The Gates of Justice*, but because the curation did not include Black community members as equal collaborative partners, any potential collaborative result from facing Black and Jewish communities in the cantata was unrealized. Brubeck's own recollection of a meaningful response to *The Gates of Justice* focused on the reflection of a Jewish college student, who told him after singing the piece, "Now I have a better understanding of my own religious tradition."[115] Created primarily by Jewish and white stakeholders for Jewish audiences, the piece ultimately offers a one-sided account of the Black-Jewish relations it intended to mend. The commission thus demonstrates an interest in using jazz (and other Black American musical genres) as a sonic signifier for blackness, but only as translated through a western classical musical form by a white composer. The lack of Black voices, authors, and stakeholders limits the cantata's effectiveness as a symbolic

---

[111] Earl Calloway, "Conductor Everett Lee Communicates with Brubeck's Cantata," *Chicago Daily Defender*, August 26, 1971, 16.

[112] Brian Ward, *Just My Soul Responding: Rhythm and Blues, Black Consciousness, and Race Relations* (Berkeley: University of California Press, 1998).

[113] Judah M. Cohen, "Hearing Echoes, Sensing History: The Challenge of Musical Diasporas," in *Theory and Method in Historical Ethnomusicology*, ed. Johnathan McCollum and David G. Hebert (Lanham, MD: Lexington Books, 2014), 153. "Facing" comes from Adam Zachary Newton, *Facing Black and Jew: Literature as Public Space in Twentieth-Century America* (Cambridge: Cambridge University Press, 1999); Wendy Zierler, "'My Holocaust Is Not Your Holocaust': 'Facing' Black and Jewish Experience in *The Pawnbroker, Higher Ground*, and *The Nature of Blood*," *Holocaust and Genocide Studies* 18, no. 1 (Spring 2004), 46–67.

[114] Cohen, "Hearing Echoes, Sensing History," 165.

[115] William Skoog, "An Interview with Dave Brubeck Regarding His Choral Music," *Choral Journal* 49, no. 11 (May 2009): 37.

model of multicultural interaction and support; the cantata instead reads primarily as a statement by and for Jewish and white allies to promote sympathy and empathy (which can only go so far in a violent struggle against those who denied Black humanity and civil rights).

One could imagine other fruitful collaborations that might have had different results; indeed, Brubeck was not the only jazz musician to compose religious music in this period. For example, Mary Lou Williams's *Black Christ of the Andes*, a devotional work dedicated to St. Martin de Porres, premiered in New York in 1962 (it was later recorded in 1963), and she composed sacred music and masses throughout the 1960s, including *The Pittsburgh Mass* (1966), *Mass for Lenten Season* (1968), and *Mass for Peace and Justice* (1969). Given the 1965 declaration from the Second Vatican Council condemning anti-Semitism and asserting for the first time that Jews were not responsible for Jesus's death, a cantata by a Black Catholic composer would certainly have been both relevant and interesting. Likewise, Duke Ellington composed three "sacred concerts," which were performed in 1965, 1968, and 1973. These are only potential Christian jazz composers: there were also a number of Jewish jazz musicians, including Black Jewish jazz musicians, or Black jazz musicians with a particular affinity for Jewishness well-known in the jazz field who might have made interesting collaborations or compositions, including Willie "The Lion" Smith, Herbie Mann, Stan Getz, Lee Konitz, Terry Gibbs, and Sammy Davis Jr. Argentinian musician Lalo Schifrin's *Jazz Suite on the Mass Texts* (1965) was also a well-regarded religious work in the jazz genre (Schifrin's father was Jewish).

However, by selecting Brubeck as the messenger of a particularly Jewish approach to Black-Jewish relations, Mintz drew an implicit comparison between the predominantly Jewish congregation in the audience and Brubeck. If Mintz had asked Ellington or Mary Lou Williams to compose a cantata, the comparison could potentially have magnified the differences between Black and Jewish communities, exacerbating an already tenuous relationship. Using Brubeck offered the congregation a chance to instead draw a contrast between Jewish whiteness and Brubeck's whiteness; in doing so, the Jewish congregation in attendance (especially those at the premiere at Rockdale Temple, seated miles away from their former predominantly Black neighborhood) could be reminded, possibly reassured, that even if they had achieved some of the benefits of whiteness, in terms of neighborhoods, education, and class relationships, they could still maintain their Jewish identity and thereby stand somewhat apart from whiteness. For Mintz and other Jewish allies and activists, maintaining a particular place as Jews in the world was crucial for Jews' continued work for human rights in the civil rights movement as non-whites.

By both offering an examination of whiteness as separate from the Jewish experience and relying on an implicit assumption of the separation between blackness and Jewishness, the cantata reflects what Brodkin describes as "a kind of double vision that comes from racial middleness: of an experience of marginality vis-à-vis whiteness, and an experience of whiteness and belonging vis-à-vis blackness."[116] The cantata shows a community uncomfortable with the elements of white privilege they had newly achieved and searching for a way to distance themselves from that whiteness.

While the various performances of whiteness throughout this book demonstrate the ways in which whiteness worked, operated, and benefited white Americans, *The Gates of Justice* offers a musical and social performance outside, within, and *against* whiteness—a performance of negotiation. As Goldstein argues, Jews have "negotiated their place in a complex racial world where Jewishness, whiteness, and blackness have all made significant claims on them."[117] As an expression of the Reform Jewish movement's position in late 1960s civil rights politics, *The Gates of Justice* demonstrates how Brubeck's whiteness could be used in a carefully crafted performance of whiteness outside the Black/white racial binary that dominated the mid-century racial landscape. Further, in performing a distinction between Jewishness and whiteness through involvement in the civil rights movement, *The Gates of Justice* also represents a performance against the political power and structural supremacy of whiteness. Another read of the cantata might be that it, along with Mintz and the Brubecks, fell into a trope of (white) moral heroism—acting in the interest of oppressed others, while at the same time benefiting from that action. But still another might interpret any action that inspired empathetic action in the civil rights movement, no matter the means, as operating against structures of white supremacy.[118]

However, by excluding Black voices in the telling of this story, the cantata ultimately reflects a degree of unexamined privilege in storytelling and history creation. Whose voices are heard in histories of discrimination and oppression? Who is allowed to document those stories? *The Gates of Justice* documented a shared history that no longer felt shared to many of the Black communities for whom Mintz and the Brubecks fought to win justice and equality. Although the stated goal of the cantata was to bring Black and Jewish communities back together, the result threatens to prioritize a

---

[116] Brodkin, *How Jews Became White Folks*, 1–2.
[117] Goldstein, *The Price of Whiteness*, 5.
[118] Indeed, many in the audience of Rockdale Temple and at the Union of American Hebrew Congregations (UAHC) Biennial Convention may have been working to recognize their privilege and put it to the work of supporting Black Americans.

performance against and outside of whiteness over a partnership with Black communities. Across these myriad interpretations of the cantata and its meaning for late civil rights era Reform Jews, one thing is clear: the cantata reflects Jewish performances within, outside, and against whiteness that were rendered invisible by the Black/white racial binary that defined American racial politics.

# Conclusion

## Evading Whiteness

Dave Brubeck looms large in many fields of music, and for many audiences, in part because he was engaged in so many different conversations across his career. It is clear to me that he thought a lot about who he wanted to be in conversation with in his compositions, jazz albums, and tours, and that he wanted those conversations to be myriad, diverse, and inclusive. I have loved researching him and telling his stories because I have been able to engage with scholars and audiences from a variety of fields and perspectives—combining classical, popular, and jazz music cultures into a broader story about mid-century American whiteness. This has perhaps been most evident in my work with *The Gates of Justice*, about which I was invited to write for the Milken Archive of Jewish Music and to speak with the Jewish Music Study Group at UCLA. I have been grateful for the generosity and feedback of editors, scholars, audiences, and listeners in these spaces. And yet as I came to the end of this project, I couldn't help but feel increasingly uncomfortable about some of the intellectual places into which Brubeck was leading me. I continue to have an uneasy relationship with this book's fifth chapter, centering as it does on connections between Jewishness and whiteness—even if it revolves around a simultaneously well-known and understudied classical piece by Brubeck (among his most performed classical pieces, in fact). Who am I, a white non-Jew raised in the Catholic Church, to explore Jewish identity in this way, given the long histories of anti-Semitism experienced by American Jews, and given the strange and often intricately bound relationships between and among whiteness, anti-Semitism, and anti-Blackness?

Whose stories should we tell? For whom do we bear knowledge, and whose knowledge do we bear? In this final entry on the relationships between Brubeck, his critics and audiences, and whiteness, I locate him in the 1990s, a period in which his relationship with Native American culture and heritage appears on full display: first, the April 1992 premiere of the choral work, *Earth Is Our Mother*, featuring a well-known text from 1854 attributed to Chief Si'ahl (1780–1866), a leader of the Suquamish and Duwamish tribes in what is now Washington State (his anglicized name is Chief Seattle, and it is also written as Sealth or Seathl); and second, the centering of Brubeck's identity around his alleged Native American ancestry in jazz critic Gene Lees's *Cats of Any Color: Jazz, Black and White* (1994).[1]

As a Brubeck scholar and as a critical whiteness scholar, whether or not and how I might engage with Brubeck's "Indianness" has been a particular challenge. Upon reviewing my book proposal, a senior scholar whose work I deeply admire suggested this as an area I might consider further. One year later, a colleague finishing her dissertation in ethnomusicology and Indigenous studies matter-of-factly responded that of course I, a non-Indigenous scholar, would not consider such work. This tension, paired with the belief that Brubeck's claims were as much, if not more, about whiteness than about Indigeneity, required me to think carefully about my methods, motives, and outcomes in this work as I considered what my relationship to Indigenous music studies might look like. I gesture here particularly to Stó:lō musicologist Dylan Robinson's crucial monograph *Hungry Listening: Resonant Theory for Indigenous Sound Studies*. Robinson theorizes hungry listening as a settler colonial orientation to listening, which privileges "'more easily digestible,' forms of Indigenous culture and narratives," which offer "palatable narratives of difference," and which "consumes without awareness of how the consumption acts in relationship with those people, the lands, the waters who provide sustenance."[2] Ultimately, Robinson asks listeners (whether settlers or Indigenous) to pay particular attention to our own positionality as we listen and choose to listen—or perhaps, as we know and choose to seek knowledge.[3]

With *Earth Is Our Mother*, I want to resist hungry listening—both the hungry listening by which I might consume Chief Si'ahl's speech and its meaning, even within a largely western classical musical setting, and Brubeck's own hungry listening in the sound curation of this piece. This conclusion is therefore not about *Earth Is Our Mother*, in terms of what the composition is about and how the text and music might make meaning. Likewise, it does not seek the "truth" of Brubeck's ancestry. Rather, it is about how Brubeck's Indigenous extraction offered another performance of whiteness, specific to

---

[1] Prior to the 1990s, the primary references to any potential Native American ancestry in the Brubeck family were largely limited to (1) the 1974 album titled *Brother, The Great Spirit Made Us All*, with cover art featuring several icons reminiscent of a vaguely Native American aesthetic (otherwise the album was a pretty typical jazz album); and (2) Paul Desmond's occasional reference to Brubeck as "the Indian," an apparent reference to Brubeck's looks and stoic demeanor at the piano when they first met.

[2] Dylan Robinson, *Hungry Listening: Resonant Theory for Indigenous Sound Studies* (Minneapolis: University of Minnesota Press, 2020), 49, 50, 53.

[3] For information on Indigenous style principles, see Gregory Younging, *Elements of Indigenous Style: A Guide for Writing by and About Indigenous Peoples* (Edmonton, ON: Brush Education, 2018). For suggestions on how to apply those style principles to musicological and ethnomusicological research, see Jessica Bissett Perea and Gabriel Solis, "Asking the Indigeneity Question of American Music Studies," *Journal of the Society for American Music* 13, no. 4 (2019): 401–410.

the context of the 1990s jazz scene. It is a critique of a white possessive investment in a settler understanding of Indigeneity and multiculturalism. And ultimately, it is about the performances of evasion that maintain whiteness and white dominance through their refusal to be named and critiqued.

## Earth Is Our Mother

*Earth Is Our Mother* was commissioned and premiered by the Marquette Choral Society for its twentieth anniversary. The premiere took place April 11, 1992, at Northern Michigan University in Marquette, Michigan. When the commission came, Dave and Iola Brubeck asked if the choral society might be interested in a setting of an 1854 speech attributed to Chief Si'ahl. Iola Brubeck later explained that the Michigan-based choral society was interested in the text and theme because "northern Michigan is Indian territory—so much of Indian lore and background and culture is there."[4] The choral piece originally featured a vocal soloist, but the part was very demanding. Wanting to re-focus the piece on the text, Iola Brubeck eventually suggested that the solo part be spoken instead for subsequent performances (Dave Brubeck conceded that in performances with Russell Means, an Oglala Lakota activist who performed the spoken role, "I know it was more powerful than singing").

The origin story for *Earth Is Our Mother* reflects a broader burgeoning fascination with spirituality from Indigenous sources (a "return to nature") in the 1980s and 1990s. Dave and Iola Brubeck originally came to the Chief Si'ahl text as quoted by Joseph Campbell on the 1988 PBS broadcast of *The Power of Myth*. At some point after acquiring the PBS transcript, the Brubecks learned of the challenging reality of the Si'ahl text: there are many versions, and the authenticity of each is highly contested, due to the dense combination of power relations, translation and transcription issues, the passage of time, and the 1970s adaptation of the text by white screenwriter Ted Perry.[5] In the published program notes for *Earth Is Our Mother*, Dave Brubeck writes that

---

[4] Dave Brubeck, "A Long Partnership in Life and Music," an oral history conducted in 1999 and 2001 by Caroline C. Crawford, Regional Oral History Office, Bancroft Library, University of California, Berkeley, 2006, 82.

[5] In 1995, poet Denise Low analyzed recent adaptations (of the 1970s–1990s) of the text, arguing that because of the limited publishing power Native Americans have had, "the created reality of recent versions of Seattle's words is fictitious and signifies a monologic domination." She further explains that "no historical or contemporary Native people have felt a need to translate or adapt the speech," essentially advocating for the original transcription and publication by Dr. H. A. Smith in 1887, thirty years after the speech, while acknowledging even the fragmentary nature of that version. Denise Low, "Contemporary Reinvention of Chief Seattle: Variant Texts of Chief Seattle's 1854 Speech," *American Indian Quarterly* 19, no. 3 (Summer 1995). More recently, Indigenous studies scholar Arnold Krupat explains inaccuracies that may be present in Smith's text but he ultimately believes "that the speech Dr. Smith published in 1887 does derive

other versions he and Iola consulted during the composition process in addition to the Campbell version included one sent by Ada Deer from the Native American Rights Fund and another from the Suquamish museum (this was the 1887 version published by Dr. Henry A. Smith, which is considered to be the first published version). The Brubecks explain that they learned of the 1970s version by Ted Perry, which was widely circulated and made popular among white ecological activists, only after setting the text.[6]

Indigenous poet Denise Low (Lenape and Cherokee) explains that the motive of Chief Si'ahl's speech was to enact "preliminary negotiations for rights of Suquamish and Duwamish people to visit their burial grounds" in the face of forced removal.[7] Low writes that the key purpose of the argument, since lost in subsequent flowery, fragmented, and commercial versions, is, "Land is sacred because of religious ties to ancestors; specific histories are part of the tribal landscapes." Indigenous studies scholar Arnold Krupat further argues that Chief Si'ahl's speech was a way of saying goodbye—that "his speech as published by Dr. Smith strongly expresses an understanding that there was *nothing* he and his people could do to ensure their *continuance* and *survivance*. [emphasis in the original]"[8]

Brubeck's version draws heavily on the Campbell/*Power of Myth* version, which itself draws much more substantially on an abbreviated Perry/ecological version than on the original Smith version (the 1887 publication by Dr. Smith that Indigenous studies scholars like Krupat hold to be the most authentic version of the speech). The Perry version is essentially a work of ecological activism, much more about white people's separation from nature and nature's impending death than a Native chief grappling with forced removal and genocide. The Brubeck version adds text that emphasizes the ecological urgency of the Campbell/Perry texts, highlighting that various aspects of nature will be gone, with the foreboding warning that "whatever happens to the beasts soon happens to man."[9] Essentially, though Brubeck acknowledges that he had access to previous versions of the text from Native American sources,

---

substantially, if not entirely, from Sealth's performance on that January day in 1854." Arnold Krupat, "Chief Seattle's Speech Revisited," *The American Indian Quarterly* 35, no. 2 (Spring 2011), 192–214, 200. Krupat continues to offer further contextualization of the Smith version.

[6] Perry wrote his version of the Chief Si'ahl speech as part of a fictional screenplay that relied on a Native American call for environmental responsibility. However, Perry was given no on-screen credit: according to later reporting, "the producer said the words sounded 'more authentic' presented as Chief Seattle's." Perry later regretted the perpetuation of the false Chief Si'ahl speech. Ann Medlock, "Chief Seattle's Screenwriter," *HuffPost* (November 17, 2007), https://www.huffpost.com/entry/chief-seattles-screenwrit_b_72510.

[7] Low, "Contemporary Reinvention of Chief Seattle."

[8] Krupat, "Chief Seattle's Speech Revisited," 205.

[9] Dave Brubeck, *Earth Is Our Mother* (Los Angeles, CA: Alfred Music, 1997).

his version becomes yet another removal of the text from its original political setting, further re-positioning the speech as by a Native elder in order to authenticate ecological activism.

In terms of the music, Brubeck writes that he "made no attempt to be 'authentic,' but hoped to capture in my composition some of their [Indigenous songs'] emotional power," which he heard on field recordings made by Ida Halpern in the Pacific Northwest in 1947. He also explained that "each tribal group had its own sociological and religious rules about their songs" that were difficult to authenticate.[10] While he acknowledges sonic distinctions and approaches between tribes, he ultimately relied more on sonic tropes frequently associated with Indigenous musical traditions than on existing Suquamish or Duwamish musical sources, explaining that many of the musical traditions had "been lost or changed by European influences." His statement also suggests that he understood Indigenous musical sounds to exist primarily and most authentically in the distant past, thereby contributing to and further normalizing settler notions of disappearance rather than acknowledging the continuance of Indigenous traditions.

Two performances in particular stood out to the Brubecks: one was a December 1997 performance in Albuquerque, New Mexico, featuring Oglala Lakota activist Russell Means (1939–2012) to benefit the Acoma schools. In an interview published just before the performance, Brubeck explained that he "like[d] the idea of performing for people in an area where it should be understood."[11] He also shed some light on who the target audience for the benefit concert was: "At first we were going to do this on the reservation, but Reginald Rodriguez decided to do it in Albuquerque. The audience can get there easier."[12] The target audience—the donor audience that could get there easier—almost certainly did not live on the reservation.

Perhaps the most meaningful performance for the Brubecks was the West Coast premiere in May 1993, in Seattle, Washington. In the days surrounding the performances, the Brubecks visited the grave of Chief Si'ahl, they met with his descendants and others in local Indigenous communities, and the performances were attended by the great-great-grandchildren of Chief Si'ahl. The concert was preceded by a talk and prayer by either a spiritual

---

[10] Dave Brubeck, "Notes on *Earth Is Our Mother*," *Earth Is Our Mother* (Los Angeles: Alfred Music, 1997).
[11] David Steinberg, "Chief's Speech Inspired Brubeck," *Albuquerque Journal*, December 19, 1997, E15.
[12] Reginald Rodriguez (d. 2001) worked for the Bureau of Indian Affairs, was superintendent of the San Felipe Pueblo schools, was a past president of the New Mexico Symphony Orchestra, and was very active in the Albuquerque arts community.

advisor or a chief of a tribe closely related to the Suquamish.[13] Toward the end of the rehearsals and performances, the spiritual advisor returned and presented Dave Brubeck with eagle feathers that Iola Brubeck explains "had been blessed with the smoke and whatever ritual that they go through."[14] In that interview, she continues, "And that's something that we prize very much because nothing could be more significant than to receive that." At Iola Brubeck's prompting, Dave Brubeck explains the feathers' significance: "To take an eagle feather from a nest is illegal today. But he said, 'Now, when I give you this, remember when you cross over, you wave that, and we'll let you in.'" Iola Brubeck continues his story, explaining that the feather meant, "We'll recognize you. We'll know who you are, that you're one of us. You're one of the people."[15] She concludes the re-telling by stating that the generous gift is kept in their dining room. For the Brubecks, the attendance of the concert by Si'ahl's descendants and participation of the spiritual advisor or chief seemed to have lent approval and authority to their setting of the text. The added gift of the feathers also potentially granted a kind of authenticity to Dave Brubeck's own alleged Native American background, and indeed, the gift may have reflected a possible reciprocal relationship that the descendants could have felt with the Brubecks.

## Brubeck's Native Story Grows

In the 1990s, Brubeck's public identity began to circulate around his claim of Native American ancestry to a greater extent than ever before. Among the first major references to his ancestry in this period was jazz critic Ted Gioia's quick reference in 1992, in his chapter on Brubeck in *West Coast Jazz: Modern Jazz in California, 1945–1960*. Gioia writes,

> Brubeck's father was probably of Native American descent (the family tree is ambiguous at this point, although musical colleagues Dave Van Kriedt and Paul Desmond took it as a certainty, the latter often referring to the pianist as "the Indian").[16]

---

[13] In Brubeck's interview with the *Albuquerque Journal*, he says that the talk was given by a chief, while in a much later interview with Shan Sutton at the University of the Pacific, Brubeck says the talk was given by a spiritual advisor. Dave and Iola Brubeck, "Dave and Iola Brubeck on Earth Is Our Mother," interview with Shan Sutton, Brubeck Oral History Project, Holt-Atherton Special Collections, University of the Pacific, 2007, https://scholarlycommons.pacific.edu/bohp/34/, accessed June 1, 2021.
[14] Dave and Iola Brubeck, "Dave and Iola Brubeck on Earth Is Our Mother," interview with Shan Sutton.
[15] Ibid.
[16] Ted Gioia, *West Coast Jazz: Modern Jazz in California, 1945–1960* (1992; Oxford: Oxford University Press; reprt., University of California Press, 1998), 70.

Though simply a passing mention in Gioia's work, Brubeck's identity takes center stage in jazz critic Gene Lees's *Cats of Any Color: Jazz, Black and White* (1994). While the book was published two years after the premiere of *Earth Is Our Mother*, the Brubeck chapter is dated December 1992—just eight months after the composition's premiere. The chapter shifts between biography, oral history, history, and interview, featuring substantial passages from Brubeck himself, along with comments and longer passages charting the history of Native Americans in California by Lees. In doing so, the chapter positions Brubeck somewhat as a storyteller, with Lees shifting between translator and advocate.

In his interview with Lees for *Cats of Any Color*, Brubeck offers more detail to support his claim for Indian American heritage:

> "There's maybe a fourth Modoc," Dave told me.
> "My dad was born in 1884 near Pyramid Lake, which is an Indian reservation." . . . "That lake still belongs to the Indians. He was born maybe twenty miles from the lake at a place called Amedee, where there's no one living, in Honey Lake Valley."[17]

He ends the passage with what would become an oft-cited nod to his ancestry: "My mother's attitude was, 'Don't tell him that nonsense' [referring to the Modoc ancestry]. And my father toward the end of his life told his grandson to be proud of what you are." In another section of the interview, Brubeck explains that his upbringing on his parent's cattle ranch brought him into contact with Native Americans as he was growing up: he says that "on our ranch there was a reservation for Indians"; conjectures that one of the last Miwok sweat houses in California was on their ranch; and explains that he had many friends who were Miwok Indians, including his mother's piano assistant and his father's top cowhand, Al Walloupe, who he clarifies was full Miwok.[18] Throughout the 1990s, Brubeck seems particularly interested in better understanding his ancestry; in the very beginning of another interview in 1999, the interviewer mentions, "It was interesting to talk to your uncle Leslie Brubeck," and Brubeck responds, "What did he have to say? Did you ask him if I'm part Indian?"[19]

Later in the chapter, Lees writes that in addition to Brubeck's "lifelong hatred of racism," Brubeck also "has an abiding interest in the welfare and

---

[17] Gene Lees, *Cats of Any Color: Jazz, Black and White* (Cambridge, MA: Da Capo Press, 1994), 42.
[18] Ibid., 43.
[19] The interviewer explains that they can't remember if they talked to him about that. Brubeck, interview by Carolyn C. Crawford, 1999, 1.

culture of the American Indians."[20] Lees describes two compositions by Brubeck that honor Native American culture in some way: *They All Sang Yankee Doodle*, which Brubeck explains begins with an Indian song taught to him by Walloupe, and *Earth Is Our Mother*.[21] In between discussions of these pieces, Lees also addresses what seems to him to be among the most convincing pieces of evidence: Brubeck's appearance. He writes, "No matter how misty the family history, the visual evidence is there. For years I've kidded Dave that he looks like the man on the buffalo nickel." Lees includes bits of conversation between himself and Dave and Iola Brubeck, in which Lees says of their children that "Darius looks a bit Indian" and Danny "really looks Indian." Dave Brubeck agrees, to which Iola Brubeck adds, "There is a photo of a young Modoc that looks almost identical to Dave at the same age."[22]

The second-to-last scene in Lees's chapter on Brubeck focuses on *Earth Is Our Mother*, and most of this passage is dedicated to a lengthy quotation of the Chief Si'ahl text. Lees introduces the text with a provocation that, though perhaps intended to critique a particular system of racial accounting, may actually threaten to re-assert the importance of "blood quantum"-type qualifications of Native American citizenship: "If Dave is one-quarter Modoc, and Seattle was all Suquamish, what do we, in our mad ethnic system of classification, call the piece of music Dave has made out of the speech? Five-eighths Indian?"[23] The last sentence of the chapter states unequivocally that based on family lore, resemblance, and two Native American-esque compositions, that "Dave Brubeck, part Modoc Indian, is one of the great jazz musicians."[24]

Lees offers an account of Indigenous history in what is now California that explains in part why Brubeck's ancestors, and others, might have hidden any potential Native American ancestry: this includes systems of peonage, forced assimilation, and widespread genocide and violence enacted against Native Americans across the territory, especially in the nineteenth century. As Lees explains, "California takes a back seat to no other state, probably even no other nation, for its record of relentless racism."[25] Likewise, Native

---

[20] Lees, *Cats of Any Color*, 57.
[21] *They All Sang Yankee Doodle* (orchestral premiere 1976, choral premiere 1978) weaves the tune of "Yankee Doodle" in and out of other folk melodies he was familiar with to demonstrate that they (all peoples, of different backgrounds) all indeed sang "Yankee Doodle," or celebrated America in their own ways. Brubeck dedicated the piece to Charles Ives, and it includes snippets from "America the Beautiful," "When the Saints Go Marching In," *La Marseilles*, and an unidentified "Indian song." Lees, *Cats of Any Color*, 13.
[22] Ibid., 58.
[23] Ibid., 59.
[24] Ibid., 61.
[25] Ibid., 41.

For more on the history of Californian Indian peoples, see Brendan Lindsay, *Murder State: California's Native American Genocide, 1846–1873* (Lincoln: University of Nebraska Press, 2012); Jack Norton, *Genocide in Northwestern California: When Our Worlds Cried* (San Francisco: Indian Historian Press, 1979).

American studies scholar Cutcha Risling Baldy (Hupa, Yurok, Karuk) writes, "California's post invasion history is framed by genocide with the aim of total annihilation of California Indian peoples."[26] Nevertheless, claims of Native American ancestry by white Americans are common (and were particularly common in the 1990s), and can be destructive to Native American sovereignty, identity, and relationality. Neither family stories passed down for generations nor a physical resemblance typically serve as "evidence" of belonging to a Native American tribe. As geneticist-ethicist Krystal Tsosie (Navajo/Diné) articulates, "Native American U.S. tribes have the sovereign right to establish their own enrollment rules."[27]

In 2018, presidential candidate Elizabeth Warren was goaded into taking a DNA test after decades of claiming Cherokee ancestry by then-presidential candidate Donald Trump.[28] Warren's DNA test indicated that she is between 1/32 and 1/1024 Native American. In the fallout of her DNA test, Warren both claimed Native ancestry *and* asserted Cherokee sovereignty in defining membership; while this soothed many white progressives, many Native Americans considered this seeming distinction a reflection of Warren's privilege in centering her own, non-Native definition of Indigenous identity. As Native studies scholar Kim TallBear (Sisseton-Wahpeton Oyate) writes of Warren's DNA test, "This shows that she focuses on and actually privileges DNA company definitions in this debate, which are ultimately settler-colonial definitions of who is Indigenous."[29] Many tribes do not use DNA or blood quantum (the fractional measurement of how much "Indian blood" a person possesses) to determine citizenship, but even those that do still tend toward using blood quantum in terms of direct lineage.[30] Similarly, Indigenous

---

[26] Cutcha Risling Baldy, *We Are Dancing for You: Native Feminisms and the Revitalization of Women's Coming-of-Age Ceremonies* (Seattle: University of Washington Press, 2018), 55. Baldy notes that the post-invasion population of California Indians was reduced by 90 percent.

[27] Krystal Tsosie, "Elizabeth Warren's DNA Is Not Her Identity," *The Atlantic*, October 17, 2018, https://www.theatlantic.com/ideas/archive/2018/10/what-make-elizabeth-warrens-dna-test/573205/.

[28] Elizabeth Warren once responded to questions about her ancestry with a similar mix of family stories and imagery, "I still have a picture on my mantel and it is a picture my mother had before that—a picture of my grandfather. And my Aunt Bea has walked by that picture at least a 1,000 times remarked that he—her father, my Papaw—had high cheek bones like all of the Indians do." Lucy Madison, "Warren Explains Minority Listing, Talks of Grandfather's 'High Cheekbones,'" *CBS News*, May 3, 2012, https://www.cbsnews.com/news/warren-explains-minority-listing-talks-of-grandfathers-high-cheekbones/.

[29] Kim TallBear, "Statement on Elizabeth Warren's DNA Test," press release posted to Twitter, October 15, 2018, https://twitter.com/kimtallbear/status/1051906470923493377?lang=en.

[30] Blood quantification, or the amount of "Indian blood" an individual possesses, was initially used to define who counted as "Indian" in federal law. As journalist Kat Chow explains, "Blood quantum minimums really restrict who can be a citizen of a tribe." It is a contested tool used by the federal government and in some cases by Native peoples in an expression of agency to define Indigenous identity that nevertheless plays a role in tribal survival and disappearance, with some Native Americans arguing that it helps tribes to survive and others arguing that it will eventually "dilute their existence." Elizabeth Rule, interviewed by Kat Chow, "So What Exactly Is 'Blood Quantum'?" NPR, February 9, 2018, https://www.

studies scholar Aileen Moreton-Robinson (Quandamooka) recalls former President Bill Clinton's failure to appoint a Native American representative to his Advisory Board on Race in 1997 while simultaneously claiming Cherokee ancestry (explaining that his grandmother was one-quarter Cherokee) as a moment that replayed centuries of white possession of Indigenous land and sovereignties: "Clinton can stake a possessive claim to Cherokee descent because there is no threat to his investment in his white identity, which carries a great deal of cultural capital and enables him to make the claim on biological grounds outside Cherokee sovereignty."[31]

In his own retellings, Brubeck is vague about his lineage, in part because he likely does not know: he tells Lees that "there's maybe a fourth Modoc," but does that mean one of his grandparents was Modoc (he also claims that his father was born on an Indian reservation)? Or that one-quarter was what his father told him, meaning one of *his* grandparents was Modoc? The lineage seems reasonably close—much closer than Warren's—but Brubeck is not able to trace his lineage to a specific relative, let alone a relative who had included themselves on the specific enrollment lists that "counted."[32]

Who counts as native, and who decides the measures by which someone counts is fraught, combining ancestry, culture, and blood with genocide, survival, and trauma. For many Native American communities, citizenship is defined more by language, kinship, tradition, and culture than DNA. For many, it would not have mattered if either Warren or Brubeck had been able

---

npr.org/sections/codeswitch/2018/02/09/583987261/so-what-exactly-is-blood-quantum; Krystal Tsosie and Matthew Anderson, "Two Native American Geneticists Interpret Elizabeth Warren's DNA Test," *The Conversation*, October 25, 2018, https://theconversation.com/two-native-american-geneticists-interpret-elizabeth-warrens-dna-test-105274; Matika Wilbur and Desi Small Rodriguez, "Can a DNA Test Make Me Native American?," *All My Relations* podcast, March 12, 2019, https://podcasts.apple.com/us/podcast/all-my-relations-podcast/id1454424563?i=1000431652242. For more on the history of blood quantum and its uses, see Paul Spruhan, "A Legal History of Blood Quantum in Federal Indian Law to 1935," *South Dakota Law Review* 51, no. 1 (2006). For more on DNA testing and tribal belonging, see Kim TallBear, *Native American DNA: Tribal Belonging and the False Promise of Genetic Science* (Minneapolis: University of Minnesota Press, 2013).

[31] Aileen Moreton-Robinson, *The White Possessive: Property, Power, and Indigenous Sovereignty* (Minneapolis: University of Minnesota Press, 2015), 56.

[32] The Modoc tribe, to which Brubeck claimed a tie, does not recognize DNA tests as proof of membership; members must demonstrate their relationship to a lineage. Tribes are under no obligation to reveal membership. A google search of birth records of Brubeck's paternal grandparents and great-grandparents offers little to support his claim. "Tribal Enrollment," *Modoc Nation*, https://modocnation.com/tribal-enrollment/, accessed June 11, 2021. However, enrollment based on a particular lineage can also be a challenge, as that lineage must be documented in a particular way; often, family members must have been enrolled in a certain time period. Not all Native peoples chose to be enrolled; for example, not enrolling could offer a potential escape from discrimination and violence. California's particularly violent legacy against Californian Native peoples could possibly have led Brubeck's family to disavow native heritage to either protect the family or protect their whiteness.

to find a more direct lineal tie: as Tsosie writes, "Warren has not experienced the traditional and cultural ways of Native American life," and indeed, despite her socioeconomic struggles, ultimately benefited from her whiteness in a way that most enrolled members of Native American tribes do not. This matters because Native American citizenship is a designation that confers certain rights and privileges based on centuries of abuse, neglect, murder, and theft enacted by the United States government and its citizens. Claims like Lees's and Brubeck's suggest that Native identity could be assumable, and, as author and activist Kelly Hayes (Menominee) and writer Jacqueline Keeler (Diné/Ihanktonwan Dakota) argue, these claims perpetuate the erasure of not only Indigenous identity, but specific treaties and policies aimed at redressing a fraction of the specific horrors those nations experience.[33] At the same time, Indigenous children adopted out, stolen by the American and Canadian governments from their families to be placed in abusive boarding schools whose purpose was to erase their language and culture, or whose family histories were altered with either racist or protective intent—these children were not able to experience the "traditional and cultural ways of Native American life," nor were people whose ancestors chose not to enroll.[34] Whether or not Brubeck's ancestry includes Modoc lineage is ultimately beside the point; what is more important is why Brubeck makes the claim, what that claim does for him, and what that claim does for the Modoc tribe.[35]

---

[33] Hayes Keeler and Jacqueline Keeler, "Elizabeth Warren Connected DNA and Native American Heritage. Here's Why That's Destructive," *NBC News*, October 17, 2018, https://www.nbcnews.com/think/opinion/elizabeth-warren-connected-dna-native-american-heritage-here-s-why-ncna921166. For more responses, see Kelly Adrienne Keene, Rebecca Nagle, and Joseph M. Pierce, "Syllabus: Elizabeth Warren, Cherokee Citizenship, and DNA Testing," *Critical Ethnic Studies Journal*, December 19, 2018, http://www.criticalethnicstudiesjournal.org/blog/2018/12/19/syllabus-elizabeth-warren-cherokee-citizenship-and-dna-testing; Debbie Reese, "A Curated List of Indigenous Responses to Elizabeth Warren," *American Indians in Children's Literature*, October 20, 2018, https://americanindiansinchildrensliterature.blogspot.com/2018/10/a-curated-list-of-native-responses-to.html.

[34] Tsosie, "Elizabeth Warren's DNA Is Not Her Identity." For a key perspective on the complicated and interrelated nature of genealogical trace, racialized blood, and cultural authenticity in Cherokee citizenship (particularly with regard to children who were adopted out), see Joseph M. Pierce, "Trace, Blood, and Native Authenticity," *Critical Ethnic Studies* 3, no. 2 (Fall 2017), 57–76.

[35] Still other Indigenous scholars explain that the true decolonial approach to Native identity would be to believe claims made by people like Brubeck and even Warren rather than litigate their "nativeness." In that case, the questions for Brubeck and Warren would lie less with proving their identity through ancestry or blood quantum and more with how they engaged with communities they claimed and the degree to which they took on more Indigenous approaches and mindsets. Editors, "Against a Politics of Disposability," July 7, 2015, https://againstpoliticsofdisposability.wordpress.com/2015/07/07/against-disposability/, accessed June 19, 2021;Andrew Jolivétte, "Rachel Dolezal and Andrea Smith: On the Politics of Racial Identity and 'Passing' from a Critical Mixed-Race Studies Perspective," *Against a Politics of Disposability*, July 5, 2015, https://againstpoliticsofdisposability.wordpress.com/2015/07/05/rachel-dolezal-and-andrea-smith-on-the-politics-of-racial-identity-and-passing-from-a-critical-mixed-race-studies-perspective-by-andrew-jolivette/, accessed June 19, 2021.

## White Jazz Backlash in the 1990s

Throughout *Cats of Any Color*, Lees, an established white jazz critic, positions his book as an argument for a more "multiethnic" approach to jazz, both in its history and appreciation.[36] However, it seems no small coincidence that Lees's approach arrived in a period in which Black jazz musicians were developing a stronger platform to argue that jazz was and is Black music. Brubeck's "Indian moment" (which, though different from Warren's own "Indian moment" in terms of the nature and use of his claims, nevertheless occurred in the same period) should likewise be viewed within this context.[37]

The 1980s and 1990s in jazz has often been referred to as a renaissance—a period in which jazz's so-called "young lions" were credited with generating more interest in and publicity for jazz. Wynton Marsalis quickly became the face of this movement: he was the feature of many interviews and articles throughout the 1980s, released several successful albums, won several Grammy Awards (he remains the only musician to win Grammy Awards in jazz and classical music during the same year), and began a series of jazz concerts at Lincoln Center in 1987. Though already well established, his authority in jazz was cemented in 1996, when Jazz at Lincoln Center was formed and he was named its artistic director, a position he still holds over twenty-five years later. Influenced by cultural critics and writers Stanley Crouch and Albert Murray, Marsalis created and promulgated a particularly canonical definition of jazz—one centered around connections between jazz, nationalism, and democracy; that advocated specific styles and particular periods in jazz (New Orleans, Swing, and Bebop); and that especially highlighted the contributions of Black musicians to jazz (however, Marsalis was careful to define jazz as a cultural inheritance, and not a racial inheritance).[38] As jazz scholar Dale Chapman explains, Crouch and Murray themselves were particularly influenced by writer Ralph Ellison, who understood jazz as a black

---

[36] The cover summary begins, "Gene Lees explores racism in the past and present of jazz—both the white racism that for decades ghettoized black musicians and their music, and the prejudice that Lees documents of some black musicians against their white counterparts" (Lees, back cover, *Cats of Any Color*).

[37] Unlike Warren, Brubeck's claims of Modoc lineage only became part of his story in the 1990s and were usually much more moderate: He would state that he was "possibly" Native American, and that this story came from his father (distancing himself from making that claim). Like Warren, Brubeck did name a specific tribe (Modoc) to which a claim of belonging might be made.

[38] Jazz scholar Tracy McMullen critiques the effect Marsalis's view of jazz had in this period: "Marsalis's face of jazz has coalesced around the visage of the sophisticated, upper-class black man. This image can partially be traced to the influence of Stanley Crouch, who has long championed the idea of black middle- (or increasingly, upper-) class values and castigated inner-city black expressions. But it also meets the needs of a white capitalist culture that understands the selling power of black male mystique." Tracy McMullen, "Identity for Sale: Glenn Miller, Wynton Marsalis, and Cultural Replay in Music," in *Big Ears: Listening for Gender in Jazz Studies*, ed. Nichole T. Rustin and Sherrie Tucker (Durham, NC: Duke University Press, 2008), 142.

vernacular expression "central to the promise of American exceptionalism," rather than as a countercultural movement.[39]

Many musicians and jazz writers criticized the narrow confines around which Marsalis defined jazz, but there was a particularly swift white backlash to Marsalis's approach. As historian Eric Porter recounts, white critic Whitney Balliett accused Marsalis of "reverse racism" in 1991. In 1993, white critic James Lincoln Collier's book, *Jazz: The American Theme Song*, argued in part that white musicians were not given enough credit for their role in the creation of jazz.[40] Sociologist Herman Gray documents white critic Terry Teachout's 1995 article, "The Color of Jazz," which blamed Marsalis for creating a racial hierarchy in jazz that privileged Black musicians, accusing Jazz at Lincoln Center of race-based hiring policies, commissions, and programming, and charging Marsalis with "harbor[ing] a general disdain for white musicians."[41] Furthermore, the 1990s featured a spate of books by white jazz critics desperate to hold onto their own supposedly race-neutral or multicultural approaches to jazz, including Collier's *Jazz: The American Theme Song* (1993), Gene Lees's *Cats of Any Color: Jazz, Black and White* (1994), and Richard Sudhalter's *Lost Chords: White Musicians and Their Contribution to Jazz, 1915–1945* (1999). Jazz scholar John Gennari summarizes the ideology behind such work (what Ingrid Monson refers to as a "white resentment narrative"): "Sudhalter, Collier, Lees, and Teachout allege a deeper historical revisionism. They claim that a hegemonic liberal jazz historiography, buttressed by post-1960s multicultural ideology, has inflated the reputations of black musicians and devalued the contributions of white ones."[42] Musicologist Christi Jay Wells offers a crucial critique of the post-racial approach Lees in particular takes:

> In a fairly glaring dismissal, Lees claims that truly great black musicians adopted a post racial perspective while "there has long been anti-white sentiment among

---

[39] Dale Chapman, *The Jazz Bubble: Neoclassical Jazz in Neoliberal Culture* (Berkeley: University of California Press, 2018), 9.

[40] The following year, Marsalis challenged Collier to a debate at Lincoln Center in response to a complimentary review of his book in the *New York Times Book Review*. Eric Porter, *What Is This Thing Called Jazz? African American Musicians as Artists, Critics, and Activists* (Berkeley: University of California Press, 2002).

[41] Terry Teachout, "The Color of Jazz," *Commentary*, September 1995, https://www.commentarymagazine.com/articles/terry-teachout/the-color-of-jazz/; Herman Gray, *Cultural Moves: African Americans and the Politics of Representation* (Berkeley: University of California Press, 2005), 42. As Gray summarizes, "Where Teachout sees (and aspires to) color blindness, Marsalis sees (and rejects) racial and cultural invisibility that is sustained by the continuing salience of racism in all aspects of American life and culture" (Gray, *Cultural Moves*, 43).

[42] John Gennari, *Blowin' Hot and Cool: Jazz and Its Critics* (Chicago: University of Chicago Press, 2006), 362; Ingrid Monson, *Freedom Sounds: Civil Rights Call Out to Jazz and Africa* (Oxford: Oxford University Press, 2008), 16.

certain jazz musicians. They, for the most part, have been the lesser ones." Lees's perspective exemplifies how these authors situated themselves as antiracist while they framed their work as an objective correction to scholarship ostensibly tainted by Afrocentrism, political correctness, or any political movement driven by the desire to advance the interests of African Americans or the attention paid to African American cultural innovators while marginalizing white musicians."[43]

This 1990s white backlash ignored the long historical view of Marsalis's achievements; as Gennari argues, "Wynton Marsalis's vision of the Lincoln Center jazz program reflects a backlog of critical work that had to strain hard to put a black face on jazz *at all*, much less put blacks in control of the jazz story."[44] For those white critics making claims of reverse racism, Marsalis's authoritative claim of the centrality of Black musicians to both jazz and American life, paired with his quickly growing platform, threatened the assumed import of white (and sometimes other non-Black) musicians—and critics and historians themselves. As Gray writes, "To present black cultural expressions within dominant mainstream cultural spaces . . . is to generate highly contentious political disputes about black cultural practices and images."[45]

Two interviews given by Brubeck in the 1990s demonstrate his own struggle to place himself within jazz's shifting racial landscape during this period. Both reflect a performance of whiteness dramatically changed from the mid-century performances on which we have focused for most of this book. The first is a long interview published in the jazz magazine *Cadence* in December 1994. The interview is dated May 21, 1993, around the time of the West Coast premiere of *Earth Is Our Mother* in Seattle, Washington.[46] For the majority of the interview, the interviewer, jazz pianist Martin Totusek, asks Brubeck questions about his contributions to jazz, unique approaches to harmony and rhythm, players he has influenced and who have influenced him, various performances he had given—in general, a standard, albeit detailed, account of Brubeck's life and connections to various other titans of jazz (specifically jazz piano). However, in the middle of the thirteen-page interview, Brubeck begins to talk at length (three and a half pages) about race in jazz and his career. Within this interview, Brubeck, who was no stranger to race-based critiques of his ability to belong in jazz, seemed to perceive a new threat to his career and legacy, perhaps sharing a sense of powerlessness to define jazz with

---

[43] Christopher J. Wells, "'The Ace of His Race': Paul Whiteman's Early Critical Reception in the Black Press," *Jazz & Culture* 1 (2018), 81.
[44] Gennari, *Blowin' Hot and Cool*, 363.
[45] Gray, *Cultural Moves*, 14.
[46] Martin A. Totusek, "Dave Brubeck Interview," *Cadence*, December 1994, 5–17.

other white musicians and critics who had formerly felt secure in their place in jazz communities.[47]

In the interview, Totusek notes that many of Brubeck's compositions and actions demonstrate his concern with human rights issues, claiming that it seems the media had ignored many of those actions.[48] Brubeck responds by recounting experiences in his integrated World War II army band, the Wolf Pack, explaining that he would try to put any enlisted musician he could into the band, black or white, though the army was at that point segregated and members of the band were physically threatened on multiple occasions. He recalls one incident in which fellow soldiers were outside of the building the band was in, calling out insults in provocation: "They were trying to get us outside where a bunch of them had knives and guns. They would have killed [Dick Flowers, trombonist] for sure." He recounts another incident, in which a Texas restaurant refused to serve returning Black soldiers and also explains that he'd seen "much, much worse things in the army," emphasizing that "they are so horrible that I don't talk about them." These moments were a catalyst, inspiring many of the moments explored in greater detail in chapter 4: refusing to segregate the quartet, the canceled 1960 southern tour, the 1958 East Carolina College incident, refusing to play for segregated audiences, and police escorts for performances in the South. Throughout the interview, Brubeck both reiterates his commitment to racial justice—in a similar manner to what critical whiteness studies scholar Robin DiAngelo refers to as "credentialing"—and issues calls for critics to put themselves on the line as he had repeatedly done.[49]

Totusek then asks Brubeck if the situation has gotten better since the 1960s. In his response, Brubeck first says yes, but though he acknowledges that there may be further to go, he quickly goes on the defensive, countering many of the criticisms he had received across his decades long career.[50] Brubeck first positions his ire toward critics, attacking their lack of knowledge about his

---

[47] It may seem odd to suggest that Dave Brubeck felt powerless, given his success and visibility within the music industry and among fans; however, in a blogpost memorializing his father, Chris Brubeck explained that it was not until the Ken Burns *Jazz* (2001) documentary that the family felt Dave Brubeck was properly recognized. Chris Brubeck recounts the story about the formerly enslaved man Dave Brubeck met with his father at the river, who showed Dave Brubeck his scarred back (detailed in this book's Introduction), and explains that following the interview, Dave Brubeck felt he had blown the interview because he had cried on camera. In his reflection, Chris Brubeck noted that jazz critics who had dismissed or been unkind to Dave Brubeck throughout his career reassessed his contributions as a result of that story, leading to a more appreciative reception in the 2000s. Chris Brubeck, "Tributes to Dave Brubeck After His Death," *Dave Brubeck Jazz.com* (n.d., copyright 2021), http://www.davebrubeckjazz.com/Bio-/Tributes.

[48] Totusek, "Dave Brubeck Interview," 11.

[49] Ibid., 12. According to DiAngelo, credentialing "describe[s] the ways in which white progressives attempt to prove that they are not racist." Robin DiAngelo, *Nice Racism: How Progressive White People Perpetuate Racial Harm* (Boston: Beach Press, 2021), 58.

[50] Totusek, "Dave Brubeck Interview," 13.

career and in particular, the instances in which they explicitly name race in their reviews of him.[51] He reminds readers that he has had multiple Black musicians in his quartet (naming bassists Wyatt "Bull" Ruther and Joe Benjamin and drummer Frank Butler, who all performed with the Brubeck quartet prior to the addition of Eugene Wright); that he led an interracial army band; that he refused to play the "Bell Telephone Hour" when they would not allow his integrated quartet to perform on television (according to Brubeck, Duke Ellington ultimately received that gig); and that the quartet played many Black schools and the Apollo Theater, and won the first Black poll ever taken in the *Pittsburgh Courier* in the small combo section.[52] Incredulously, possibly angrily, and with no small amount of in-group protection, Brubeck concludes this portion, "Then enough guys who wanted to say something untrue, mean, not historically correct, said things against us, and against anyone White."[53]

Brubeck continues on, offering a meta-critique of jazz history through his own experiences in jazz, replaying arguments familiar to the 1990s backlash: that jazz musicians had previously enjoyed colorblind relationships and the field now was being "turned around by ignorance and lies." Eventually, his focus shifts from critics and historians to present-day musicians: "There's good, young intelligent Black and minority players out there today, who have no idea what we've done or the risks we took."[54] Given the success of and media attention given to the so-called Young Lions of jazz, and especially Wynton Marsalis, it seems clear on whom Brubeck's irritation was focused. He finishes with a standard plea for colorblindness: "I don't like the idea of people even thinking or judging people in terms of Black or White skin colors, or Black or White bands. We are *all* human beings and can learn so much from each other, if we don't shut each other out."

The second interview revealing Brubeck's understanding of his place in the context of jazz's shifting racial politics in the 1990s is an oral history interview sponsored by the University of California, Berkeley's Regional Oral History Office. The interview, a three-day process that stretched across 1999–2001, featured both Dave and Iola Brubeck. On the second interview day, which

---

[51] For example, Brubeck highlights a March 1993 record review of a 4-CD career retrospective boxset (*Dave Brubeck: Time Signatures*), in which the critic wrote that Brubeck's music "was indeed the rage of college campuses. Make that *white* college campuses" (the review goes on to highlight the Black musicians like Duke Ellington and Louis Armstrong who endorsed Brubeck, insisting that he had been dismissed "out of hand"). Brubeck reflected that the review wasn't bad, "but he just had to stick this jive in." Lawrence B. Johnson, Review of *Dave Brubeck: Time Signatures—A Career Retrospective* (Columbia/Legacy), by Dave Brubeck, *Detroit News*, March 13, 1993, 16D.

[52] Amiri Baraka also attested to Brubeck's popularity among Black college students. LeRoi Jones [Amiri Baraka], *Blues People: Negro Music in White America* (1963; New York: William Morrow, 1999), viii.

[53] Totusek, "Dave Brubeck Interview," 14.

[54] Ibid.

took place in February 1999, interviewer, Caroline Crawford, asked Brubeck an open-ended question: "Well, what has been the most frustrating part of this profession you're in?"[55] He responded, "When people get on the race thing, that is the most frustrating part of it." The generic "race thing" suggests both a dismissiveness and a discomfort with using explicit labels to describe which "race thing" he might mean.

Brubeck offers an overview of jazz history, pointing out a number of points common to "race things" in jazz: (1) he highlights moments in which Black musicians seemed to express a colorblind ideology or support for a meritocratic approach to playing, such as when Louis Armstrong referred to Jack Teagarden as "my real brother" and his favorite person to play with, or when Duke Ellington hired white drummer Louis Bellson; (2) by insisting that Count Basie's band with white drummer Butch Miles was the "most swinging jazz band that's ever been," Brubeck reiterates the use of swing as a marker of jazz authenticity, but not one of racial authenticity; (3) by highlighting the hiring of white jazz musicians by Ellington and Basie, two widely regarded titans of jazz, and definers of the swing era, Brubeck asserts that people who believe in "the race thing" are simply wrong, or lack the necessary qualifications to hold such a perspective; and (4) Brubeck makes clear that "the race thing" to which he refers is about dismissiveness toward white jazz musicians in particular: "So Basie must not have been against white guys, if you are going to get a white drummer."

Though Brubeck's recollections are not untrue, they lay blame in curious places. For example, some jazz groups and venues in the 1940s and early 1950s could be more integrated than in the late 1950s and 1960s, as the civil rights movement blossomed and a strong backlash ensued. But rather than blame policymakers who created segregated policies following *Brown v. Board of Education*, thereby resulting in more segregated performing experiences, Brubeck appears instead to place responsibility for jazz's rising racial tensions on critics' discussions of race and racial inequality, as he did in the earlier *Cadence* interview.

Toward the end of this portion of the interview, Dave Brubeck turns to Iola Brubeck to back him up, and she does, insisting that the crux of the matter lay in contemporary perceptions of jazz history, like those promoted by writers like Murray and Crouch and musicians like Marsalis: "I think it's part of the myth of the jazz legend, that jazz is supposed to be a black people's

---

[55] Dave Brubeck, "A Long Partnership in Life and Myth," an oral history conducted in 1999 and 2001 by Caroline C. Crawford, Regional Oral History Office, Bancroft Library, University of California, Berkeley, 2006, 83.

music." She clarifies Dave Brubeck's comments about jazz critics, explaining that European writers were the first to place undue emphasis on jazz's roots in the blues and spirituals without also noting its European influences, and that "it takes only a cursory listen to realize that the two elements [African and European] are there." Iola Brubeck's addition recalls the Brubecks' two-part jazz history survey article published in *Down Beat* in 1950 (discussed in chapter 1), which likewise asserted that "African" rhythm and "European" harmony combined out of spiritual necessity to create jazz music, as well as another article from 1964 that re-visited and re-asserted the points of that article.[56] Throughout this lengthy passage, one thing is clear: for Dave Brubeck, in this moment, to speak about race in the context of jazz means to speak about whiteness.

## "Playing Indian" and *Earth Is Our Mother*

I have examined both of these interviews at length because they offer an important contextualization of Brubeck's relationship with Native American culture and interest in his own multicultural ancestry in the 1990s. Both interviews are introduced with discussions of *Earth Is Our Mother*, and yet both consistently frame Brubeck's experience with race specifically within jazz, not classical music. This could easily be because jazz remained the musical community in which Brubeck was (and is) best known. Or, it could reflect the contemporary conversations that most bothered him at the time of the interviews. But it may also indicate his experience of the difference between the white dominance of western classical musical spaces and communities, and jazz's blackness.

According to Brubeck, *Earth Is Our Mother*, *The Gates of Justice*, and other compositions that similarly fuse western classical compositional techniques with texts or sonic borrowings outside the classical or jazz traditions provide proof of his multicultural approach based in love and unity. He explained this compositional approach (and Iola Brubeck's paired approach to lyrics) in his 1994 *Cadence* interview: "We have consciously used an inclusive multicultural philosophy in most of these pieces. I have always been aware of my multi-ethnic ancestry. It includes German, Polish, Russian, English and, according to my Father, (possibly) Native American (Modoc Tribe) roots."[57]

---

[56] David Brubeck, "Jazz' Evolvement as Art Form," *Down Beat*, January 27, 1950; Les Tomkins, "Jazz? It's as Much European as African, Claims Dave Brubeck," *Crescendo*, June 1964, 18–19.

[57] Totusek, "Dave Brubeck Interview," 6.

For Brubeck, inclusion of Chief Si'ahl's words in *Earth Is Our Mother*, a composition that deeply values nature and critiques the buying and selling of land (which was ultimately not in Chief Si'ahl's power to deny), is proof of his own inclusive approach to western classical composition. It was his way of diversifying the sounds and sources of the classical tradition in which he was trained—notably by Darius Milhaud, who, in Brubeck's telling, taught Brubeck and his other American students that jazz "made a composer a more authentic American voice."[58] Brubeck thus became part of a tradition of white western classical composers extracting Native and Black sounds in order to simultaneously reinvigorate classical art forms and produce a uniquely American sound. In the United States, this tradition was notably promoted by Antonín Dvořák (1841–1904), who urged white composers to claim Native and Black traditions as their own folk heritage. However, Brubeck's case holds a key difference, in that he simultaneously claimed Native American sounds (even if non-specific, stereotypical versions of those sounds) *and*, to some extent, claimed Native ancestry.

Though Brubeck's compositional approach carried different political motivations, he, like Lees and other white critics in the 1990s, nevertheless demonstrated a possessive investment in multiculturalism that denied the social and political realities of the communities he sought to combine. Historian Philip Deloria (Standing Rock Sioux) refers to this culture-focused multiculturalism as "incorporative multiculturalism," writing:

> As the United States has enshrined a multiculturalism that emphasizes culture more than multi-, simply knowing about Indians, African Americans, Asian-Americans, and Latino/as has become a satisfactory form of social and political engagement. As a result, the ways in which white Americans have used Indianness in creative self-shaping have continued to be pried apart from questions about inequality, the uneven workings of power, and the social settings in which Indians and non-Indians might actually meet.[59]

Deloria argues that white Americans from the Boston Tea Party through the 1990s have "played Indian" in myriad and paradoxical ways, writing that "playing Indian has been central to efforts to imagine and materialize distinctive American identities."[60] For example, Brubeck's gesture toward Indianness in *Earth Is Our Mother* and the 1990s framing of his ancestry may reflect an

---

[58] William Skoog, "An Interview with Dave Brubeck Regarding His Choral Music," *Choral Journal* 49, no. 11 (May 2009), 36.
[59] Philip J. Deloria, *Playing Indian* (New Haven, CT: Yale University Press, 1998), 189–190.
[60] Ibid., 129.

interest in self-definition away from whiteness and toward a kind of timeless authenticity many white people assumed of Native Americans; these are characteristics Deloria recognizes in Cold War Indian play, which he found "addressed anxieties focused on a perceived lack of personal identity."[61] As Deloria explains, "Indianness gave the nation a bedrock, for it fully engaged the contradiction most central to a range of American identities—that between an unchanging, essential Americanness and the equally American liberty to make oneself into something new."[62] But while "playing Indian" offered Brubeck and others access to a particular cultural capital that became tied to a white American narrative, it also repressed and obscured the genocidal histories of colonization on which that narrative was built. As Moreton-Robinson writes, "It is not as easy to distance one's self from a history of Indigenous dispossession when one benefits every day from being tied to a nation that has and continues to constitute itself as a white possession."[63]

## Conclusion

It would be no great surprise to suggest that Dave Brubeck's responses to the 1990s racial shifts in jazz speak from a place of grievance, resulting from a half century's worth of race-based critiques about his authenticity from jazz critics and musicians who used him as an example of a white musician who had unfairly received more recognition and more profit than he was due. By the 1990s, Brubeck was in his seventies and could likely have expected to be treated as an elder statesman of jazz.[64] Instead, these interviews show him dealing with a perceived loss of status and power as jazz reoriented more forcefully around Black musicians, as Black musicians and writers began to be recognized more broadly in key roles in defining jazz, and as Black musicians like Wynton Marsalis achieved positions of institutional power. Throughout these interview passages, Brubeck seems to shift between fragility, rage, resentment, and back as he navigates his experience of insecurity in the 1990s jazz landscape—an insecurity that perhaps was not new, given his long career in jazz, but one that was expressed in a new manner.[65] At the same time, he

---

[61] Ibid., 129.
[62] Ibid., 182.
[63] Moreton-Robinson, *The White Possessive*, 52.
[64] He eventually was valorized as such in the 2000s: he was named an NEA jazz master in 1999, played a key role as an interviewee in Ken Burns's *Jazz* documentary (2000), accumulated honorary degrees and places in prestigious halls of fame, and was a Kennedy Center Honors recipient in 2009.
[65] Carol Anderson, *White Rage: The Unspoken Truth of Our Racial Divide* (London: Bloomsbury, 2016); Robin Diangelo, *White Fragility: Why It's So Hard for White People to Talk About Racism* (Boston,

also began to claim Native American ancestry in a new way, asserting something of a new (at least to the public), non-white identity that was ultimately used to support calls for a colorblind multiculturalism. Bowled over by legitimate structural critiques of white musicians' success in jazz, which he perceived as attacks on himself as an individual, and despite a nearly lifelong dedication to racial justice that was evident in both actions and compositions, Brubeck became part of the growing white backlash against Marsalis, Murray, and Crouch's assertions of blackness as a key cultural definer of jazz.

I've ended with Brubeck in this moment in part because these interviews show a very different performance of whiteness than the earlier performances analyzed throughout the book—one that highlights whiteness's adaptivity and evasiveness. When I first read these interviews, I was surprised at the Brubeck I encountered: this Brubeck seemed more desperate, more afraid, and more angry than either the Brubeck of the mid-twentieth century or of the early twenty-first century, when he received more recognition for his contributions to the field of jazz. Frankly, my first impulse was to refuse this Brubeck—to ignore the parts that didn't fit his mid-century performances of "nice" whiteness.[66] However, though this performance by Brubeck in the 1990s was to some degree situational, it was nevertheless sustained to varying degrees for around a decade. My own impulse to ignore or excuse this particular performance was yet another performance that evaded whiteness in order to protect Brubeck. Whiteness and white supremacy maintain their power through such performances of evasion, in which whiteness goes unnamed, unrecognized, and uncriticized.

Admittedly, it's not an optimistic place to end—that one of whiteness's most sustaining performances is evasion, made manifest today through colorblind discourse, the expansive fragility of white emotion, and anti-education sentiment; but then, any optimism in a book about performances of whiteness would be its own performance, one that would encourage white readers to perpetuate the myth that dismantling white supremacy can be anything but uncomfortable and can result in anything other than whiteness losing its place of dominance over others. That is the struggle Dave Brubeck faced in encountering, or in being made to encounter, his whiteness in *Down Beat* reviews of his music, or when Black musicians expressed their experiences of racism

---

MA: Beacon Press, 2018); Ingrid Monson, *Freedom Sounds: Civil Rights Call Out to Jazz and Africa* (Oxford: Oxford University Press, 2008), 16.

[66] Robin DiAngelo, *Nice Racism: How Progressive White People Perpetuate Racial Harm* (Boston, MA: Beacon Press, 2021); Shannon Sullivan, *Good White People: The Problem with Middle-Class White Anti-Racism* (Albany: State University of New York Press, 2014).

within the music industry to him. It's a struggle he faced even as he engaged in meaningful anti-racist actions, which he later instrumentalized to evade critique of systems of whiteness that he interpreted as critiques of his own whiteness as an individual.

But this story—this performance of whiteness—is ultimately about more than Dave Brubeck. From the critics who wrote about him, to the diverse audiences who heard his music, to myself as I researched and wrote about him, and finally to Brubeck himself, each was simultaneously engaged in their own performances of whiteness, and their performances responded to and intertwined with others' performances. All of these performances—from the highly visible to the nearly invisible—are part of a broader system of white supremacy that constantly evades direct contact in the maintenance of its power. As Black writers have indicated for more than two centuries, naming the modes of privilege associated with whiteness and analyzing its performances reveals the limits of whiteness, decenters it as a universal norm, and offers a chance at tracing its adaptations through to the present day. It offers a chance at disrupting white supremacy. If there is optimism in the close of this book, let it be in the potential for such disruption, which can only happen through relentless, focused critique of the performances of whiteness that surround us, and in which we ourselves must be engaged.

# Selected Bibliography

## Archival Collections

Brubeck Collection. Previously at Holt-Atherton Special Collections, University of the Pacific, Stockton, CA; now at Wilton Library, Wilton, CT.
Institute of Jazz Studies. Rutgers University, Newark, NJ.
Iowa Women's Archive. University of Iowa, Iowa City, IA.
Library of Congress. Washington, DC.
National Museum of American History. Smithsonian Institution, Washington, DC.
Paul Desmond Papers. Holt-Atherton Special Collections, University of the Pacific, Stockton, CA.

## Sources

Adler, Cyrus, Francis L. Cohen, Abraham De Harkavy, and Judah David Eisenstein. "Shofar." In *The Jewish Encyclopedia*. New York: Funk & Wagnalls, 1906. http://www.jewishencyclopedia.com/articles/13602-shofar.
Agawu, Kofi. "The Invention of 'African Rhythm.'" In *Representing African Music*, 55–70. New York: Routledge Press, 2003.
Ahmed, Sara. "Declarations of Whiteness: The Non-Performativity of Anti-Racism." *Borderlands E-Journal* 3, no. 2 (2004).
Ahmed, Sara. "In the Name of Love." In *The Cultural Politics of Emotion*, 122–143. Edinburgh: Edinburgh University Press, 2014.
Ahmed, Sara. *On Being Included: Racism and Diversity in Institutional Life*. Durham, NC: Duke University Press, 2012.
Ake, David. *Jazz Cultures*. Berkeley: University of California Press, 2002.
Ake, David. "Re-Masculating Jazz: Ornette Coleman, 'Lonely Woman,' and the New York Jazz Scene in the Late 1950s." *American Music* 16, no. 1 (Spring 1998): 25–44.
Alcoff, Linda Martín. *The Future of Whiteness*. Cambridge: Polity Press, 2015.
Anderson, Carol. *White Rage: The Unspoken Truth of Our Racial Divide*. New York: Bloomsbury, 2016.
Arendt, Hannah. "A Way Toward the Reconciliation of Peoples." In *Hannah Arendt: The Jewish Writings*, edited by Jerome Kohn and Ron Feldman. New York: Schocken Books, 2007.
Baldwin, James. *The Fire Next Time*. New York: Vintage Books, 1992.
Baldwin, James. "From the American Scene: The Harlem Ghetto: Winter 1948." *Commentary*, February 1948.
Baldwin, James. *Notes of a Native Son*. Boston: Beacon Press, 1984 [1955].
Baldwin, James. *The Price of the Ticket: Collected Nonfiction, 1948–1985*. New York: St. Martin's/Marek, 1985.
Baldy, Cutcha Risling. *We Are Dancing for You: Native Feminisms and the Revitalization of Women's Coming-of-Age Ceremonies*. Seattle: University of Washington Press, 2018.
Baughman, James L. *Henry R. Luce and the Rise of the American News Media*. Boston: Twayne, 1987.

Baraka, Amiri [LeRoi Jones]. *Blues People: Negro Music in White America*. New York: HarperCollins, 1963.

Baraka, Amiri [LeRoi Jones]. *Black Music*. New York: Murrow, 1960.

Biale, David. "The Melting Pot and Beyond: Jews and the Politics of American Identity." In *Insider/Outsider: American Jews and Multiculturalism*. Berkeley: University of California Press, 1998.

Birtwistle, Andy. "Marking Time and Sounding Difference: Brubeck, Temporality and Modernity." *Popular Music* 29 (2010): 351–371.

Bonilla-Silva, Eduardo. *Racism Without Racists: Color-Blind Racism and the Persistence of Racial Inequality in the United States*. 3rd ed. New York: Rowman & Littlefield, 2010.

Bourdieu, Pierre. *Outline of a Theory of Practice*. Cambridge: Cambridge University Press, 1977.

Braxton, Anthony. *Tri-Axium Writings*, vol. 1. Dartmouth, NH: Synthesis/Frog Peak, 1985.

Brodkin, Karen. *How Jews Became White Folks: And What That Says About Race in America*. New Brunswick, NJ: Rutgers University Press, 1994.

Brooks, Daphne. "'This Voice Which Is Not One': Amy Winehouse Sings the Ballad of Sonic Blue(s)face Culture." *Women and Performance: A Journal of Feminist Theory* 20, no. 1 (March 2010): 37–60.

Brubeck, Darius. "1959: The Beginning of Beyond." In *The Cambridge Companion to Jazz*, edited by Mervyn Cooke and David Horn, 177–201. Cambridge: Cambridge University Press, 2002.

Bryer, Marjorie Lee. "Representing the Nation: Pinups, Playboy, Pageants and Racial Politics, 1945–1966." PhD diss., University of Minnesota, 2003.

Burke, Patrick. *Come In and Hear the Truth: Jazz and Race on 52nd Street*. Chicago: University of Chicago Press, 2008.

Burke, Patrick. "Race in the New Jazz Studies." In *The Routledge Companion to Jazz Studies*, edited by Nicholas Gebhardt, Nichole Rustin-Paschal, and Tony Whyton, 185–195. New York: Routledge Press, 2019.

Butler, Judith. "Performative Acts and Gender Constitution: An Essay in Phenomenology and Feminist Theory." *Theatre Journal* 40, no. 4 (December 1988): 519–531.

Butler, Judith. *Undoing Gender*. New York: Routledge, 2004.

Butterfield, Matthew. "Race and Rhythm: The Social Component of the Swing Groove." *Jazz Perspectives* 4, no. 3 (2010): 301–335.

Campbell, Gavin James. "Classical Music and the Politics of Gender in America, 1900–1925." *American Music* 21, no. 4 (Winter 2003): 446–473.

Casey-Leininger, Charles F. "Making the Second Ghetto in Cincinnati: Avondale, 1925–1970." In *Race and the City: Work, Community, and Protest in Cincinnati*, edited by Henry Louis Taylor Jr., 232–257. Urbana, IL: University of Illinois Press, 1993.

Carson, Clayborne. "Blacks and Jews in the Civil Rights Movement: The Case of SNCC." In *Bridges and Boundaries: African Americans and American Jews*, edited by Jack Salzman, 36–49. New York: George Braziller, 1992.

Cawthra, Benjamin. *Blue Notes in Black and White: Photography and Jazz*. Chicago: University of Chicago Press, 2011.

Chapman, Dale. *The Jazz Bubble: Neoclassical Jazz in Neoliberal Culture*. Berkeley: University of California Press, 2018.

Cheng, William. *Loving Music Till It Hurts*. Oxford: Oxford University Press, 2019.

Clark, Philip. *Dave Brubeck: A Life in Time*. New York: Da Capo Press, 2020.

Coady, Christopher. *John Lewis and the Challenge of 'Real' Black Music*. Ann Arbor: University of Michigan Press, 2016.

Coates, Ta-Nehisi. *Between the World and Me*. New York: Spiegel & Grau, 2015.

Cohen, Judah M. "Hearing Echoes, Sensing History: The Challenge of Musical Diasporas." In *Theory and Method in Historical Ethnomusicology*, edited by Johnathan McCollum and David G. Hebert, 149–174. Lanham, MD: Lexington Books, 2014.

Crist, Stephen. *Dave Brubeck's* Time Out. Oxford: Oxford University Press, 2019.
Crist, Stephen. "Jazz as Democracy? Dave Brubeck and Cold War Politics." *Journal of Musicology* 26 (2009): 133–174.
Crist, Stephen. "The Role and Meaning of the Bach Chorale in the Music of Dave Brubeck." In *Bach Perspectives: Bach in America*, edited by Stephen Crist, 179–216. Urbana, IL: University of Illinois Press, 2003.
Cruse, Harold. "My Jewish Problem and Theirs." In *Black Anti-Semitism and Jewish Racism*, edited by Nat Hentoff, 143–188. New York: Richard W. Baron, 1969.
Davis, Miles with Quincy Troupe. *Miles: The Autobiography*. New York: Simon and Schuster, 1990.
Decker, Todd. *Who Should Sing "Ol' Man River"?* Oxford: Oxford University Press, 2015.
Deloria, Philip J. *Playing Indian*. New Haven, CT: Yale University Press, 1998.
Derrida, Jacques. *Margins of Philosophy*. Translated by Alan Bass. Chicago: University of Chicago Press, 1984.
DeVeaux, Scott. *The Birth of Bebop: A Social and Musical History*. Berkeley: University of California Press, 1997.
DeVeaux, Scott. "Constructing the Jazz Tradition: Jazz Historiography." *Black American Literature Forum* 25, no. 3 (Autumn 1991).
DeVeaux, Scott. "The Emergence of the Jazz Concert, 1935–1945." *American Music* 7, no. 1 (Spring 1989): 6–29.
DiAngelo, Robin. *Nice Racism: How Progressive White People Perpetuate Racial Harm*. Boston, MA: Beacon Press, 2021.
DiAngelo, Robin. *White Fragility: Why It's So Hard for White People to Talk About Racism*. Boston, MA: Beacon Press, 2018.
Dinnerstein, Joel. *Anti-Semitism in America*. Oxford: Oxford University Press, 1995.
Dollinger, Marc. *Black Power, Jewish Politics: Reinventing the Alliance in the 1960s*. Waltham, MA: Brandeis University Press, 2018.
Dorff, Elliott N. *The Way Into Tikkun Olam: Repairing the World*. Woodstock, VT: Jewish Lights, 2005.
Du Bois, W. E. B. *The Souls of Black Folk*. Chicago: A. C. McClurg, 1903.
Du Bois, W. E. B. "The Souls of White Folk." In *Darkwater: Voices from Within the Veil*, 17–31. New York: Harcourt, Brace, 1920.
Dyer, Richard. *White: Essays on Race and Culture*. New York: Routledge Press, 1997.
Early, Gerald. *Tuxedo Junction: Essays on American Culture*. Hopewell, NJ: Ecco Press, 1989.
Eddo-Lodge, Reni. *Why I'm No Longer Talking to White People About Race*. London: Bloomsbury, 2017.
Ehrenreich, Barbara. "Playboy Joins the Battle of the Sexes." In *The Hearts of Men: American Dreams and the Flight from Commitment*, 42–51. Garden City, NJ: Anchor Press/Doubleday, 1983.
Eidsheim, Nina Sun. "Marian Anderson and 'Sonic Blackness' in American Opera." *American Quarterly* 63, no. 3 (September 2011): 641–671.
Eidsheim, Nina Sun. *The Race of Sound: Listening, Timbre, and Vocality in African American Music*. Durham, NC: Duke University Press, 2018.
Ellison, Ralph. *Invisible Man*. New York: Vintage International, [1952] 1995.
Ellison, Ralph. *Living with Music: Ralph Ellison's Jazz Writings*. Edited by Robert G. O'Meally. New York: Modern Library, 2002.
Ellison, Ralph. *Shadow and Act*. New York: Vintage International, [1964] 1995.
Ewell, Philip A. "Music Theory and the White Racial Frame." *Music Theory Online* 26, no. 2 (September 2020). https://mtosmt.org/issues/mto.20.26.2/mto.20.26.2.ewell.html.
Fanon, Frantz. *Black Skin, White Masks*. Translated by Richard Philcox. New York: Grove Press, 1967 [1952].

Feagin, Joe R. *The White Racial Frame: Centuries of Racial Framing and Counter-Framing*. 3rd ed. New York: Routledge, 2020 [2009].

Feather, Leonard. *Jazz: An Exciting Story of Jazz Today*. Los Angeles, CA: Trend Books, 1958.

Fellezs, Kevin. "Silenced But Not Silent: Asian Americans and Jazz." In *Alien Encounters: Popular Culture in Asian America*, edited by Mimi Thi Nguyen and Thuy Linh Nguyen Tu, 69–108. Durham, NC: Duke University Press, 2007.

Fiske, John. *Media Matters: Race and Gender in U.S. Politics*. 2nd ed. Minneapolis: University of Minnesota Press, 1996.

Frankenburg, Ruth. *White Women, Race Matters*. Minneapolis: University of Minnesota Press, 1993.

Fraterrigo, Elizabeth. *Playboy and the Making of the Good Life in Modern America*. Oxford: Oxford University Press, 2009.

Frith, Simon. "Rhythm: Race, Sex, and the Body." In *Performing Rites: On the Value of Popular Music*, 123–144. Cambridge, MA: Harvard University Press, 1996.

Gabbard, Krin. "How Many Miles? Alternate Takes on the Jazz Life." In *Thriving on a Riff: Jazz and Blues Influences in African American Literature and Film*, edited by Graham Lock and David Murray, 184–202. Oxford: Oxford University Press, 2009.

Gabbard, Krin. *Jammin' at the Margins: Jazz and the American Cinema*. Chicago: University of Chicago Press, 1996.

Gates, Henry Louis, Jr. *The Signifying Monkey: A Theory of Afro-American Literary Criticism*. Oxford: Oxford University Press, 1988.

Gennari, John. *Blowin' Hot and Cool: Jazz and Its Critics*. Chicago: University of Chicago Press, 2006.

Gill, Denise. "On Theory, Citational Practices and Personal Accountability in the Study of Music and Affect." *Culture, Theory and Critique* 61, no. 2–3 (2020).

Gillespie, Dizzy. *To Be or Not . . . to Bop*. Minneapolis: University of Minnesota Press, 2009 [1979].

Gioia, Ted. *West Coast Jazz: Modern Jazz in California, 1945–1960*. Berkeley: University of California Press, 1992.

Gioia, Ted. "Jazz and the Primitivist Myth." In *The Imperfect Art*, 19–50. New York: Oxford University Press, 1988.

Glenn, Evelyn Nakano. *Unequal Freedom: How Race and Gender Shaped American Citizenship and Labor*. Cambridge, MA: Harvard University Press, 2002.

Goldberg, Joe. *Big Bunny: The Inside Story of Playboy*. New York: Ballantine Books, 1967.

Goldberg, Joe. *Jazz Masters of the Fifties*. New York: Da Capo Press, 1983.

Goldstein, Eric L. *The Price of Whiteness: Jews, Race, and American Identity*. Princeton, NJ: Princeton University Press, 2006.

Goodman, Glenda. "Bound Together: The Intimacies of Music-Book Collecting in the Early American Republic." *Journal of the Royal Musical Association* 145, no. 1 (2020): 1–35.

Graber, Naomi. "Colliding Diasporas: Kurt Weill's *Ulysses Africanus* and Black-Jewish Relations During the Great Depression." *Musical Quarterly* 99 (2017): 321–355.

Greenberg, Cheryl Lynn. *Troubling the Waters: Black-Jewish Relations in the American Century*. Princeton, NJ: Princeton University Press, 2006.

Guillory, Monique. "Black Bodies Swingin': Race, Gender, and Jazz." In *Soul: Black Power, Politics, and Pleasure*, edited by Monique Guillory and Richard C. Green, 191–215. New York: New York University Press, 1998.

Hall, Fred M. *It's About Time: The Dave Brubeck Story*. Fayetteville: University of Arkansas Press, 1996.

Hall, Stuart. "Whites of Their Eyes." In *Gender, Race and Class in Media: A Text Reader*, edited by Gail Dines and Jean M. Humez, 89–93. Thousand Oaks, CA: Sage, 1995.

Hatschek, Keith. "The Impact of American Jazz Diplomacy in Poland During the Cold War." *Jazz Perspectives* 4, no. 3 (2010): 253–300.

Hatschek, Keith. *The Real Ambassadors: Dave and Iola Brubeck and Louis Armstrong Challenge Segregation*. Jackson: University Press of Mississippi, 2022.
Hersch, Charles. *Jews and Jazz: Improvising Ethnicity*. New York: Routledge, 2017.
Hersch, Charles. "Poisoning Their Coffee: Louis Armstrong and Civil Rights." *Polity* 34, no. 3 (Spring 2002): 371–392.
Higginbotham, Evelyn Brooks. "The Politics of Respectability." In *Righteous Discontent: The Women's Movement in the Black Baptist Church, 1880–1920*, 185–229. Cambridge, MA: Harvard University Press, 1993.
Hisama, Ellie. "Considering Race and Ethnicity in the Music Theory Classroom." In *Norton Guide to Teaching Music Theory*, edited by Rachel Lumsden and Jeffrey Swinkin, 252–266. New York: Norton, 2018.
hooks, bell. "Representing Whiteness in the Black Imagination." In *Displacing Whiteness: Essays in Social and Cultural Criticism*, edited by Ruth Frankenberg, 165–179. Durham, NC: Duke University Press, 1997.
Ioanide, Paula. *The Emotional Politics of Racism: How Feelings Trump Facts in an Era of Colorblindness*. Stanford, CA: Stanford University Press, 2015.
Isenberg, Nancy. *White Trash: The 400-Year Untold History of Class in America*. New York: Penguin Random House, 2016.
Jacobson, Matthew Frye. *Whiteness of a Different Color: European Immigrants and the Alchemy of Race*. Cambridge, MA: Harvard University Press, 1999.
Johnson, Walter. *The Broken Heart of America: St. Louis and the Violent History of the United States*. New York: Basic Books, 2020.
Kajikawa, Loren. "The Possessive Investment in Classical Music: Confronting Legacies of White Supremacy in U.S. Schools and Departments of Music." In *Seeing Race Again: Countering Colorblindness Across the Disciplines*, edited by Kimberlé Crenshaw, Luke Charles Harris, Daniel Martinez HoSang, and George Lipsitz, 155–174. Berkeley: University of California Press, 2019.
Kelley, Robin D. G. *Africa Speaks, America Answers: Modern Jazz in Revolutionary Times*. Cambridge, MA: Harvard University Press, 2012.
Kelley, Robin D. G. "Foreword." In *Black Marxism: The Making of the Black Radical Tradition*. Durham, NC: University of North Carolina Press, 2000 [1983].
Kelley, Robin D. G. "The Jazz Wife: Muse and Manager." *New York Times*, July 21, 2002.
Kelley, Robin D. G. *Thelonious Monk: The Life and Times of an American Original*. New York: Free Press, 2009.
Kendi, Ibram X. *How to Be an Anti-racist*. New York: One World, 2019.
Kendi, Ibram X. *Stamped from the Beginning: The Definitive History of Racist Ideas in America*. New York: Nation Books, 2016.
Kernodle, Tammy. "Black Women Working Together: Jazz, Gender, and the Politics of Validation." *Black Music Research Journal* 34, no. 1 (Spring 2014): 27–55.
King, Martin Luther, Jr. The Martin Luther King, Jr. Research and Education Institute. https://kinginstitute.stanford.edu.
King, Martin Luther, Jr. *The Papers of Martin Luther King, Jr.*, vol. 4, *Symbol of the Movement, January 1957–December 1958*. Edited by Clayborne Carson. Berkeley: University of California Press, 2000.
King, Martin Luther, Jr. *The Trumpet of Conscience*. Boston: Beacon Press, 2011 [1968].
King, Martin Luther, Jr. *Where Do We Go from Here: Chaos or Community*. Boston: Beacon Press, 2010.
Klotz, Kelsey A. K. "Dave Brubeck's Southern Strategy." *Dædalus* 148, no. 2, special issue "Jazz Still Matters." Edited by Ingrid Monson and Gerald Early (Spring 2019): 52–66.
Klotz, Kelsey A. K. "Negotiating Jewish Identity in Dave Brubeck's *The Gates of Justice*." *Milken Archive of Jewish Music* (2020). https://www.milkenarchive.org/articles/view/negotiating-jewish-identity-in-dave-brubecks-the-gates-of-justice/.

Klotz, Kelsey A. K. "On Musical Value: John Lewis, Structural Listening, and the Politics of Respectability." *Jazz Perspectives* 11, no. 1 (Fall 2018): 25–51.

Klotz, Kelsey A. K. "Performing Authenticity 'In Your Own Sweet Way.'" *Journal of Jazz Studies* 12, no. 1 (2019): 72–91.

Klotz, Kelsey A. K. "Racial Ideologies in 1950s Cool Jazz." PhD diss., Washington University in St. Louis, 2016.

Klotz, Kelsey A. K. "'Your Sound Is Like Your Sweat': Miles Davis's Disembodied Sound Discourse." *American Studies* 58, no. 4 (2019): 5–23.

Krasner, Jonathan. "The Place of Tikkun Olam in American Jewish Life." *Jewish Political Studies Review* 26, no. 3 & 4 (November 1, 2014).

Kuhlman, Martin Herman. "The Civil Rights Movement in Texas: Desegregation of Public Accommodations, 1950–1964." PhD diss., Texas Tech University, 1994.

Landau, Emily Epstein. *Spectacular Wickedness: Sex, Race, and Memory in Storyville*. Baton Rouge: Louisiana State University Press, 2013.

Laver, Mark. *Jazz Sells: Music, Marketing, and Meaning*. New York: Routledge, 2015.

Lees, Gene. *Cats of Any Color: Jazz, Black and White*. Cambridge, MA: Da Capo Press, 2001.

Lesesne, Henry H. *A History of the University of South Carolina: 1940–2000*. Columbia: University of South Carolina Press, 2001.

Lester, Julius. "The Lives People Live." In *Blacks and Jews: Alliances and Arguments*, edited by Paul Berman, 164–177. New York: Delacorte Press, 1994.

Lester, Julius. "A Response." In *Black Anti-Semitism and Jewish Racism*, edited by Nat Hentoff, 231–232. New York: Richard W. Baron, 1969.

Lewis, George. "Improvised Music After 1950: Afrological and Eurological Perspectives." *Black Music Research Journal* 16, no. 1 (Spring 1996): 91–122.

Lipsitz, George. *How Racism Takes Place*. Philadelphia, PA: Temple University Press, 2011.

Lipsitz, George. *The Possessive Investment in Whiteness: How White People Profit from Identity Politics*. Philadelphia, PA: Temple University Press, 1998.

Loeffler, James. *Rooted Cosmopolitans: Jews and Human Rights in the Twentieth Century*. New Haven, CT: Yale University Press, 2018.

Long, Alecia P. *The Great Southern Babylon: Sex, Race, and Respectability in New Orleans, 1865–1920*. Baton Rouge: Louisiana State University Press, 2004.

Lopes, Paul. *The Rise of a Jazz Art World*. Cambridge: Cambridge University Press, 2002.

Lott, Eric. *Black Mirror: The Cultural Contradictions of American Racism*. Cambridge, MA: Harvard University Press, 2017.

Lott, Eric. *Love and Theft: Blackface Minstrelsy and the American Working Class*. New York: Oxford University Press, 1993.

Lutz, Catherine A. and Jane L. Collins. *Reading National Geographic*. Chicago: University of Chicago Press, 1993.

Maher, Erin K. "Darius Milhaud in the United States, 1940–71: Transatlantic Constructions of Musical Identity." PhD diss., University of North Carolina at Chapel Hill, 2016.

MacDonald, Dwight. "Masscult & Midcult." In *Essays Against the American Grain*, edited by John Summers, 3–71. New York: New York Review of Books, 2011.

Malcolm, Douglas. "'Myriad Subtleties': Subverting Racism Through Irony in the Music of Duke Ellington and Dizzy Gillespie." *Black Music Research Journal* 35, no. 2 (2015): 185–227.

Marin, Reva. *Outside and Inside: Race and Identity in White Jazz Autobiography*. Jackson: University of Mississippi Press, 2020.

McFarland, Mark. "Dave Brubeck and Polytonal Jazz." *Jazz Perspectives* 3 (2009): 153–176.

McIntosh, Peggy. "White Privilege: Unpacking the Invisible Knapsack." *Peace and Freedom* (July/August 1989): 10–12.

McMichael, Robert K. "'We Insist-Freedom Now!': Black Moral Authority, Jazz, and the Changeable Shape of Whiteness." *American Music* 16, no. 4 (Winter 1998): 375–416.

McMullen, Tracy. *Haunthenticity: Musical Replay and the Fear of the Real*. Middletown, CT: Wesleyan University Press, 2019.

Miller, Karl Hagstrom. *Segregating Sound: Inventing Folk and Pop Music in the Age of Jim Crow*. Durham, NC: Duke University Press, 2010.

Mills, Charles W. "White Ignorance." In *Race and Epistemologies of Ignorance*, edited by Shannon Sullivan and Nancy Tuana, 11–38. Albany: State University of New York Press, 2007.

Monson, Ingrid. "Fitting the Part." In *Big Ears: Listening for Gender in Jazz Studies*, edited by Nichole T. Rustin and Sherrie Tucker, 267–287. Durham, NC: Duke University Press, 2008.

Monson, Ingrid. *Freedom Sounds: Civil Rights Call Out to Jazz and Africa*. Oxford: Oxford University Press, 2007.

Monson, Ingrid. "On Ownership and Value: Response." *Black Music Research Journal* 30, no. 2 (Fall 2010): 375–378.

Monson, Ingrid. "The Problem with White Hipness: Race, Gender, and Cultural Conceptions in Jazz Historical Discourse." *Journal of the American Musicological Society* 48, no. 3 (Autumn 1995): 396–422.

Moreton-Robinson, Aileen. *The White Possessive: Property, Power, and Indigenous Sovereignty*. Minneapolis: University of Minnesota Press, 2015.

Morgenstern, Dan. *Living with Jazz: A Reader*. New York: Pantheon Books, 2004.

Morrison, Matthew D. "Race, Blacksound, and the (Re)Making of Musicological Discourse." *Journal of the American Musicological Society* 72, no. 3 (Fall 2019): 781–824.

Morrison, Matthew D. "The Sound(s) of Subjection: Constructing American Popular Music and Racial Identity Through Blacksound." *Women & Performance: A Journal of Feminist Theory* 27, no. 1 (2017): 13–24.

Morrison, Toni. *Playing in the Dark*. Cambridge, MA: Harvard University Press, 1992.

Mueller, Darren. *At the Vanguard of Vinyl: A Cultural History of the Long-Playing Record*. Durham, NC: Duke University Press, Forthcoming.

Murch, Donna Jean. *Living for the City: Migration, Education, and the Rise of the Black Panther Party in Oakland, California*. Chapel Hill: University of North Carolina Press, 2010.

Newton, Adam Zachary. *Facing Black and Jew: Literature as Public Space in Twentieth-Century America*. Cambridge: Cambridge University Press, 1999.

Obama, Barack. *Dreams from My Father: A Story of Race and Inheritance*. New York: Crown, 2007.

Oja, Carol J. "Segregating a Great Singer: Marian Anderson and the Daughters of the American Revolution." *Times Literary Supplement*, July 17, 2020, 10–11.

Painter, Nell Irvin. *The History of White People*. New York: W. W. Norton, 2010.

Panish, Jon. *The Color of Jazz: Race and Representation in Postwar American Culture*. Jackson: University Press of Mississippi, 1997.

Perea, Jessica Bissett and Gabriel Solis. "Asking the Indigeneity Question of American Music Studies." *Journal of the Society for American Music* 13, no. 4 (2019): 401–410.

Peretti, Burton. *The Creation of Jazz: Music, Race, and Culture in Urban America*. Urbana: University of Illinois Press, 1992.

Piekut, Benjamin. "When Orchestras Attack! John Cage Meets the New York Philharmonic." In *Experimentalism Otherwise: The New York Avant-Garde and Its Limits*, 20–64. Berkeley: University of California Press, 2011.

Pitzulo, Carrie. *Bachelors and Bunnies: The Sexual Politics of Playboy*. Chicago: University of Chicago Press, 2011.

Porter, Eric. *What Is This Thing Called Jazz? African American Musicians as Artists, Critics, and Activists*. Berkeley: University of California Press, 2002.

Ramsey, Guthrie. *The Amazing Bud Powell: Black Genius, Jazz History, and the Challenge of Bebop*. Berkeley: University of California Press, 2013.

Ramsey, Guthrie. *Race Music: Black Cultures from Bebop to Hip-Hop*. Berkeley: University of California Press, 2003.

Robinson, Cedric J. *Black Marxism: The Making of the Black Radical Tradition*. Chapel Hill: University of North Carolina Press, 2000 [1983].

Roediger, David R. *The Wages of Whiteness: Race and the Making of the American Working Class*. London: Verso, 1991.

Roediger, David R., ed. *Black on White: Black Writers on What It Means to Be White* New York: Schocken Books, 1998.

Rothstein, Richard. *The Color of Law: A Forgotten History of How Our Government Segregated America*. New York: Liveright, 2017.

Rustin-Paschal, Nichole. "*Cante Hondo*: Charles Mingus, Nat Hentoff, and Jazz Racism." *Critical Sociology* 32, no. 2–3 (2006): 309–331.

Rustin-Paschal, Nichole. *The Kind of Man I Am: Jazzmasculinity and the World of Charles Mingus Jr*. Middletown, CT: Wesleyan University Press, 2017.

Sales, Grover. *Jazz: America's Classical Music*. New York: Da Capo Press, 1992 [1984].

Sarna, Jonathan D. and Karla Goldman. "From Synagogue-Community to Citadel of Reform: The History of K. K. Bene Israel (Rockdale Temple) in Cincinnati, Ohio." In *American Congregations*. Vol. 1, edited by James P. Wind and James W. Lewis, 201–207. Chicago: University of Chicago Press, 1998.

Sarna, Jonathan D. and Karla Goldman. *The Jews of Cincinnati*. Teaneck, NJ: Holmes & Meier, 1986.

Savage, Barbara Dianne. *Broadcasting Freedom: Radio, War, and the Politics of Race, 1938–1948*. Chapel Hill: University of North Carolina Press, 1999.

Shirey, Theresa E. "Common Patterns in an Uncommon Place: The Civil Rights Movement and Persistence of Racial Inequality in Waterloo, Iowa." Honors Project, Bowdoin College, 2014.

Shotwell, Alexis. "The Problem with Loving Whiteness: A Response to S. Sullivan's *Good White People: The Problem with Middle-Class White Anti-Racism*." *Philosophy Today* 60, no. 4 (Fall 2016): 1003–1013.

Smith, Julie Dawn and Ellen Waterman. "Listening Trust: The Everyday Politics of George Lewis's 'Dream Team.'" In *People Get Ready: The Future of Jazz Is Now!*, edited by Ajay Heble and Rob Wallace, 59–87. Durham, NC: Duke University Press, 2013.

Solis, Gabriel. *Monk's Music: Thelonious Monk and Jazz History in the Making*. Berkeley: University of California Press, 2008.

Spencer, Michael. "'Jazz-mad Collegiennes': Dave Brubeck, Cultural Convergence, and the College Jazz Renaissance in California." *Jazz Perspectives* 6 (2012): 337–353.

Starr, Kevin. "Brubeck! Jazz Goes to College." *Golden Dreams: California in an Age of Abundance, 1950–1963*, 381–410. Oxford: Oxford University Press, 2009.

Stearns, Marshall. *The Story of Jazz*. Oxford: Oxford University Press, 1970.

Stoever, Jennifer Lynn. *The Sonic Color Line: Race and the Cultural Politics of Listening*. New York: New York University Press, 2016.

Storb, Ilse. *Dave Brubeck: Improvisations and Compositions—The Idea of Cultural Exchange*. New York: Peter Lang, 1994.

Suisman, David. *Selling Sounds: The Commercial Revolution in American Music*. Cambridge, MA: Harvard University Press, 2009.

Sullivan, Shannon. *Good White People: The Problem with Middle-Class White Anti-Racism*. Albany: State University of New York Press, 2014.

Sullivan, Shannon. *Revealing Whiteness: The Unconscious Habits of Racial Privilege*. Bloomington: Indiana University Press, 2006.

Sutherland, Wendy. *Staging Blackness and Performing Whiteness in Eighteenth-Century German Drama*. New York: Routledge, 2016.

Suzuki, Yoko. "Two Strikes and the Double Negative." *Black Music Research Journal* 33, no. 2 (2013): 207–226.

Sweetser, Frank L. *The Social Ecology of Metropolitan Boston: 1950*. Boston University, Division of Mental Hygiene, Massachusetts Department of Mental Health, 1961.

Taylor, Diana. *The Archive and the Repertoire*. Durham, NC: Duke University Press, 2003.

Taylor, Diana. *Performance*. Translated from Spanish by Abigail Levine, adapted into English by Diana Taylor. Durham, NC: Duke University Press, 2016.

Teal, Kimberly Hannon. *Jazz Places: How Performance Spaces Shape Jazz History*. Berkeley: University of California Press, 2021.

Tick, Judith. "Charles Ives and Gender Ideology." In *Musicology and Difference: Gender and Sexuality in Music Scholarship*, edited by Ruth A. Solie, 83–106. Berkeley: University of California Press, 1993.

Tuck, Eve and K. Wayne Yang. "Decolonization Is Not a Metaphor." *Decolonization: Indigeneity, Education & Society* 1, no. 1 (2012): 1–40.

Tucker, Mark, ed. *The Duke Ellington Reader*. Oxford: Oxford University Press, 1993.

Tucker, Sherrie. *Dance Floor Democracy*. Durham, NC: Duke University Press, 2014.

Tucker, Sherrie. *Swing Shift: "All-Girl" Bands of the 1940s*. Durham, NC: Duke University Press, 2000.

von Eschen, Penny. *Satchmo Blows Up the World: Jazz Ambassadors Play the Cold War*. Cambridge, MA: Harvard University Press, 2004.

Vorspan, Albert. "Blacks and Jews." In *Black Anti-Semitism and Jewish Racism*, edited by Nat Hentoff, 191–228. New York: Richard W. Baron, 1969.

Walser, Robert, ed. *Keeping Time: Readings in Jazz History*. Oxford: Oxford University Press, 2014.

Ward, Brian. *Just My Soul Responding: Rhythm and Blues, Black Consciousness, and Race Relations*. Berkeley: University of California Press, 1998.

Waters, Charles. "Anatomy of a Cover: The Story of Duke Ellington's Appearance on the Cover of *Time* Magazine." *Annual Review of Jazz Studies* 6 (1993): 1–46.

Wein, George, with Nate Chinen. *Myself Among Others*. Cambridge, MA: Da Capo Press, 2003.

Wells, Christi Jay. *Between Beats: The Jazz Tradition and Black Vernacular Dance*. Oxford: Oxford University Press, 2021.

Wells, Christopher J. "'The Ace of His Race': Paul Whiteman's Early Critical Reception in the Black Press." *Jazz & Culture* 1 (2018): 77–103.

Wells, Christopher J. "'*You* Can't Dance to It': Jazz Music and Its Choreographies of Listening." *Dædalus, Journal of the American Academy of Arts & Sciences* 148, no. 2 (Spring 2019): 36–51.

Wright, Richard. *Black Boy*. New York: Harper & Brothers, 1945.

Yancy, George. "Guidelines for Whites Teaching About Whiteness." In *Teaching Race: How to Help Students Unmask and Challenge Racism*, edited by Stephen D. Brookfield, 19–41. Hoboken, NJ: John Wiley, 2019.

Yancy, George. *Look, A White! Philosophical Essays on Whiteness*. Philadelphia, PA: Temple University Press, 2012.

Zierler, Wendy. "'My Holocaust Is Not Your Holocaust': 'Facing' Black and Jewish Experience in The Pawnbroker, Higher Ground, and The Nature of Blood." *Holocaust and Genocide Studies*, 18, no. 1 (Spring 2004): 46–67.

## Long-form Interviews and Oral History Interviews with Dave and Iola Brubeck

Brubeck, Dave. "Dave and Iola Brubeck: *The Gates of Justice*." Interview with Eugenia Zukerman. *Milken Archive of Jewish Music*, September 23, 2003. Audio: https://www.milkenarchive.org/oral-history/category/audio/dave-and-iola-brubeck.

Brubeck, Dave. "The Jazz of Dave Brubeck." Interview by Walter Cronkite. *The Twentieth Century*, CBS, August 15, 1961. Television.

## Selected Bibliography

Brubeck, Dave. "A Long Partnership in Life and Music." An Oral History conducted in 1999 and 2001 by Caroline C. Crawford. Regional Oral History Office, Bancroft Library, University of California, Berkeley, 2006.

Brubeck, Dave. Monterey Jazz Festival 2002. Interview with Herb Wong. *Jazz on My Mind: Liner Notes, Anecdotes and Conversations from the 1940s to the 2000s*, 165–173. Jefferson, NC: McFarland, 2016.

Brubeck, Dave. "Summer Music Interview." Interview by Howard Reich. *Moment Magazine* (July–August 2010). https://www.momentmag.com/summer-music-interview/.

Brubeck, Dave. "Talking with Dave Brubeck." Interview with Hedrick Smith. *Rediscovering Dave Brubeck*, PBS, December 16, 2001. Print: http://www.pbs.org/brubeck/documentary/facts.htm.

Brubeck, Dave and Iola Brubeck. "Brubeck Oral History Project." Interviews with Shan Sutton. Brubeck Oral History Project, University of the Pacific Library, 2007. Video: https://scholarlycommons.pacific.edu/bohp/. Accessed May 26, 2021.

Brubeck, Dave and Iola Brubeck. Jazz Oral History Program Collection, Archives Center, National Museum of American History, Smithsonian Institution, August 6–7, 2007. Audio.

Brubeck, Iola. "Jazz Conversation: Lyricist Iola Brubeck." Interview with Denise Gallo. Library of Congress, April 10, 2008. Video: https://www.loc.gov/item/webcast-4797/.

Totusek, Martin A. "Dave Brubeck Interview." *Cadence* (December 1994), 5–17.

# Index

*For the benefit of digital users, indexed terms that span two pages (e.g., 52-53) may, on occasion, appear on only one of those pages.*

Tables and figures are indicated by *t* and *f* following the page number

ABC (Associated Booking Corporation), 180-81, 184-85, 190
Adderley, Cannonball, 190-92
advertising campaigns, 78-82, 148-49
Ahmed, Sara, 8-9, 26
Ake, David, 50-51, 94, 95-96
Alcoff, Linda Martín, 6-8, 30n.90
Amberley Village Rockdale Temple, Cincinnati (Ohio), 209-12, 210f
American democracy, 197-98
Anderson, Carol, 170
Anderson, Marian, 26-27n.87
anti-racism, 5, 16-17, 24-26
anti-Semitism, 213, 218-22, 237-39
Armstrong, Louis
  on Little Rock integration crisis, 162-64
  public persona of, 126-30
  *The Real Ambassadors*, 1, 24, 164, 250-51
  *Time* cover article on, 130-31, 130f
"Arts in Struggle: An Afternoon of Creativity, Community and Dialogue on the Struggle for Racial Justice" event, St. Louis's Center for the Humanities, 22-23
Artzybasheff, Boris, 130-31, 130f, 142, 142f
Associated Booking Corporation (ABC), 180-81, 184-85, 190
Athens (Georgia), cancelation of 1959 concert in, 168-71
Atlantic Records, 37
attentive listening, 86-87
"At the Darktown Strutters' Ball" (Dave Brubeck Quartet), 177
audiences. *See also* mainstream audiences
  Black, 76-77, 123-24
  feeling, 145-46
  participation, 145
  at Storyville, 88-92
  trust of, 144-45, 153

authenticity
  Black masculinity, 93
  of Brubeck, 67-68
  swing, 55-58, 62
Avakian, George, 83
Avondale Village Rockdale Temple, Cincinnati (Ohio), 207-11, 210f

Bach, Johann Sebastian, 225-29
  DBQ counterpoint, 46-47
  MJQ counterpoint, 45-49, 48f
  white intellectual privilege, 48-51
Baldwin, James, 6, 15-16, 93-94, 125, 235-36, 238n.77, 240
Baldy, Cutcha Risling, 266-67
Balliett, Whitney, 271
Baraka, Amiri, 74-75, 139-40
baritone, role in *Gates of Justice*, 215, 235-37
Bates, Bob, 171
bebop, 87, 87n.38, 91-92, 147-48
Bernstein, Leonard, 246n.98
Bethlehem Steel advertisement, 80-82, 80f
*Between the World and Me* (Coates), 149
Biale, David, 239-40
Biennial Convention of Union of American Hebrew Congregations, 203, 206-7
*Billboard* charts, 37-38
Black audiences, 76-77, 123-24
blackface minstrelsy, 11, 93, 125-27
Black jazz musicians. *See also* musicians by name
  civil rights involvement, 159
  masculinity of, 93-94, 95-96
  primitivist discourses, 93-94, 132, 136-37, 139
  public personas of, 126-30, 132-36
  recognition of racial capitalism, 190-91
  relationship with audience, 148-49
  visibility of, 121-26, 124n.15, 128-30, 136

Black-Jewish relations, 29
  divide in, 199, 200–1, 237–41
  ideal partnership in, 242–46
  particularism and universalism in multicultural soundscape, 247–53
  shared history and Jewish moral imperative, 218–22, 239–40
Blacksound, 122
Black/white racial binary, 12–13
Blindfold Test (*Down Beat* magazine), 34–36, 58–59, 67
blood quantification, 267–68, 267–68n.30
"Blue Rondo à la Turk" (Dave Brubeck Quartet), 153
Bonilla-Silva, Eduardo, 65–66
Brodkin, Karen, 203–4, 212–13, 247, 256
"Brother, Can You Spare a Dime?" (Dave Brubeck Quartet), 59–60
*Brown v. Board of Education* (1954), 158–59, 178–79
Brubeck, Chris, 21, 21n.74
Brubeck, Darius, 67–68
Brubeck, David. *See also* Dave Brubeck Quartet
  on ability to swing, 59–60, 71–72, 71n.123
  anti-racism, 24–26
  anti-racist decisions on behalf of band, 195–96, 196n.106
  approach to integration, 179–80
  on attracting new audiences, 82
  on being cool, 69–71
  on chorales, 225–29
  civil rights involvement, 193–94, 199–202
  colorblind ideology of, 2–3, 63–64, 65–67, 150, 154–55, 251
  on commercial success, 149
  on East Carolina College concert, 167–68
  entry into jazz, 31
  interview in *Jazz* documentary, 20–21
  as jazz educator, 82
  on jazz history, 64–65
  masculinity of, 95–96
  on music as universal language, 152
  on racial prejudice, 153–54, 165–66
  on racism in business practices, 190–91
  on relationship with audience, 144–46, 153
  religion of, 204–5, 205n.20
  respectability of, 74, 75, 76–84, 108
  on role of race in jazz and career, 2–3, 272–76
  on Storyville performances, 89–90
  switch to classical composition, 201
  *Time* cover article on, 28, 33, 95–96, 115–16, 119, 140–44, 142*f*, 146
  on Wright's political stance, 193–95
Brubeck, Elizabeth, 97
Brubeck, Iola
  on baritone in *Gates of Justice*, 235–36
  on college tours, 73–74n.2, 97n.70
  on Daves' mother's conception of jazz musicians, 97
  on Dave's relationship with audience, 146
  on gift from Si'ahl's descendants, 263–64
  letter-writing campaign for trio and octet, 31–32
  on prejudice in northern states, 195n.105
  pride in success in *Playboy* polls, 109–10
  Regional Oral History Office interview with, 274–76
  role in Dave's appeal to mainstream audiences, 115–17
  on selection of texts for *Gates of Justice*, 237
  "She Also Cooks ..." (Wahl), 117–18
  southern tour preparations, 181
  thank-you note to Smith from, 67
*Brubeck Time* (Dave Brubeck Quartet), 37–38
Bruff, Barbara, 197
Bryer, Marjorie Lee, 114–15
Bundy, Bob, 180–81, 185–86, 187–88, 190
Burke, Patrick, 123
*Business Week* magazine, 80–82, 80*f*
Butler, Judith, 14, 120, 124, 142–43
Butterfield, Matthew, 55–56

*Cadence* magazine, 272–74, 276–77
Calloway, Earl, 253–54
cancelations of concerts
  in Athens, Georgia in 1959, 168–71
  in Dallas, Texas in 1957, 159–65
  near-cancelation at East Carolina College in 1958, 166–68
  South African tour in 1958, 165–66
  in southern tour, 157–59, 180–87
capitalism, racial, 187–93
Carter, Dick, 40–42
Cartesian dualisms, 49–50, 51–52
Casey-Leininger, Charles, 211
Catholicism, 205n.23
*Cats of Any Color: Jazz, Black and White* (Lees), 265–67

Cawthra, Benjamin, 123–24
Chaliapin, Boris, 138, 138f
Chapman, Dale, 20
Chief Si'ahl, 259–60, 261–62, 263–64
choir, role in *Gates of Justice*, 222–32
choreographies of listening, 84–87
Chow, Kat, 267–68n.30
Christianity, 82–83, 82n.18, 204–5, 205n.20
civil rights movement. *See also* cancelations of concerts; southern tour
   Black-Jewish relations during, 199, 200–1, 237–41
   Brubeck's engagement with, 1, 28, 157–59, 193–94
   Jewish moral imperative, 199, 218–22
   school integration, 178–79, 185–86
   successes during 1960s, 214
   Thelonious Monk and, 137–38
   UAHC and, 206–7
   Wright's position on political activism, 193–97, 196n.107
Clark, Kenneth, 245–46
Clark, Philip, 49n.44
Clinton, Bill, 267–68
clowning, 126–30
Coady, Christopher, 54n.57, 62, 91
Coates, Ta-Nehisi, 149, 189–90
Cohen, Francis L., 216–17
Cohen, Judah, 254–55
Cohen, Philip, 207
Coleman, Ornette, 94
college tours, 38–39, 73–74, 75, 109–10
Collier, James Lincoln, 271
colorblindness
   of Brubeck, 2–3, 63–64, 65–67, 150, 154–55, 251
   in jazz, 63–69
   paradox of, 21–22
   revealing whiteness, 5–9
Columbia Records, 37, 83
commercial music industry
   economic opportunities for DBQ versus MJQ in, 36–40
   racial capitalism, 187–93
   success of Brubeck, 148–49
*Concorde* (Modern Jazz Quartet), 38
consumerism, 106–7, 108–9
cool jazz, white racialization of, 51–55
counterpoint
   DBQ's approach to, 40–45, 41f, 42f
   MJQ's approach to, 45f, 45–47, 48f

   overview, 40
   white intellectual privilege, 48–51
   white racialization of cool jazz, 51–55
Crawford, Caroline, 274–76
credentialing, 66–68, 67n.106
Crist, Stephen, 67–68, 151n.94, 163–64, 169n.31, 174–75, 185n.69, 225–29
critical whiteness studies, 5–9, 26
Cronkite, Walter, 152
Cruse, Harold, 239–40
Cunningham, Bill, 51

Dallas (Texas), cancelation of 1957 concert in, 159–65
Damon, Maria, 213
Daughters of the American Revolution (DAR), 26–27n.87
Dave Brubeck Quartet (DBQ). See also *songs and albums*; southern tour
   approach to counterpoint, 40–45, 41f, 42f
   Athens (Georgia) concert, cancelation of, 168–71
   audience noise in live recordings from Storyville, 89
   "Blindfold Test" with Rogers, 34–36
   concert at East Carolina College in 1958, 166–68
   Dallas (Texas) concert, cancelation of, 159–65
   economic and marketing disparities between MJQ and, 36–40
   formation of, 31–33
   jazz legacy, 62–63
   on *Playboy's Penthouse*, 111–13
   relationship to Bach, 46–47, 49n.44
   South African tour in 1958, cancelation of, 165–66
   State Department tour, 151–54, 151n.94
   swing of, 56–59
   swing spectrum of, 59–61
"Dave Teaches Teachers" program, Alameda County, California, 98–101, 99f, 100f, 101f
*Davidsonian, The* (magazine), 51
Davis, Angela, 189–90
Davis, Miles, 54–55, 57–58, 64n.94, 78–79n.15, 128
Davis, Sammy, Jr., 112
DBQ. *See* Dave Brubeck Quartet
Decker, Todd, 175–76
Deloria, Philip, 277–78

DeMichael, Don, 56–57, 61–62, 178
Derrida, Jacques, 14–15
Desmond, Paul. *See also* Dave Brubeck
    Quartet
  ability to swing, 59–60, 60n.81
  formation of Brubeck Quartet, 31–33
  on Harris, 140
  "The Way You Look Tonight," 40–44, 41*f*,
    42*f*
*Detroit Times*, 73–74
DeVeaux, Scott, 9–10, 74n.5, 87
DiAngelo, Robin, 17–19, 20, 67n.106
Dinnerstein, Leonard, 237–39, 244–45
Dixon, Bill, 65–66
Dollinger, Marc, 213–14, 239–40, 247
double-voicedness, 134
*Down Beat* magazine, 31
  Black jazz musicians on cover of, 124n.15
  "Blindfold Test," 34–36, 58–59, 67
  "Coronation Ceremonies Nearing for
    Brubeck," 68–69
  debate on legitimacy of Brubeck's music,
    33–36
  economic opportunities debate in, 36–40
  *Gone With the Wind* review, 178
  readers polls, 38–39
  spontaneity versus composition debate in,
    40–55
  swing debate in, 55–63
  "Zombies Put Kiss of Death on 52nd St.
    Jazz," 87n.38
Drummer, Dotti, 103–4
Durgin, Cyrus, 86–87
Dvořák, Antonín, 276–77
Dyer, Richard, 6, 19

*Earth Is Our Mother* (Brubeck), 261–64, 266,
    276–77
East Carolina College concert (Greenville,
    North Carolina), 166–68, 195
economic opportunities in music industry,
    36–40
Eddo-Lodge, Reni, 6, 17–18, 19n.70, 23–24
Ehrenreich, Barbara, 106–7, 110
Eidsheim, Nina, 215–16
Ellington, Duke, 132–35, 133*f*, 136, 143–44,
    255
Ellison, Ralph, 119–21, 124–26, 128–29,
    132–34
Elworth, Steven, 73–74
endorsements, 78–82, 148–49

*Esquire* magazine, 51–52
European classical musical traits
  cool jazz, 51–55
  DBQ counterpoint, 46–47, 49n.44
  MJQ counterpoint, 45–49, 48*f*
  white intellectual privilege, 48–51
Evans, Bill, 50–51
evasion, 279–80
Ewell, Philip, 14n.52, 50n.48
"Except the Lord Build the House" (*Gates of
    Justice*), 208–9
exnomination, 6–7

facing, 254–55
Fanon, Frantz, 235–36
Farrell, Barry, 135–36, 137–38
Feagin, Joe R., 14, 49–50
Feather, Leonard, 55
  "Blindfold Test" with Rogers, 34–36
  on Brubeck Quartet's appeal to audiences,
    141
  on economic and marketing disparities
    between MJQ and DBQ, 36–37, 39–40
  on *Time* article featuring Monk, 139
feeling with the audience, 145–46
feeling white, 18–24
female jazz audience, 92–96, 98–105, 99*f*,
    100*f*, 101*f*
Fineberg, S. Andhil, 240–41
Fiske, John, 6–8
Frankenberg, Ruth, 6, 63–64
Fraterrigo, Elizabeth, 106
Freeman, Don, 59–60
Frith, Simon, 49–50, 84, 85
Frumkin, Kerry, 167–68
Fuerbringer, Otto, 143–44
fugue form, 45–47, 49n.42, 49n.44
Fuller, Gil, 241
Furgerson, Betty Jean, 160–63, 160n.7,
    161n.8, 197

Gabbard, Krin, 4n.7
Gallaghan, Nettie W., 98–100, 101*f*
Garroway, Dave, 74
Gates, Henry Louis, 134
*Gates of Justice* (Brubeck), 24, 29
  Black baritone, role in *Gates of Justice*, 215,
    235–37
  Black-Jewish relations, 215, 237–41
  choice of Brubeck as composer of, 255
  commission for, 201–5

ideal partnership in, 242–46
imperative of "unheard millions," 222–32
Jewish identity as distinct from whiteness, 212–14
lack of Black voice in, 253–55, 256–57
overview, 199–201
particularism and universalism in multicultural soundscape, 247–53
Rockdale Temple dedication, 207–12
role at UAHC, 206–7
role of Black baritone in, 235–37
shared history and Jewish moral imperative, 218–22
soundscape, 215–18
gaze of musicians, on *Time* covers, 142–44
Gennari, John, 10–11, 83, 117, 188–89, 271, 272
Gerry Mulligan Quartet, 88
Gillespie, Dizzy
  on bebop, 87, 147–48
  on cool musicians' masculinity, 95
  on Louis Armstrong's image, 127–28
  "Manteca," 241
  on *Playboy's Penthouse*, 111n.93
  on racism in business practices, 190–91
  on Tomming, 134
Gioia, Ted, 33, 49n.44, 70–71, 93, 264
Glaser, Joe, 163–64
Gleason, Ralph
  article about South African tour cancelation, 165–66
  *Down Beat* debates about DBQ and MJQ, 35–36, 39, 55
  *Gone With the Wind* review, 178
  interview with Brubeck after State Department tour, 153–54
  on jazz legacy, 62
  on Louis Armstrong, 129–30
  on masculinity of Brubeck, 95
  on racism in business practices, 191–92
  on *Time* article featuring Monk, 139
Glenn, Evelyn Nakano, 17–18, 192–93
Goldstein, Eric, 213–14, 247, 256
*Gone With the Wind* (Dave Brubeck Quartet), 172–80, 174*f*
*Good Housekeeping* magazine, 77, 96–97
Goodman, Benny, 78n.12, 123–24, 158–59
goodness, construct of, 23–24
"Grandma and le jazz hot: California Housewives Learn to Beat It Out in Modern Manner" (*New York Daily News*), 98–101, 99*f*, 100*f*, 101*f*

Granz, Norman, 157n.3, 158–59
Gray, Herman, 271, 272
Greenberg, Cheryl Lynn, 211, 212–14, 219–20, 244–45

habit, whiteness as, 13–14
Hall, Stuart, 189–90
"Happy Times" (Dave Brubeck Quartet), 176–77
Harman, Carter, 132–34, 136
Harris, T. George, 44, 95–96, 115–16, 140–41
Hefner, Hugh, 106–7, 110–13, 111n.93
Hentoff, Nat
  *Down Beat* debates about DBQ and MJQ, 35–36, 39, 48–49, 55, 56–57, 58–59, 61–62
  on jazz legacy, 62
  Jewish identity of, 214
  on media focus on white jazz musicians, 147
  on racism in business practices, 190–91
"Here Lies Love" (Dave Brubeck Quartet), 35
Hersch, Charles, 131
Higginbotham, Evelyn Brooks, 90–91
Hirsch, Arnold, 73–74
"His Truth is a Shield" (*Gates of Justice*), 241, 242*f*
Holland, Dave, 82–83
Hollywood, Black stereotypes in, 125–26
Holmgren, Ilene, 98–100, 100*f*
Hood, James, 185–86
hooks, bell, 142–43
housewives, as jazz audience, 98–105, 99*f*, 100*f*, 101*f*
Hughes, Langston, 192
hungry listening, 260–61
Hurd, Peter, 132–34, 133*f*

ideal partnership, in *Gates of Justice*, 242–46
inaudibility of whiteness, 11
Indigeneity
  blood quantification, 267–68, 267–68n.30
  Brubeck's identification with, 264–69, 268n.32, 270n.37
  *Earth Is Our Mother*, 261–64
  overview, 29, 259–61
  playing Indian, 276–78
  white jazz backlash, 270–76
integration, racial, 178–80, 185–86
intent, in performance of whiteness, 16–17
intersectionality, 4, 4n.8, 13

## Index

invisibility of Blacks
   Louis Armstrong, 128–30
   overview, 119–21
   Thelonious Monk, 136
   in *Time* magazine and mainstream audiences, 121–26
invisibility of whiteness, 6–9, 11, 124–25
*Invisible Man* (Ellison), 119–21
Ioanide, Paula, 18–19

Jacobson, Matthew Frye, 4, 212–13
James, Gavin, 103
James, Willis, 67–68
jazz. *See also* counterpoint; swing
   authenticity, 55–58, 62, 67–68, 93
   colorblindness in, 63–69
   legacy, 62–63
   masculinity of musicians, 93–94, 95–96, 112
   racial capitalism in industry, 187–93
   racial coding of, 33–34, 54, 68–69
   serious listening, 86–87, 89–90
   sounding white, 9–13
   white racialization of cool, 51–55
*Jazz* (documentary), 20–21
*Jazz at Oberlin* (Dave Brubeck Quartet), 40–44
jazz converts. *See* mainstream audiences
jazz critics, debate of Brubeck's legitimacy by, 27
   colorblindness, 63–69
   *Down Beat* debate, 34–36
   economic opportunities in music industry, 36–40
   overview, 31–34
   spontaneity versus composition, 40–55
   swing, 55–63
*Jazz Goes to College* (Dave Brubeck Quartet), 37–38
jazzmasculinity, 112
*Jazz: Red, Hot and Cool* (Dave Brubeck Quartet), 37–38, 78–80, 79f
Jewish cantorial style, 217–18, 217–18n.57, 218f
Jewish identity, in *Gates of Justice*, 29
   Black-Jewish relations, 215, 237–41
   as distinct from whiteness, 212–14
   ideal partnership in, 242–46
   imperative of "unheard millions," 222–32
   particularism and universalism in multicultural soundscape, 247–53
   role of Black baritone, 235–37
   shared history and Jewish moral imperative, 218–22
   soundscape, 215–18
Jewish jazz musicians, 213
Jewish moral imperative, 218–22
Jim Crow, in music industry, 190–92
Johnson, Walter, 189–90

Kajikawa, Loren, 17–18n.63
Kaminsky, Max, 217–18n.57
Kelley, Robin D. G., 116–17, 135–36, 135n.55, 137–38, 189–90
Kendi, Ibram X., 24–26, 63–64, 178–79, 194n.100
Kenton, Stan, 198n.111
King, Martin Luther, Jr., 169–70, 207–8, 238–39, 242–44
Konitz, Lee, 52–53
Krupat, Arnold, 261–62n.5, 262
Kugle, Ginger, 197

Landau, Emily Epstein, 85–86
Laporta, John, 52–53
Laver, Mark, 108–9
Lees, Gene, 57, 66n.105, 265–67
Lelyveld, Arthur, 219, 219n.60, 240–41
Lerner, Michael, 214
Lester, Julius, 239–40, 246n.98
Lewis, George, 53–54
Lewis, John, 34–35. *See also* Modern Jazz Quartet
   approach to counterpoint, 45–46, 47
   economic and marketing disparities between Brubeck and, 37
   respectability of, 91
   on swing, 62
   use of European classical techniques, 54, 54n.57
Lewis, Mort, 102n.75, 166, 169
*Life* magazine, 123–24
*Light in the Wilderness, The* (Brubeck), 201, 204
"Limelight" (Gerry Mulligan Quartet), 88
Lion, Lorraine, 135–36
Lipsitz, George, 3, 6, 13, 17n.62, 30, 85, 187–88
lipstick advertisement, 78–80, 79f
listening trust, 144–45
Little Rock integration crisis, 159, 162–65
live recordings from Storyville, audience noise in, 88–89

living rooms, as spaces for jazz, 96–105
Loeffler, James, 219–20, 247–48, 247n.102
"Look for the Silver Lining" (Dave Brubeck Quartet), 46, 69–70
Lopes, Paul, 75
"Lord Is Good, The" (*Gates of Justice*), 248–50, 249t, 251–53, 251f
Lovette, Harold, 126–27, 128
Low, Denise, 261–62n.5, 262
Luce, Henry, 121–22

MacDonald, Dwight, 122
Madhattan Room, Pennsylvania, 123–24
Maher, Jack, 56
mainstream audiences, 27–28
    Brubeck's role in attracting, 73–77
    criticism of Brubeck's success with, 148–49
    housewives, 98–105, 99f, 100f, 101f
    image of respectability, 77–84
    *Playboy*, 105–15
    recognition by, 144–46
    role of Iola in Dave's appeal to, 115–17
    Storyville club, 84–92
Malcolm, Douglas, 134–35
Malone, Vivian, 185–86
"Man on Cloud No. 7, The" (Harris), 28, 33, 95–96, 115–16, 119, 140–44, 142f
"Manteca" (Gillespie, Pozo & Fuller), 241, 242f
Marek, George, 96–98
Marin, Reva, 15n.58, 65–66, 78n.12, 158–59
Marsalis, Wynton, 193, 270–72, 270n.38
masculinity
    of Black jazz musicians, 93–94, 95
    of cool musicians, 95–96
    jazzmasculinity, 112
    in *Playboy*, 106–10, 114
    in *Playboy's Penthouse*, 110–13
    respectability of Brubeck, 92–94
Maxwell, Roger, 161
McIntosh, Peggy, 6–7
McMichael, Robert K., 111n.93
McMullen, Tracy, 270n.38
Means, Russell, 263
Messick, John, 167–68
Mezzrow, Mezz, 217–18n.57
middle-class status, 77–78, 77n.11
*Miles Ahead* (Davis), 78–79n.15
Milhaud, Darius, 31–32, 65–66, 204n.17
Miller, Karl Hagstrom, 172–73
Mills, Charles W., 6–7

Mingus, Charles, 57–59, 192
Mintz, Charles D., 199, 202–4, 203n.13, 242
Modern Jazz Quartet (MJQ)
    approach to counterpoint, 45–47, 45f, 48f
    "Blindfold Test" with Rogers, 34–36
    economic and marketing disparities between DBQ and, 36–40
    jazz legacy, 62–63
    relationship to Bach, 45–49, 48f, 49n.42
    respectability of, 91
    swing of, 61–62
*Modern Jazz Quartet* (Modern Jazz Quartet), 38
Modoc ancestry, 265, 266, 268, 268n.32, 270n.37
Monk, Thelonious, 135–40, 138f
monolithic whiteness, 4, 7–8, 13
Monson, Ingrid
    on advanced consciousness, 3
    on bebop artists, 147–48
    on Black jazz musicians on cover of *Down Beat*, 124n.15
    on Black masculinity, 91, 93–94
    on colorblindness in jazz, 63–64, 64n.94
    on inaudibility of whiteness, 11
    on Monk, 137–38
    on racial coding of jazz, 33–34, 54, 68–69
    on segregation in music industry, 164n.18, 190n.86
    on sexuality of jazz culture, 94
    on structural white privilege, 16–17
    on swing, 55–56
    on *Time* article featuring Brubeck, 141–42
Morello, Joe, 32–33, 152. *See also* Dave Brubeck Quartet
Moreton-Robinson, Aileen (Quandamooka), 12–13, 277–78
Morgenstern, Dan, 128
Morrison, Matthew, 122
Morrison, Toni, 8–9
Mueller, Darren, 83
Mulligan, Gerry, 88
multiculturalism, 276–78
musical intellect, 50–51
music as universal language, 152
music industry
    commercial success of Brubeck, 148–49
    economic opportunities for DBQ versus MJQ in, 36–40
    racial capitalism, 187–93
mutual recognition, 142–43, 150

National Student Association (NSA), 180n.59
Native American ancestry, 29
  blood quantification, 267–68, 267–68n.30
  Brubeck's identification with, 264–69, 268n.32, 270n.37
    *Earth Is Our Mother*, 261–64
    overview, 259–61
    playing Indian, 276–78
    white jazz backlash, 270–76
"New Jazz Audience, The" (*Playboy*), 107–8
New Jazz Studies, 9–10
*New York Daily News*, 98–101, 99f, 100f, 101f
niceness, 20
Nordell, Red, 40–42
NSA (National Student Association), 180n.59
Ntoni, Victor, 196n.106

*Oakland Tribune*, 116–17
O'Connor, Norman J., 205n.23
Oja, Carol J., 26–27n.87
"Ol' Man River" (Dave Brubeck Quartet), 175–76
"Open the Gates" (*Gates of Justice*), 223–25, 223f, 224f, 225f, 226f, 227f, 229f
"Open the Gates chorale" (*Gates of Justice*), 225–32, 232f, 233f, 234f

Panish, Jon, 63–64
Parker, Charlie, 147–48
Parker, Suzy, 78–80, 79f
particularism in multicultural soundscape, 247–53
Peretti, Burton, 50–51n.49, 54, 123, 132
performance of whiteness, 13–16, 279–80
Perry, Ted, 261–63, 262n.6
phobias of Duke Ellington, 132
Piekut, Benjamin, 107
Pitts, George, 193–94
Pitzulo, Carrie, 108–9
*Playboy* magazine, 77, 105–15
*Playboy's Penthouse* (television series), 110–13
playing Indian, 276–78
politics of respectability, 90–91, 91n.49
Pollard, William, 196
Porter, Eric, 58–59, 141, 271
Porter, Lewis, 71–72
possessive investment in whiteness, 3
Pozo, Chano, 241
Prestige, 37
Pribyl, Ashley, 29–30

primitivist discourses, 93–94, 132, 136–37, 139
progressive approach to race and race relations, 3

Race, Steve, 59–60
race clause, in contracts, 184–85
racial capitalism, 187–93
racial mixing, 94–95
Ramsey, Guthrie, 74–75, 91–92
*Real Ambassadors, The* (musical), 1, 24, 164, 250–51
recognition
  Armstrong's *Time* cover article, 126–31, 130f
  Brubeck's "new" audience and, 144–49
  Brubeck's *Time* cover article, 140–44, 142f
  commercial success, 148–49
  Ellington's *Time* cover article, 132–35, 133f
  Monk's *Time* cover article, 135–40, 138f
  overview, 28, 119–21
  in *Time* magazine, 121–26
  of whiteness, 150–54
respectability
  Brubeck's image of, 74, 75, 76–84, 108
  of MJQ, 91
  politics of, 90–91
  of Storyville audiences, 88–89
  in *Time* article featuring Brubeck, 140–41
reverse colorism, 194n.100
Robert, Sarah Corbin, 26–27n.87
Robinson, Cedric J., 189–90
Robinson, Dylan, 260
Rockdale Temple, Cincinnati (Ohio), 199, 207–12, 210f
Roediger, David, 3
Rogers, Shorty, 34–35, 40n.27
Rowand, Wilbur, 187
Rustin-Paschal, Nichole, 93, 112

Sales, Grover, 33
Salmon, John, 204n.17
Sarkesian, Ed, 73–74
Savoy Ballroom, New York, 123–24
Schlesinger, Arthur, Jr., 106–7
school integration, 178–79, 185–86
Schuller, Gunther, 46–47, 190–91
segregation policies, cancelations of concerts due to
  in Athens, Georgia in 1959, 168–71
  in Dallas, Texas in 1957, 159–65

near-cancelation at East Carolina College in 1958, 166–68
South African tour in 1958, 165–66
in southern tour, 157–59, 180–87
self-critique, 25–26
serious listening, 86–87, 89–90
sexuality, 93–96, 114–15
shared Black-Jewish experiences, 218–22, 239–40
Shaw, Arnold, 51–52
Shaw, Artie, 158–59, 213
sheet music, 104–5
shofar call, 216–18, 216f, 216n.52, 217f
"Shout unto the Lord" (*Gates of Justice*), 242–44, 243f, 244f, 245f
Sigg, Clarine, 100–1
Signifyin(g), 132–35
Silver, Horace, 95
Simon, George T., 126–27
Smith, Hedrick, 2–3, 76–77, 195
Smith, Julie Dawn, 144–45
Smith, Willie "The Lion," 67
"Softly, as in a Morning Sunrise" (Modern Jazz Quartet), 47, 48f, 61
Solis, Gabriel, 135–36
*Someday My Prince Will Come* (Davis), 78–79n.15
sonic color line, 9–10, 33–34, 174–75
sounding white, 9–13
soundscape, in *Gates of Justice*, 215–18
South Africa, tours in
in 1976, 196n.106
cancelation of 1958 tour in, 165–66
*Southern Scene* (Dave Brubeck Quartet), 172–80, 175f
southern tour, 28
cancelations of concerts in, 157–59, 180–87
preparations for, 180–82
return to south after, 184–87, 190
revised itinerary for, 182, 183t
strategy for, 172–80
Southern Universities Student Government Association (SUSGA), 180n.59
spontaneity versus composition, 40–55
DBQ's approach to counterpoint, 40–45, 41f
MJQ's approach to counterpoint, 45f, 45–47, 48f
overview, 40
white intellectual privilege, 48–51
white racialization of cool jazz, 51–55

State Department tour, 151–54, 151n.94, 196n.107
Stearns, Marshall, 83
Steinberg, L. M., 166
stereotypes of Blacks, 125–26, 132–35
Stewart, Rex, 192
"St. Louis Blues" (Dave Brubeck Quartet), 67
Stoever, Jennifer Lynn, 9–10, 11, 12–13, 33–34, 64, 174–75
Storck, Jacqueline, 101–3, 102n.75, 104–5
Storyville, New Orleans, 85–86, 85n.29
Storyville club, Boston, 84–92
audience noise in live recordings from, 88–89
respectability of audience, 89–92
serious listening in, 84–87, 89–90
subjectivity of swing, 57–58
Sullivan, Shannon, 6, 13, 16, 19, 77n.11, 169–70, 195
SUSGA (Southern Universities Student Government Association), 180n.59
Sutherland, Wendy, 11–12
Sutton, Shan, 196n.106
swing, 55–63
of DBQ, 56–59
defined, 55–56
jazz legacy, 62–63
of MJQ, 61–62
swing spectrum of Brubeck, 59–61

Talbert, Bob, 51
TallBear, Kim, 267–68
Taylor, Diana, 14–15
Taylor, Timothy, 77–78
Teachout, Terry, 271
Teal, Kimberly Hannon, 75–76
tenor, role in *Gates of Justice*, 215, 217–18, 218f
theft of black capital, 4n.7
"They Say I Look Like God" (*The Real Ambassadors*), 250–51
Third Stream movement, 49n.42
"This Can't Be Love" (Dave Brubeck Quartet), 69–70
Tick, Judith, 103
*Time* magazine
Armstrong's cover article in, 126–31, 130f
Brubeck's cover article in, 28, 33, 95–96, 115–16, 119, 140–44, 142f
discussion of DBQ counterpoint in, 44
Ellington's cover article in, 132–35, 133f, 136
Monk's cover article in, 135–40, 138f
recognition in, 121–26

*Time Out* (Dave Brubeck Quartet), 1, 152
Tomming, 126–30
Totusek, Martin, 272–74
Tracy, Jack, 69
transcriptions of compositions, 104–5
Tristano, Lennie, 52–53
trust of audience, 144–45, 153
Tsosie, Krystal, 266–67, 268–69
Tucker, James, 166–67
Tucker, Sherrie, 7–8, 94
Turner, Victor, 16
"Two Part Contention" (Dave Brubeck Quartet), 60–61, 60n.82

Ulanov, Barry, 52–53, 70
*Undoing Gender* (Butler), 120
"unheard millions" chorus, in *Gates of Justice*, 222–32
Union of American Hebrew Congregations (UAHC), 199, 206–7, 214
universalism in multicultural soundscape, 247–53
University of Alabama (UA) concert in 1964, 185–87
University of Georgia (UGA), cancelation of 1959 concert at, 168–71

"Vendôme" (Modern Jazz Quartet), 35, 45–46, 45*f*, 61
visibility
  Armstrong's *Time* cover article, 126–31, 130*f*
  Brubeck's *Time* cover article, 140–44, 142*f*
  Ellington's *Time* cover article, 132–35, 133*f*
  Monk's *Time* cover article, 135–40, 138*f*
  overview, 119–21
  in *Time* magazine, 121–26
*Vogue* magazine, 52–53, 77
von Eschen, Penny, 151–52
Vorspan, Albert, 211, 245–46

wages of whiteness, 3
Wahl, Kay, 116–17
Wallace, George, 185–86
Ward, Brian, 172–73
Warren, Elizabeth, 267–69, 267n.28
Waterman, Ellen, 144–45
"Way You Look Tonight, The" (Dave Brubeck Quartet), 40–44, 41*f*, 42*f*, 59–60
Wein, George, 85–86, 86n.30, 89
Wells, Christi Jay, 84–85, 271–72

"When the Saints Go Marching In" (Dave Brubeck Quartet), 44–45
white ally, 1
white flight in Cincinnati, 209, 211
white fragility, 18–19, 18–19n.67, 22–23
white habitus, 65–66
white ignorance, 6–7
white innocence, 20–23
white intellectual privilege, 27, 48–51, 54–55
white jazz musicians
  autobiographers, 15n.58
  backlash in 1990s, 270–76
  colorblindness in jazz, 63–69
  racially integrated bands, 158–59
white mainstream audiences. *See* mainstream audiences
"White Man" (Hughes), 192
white masculinity, 106–7
white moderates, 169–70
white moral supremacy, 12
whiteness
  anti-racism, 24–26
  feeling white, 18–24
  Jewish identity as distinct from, 212–14
  monolithic, 4, 7–8, 13
  performance of, 13–16, 279–80
  recognition of, 150–54
  revealing, 5–9
  sounding white, 9–13
white privilege, 6–8
  habits of, 13–14
  in music industry, 187–93
white racial frame, 14, 14n.52, 49–50, 50n.48, 192
white rage, 170–71
white resentment narrative, 271
white spaces, 74–76
  living rooms, 96–105
  *Playboy* penthouses, 105–15
  Storyville club, 84–92
white supremacy, 4, 16–18
  anti-Semitism, 213
  racial capitalism, 187–93
white women on jazz albums, 78–80, 78–79n.15, 79*f*
Williams, Mary Lou, 255
Willis, Robert S., 197
Wilson, John, 47, 61–62
Wolfe, Tom, 246n.98
women, as jazz audience, 92–96, 98–105, 99*f*, 100*f*, 101*f*

Woods, Stuart, 168–70, 169n.30, 169n.31, 197
Wright, Eugene, 1, 24. *See also* Dave Brubeck Quartet
    Brubeck's appreciation for talent of, 171
    featured on albums for southern tour, 173–78
    formation of Brubeck Quartet, 31–32
    "Happy Times," 176–77
    position on political activism, 193–97, 196n.107
    South African tour in 1958, cancelation of, 165–66
    State Department tour, 151–54
Wright, Richard, 238–39

Yancy, George, 21–24, 142–43
"Ye Shall Be Holy" (*Gates of Justice*), 220–22, 220*f*, 221*f*

Zeiger, Al, 56–57
Zukerman, Eugenia, 236–37